AISIIO

Welfare States and the Future

Also by B. Vivekanandan

AS THE MIND UNFOLDS: Issues and Personalities (*editor*)

BUILDING ON SOLIDARITY: Social Democracy and the New Millennium (*editor*)

CONTEMPORARY SOCIALISM: An Analysis (*co-editor*)

ECHOES IN PARLIAMENT: Madhu Dandavate's Speeches, 1971–1990 (*editor*)

CONTEMPORARY EUROPE AND SOUTH ASIA (*co-editor*)

INDIA LOOKS AHEAD: Jayaprakash Narayan Memorial Lectures, 1990–2001 (*editor*)

INTERNATIONAL CONCERNS OF EUROPEAN SOCIAL DEMOCRATS

PATHFINDERS: Social Democrats of Scandinavia

THE ISSUES OF OUR TIMES (*editor*)

THE MODERN COMMONWEALTH

THE SHRINKING CIRCLE: The Commonwealth in British Foreign Policy, 1945–1974

IN RETROSPECT: Reflections on Select Issues in World Politics, 1975–2000

Also by Nimmi Kurian

THE HIGH NOON: Anglo–American Special Relationship under Thatcher and Reagan

EMERGING CHINA AND INDIA'S POLICY OPTIONS

Welfare States and the Future

Edited by

B. Vivekanandan
Professor of European Studies
School of International Studies
Jawaharlal Nehru University
New Delhi, India

and

Nimmi Kurian
Associate Research Professor
Centre for Policy Research
New Delhi, India

First published 2005 by
PALGRAVE MACMILLAN
Houndmills, Basingstoke, Hampshire RG21 6XS and
175 Fifth Avenue, New York, N. Y. 10010
Companies and representatives throughout the world

PALGRAVE MACMILLAN is the global academic imprint of the Palgrave
Macmillan division of St. Martin's Press, LLC and of Palgrave Macmillan Ltd.
Macmillan® is a registered trademark in the United States, United Kingdom
and other countries. Palgrave is a registered trademark in the European
Union and other countries.

ISBN 1–4039–4364–8

This book is printed on paper suitable for recycling and made from fully
managed and sustained forest sources.

A catalogue record for this book is available from the British Library.

Library of Congress Cataloging-in-Publication Data

Welfare states and the future / edited by B. Vivekanandan and
Nimmi Kurian.
    p. cm.
    Includes bibliographical references and index.
    ISBN 1–4039–4364–8 (cloth)
    1. Welfare state. 2. Welfare state – Cross-cultural studies.
  I. Vivekanandan, B. II. Kurian, Nimmi.
  HB846.W444 2004
  330.12'6 – dc22   2004054465

10 9 8 7 6 5 4 3 2
14 13 12 11 10 09 08 07 06

Printed and bound in Great Britain by
Antony Rowe Ltd, Chippenham and Eastbourne

To Vimala Vivekanandan

The Light That Illumines Our Home

Contents

Foreword

Nineteen outstanding scholars from 11 countries and four continents, all of them social scientists of international repute, have authored this book edited by Professor B. Vivekanandan and Dr Nimmi Kurian. It is a significant piece of work which provides a unique high-quality international assessment of the present state and future prospects of welfare states of 14 countries of Asia, Africa, Europe, America and Latin America. The title of the book – *Welfare States and the Future* – raises an alarm which gets echoed in every chapter of the book and in the Preface and Introduction by the editors.

The concerns of the authors and editors are partly rooted in the globalization and liberalization processes born out of the Uruguay Round which was brought to a close with the adoption of the Marrakesh Treaty, with the developing countries coerced into signing on the dotted line. Aptly, Professor Ramesh Mishra and Dr Joakim Palme introduce their chapters by focusing on the challenges of globalization and liberalization to the welfare state, especially its core element of a social protection scheme.

Pradip Bose in a perspectival analysis of the state of welfare states in the world has come to the conclusion that 'in recent times the concept of the welfare state is being questioned from different angles and even being undermined in some countries', and then goes on to add that 'a situation where the people who are used to obtaining social benefits and the governments, committed to maximizing the benefits, now find themselves in a situation where many of these benefits are not economically viable'. The key words are 'not economically viable'. The fact, however, is that the social benefit schemes of the Western world, by and large, are in doldrums today.

The Western concept of the welfare state has meant helping working people and other deprived people of their states through various programmes undertaken by the state and municipalities. Tom Burden in his chapter has focused on the key phases of social policy development in the UK and lists the laws enacted by Britain starting with the Poor Law Act of 1601. Whether it was new liberalism or the Keynesian welfare state or the Beveridge reform or communitarianism, the point to be noted is that it was the transfer of a small portion of the wealth generated by the working population, in the form of employers/employees contributions, in addition to certain state/municipal taxes, that financed the social protection schemes.

Long before J.M. Keynes and William Beveridge developed their ideas of welfare states, and perhaps around the time when the Swedish social democratic economists like Gustav Möller and Ernst Wiggfors were preparing the layout of the welfare state scheme for Sweden, Mahatma Gandhi, a great Indian, had clearly enunciated his concept of people's welfare. At the height of India's struggle for independence, which he led, Gandhi said in 1931: 'The Swaraj [self-government/independence] of my dreams is the poor man's Swaraj. The necessaries of life should be enjoyed by you in common with those enjoyed by the princes and the moneyed men. But that does not mean that you should have palaces like theirs. They are not necessary for happiness. You or I would be lost in them. But you ought to get all the ordinary amenities of life that a rich man enjoys. I have not the slightest doubt that Swaraj is not Poorna Swaraj until these amenities are guaranteed to you under it.'

In three pithy statements made on three different occasions Mahatma Gandhi defined his concept of welfarism:

> According to me the economic Constitution of India and for the matter of that of the world, should be such that no one under it should suffer from want of food and clothing. In other words, everybody should be able to get sufficient work to enable him to make the two ends meet. And this ideal can be universally utilized only if the means of production of the elementary necessaries of life remain in the control of the masses. These should be freely available to all as God's air and water are ought to be; they should not be made a vehicle of traffic for the exploitation of others. Their monopolization by any country, nation or group of persons would be unjust. The neglect of this simple principle is the cause of the destitution that we witness today not only in this unhappy land but in other parts of the world too . . . .

> True economics never militates against the highest ethical standard, just as all true ethics to be worth its name must at the same time be also good economics. An economics that inculcates Mammon worship, and enables the strong to amass wealth at the expense of the weak, is a false and dismal science. It spells death. True economics, on the other hand, stands for social justice, it promotes the good of all equally including the weakest, and is indispensable for decent life . . . .

> I want to bring about an equalization of status. The working classes have all these centuries been isolated and relegated to a lower status. They have been *shoodras*, and the word has been interpreted to mean an inferior status. I want to allow no differentiation between the son of a weaver, of an agriculturist and of a schoolmaster.

'Welfare State' means different things to different people and states. There is of course no ideal model. The plans provided by Keynes and Beveridge for the UK, by Gustav Möller and Ernst Wiggfors for Sweden, and by Leonard Marsh for Canada were great leaps forward in providing against the mischances of life like old age, unemployment, health hazards and so on. Conventionally understood social security from the 'cradle-to-the-grave' was the welfare state at its best.

The welfarist models that the developed societies have pursued – the welfare state in the United Kingdom, the social market in Germany, social protection in France and the institutional-redistributive model in the Scandinavian countries – may have worked in Europe but they cannot easily be replicated in India and other developing countries.

No matter how one defines welfarism, the *sine qua non* for the sustenance of the welfare state is the creation of more resources, to provide social protection to the less-privileged and to the jobless. While the Beveridge and Marsh plans sought to generate this resource through a system of national insurance based on a single weekly contribution to provide for the needy, Guslav Möller and Wiggfors prescribed progressive taxation to mobilize resources for the purpose.

India is a classic example of how, in the absence of the requisite resources, the concept of welfare state was allowed to wilt. Article 38 of the Directive Principles of State Policy, in India's Constitution, enjoins the state to secure a social order to promote the welfare of the people by securing and protecting as effectively as it may a social order in which justice – social, economic and political – shall inform all the institutions of national life. The State shall, in particular, strive to minimize inequalities in income, and endeavour to eliminate inequalities in status, facilities and opportunities, not only amongst individuals but also amongst groups of people residing in different areas or engaged in different vocations. Article 39 spells out in some detail how to go about this. To state here that the state has failed to live by the lofty ideals enshrined in the Constitution is not to put the state in the dock and question its bona fides; it is to emphasize that resource deficiencies have prevented the Indian state from fulfilling its constitutional commitments.

Why confine ourselves only to India. On 10 December 1948, the UN General Assembly proclaimed the Universal Declaration of Human Rights as a common standard for all peoples and all nations. Article 1 of the Declaration asserts 'All human beings are born free and equal in dignity and rights. They are endowed with reason and conscience and should act towards one another in a spirit of brotherhood.' Articles 25 and 26 of the Declaration were all about what welfare states should be. They proclaimed, *inter alia*: 'Everyone has the right to a standard of living adequate for the health and well-being of himself and of his family, including food, clothing, housing and medical care and necessary social services, and the right to security, in the event of unemployment, sickness, disability, widowhood, old age or other lack of livelihood in circumstances beyond his control.'

The advent of globalization has led to paradigm shifts in many spheres. The spread of democracy in more and more countries and the new mantra of the market have led to a fundamental restructuring of production, finance and significant growth in world trade and global investment flows. Besides dismantling barriers, globalization has revolutionalized the thinking of political regimes at all levels across the world. The traditional role of the state itself has undergone a sea change, and today its role is becoming increasingly catalytic. It is against this background that the concept of the welfare state and its future needs to be reviewed and reexamined.

These challenges notwithstanding, the core values of the welfare state remain valid the world over. A state like India should attempt to bridge the India–Bharat divide by a judicious blend of high economic growth and distributive justice. India's central problem is poverty and economic marginalization, with nearly half of the population living on less than $2 per day. While the richest 20 per cent of the world's population in the highest income countries account for 86 per cent of the total private consumption expenditure, the poorest 20 per cent consume just 1.3 per cent. Among the 4.4 billion people in the developing countries, almost one-third are without proper drinking water, one-fourth do not have adequate housing and one-fifth are without access to modern health services. During the past 15 years or so, per capita income has declined in more than 100 countries. As Professor Amartya Sen rightly argues, poverty stems not just from a lack of resources, but from lack of entitlements. Famines occur not because there is not enough food to eat, but because poor people are deprived of earning the much needed exchange entitlements, be it income, land, employment or whatever.

It is widely believed that the market economy limits the capacity of states to undertake national welfare policies. Hundreds of thousands of people have been rendered jobless, and there is a huge army of unemployed youth. The state can afford to ignore their plight at its own peril. India is bound by the Constitution to promote a policy of social and economic justice to include the excluded communities like *Dalits* (depressed classes) and *Adivasis* (tribal communities) into the decision-making process. It would be naïve to imagine that protection of women's rights, empowerment of Dalits and the amelioration of the conditions of poor and the indigent can be left to market forces. Freedom from want, disease and fear is best suited to promote social justice and human development. Therefore, the welfare state is here to stay as an instrument to empower the needy and the marginalized. In a world where democratic citizenship is a key issue, where the construction of economic societies is paramount, there is an imperative need to reinvent the welfare state.

Welfarism must be viewed as a redistributive measure. This is not to say that the state should see its role as a dispenser of doles to the people. Giving alms to the poor may be an act of charity, but that is not what the state is for. The state's role should be primarily one of a facilitator and a catalyst. In the global world, creation of resource is no longer the job of the state only. What the state is required to do is provide an ideal framework for the generation of resources and structural possibilities for its redistribution. The provision of mass education, healthcare and social security cannot be left to non-state actors, though they can play a complementary role.

I conclude with a specific reference to the title of this volume, viz. *Welfare States and the Future.* The concept of a welfare state of the future needs to be seen in a dynamic sense. Gross inequalities in social arrangements can be a threat to a good life and cohesive human well-being. I would even say it is barbaric. So the welfare state of the future will have to address this issue. Again, expanding social opportunities and widening employment is far better than providing unemployment insurance or dole. Providing basic healthcare, educational facilities, building capabilities and enhancing freedom should be the hallmark of the welfare state of the future rather than the offering of social security *per se* in a narrow sense. Fighting gender asymmetries has to be done as part of policy choices and affirmative action in the welfare state of the future. In brief, while economic reform in favour of allowing more space for the market cannot be ignored in promoting economic growth and generation of resources, other social arrangements are needed to expand employment and to ensure social and economic equity. Economy is important, but it has to be socially embedded. That is the highway to the welfare state of the future.

Therefore, I am of the view that the welfare state idea in action must return to centre-stage in the twenty-first century. If policy-makers fail to do so, the social consequences are not hard to imagine. This highly readable volume of essays written by well-known specialists on the subject is a timely and valuable contribution of great significance.

New Delhi   GEORGE FERNANDES

Preface

This book occupies a unique space in the global literature on welfare state systems. It presents a comprehensive analysis and provides a macro-level international assessment of welfare states in four continents and 14 countries, providing an important input into transnational policy formulations for building modern societies. So far, welfare states have been studied either from a national perspective or from a regional perspective, and that too mostly at micro-levels, which, of course, in itself is very important. Moreover, generally they have been studied as a feature of the developed world. Very little has been done to look at this feature at a macro-level, from a larger global perspective transcending various cultures and continents, and its gradual positioning in the agenda of states, including developing countries, across the world as a guiding force for the establishment of a stable and harmonious world society based on principles of equity, justice, democracy and solidarity. This book tries to fill the void by generating a confluence of analyses of a number of welfare state systems evolved in the world during the last seven decades, contributed to by 20 outstanding experts drawn from different parts of the world. These analyses are complemented by presentations of a few important general theoretical aspects which underpin the construction of welfare state structures.

In the ultimate analysis, the welfare state is all about the quality of day-to-day life for ordinary people everywhere in the world. Therefore, its long-term validity is not in doubt. Moreover, at this juncture of the development of human civilization, the welfare state agenda has a critical role to play in shaping the future of millions of people across the world. Anchored in the basic human psyche of concern for the well-being of fellow human beings, during the last seven decades the welfare state system has unmistakably promoted a sense of solidarity, and cultivated a sense of sharing without heartburn, in due recognition of human beings' social rights, in many countries, evolving a credible welfare state system where the state was made the chief custodian of those systems both as a regulator and a provider. Though a consensus has been carefully built among the major political streams everywhere regarding the necessity of having welfare provisions to meet the basic necessities of life, there has remained a debate on whether their entitlement should be made universal, as a social right, or targeted, whether the public sector should undertake it or it be left to the free market, or should there be a mixed involvement of both public and private sectors. That debate is still going on. However, it has been generally found that while a dominant public sector role, enjoined by a universalistic approach, has promoted egalitarianism in society (in all such states people remain overwhelmingly welded to welfare statism), a market-dominated system seems to have helped to preserve or even heighten inequality and hit hard on the poorer sections of society who could not afford to purchase adequate services from the market.

However, this book should be read not only as a contribution to the growing literature on welfare state systems, but also as a unique intercontinental study which presents a comprehensive macro-picture of the state of welfare state systems across the world at the turn of the new millenium, and what they beckon for future both in the global context and also in the context of developing countries. In the context of the developed world, chapters on welfare state systems in the United States, Canada, Britain, France, Germany, Austria, Sweden, Finland and Denmark are significant. As far as the developing countries of Asia, Africa and Latin America are concerned, chapters on the welfare state systems in India, China, Brazil and South Africa are of special significance since they, in a way, constitute the representative samples of the developing world and are also pointing the way to the future. The system in Japan presents a different model altogether.

In the preparation of this volume, we have accumulated considerable indebtedness. In particular, we are very grateful to all contributors. Similarly, we are grateful to the Jawaharlal Nehru University (JNU), New Delhi, and the Jean Jaures Foundation, Paris, for sponsoring the international seminar on welfare states in April 2001 where the idea of publishing this book was first mooted. Similarly, we are grateful to Prof. Asis Datta, former JNU Vice Chancellor, Prof. Harbans Mukhia, former Rector, and other JNU faculty members like Prof. T.K. Oommen, Prof. Girijesh Pant, Prof. Nirmala Joshi, Prof. C.S.R. Murthy, Prof. Arun Kumar, Dr Madhu Bhalla, Prof. R.N. Mehra of Lucknow, Prof. Ashok Mukhopadhyay of Calcutta, Prof. J.P. Roos, University of Helsinki, Dr Peter Abrahamson of the University of Copenhagen, and late Mr Surur Hoda OBE for their cooperation and support. We are also thankful to Dr Susan Mathai, Ms Jayashree Vivekanandan, Research Scholar, School of International Studies, JNU, and Mrs Vimala Vivekanandan, Assistant Registrar, JNU.

We are also grateful to Mr Kalevi Sorsa, Finland's former social democratic Prime Minister and international statesman, for his active support and encouragement of this venture. Similarly, we are grateful to Mr Axel Queval, Jean Jaures Foundation, Paris, for his spirited support. Our special thanks go to Dr Cherian Samuel for the sincere assistance he had extended to us at all stages of the preparation of this volume.

We are grateful to Mr George Fernandes, outstanding Indian socialist and presently India's Defence Minister, for writing a scintillating Foreword to this book. It was very kind of him to find time within his extremely busy schedule dealing with national and global security problems.

Finally, we are grateful to our publishers, Palgrave Macmillan Ltd, and its Senior Commissioning Editor, Ms Amanda Hamilton, for excellent support and diligence.

New Delhi

B. VIVEKANANDAN
NIMMI KURIAN

Notes on the Contributors

Christian Aspalter is an Assistant Professor, Department of Social Welfare, Seoul National University, Seoul, Korea; Honorary Lecturer, Department of Social Work and Social Administration, University of Hong Kong, Hong Kong; and Director, Research Centre on Societal and Social Policy, Hong Kong.

Pradip Bose is a well-known author, a leading social democratic ideologue, and President of the Indian Centre for Democratic Socialism, New Delhi, India.

Tom Burden is Principal Lecturer in Political Science, Leeds Metropolitan University, UK.

Sandwip Kumar Das is Professor of International Economics and former Dean, School of International Studies, Jawaharlal Nehru University, New Delhi, India.

Hartmut Elsenhans is Professor, Institute of Social Sciences, University of Leipzig, Germany.

George Fernandes is an eminent Indian socialist leader and Minister of Defence, Government of India.

Marcel Fink is a Lecturer in the Department of Political Science, University of Vienna, Austria.

Asha Gupta is the Principal of Bharati Mahila College, Delhi University, India.

Anand Kumar is Professor of Social Systems, School of Social Sciences, Jawaharlal Nehru University, New Delhi, India.

Nimmi Kurian is an Associate Research Professor, Centre for Policy Research, New Delhi, India.

Lutz Leisering is Professor of Sociology, Department of Sociology, Bielefeld University, Germany.

Dilip Loundo is Professor and the Brazilian Chair, Department of Sociology, Goa University, Goa, India.

Ramesh Mishra is Professor Emeritus, York University, Canada.

Sophie Nadal is an Associate Professor, Department of Law, University of Cergy-Pontoise, Paris, France.

Joakim Palme is Director, Institute for Future Studies, Stockholm, Sweden.

Jukka Pekkarinen is Director, Labour Institute for Economic Research, Helsinki, Finland.

Jørn Henrik Petersen is Professor of Social Policy, University of Southern Denmark, Odense, Denmark.

Emmerich Talos is Professor of Political Science, University of Vienna, Austria.

Albert J. Venter is Professor of Government and Politics, Rand Afrikaans University, Johannesburg, South Africa.

B. Vivekanandan is Professor of European Studies, School of International Studies, Jawaharlal Nehru University, New Delhi, India.

1

Introduction: Welfare States and the Future

B. Vivekanandan and Nimmi Kurian

Fundamentally, the welfare state draws its very *raison d'être* from a range of state policies aimed at promoting the welfare of its population. The welfare orientation thus sees the state devoting considerable fiscal resources aimed at the socialization of risk and the enhancement of cohesion in society. It presupposes substantial governmental responsibility for the provision of social security, healthcare, education, housing, social services, unemployment insurance, family allowances, pensions and so on.

The concept of a welfare state drew its ideological basis from economists like Ernst Wiggfors, Gustav Möller and John Meynard Keynes. Gustav Möller, the architect of the Swedish welfare state used the term 'welfare state' for the first time in the Swedish Social Democratic Party's election manifesto in 1928. Keynes elaborated the concept in his influential work, *The General Theory of Employment, Interest and Money*, published in 1936. Contesting the orthodox view that unemployment was a temporary phenomenon that could be ameliorated by the free play of market forces, Keynes pioneered the theory of full employment and advocated an activist economic policy by government. These ideas were further strengthened by the recommendations contained in William Beveridge's *Report on Social Insurance and Allied Services* (1942), which sought to establish a minimum standard of living 'below which no one should be allowed to fall'. Another influential report was Leonard C. Marsh's *Report on Social Security for Canada* (1943), which recommended a social security net, with a comprehensive spread of benefits.

In many countries, the impetus to build welfare states came from the widespread hardships caused by the Second World War. The welfare state system was established early in Scandinavia as a response to the Great Depression of the late 1920s and early 1930s. In the 1930s, Swedish Social Democrats made it their plank for restructuring society on egalitarian lines and built a cradle-to-the-grave welfare state system. Möller and Wiggfors were the moving spirits of this. Having thus pioneered these achievements, the welfare state system has since become almost synonymous with social

1

democracy. Universalism and non-discrimination were the bases on which Sweden had built up a new caring welfare society. Nurtured by the social democratic principles of distributive justice and solidarity, the state set its sights beyond the mere alleviation of poverty to cast a wide social security net and provide universal welfare rights without exception. Social democrats everywhere have adopted the welfare state system as one of their principal goals and tried to emulate the Swedish example.

The principle that some sort of welfare provision is necessary is today undisputed and enjoys universal adherence. Beyond this, however, the field of welfare state research is a contested one, with key organizing principles being fiercely debated. At the root of this debate lies the classic dilemma as to whether welfare is a public or a private good. When defined as a public good, it enjoins upon the state to provide a range of services to be shared collectively. On the contrary, when it is defined as a private good, public provision is opposed on the grounds that it infringes the freedom of the individual. Whereas the former identifies the agency of the state as the provider of social security, the latter sees the market as the most efficient dispenser of services. If public provision is the guiding principle, the state mobilizes resources to this end through tax revenues, with characteristically large public sectors providing substantial employment. Conversely, where public provision is not the norm, the tax burden is low and state employment levels, too, are noticeably far lower.

Again, some countries anchor their policies in a full employment policy, which maximizes tax revenue and minimizes unproductive public expenditure on the grounds that it limits the obligation of the state to provide income security only to a small minority. Some welfare states attune their welfare spending to paying compensation for social ills. This is generally the case with residual welfare states. But institutional welfare states pursue preventive social policies, so that they spend relatively less for paying compensation, and invest more in job-creation, job-preservation and enhancement of employability through measures like training and retraining programmes. The objective is to minimize social need and maximize employment. What comes across is the sheer diversity in welfare state regimes, each with its own structures of employment, taxation and welfare benefits.

Outline of the book

The idea for this book emerged from the conviction that while the concept of the welfare state has won widespread acceptance in many countries across the world, significant temporal and spatial variations have been the norm rather than the exception. The domain of the welfare state as traditionally understood has also expanded over the past decades to include a large non-European membership of developing countries. These nascent welfare states are emerging within distinctive, socio-historical contexts with developmental priorities vastly different from their affluent counterparts in Europe. Thus, models and categorizations cannot be transposed as each country brings its own specific experience into the crafting of its welfare system, affirming the salience of multiple developmental trajectories. This volume thus attempts to map the sheer diversity of welfare state systems across the world by bringing out the significant spatial and temporal variations that exist. By bringing together academics from Europe, Asia, Africa and the Americas, the contribution hopes to considerably enrich the research on welfare states that has for various reasons been predominantly Eurocentric in its focus and methodology.

A second intellectual concern has been to examine the prospects of the welfare state as an institution in the light of the challenges posed by the forces of globalization and the neo-liberal ideology. Despite the existence of variations across welfare states in terms of organization, functioning and the relative spread of benefits, there existed, nonetheless, a high degree of social and political consensus in favour of the welfare state. The first cracks in this consensus appeared in the mid-1980s in the face of a sustained attack from neo-liberal philosophy, which stood for a rolling back of the state, leaving welfare activities to the free market. The neo-liberals opposed the pursuit of a full employment policy and universal welfare provisions on the ground that collective decisions constituted a negation of individual freedom, which the free market upheld. They stressed instead a range of diverse paid-for services, transfer arrangements and voluntary help activities. One of the main targets of their attack has been the taxation system, a drastic reduction of which would directly weaken the state's capacity as a provider of welfare. Conceptually, these arguments posed a direct challenge to the fundamental principles of the welfare state system.

The phenomenon of globalization is also widely believed to present a grave challenge to the state's capacity for autonomous decision-making, particularly to its redistributive functions. The challenge of an increasingly competitive international economy was seen as gravely undermining the state's capacity to use fiscal instruments to finance and provide social insurance. Globalization is said to thus strike at the very edifice of the welfare state. The state is said to be under retreat, with its functional autonomy greatly compromised in the face of what appears to be the inexorable march of global markets. The forces of globalization are perceived as working at cross-purposes to that of the welfare state, since each derives its motivational impetus from conflicting ideological moorings. Thus, the goals of social democracy with its pursuit of national goals of full employment, egalitarianism and a widespread social security net are seen as inherently anachronistic in the neo-classical age of rapidly converging economies and the internationalization of economic activity. The state gets bypassed literally, as global production networks and the resultant 'deterritorialization' that is produced, pays scant regard to the traditional /hitherto sacrosanct concepts of territorial spaces and borders.

This volume attempts to critically evaluate emerging trends in welfare state systems and to analyse whether these point to its declining or to its continuing relevance. A related aim is to also study the response strategies adopted by different regimes to these similar challenges and to ascertain whether these point to any convergence or to multiple response patterns. The volume brings together an interdisciplinary perspective on these central issues with 20 contributors drawn from diverse scholarly disciplines across four continents – Asia, Europe, Africa and America – and 10 countries – Austria, Canada, Denmark, Finland, France, Germany, India, South Africa, Sweden and the United Kingdom.

Placing the welfare state systems in the context of the march of history, Pradip Bose finds that the construction of the welfare state was 'a civilizational leap in human history', and that the idea retains broad-based support and mass appeal since it addresses basic human problems. At a time when globalization is fundamentally altering economic and social activity and creating 'deep uncertainties and disruptions', the core values of the welfare state system, namely equality, liberty and community, could be the guiding principles of countries to protect their citizens. He is confident that the welfare state system will endure in the twenty-first century if it reaffirms its traditional values, but at the same time adopts a radical revision of the means for achieving them.

The economic aspects of modern welfare state systems are analysed by Sandwip Kumar Das, Hartmut Elsenhans and Ramesh Mishra. Professor Das examines the fundamental relationship between economic growth and distributive justice through income transfers to promote economic and social equality. He observes that in running the welfare state, policy-makers cannot depend entirely on the market, and the extent of state intervention in the market varies from country to country depending upon the political system prevailing in various countries. He notes the strong tradition of state intervention in developing countries where governments 'do much more than just redistribute income as they have been engaged directly in the production process and performing functions that are normally in the domain of the private sector'. In his chapter, Das introduces the concept of 'uniform income transfers' under which 'income is transferred from an above-average earner to a below-average earner with the size of transfer being proportional to the difference between the actual and average incomes'. He underlines the need to strike a balance between the market-generated growth impulses and the need to achieve an equitable distribution of income at all levels.

Professor Elsenhans examines the possibility of building a world economy based on the principles of the welfare state. According to him, 'today's world economy is characterized by the participation of economies in the international division of labour which are sectorally competitive without, however, being able to achieve full employment, neither through export growth (including the induced multiplier effects) nor by internal-market-oriented growth, possibly combined with export growth'. Arguing for the globalization of the welfare state to enable a globalization of profit as opposed to the globalization of rent, Elsenhans says that globalization has to be complemented by appropriate development policies for marginalized societies. He also presents a model of the world economy which offers a perspective for the 'globalization of profit accompanied by full employment, an autonomous civil society, high levels of competition, and lower levels of state interventionism'. He concludes: 'There is no alternative between globalization and autarky. The only option is between a rentier system and the globalization of the welfare state. A sustainable process of globalization has to promote the welfare state, and can be achieved with a limited bureaucracy if capital fails in its attempt to disempower labour.'

Professor Mishra examines the destabilizing effect of financial openness and the influence of international financial institutions on social policy, arguing that it is necessary to study the welfare state system in a larger international context as national economic and social policies are increasingly coming under the pressure of global intergovernmental organizations. He explains how international debt and the IMF-World Bank sponsored structural adjustment programmes (SAP) have curtailed national autonomy in policy-making and led to increased unemployment and the curtailment of provisions for social protection and social development. He draws up a typology of four groups of countries to study the relationship between globalization and social protection – less-developed, newly industrializing, ex-communist and Western industrial. Given the differentials within the various sets of relationships, Mishra argues for an integrated approach to the issue.

Tom Burden traces the evolution of the British welfare state along four key phases – the Tudor Poor Law, the Poor Law Amendment Act of 1834, the Edwardian period and the Second World War. He explains at length New Labour's perception of the British welfare state and comes to the conclusion that the 'New Labour social policies have much in common with neo-liberalism' in terms of its policies on work, education and poverty among others. As an alternative welfare strategy, Burden supports a new social policy initiative – the 'Citizen's Income', which can be used to expand employment, reduce social inequality and eliminate poverty. He explains: 'A guaranteed Citizen's Income would be distributed irrespective of social status and set at an amount deemed necessary to meet subsistence needs. Each citizen would receive the same basic amount, with extra-supplements paid in line with higher living costs due to, for instance, child care responsibilities or disability.' He concludes that the 'Citizen's Income may prove an important strategic idea which could take forward the historic concern of the left to create a more equal and just society.'

Sophie Nadal analyses the welfare state system in France, its salient features and the current problems facing it. She stresses the pivotal role the concept of equality plays in the construction of the welfare state in France and how the system has been attuned to the promotion of egalitarian principles by increasing social rights, reducing wage gaps, and by developing social benefits. Nadal asserts that the changes made in the French model in 1996 have not altered the basic premises of the French welfare state since the new thrust is also on the concept of 'equal chances for all'. The problems facing the French welfare state today include the high expenditure on public health, growing expenditure on pensions and social security, growing unemployment and an ageing population. The European Union's policy of free movement of people is also a problem, though not an insurmountable one. She observes that although many countries in Europe have pursued policies of privatization, France continues to follow the Republican model with emphasis on the ideals of equality and fraternity.

Professor Leisering traces the evolution of the welfare state in Germany since the 1880s when Chancellor Otto von Bismarck introduced social insurance schemes to protect workers. He explains how the Basic Law of 1949 made the welfare state a cardinal feature of Germany and the subsequent expansion of the programme after the Social Democratic Party joined the government in 1966. Leisering contends that Chancellor Helmut Kohl's neo-conservatism remained largely rhetorical during his 16 years in office from 1982. Though welfare benefits were repeatedly cut during this period, the basic structure remained intact. Significantly, after German reunification in 1990, social spending in 1996 had shown a record level of 35 per cent of GDP. Focus is also given to the welfare mix – public and private – in Germany, both at the macro and micro levels, as illustrated by the financing of the social budget at the three levels of government (federal, provincial and municipal), employers and employees. Leisering notes that while the coverage of the social insurance system in Germany is nearing universality, the programme is not egalitarian since the bulk of the welfare state is not directed to the poor but to the broad middle classes. Thus, the system results in the 'redistribution over the individual life course, not between rich and poor.' Liesering argues that changes in the German welfare state structure in the postwar period have evolved over time and are not part of a radical reform programme.

In their joint paper, Professor Emmerich Talos and Marcel Fink provide a historical overview of the development of social policy in Austria. They explain how, in the aftermath of the Second World War, Austria introduced universal insurance for the entire population by enacting the 'Universal National Security Law' in 1955. They focus on the moves of the Centre-Right government, which assumed power in 2000, to introduce neo-liberal and conservative ideas in the pursuit of a restrictive social policy in Austria.

According to them, there is a clear shift in Austria's social policy since February 2000, and efforts are being made to align it with neo-liberal, neo-conservative social and welfare policy. The authors note that the 'progressive enforcement of the individualization and privatization of social risks, as it is already being carried out and strived for even more by the ÖVP-FPÖ-Government between 2000 and 2002, will not be able to remove the deficiencies in modern societies' ability to solve social problems. Far from it. The general and extensive reduction of the welfare state would have precarious consequences even in a rich country like Austria.'

The texture of Nordic welfare states and the new challenges they are faced with are analysed in detail by Nimmi Kurian, Jukka Pekkarinen and Professor Jørn Henrik Petersen. Nimmi Kurian has analysed the Swedish welfare state model and the new challenges confronting it, explaining how Sweden has built up a universalistic, cradle-to-the-grave welfare state system around the concept *Folkhemmet*. She underlines the pivotal role that a full employment policy has played in harnessing the Swedish welfare state and the parts played by the state and municipalities as the regulator and providers respectively. The way Sweden had handled the crisis of the early 1990s and how it came out of it unscathed only by making marginal changes to its welfare programmes is also explained. An ageing population, diminished contributory revenue, increased social security expenditure, and so on, are some of the potential problems of the Swedish welfare state. Despite these, the short point that needs to be stressed is that change is not crisis and, challenges not withstanding, the fundamental tenets of the Swedish welfare state with its active social service orientation remain intact and it continues to enjoy popular support.

Jukka Pekkarinen analyses the impact of late industrialization in shaping the political economy of the Finnish welfare state. He points to the tight fiscal constraints under which welfare expenditures have always operated in Finland, with the growth potential of the economy determining expansion and contraction of welfare spending. The welfare state enjoys support of political parties cutting across ideological lines. Finland's income policy has promoted consensus on taxation and social expenditure, and it is this broad support base that has enhanced the adaptive capacity of the Finnish system and allowed it to make systemic adjustments in crisis situations.

In his analysis of the Danish welfare state system, Professor Jørn Henrik Petersen notes that the forces of globalization pose a challenge to the welfare state by constraining the independent decision-making capacity of the government's fiscal and monetary policies. The mobility of capital can cause erosion of national tax basis, the main source of welfare funding. However, in spite of vicissitudes, the Danish welfare state has remained more or less intact. He says: 'Despite the rhetoric of dismantling and retrenching the welfare state, major social programmes and the levels of social expenditures in almost all developed countries remain largely unaffected. There are no empirical signs of crisis and emphasis should rather be directed at analyzing the welfare states' capacity to adapt to changed circumstances.'

In his chapter, Joakim Palme examines the issue of modernization of social protection in Europe in the context of ongoing European integration. Palme points out how the universal mode of social protection adopted and established by the Nordic countries has followed a distinctive development path and, over the years, has become a natural reference point to many countries. According to Palme, the globalization of economies, demographic changes, exit/entry problems in the labour market, unemployment, issues of social integration/exclusion, and problems associated with the Europeanization of politics have posed serious challenges to social protection in Europe. Examining each of these challenges and the means to deal with them in detail, Palme concludes: 'Social security is ultimately about creating social identities. By sharing the costs of universal risks, the ground appears to be more fertile for building coalitions between different groups in society, groups that would otherwise have a more narrow basis for forming social identities. National identities or even nationalism, organized around social support systems for the whole population, is a more attractive scenario than nationalism based on real or believed, ethnic, religious or other divisions.'

Welfare states in North America are analysed by Asha Gupta and Professor B. Vivekanandan. Dr Gupta has focused on the recent welfare reforms in the United States by which 'welfare' gets increasingly replaced by 'workfare'. She explains how the traditional US notion of 'entitlement' has now been replaced by new notions of 'social contract' and 'reciprocity' in the disbursements of welfare benefits to the people, and she underlines the fact that in recent decades welfare provisions in the United States have become both a challenge and a constraint since the democratic governments are finding it difficult to maintain welfare programmes and policies within the existing framework of fiscal constraints. The institutional arrangements are found to be inadequate to accommodate the new demands made by the large number of social groups. She finds that, due to 'potential adverse reaction to post-modern and post-industrial capitalist economy, the welfare programmes and policies in the United States tend to be more reactive than active. She says: 'As a legacy of political culture prevailing in the United States, the recent welfare reforms aim at "more individual responsibility and less government" and "not individual liberty through government".'

Professor Vivekanandan analyses the changes in Canada's welfare state over the past two decades. His conclusion is that 'The vicissitudes of the welfare state system in Canada during the last two decades had been punctuated by several moves to hollow out the Canadian state from the welfare sector. Without making any frontal attack on the welfare state system itself or its universalistic character, the undercutting of the system was carried out by and large in stealth, with cost cutting process launched on the basis of debt, competitiveness and budget deficit. While some mutilation of the system has taken place as a result, and made it less universalistic, the core elements of the system still remain more or less intact. Key sectors like health care and education still remain universalistic and state funded.'

Tracing the history of Brazil's experience with the welfare state from 1930, Professor Dilip Loundo observes that the development process was always marked by a high degree of state intervention, regardless of the political system. The objective of this intervention was either to promote industrialization or to provide social protection to the marginalized sections of society. He focuses on the Real Plan of 1993, conceived by Fernando Henrique Cardoso, the then Finance Minister, to bring about economic transformation in the country through trade liberalization, revision of the fiscal system and social security, and flexibility of the labour market. Cardoso's election as President the following year saw the advancement of social policies in Brazil as he redefined the role of the state and drew social programmes to ameliorate poverty and social exclusion. Barring areas like education, unemployment insurance and poverty alleviation, its positive effects are yet to manifest. The politico-economic environment in the country remains still fluid. Loundo observes: 'Brazil is not Europe. To reform an accomplished welfare state is something quite different from reforming "an illfare state that takes from the poor to give to the rich and well-to-do". It demands (i) institutional/structural alternatives and (ii) effective/lasting social results.'

Progress towards the establishment of a welfare state in post-apartheid South Africa since 1994 is examined by Professor Albert J. Venter. His analysis takes into context the political economy of South Africa, its vast income disparities and widespread poverty, which was the legacy inherited from the dual economy maintained by the apartheid regime. However, the post-apartheid regime's macro-economic policy contains elements which can strengthen the construction of a welfare state in South Africa. These include the policies aimed at the redistribution of income to the poor, job-creation, building homes for the poor and poverty alleviation. In the national budget, too, priority has been given to the sectors of education, health and welfare. A notable feature of the South African welfare state has been the existence of redistributive policies alongside provisions for a free market. To quote Venter: 'In constructing and reconstructing South Africa's political economy, the South African government has chosen to let a free market economy take its place alongside the cautious welfarist policies it has embarked upon. Wealth has to be created before it can be redistributed. Private and the NGO welfare, private insurance and extended family care – leaving part of the welfare functions to private individuals and respecting their autonomy – augment state welfare in South Africa.'

Welfare state systems in three major Asian countries – China, Japan and India – are analysed by Christian Aspalter and Professor Anand Kumar. Dr Aspalter has examined the development of welfare states in Japan and China and the challenges they are faced with, finding striking similarities between the 'iron rice bowl system' of China and the occupational welfare state system in Japan, as both create strong company–labour relationships. The comparative positions of the these two East Asian countries are given in a nutshell in a chart. Aspalter explains how, in the postwar period, Japan established a residual welfare state system with provisions for meagre welfare benefits. He gives a graphic account of the series of welfare legislations Japan has enacted since then to expand the welfare programme, prompted partly by the socialist and communist-ruled local governments which had already implemented several progressive welfare measures. Significantly, a substantial portion of the welfare schemes in Japan are organized and administered by enterprises; state funding is confined mainly to healthcare and pensions. According to Aspalter, even now 'the Japanese welfare state system is still characterized by its dualism between the separately administered social security schemes of employees and that of the rest of the population'. In a graphic account of the evolution of social security system in China since 1948 and the changes introduced thereafter, he notes that a notable feature of the Chinese welfare state system is the dualism of the welfare rights of people living in the countryside. While about 81 per cent of the population lived in the countryside in the 1970s, the welfare state system was designed particularly for workers and employees in the cities. However, with the traditional economic and social system of China's rural areas set to undergo change in the coming years, he notes: 'This inevitable trend will cause the necessity of implementing a welfare state system in the countryside. . . . With the ongoing industrialization of Chinese hinterland, the Chinese welfare state system will certainly be extended to include more and more of China's vast rural population.'

Professor Kumar explains the trajectory of the construction of the welfare state in India during the last five decades. According to him the conceptualization of the Indian welfare state was accomplished partly during the freedom struggle, and partly at the Constituent Assembly where free India's constitution was framed. Indeed, in the Constituent Assembly, the construction of a welfare state was projected as a major objective. The welfare state principles envisaged for India's future reconstruction finds expression in Part IV of the Constitution dealing with the Directive Principles of State Policy. Kumar explains how India's first three Five-Year Plans were attuned to advance the construction of a welfare state in the country, with eradication of poverty being the central concern of Indian planning. However, to meet the challenges thrown up by the liberalization process, the state has reoriented itself *vis-à-vis* civil society and the market to ensure its active participation in state-supported welfare programmes.

Welfare states and the future

The contributions that follow attempt to expose the fallacy of several prevalent assumptions regarding the viability and relevance of welfare states. One such faulty formulation is the one that treats globalization as a uniform, monolithic phenomenon and paints all societies with broad brushes of uniformity. Nothing could be farther from the truth. The evidence that emerges shows that there are no proclivities towards convergence to a single model. On the contrary, the response patterns point to the adaptability of the welfare state regimes in keeping with national particularities and specificities. This further gives short shrift to the erroneous notion of a linear path of development and underscores the salience of multiple pathways and imageries.

As the contributions reveal, there is no single welfare state model that can be presented as universal and which can be applied to all countries transcending various cultures and continents. The development and expansion of welfare states across the world is marked by increased variation in models, emphasis and methods, and countries have followed their own variants of the system. This is evident not only in the developed world but also in the developing world, where many countries evolved their own distinct models conducive to their socio-economic contexts and ideological dispensations. The resultant variations are manifest in their policies on social security, social assistance, childcare, pensions, unemployment insurance, healthcare schemes, cash transfers, public expenditure levels, taxation levels, public and private arrangements for the provision of welfare benefits, and so on. Therefore, while an approximation of various welfare state models based on fundamental principles is possible, it seems impractical to transplant a particular model lock, stock and barrel to another country or region situated in a different environment, level of development or economic conditions.

A disparity in the quality of welfare benefit entitlements and a duality in their coverage of the population entitled for such benefits are also manifest. In the developed world, while in some countries welfare state construction has reached advanced levels and provides people with high-quality universal welfare benefits, in other equally resourceful countries, the benefit level remains minimal or residual. In Asian countries, such as China and Japan, welfare benefits are confined largely to the urban population or to the industrial labour force organized around enterprises. In other countries, social security schemes are largely job-based and income-based, and there exists dualism in the provision of welfare benefits as well. But there are indications that such dualism practised in some important Asian countries cannot endure since extension of benefits to everybody is on the cards.

Another faulty presupposition is the assumption that there is a basic incompatibility between the welfare state and globalization. This again rests on the misguided premise of a basic incompatibility between the market and the state. The interface between the market and the state is often portrayed as a zero-sum game, in which the terms of reference are stacked against the state and the gains of the market are always seen to be at the expense of the state. The functioning of welfare regimes so far, however, turns this thesis on its head. In fact, what emerges from the track record so far is the enabling role that the state has played in ensuring the smooth functioning of the market. The rapid expansion of economies in Europe after the Second World War was not without significant social risks and costs. Left to itself, the market would, in its drive towards competition and efficiency, produce serious social dislocations and economic disparities, which would ultimately eat into its entrails and enervate it.

It is the state, through the creation of a vast social security net, that bears these considerable social costs, thus contributing in no mean measure to the preservation of social cohesion, generating in the process widespread societal support for continued economic activity. It is no coincidence that welfare expenditures expanded substantially across Europe, with the greatest increase being recorded in countries with the maximum external exposure and, by inference, the greatest need for a sound welfare apparatus. The state also traditionally stepped in to provide investments in critical sectors that were unattractive propositions for the market on account of long gestation periods and slow returns. The state thus creates an enabling environment for market forces to operate successfully with the state reducing social dislocations through its myriad regulatory and welfare functions.

The ultimate yardstick of the relevance of the welfare state is its mandate to meet social needs and alleviate social risks. However, social needs are not cast in a mould forever, and the inventory and hierarchization of needs in a society undergo transformation over time. Thus the state will need to look beyond covering traditional social risks such as unemployment, disability, old age and so on, towards addressing new challenges as social norms undergo change. State policies need to factor in changing social patterns such as the erosion of the idea of the family as conventionally understood with the growing incidence of single parenthood, households without children, single-women households, and so on. The gender balance in society, too, is changing with the growing participation of women in the labour force, which has necessitated redefining traditional concepts such as full employment. Given the feminization of the labour market, the concept of full employment, traditionally based on the male breadwinner model, becomes redefined to mean full employment for both men and women. Thus the ambit of social policy needs to be continually redrawn to accommodate newly emerging social patterns.

It is the redistributive function of the welfare state and its role in redressing differences and disadvantages in the social context that assumes increased salience in the age of globalization. At its core, the globalization ethic is dehumanizing with human labour reduced to being little more than a mere factor of production, dispensable and liable to be substituted by the market in its search for ever cheaper replacements. It is here that the welfare state steps in to redress and temper the social and economic inequalities that market competition produces in its wake. Thus, the welfare apparatus of the state soaks in the imperfections and costs generated by the market and thereby helps contain social fissures and preserve cohesion in society.

2
Welfare States in Perspective

Pradip Bose

A perspectival analysis of welfare states in the world is a challenging task, since the subject is vast and complex. Each country has its own story to tell in the context of its own historical background, the state of its economic development and the level of its people's social and political consciousness. In spite of these perceptible difficulties, the subject merits deep and wide study. Giving shape within a democratic structure to a fully-fledged welfare state, first in Sweden and thereafter in Britain and the rest of Western Europe and across the Atlantic after the Second World War, was indeed a civilizational leap in human history. For the first time the welfare of common people became the central concern of the state.

However, in recent times the concept of the welfare state is being questioned from different angles and even being undermined in some countries. Therefore, a collective, international and in-depth study is called for to indicate what is in store for the twenty-first century.

In India the idea of a welfare state is an alluring mirage. The country does not even have a semblance of a welfare state; only a minuscule section of the country's vast population of a little more than one billion, such as government servants and employees of big industries, enjoy a degree of social benefits. But, all the same, the idea has a powerful attraction because the human problems which a welfare state deals with abound in the country, and there is an increasing urge among the people to improve their condition. The sheer accident of one's birth should not condemn a person to eternal damnation in terms of deprivation of his/her most basic needs and rights. Yet this is the position which affects the overwhelming majority of the people of India, who are no longer prepared to accept their fate as 'god's will', or the consequences of one's past deeds.

Their minimum aspirations in terms of nutrition, health, education, housing and economic well-being as a whole can be assured only in a welfare state, whatever might be its exact form or content. But this, unfortunately, is a distant dream for India and most of the countries in the Third World. With India's per capita GNP at around $350 and China's

14

$550, the welfare state, in a comprehensive sense, is a far cry for all these countries.

In the erstwhile so-called Second World, that is Russia and East European countries, there were fairly developed welfare systems which virtually collapsed with the demise of the Communist regimes. The economic dislocation which followed naturally impinged on the welfare systems in an adverse way. A significant portion of the populations of these countries, especially those belonging to the older generation, have a nostalgic longing for the old system, not for its dark side of dictatorships, but for the social benefits that people enjoyed then, even though they were of inferior quality to those of Western Europe. Until those economies revive and reach a higher stage of development, the welfare system which was a part of their culture cannot be satisfactorily restored.

The most developed welfare state systems still prevail in Western Europe. However, since the mid-1970s some serious questions have been raised about their character and functioning. This occurred soon after the oil crisis in the early 1970s, which shook the whole global economic system in a disturbing way. Countries in Western Europe began to experience structural changes which affected labour markets, and this period was the beginning of substantial, long-standing and 'stable' unemployment. For instance, in 1985 unemployment in West Germany, 'the engine of West European economy', reached approximately 10 per cent. This situation has, more or less, continued in most West European countries.

Unemployment and social security

Unemployment affects social security systems in several ways. First there are fewer people making contributions; second, the increase in wages falls and thus the increase in contributions falls as well; and third, the number of those claiming unemployment benefits rises. In addition to the problems of unemployment, there has also been a shift in the demographic balance of the population – an ever-increasing percentage reaching retirement age. All these factors have led to larger contributions demanded from employers and workers. The increasing deficit in the state budget results in cuts in benefits offered to unemployed and old-age pensioners, while payments made to the health services are substantially reduced. This is indeed a vicious circle.

Experts are of the opinion that there are limits to 'the equilibrating game' – the attempt to equilibrate incoming contributions and outgoing benefits, since this leads to a situation where the employment of labour becomes increasingly uneconomic. In Western Europe today we witness a situation where people are used to obtaining social benefits, and governments committed to maximizing benefits now find themselves in a situation where many of these benefits are not economically viable. Herein lies the basic crisis of the welfare state system in most industrially advanced countries today.

There are also problems relating to the beneficiaries. A social category called the 'marginal working class' has substantially increased in all these countries, comprised of low-wage workers with low employment security. After 40 years of employment, the social security benefits they are entitled to are only slightly higher than they would have been if they had received social assistance as unemployed. Such a worker might then justifiably ask why he/she should continue to pay money into the social security fund. On the other hand, upper-middle-class professional employees from another group have doubts about the value of social security. They accumulate assets throughout their working careers, but given the available avenues of investment in the private sector, such persons might reach the conclusion that they would do better in the private sector than putting their money into social security schemes.

Thus the fragmentation of the labour market is undermining the concept of class solidarity and the commonality of economic fate and interest among the working class.

The new right

Under these circumstances, the New Right or neo-liberals, went on the offensive from the late 1970s onwards, mainly under the leadership of Margaret Thatcher in Britain and Ronald Reagan in the USA. The economic objective of the New Right was to reduce public expenditure, which means the reduction of the tax burden; the political objective was to 'roll back' the welfare frontiers of the state; and the social objective was to encourage people to assume greater responsibility for their own welfare and thus become less dependent on the state. Other aims were to encourage 'choice' and 'freedom', and to bolster the caring role of the so-called traditional family. All this added up to a move towards the 'residual welfare state' model. In other words, an individual's needs are properly met by the 'private market' and the family. Only when these break down, should social welfare institutions come into play and that also temporarily.

This is, in brief, the New Right position and here the crucial debate on ideological issues becomes unavoidable. However, before dealing with this point, two brief comments on the New Right's approaches are pertinent. President Ronald Reagan's Republican successor in the office, George Bush Sr., had publicly referred Reaganomics as 'voodoo economics', and advocated 'compassionate conservatism'. Even then he was defeated by the rival Democratic Party's candidate William Jefferson Clinton. However, eight years later, George W. Bush Jr. became the new President of the USA and he would like to pursue some form of Reaganomics. This approach was dealt a most severe shock by the 11 September 2001 carnage caused by the terrorist attacks on the USA. The government of George W. Bush Jr., with a pronounced rightwing Republican orientation, had to make massive and energetic state interventions into the economy to give it a semblance of confidence and strength. Thus the basic postulates of the New Right's economic thinking was given a severe jolt.

Changes in Britain

The other comment concerns Britain. After the first six years' rule by Mrs Thatcher's Conservative government its public expenditure was 44.2 per cent, while the last Labour government's public expenditure in the 1978–79 period was 44 per cent. However, during the 18-year rule of the Conservative government it succeeded in bringing public expenditure to nearly 37 per cent, causing severe damage to the National Health Service, the education system and the mass transport sector. The widespread public discontent caused by this development was one of the major contributory factors to the victory of the opposition Labour Party in the 1997 elections.

The point is that it is politically unrewarding to reduce public expenditure below an 'acceptable degree' in industrially advanced countries because the population, having lived for long period in a welfare state, has certain minimum expectations which no democratic government can afford to ignore for purely ideological reasons. There has been considerable discussion in British Labour circles about the nature of reforms in the British welfare system. This is because there has been a general disappointment about the record of the Labour government to improve public services – especially health services and education – during its four years in office during the 1997–2001 period. The main debate has been around the extent of the involvement of private companies in rendering public services.

The British Prime Minister, Tony Blair, is of the opinion that while sticking strictly to social democratic values and goals, one should be open-minded regarding the means to be adopted to achieve these values and goals. For instance, one may employ private finances and expertise to improve the public services. While there is no intellectual objection to such a proposition as such, the main differences arise over the extent of the involvement of the private sector and also the fields in which it should be allowed to enter. Here the ideological issues come in.

Core concepts and values

The core concepts and values of the welfare state system – equality, liberty and community – could be the guiding principles of any country to protect its citizens. Equality means that access to decent housing, good health services and education should be a basic right for all, regardless of birth, race, gender and inheritance of wealth. Equality seeks social integration. From this emerges the unifying concept of citizenship, which leads to the development of an active and responsible society. Such a society is pledged to combat poverty, dependency and exclusion. 'Social security', therefore, is not just about obtaining social benefits; it involves wider policies and programmes for the creation of full employment to promote social security by the fostering of individual dignity and family independence. Ultimately, the success of social policies will depend on a proper balance between individuals, the family and society.

In this broader context, public-sector institutions embody an ideal of public service, based on the principle of the needs of service-users, and not on his or her money power. This is 'owned' by the people and is a concrete manifestation of the idea of community and, therefore, the quality of its performance has to be consciously raised to a higher level. It creates a public realm – a space where a wide variety of individuals come together for their collective needs and where non-market values prevail.

In a society in which public services are largely provided by private firms, mainly geared to making profits, the social outcome will be different because it expresses different values and social relations. Therefore, private means are not entirely value-neutral as they do not generate the public spirit which underlines the welfare state system. Therefore, private participation in public services should be limited so as not to change the fundamental ethos of the welfare state system.

Challenges of globalization

Pertinent in this context is the challenge of globalization and its impact on the welfare state system. Challenges emanate from the economic and political spheres, and here I shall deal with only two aspects of this very complex subject.

The globalization of information, the economy, commerce and capital movement has opened up new opportunities. The neo-liberal doctrine is now operating on the global level and as a result the more visible results have been the spectacular increases in inequality within nations and also in different regions of the world.

Globalization is substantially altering the dimensions and structures of companies, markets, investment and industrial relations. Productivity is increasing but new technology is breeding redundancies in existing jobs while creating a few new ones; surpluses are distributed unfairly and the traditional concept of employment is changing. No country in the world today can be a safe haven from this kind of disturbance and even well-developed welfare state systems are likely to be seriously threatened.

The globalization of the financial system has brought about an exponential increase in short-term capital investment, without any efficient regulatory framework to make it predictable. As a result, entire countries and regions have been subject to a series of crises which have seriously curtailed growth, earning and employment in the areas affected. This seriously affects social and public services because optimization of profit is placed before public obligation.

From the middle of the nineteenth century, advanced capitalist economies increased their productive capacities manifoldly, which simultaneously caused misery to the majority of the peoples of those countries. From then on there have been continuous struggles by working people to regulate the capitalist system through the powers of the state. Over a hundred years they succeeded in achieving their goal to a large extent and the result was the welfare state. In a similar way, in the twenty-first century global capitalism needs to be confronted by coordinated international action so that the process of globalization can work in the service of human progress. For this, a high level of public service is an essential ingredient.

The political aspect of globalization is that the character of the nation-state, which is the main provider of public services, is changing in a two-fold process. Its sovereignty is gradually 'leaking away', both upwards to supra-national institutions and downwards to sub-national ones. Therefore, no country is now in complete control of its economic life, which is why despite the best will in the world, it is often incapable of pursuing policies which it has set for itself. Therefore, some of the problems of the nation-state can be tackled only on a global scale. It is not an easy task to put public services, rather than the private profit of MNCs at the centre of international economic life, but this must be achieved for the sake of humanity.

The future

The welfare state system will survive in the twenty-first century if it reaffirms its traditional commitments, but, at the same time, adopts a revision of the means of achieving them without losing sight of its basic underlying values. In this way it will eventually triumph because it represents the interests of the overwhelming majority of the peoples of the world.

In this context, current experiments in the welfare state systems in different countries, besides their theoretical aspects which are analysed separately in this volume by competent experts, will be the input for the creation of a new kind of welfare state to meet the challenges of the twenty-first century.

3
Economic Foundations of Welfare State Systems

Sandwip Kumar Das

Introduction

In the postwar period almost all countries of the world adopted the welfare state system in various forms, and as a result there is no uniformity in the welfare state objectives pursued by governments. The basic principle behind the welfare state, however, is to bring about economic and social equality through income transfers, but there is wide divergence among countries in the ways in which income redistribution policies are adopted and implemented. The two crucial elements in income redistribution are the role of the state and dependence on markets in respect of which the countries differ to a great extent. In Western Europe, for instance, the state tends to go beyond the three economic objectives – namely full employment, price stability and an equitable distribution of income – with the state taking an active part in pursuing these objectives. Daniel Bell (1974)[1] represents one extreme position on the extent to which the welfare state is expected to intervene in the market. What he refers to as 'the revolution of the rising entitlements' is not just the claim of the minorities, the poor or the disadvantaged for a better future, but the claims of *all* groups in society for protection of rights. On the other hand, many observers would put North America in the category of those countries that use market instruments more often than an active intervention of the state in trying to achieve the liberal welfare state objectives.

Schumpeter traces the origin of the concept of the welfare state to the writings of Johann Heinrich Gottlob von Justi (1717–71) who came amazingly close to what we know as the economic objectives of the contemporary welfare state:

> . . . he dealt with economic problems from the standpoint of a government that accepts responsibility for the moral and economic conditions of life – just as modern governments do – in particular for everyone's employment and livelihood, for the improvement of the methods and

organization of production, for a sufficient supply of raw materials and foodstuffs and so on through a long list of topics that include beautification of cities, fire insurance, education, sanitation, and what not. Agriculture, manufacturing, commerce, money, banking – all come in for discussion from this point of view, technological and organizational aspects receiving much attention. But having thus pinned his faith to a principle of comprehensive public planning, he, like Seckendorf and most of the writers between these two, did not arrive at the practical conclusions this principle might lead us to expect. On the contrary, he was by no means blind to the inherent logic of economic phenomena, and did not wish to replace it by government fiat. Price fixing, for instance, was a measure to which the government had the right and duty to resort for particular purposes in particular circumstances, but it was to be avoided as much as possible . . . nor was he blind to the potentialities of free enterprise, on which he looked with detachment but without hostility. In fact, notwithstanding his approval of government regulation, which goes as far as to make him admit the expediency of enforcing the production of certain things by government decree, he stated as a general principle that all industry and commerce really needed was freedom and security.[2]

In the above quotation from Schumpeter the issue is comprehensive public planning *versus* free enterprise that requires freedom and security. In fact, even today there is no general agreement as to the extent to which the state should interfere with market forces directly rather than depend on the market and use taxes and subsidies in order bring about an equitable redistribution of income. Macroeconomic policies such as monetary and fiscal policies are used to achieve full employment and stable prices. While these policies may also affect income distribution, the state depends on direct and indirect taxes along with direct income transfers through welfare payments for arriving at a desired income distribution. Direct intervention, if attempted, is in the form of control of prices and payments to the factors of production.

It is necessary to mention two main criticisms of the concept of the welfare state. The first is the point raised by developing countries against the way that welfare state policies have been implemented in developed countries to reduce imports from them. The redistribution of income from capital to labour reduces the average propensity to import as the capital owners have a higher import propensity than the workers whose consumption expenditure is biased in favour of non-traded goods. Even the environmental policies are reported to have been used to curtail the flow of trade. Thus the entire gamut of welfare state interventions in developed countries has been branded as 'the new protectionism'[3] against trade with developing countries.

The second criticism is related to the inner contradiction in the concept of the welfare state, and includes various layers. The objectives of full employment and price stability may contradict each other as the short-run Phillips curve depicts a trade-off between the proportion of people employed and the rate of inflation. In other words, in order to have stable prices the unemployment rate would have to be rather high. In the long run the situation is worse as policy intervention in the form of monetary and fiscal actions would only raise the rate of inflation without changing the rate of unemployment. Conflict may arise between two countries applying macro demand-management policies in pursuit of welfare state objectives. For instance, a country faced with high unemployment and low inflation rates would follow an expansionary policy which will damage its trading partners that are confronted with low unemployment and high inflation rates. Such policy conflicts provide the rationale for economic cooperation and it is well-known that the genesis of the European Union is primarily based on such conflicts. But perhaps a more fundamental argument showing the inner contradiction in welfare states is related to economic growth and income redistribution. Critics such as Daniel Bell, Charles Kindleberger[4] and Melvyn Krauss have all tried to argue that redistribution of income from capital to labour may tend to reduce the rate of economic growth because (i) redistribution causes total savings to fall as workers have a lower propensity to save than the owners of capital, (ii) higher taxes and other deductions from income raise the demand for leisure, and (iii) welfare state policies encourage resources to stay in low-productivity and out of high-productivity uses.[5]

Objectives of the study

The purpose of this chapter is to examine the relationship between economic growth and income distribution in the context of income transfers that take place in welfare state systems. I shall examine the theoretical relationship between growth and distribution, retaining the growth mechanism of the traditional growth models in which the market absorbs the savings of the accumulators to raise the capital stock, but introducing a concept of 'uniform income transfers' by which income is transferred from an above-average earner to a below-average earner. I will show that a particular measure of inequality, namely Theil's entropy measure, is able to capture deviations from uniform income transfers. In one application of this measure, international income inequality is decomposed into inequality among groups of countries, to demonstrate that with uniform income transfers inequality falls at every level of disaggregation. The ultimate effect of income transfers on growth rates will be shown to be a combination of two factors: accumulation and redistribution, and it will be seen that it is not necessarily true that income transfer invariably reduces growth rates, as the Indian experience clearly shows to some extent.

If one is sure that income redistribution weakens the growth machinery, then the welfare state is not economically viable because in the long run the size of the cake that is being redistributed will steadily decline with less of it available for everybody. The economic foundation of the welfare state lies in the demonstration that this is not necessarily the case and that it is theoretically possible to achieve both economic growth and an equitable distribution of income. There is, however, a very large empirical literature on this issue. The observed relationship between growth and distribution depends largely on the stage of economic development.[6] Welfare state policy-makers have to deal with inequality in its various dimensions. For instance, in a large federal economy like the USA, Canada or India, income inequality is interpersonal, interregional and intraregional. Inequality among castes and races as well as sexual inequality may concern the welfare state planner.

Interpersonal income inequality is composed of interstate as well as intrastate income inequalities, all three of them being jointly determined by whatever redistribution policy the government may pursue. We propose to demonstrate that if a policy of uniform income transfers[7] is followed, then interpersonal, interstate and intrastate income distributions change in the same direction. The policies that result in a uniform redistribution of income without discriminating between regions or between groups within a region are the direct taxes such as income, wealth and property taxes. Redistribution through indirect taxes is not uniform, because these taxes are based on expenditure and therefore discriminate against an individual or a region having a lower-than-average income but higher-than-average expenditure.

The bias in income transfer brought about by the presence of indirect taxes is, however, partly offset by the fact that the inequality in consumption expenditure can be expected to be uniformly lower than the inequality in income, as the proportion of income saved rises with the size of income across income-earners.[8] While this may be a partial justification for restricting our analysis only to uniform transfers, there are other considerations that suggest that the income transfers actually taking place in a society are not uniform. A deviation from uniformity occurs when public spending does not discriminate between the rich and the poor. Because of the character of non-exclusivity of public goods, such non-uniformity cannot be avoided, but progressive direct tax rates that prevail in almost all countries can be expected to correct some of this non-uniformity. On the whole, it may not be too unrealistic to base a conceptual framework to study income distribution on income transfers that are uniform.[9] If income transfers are uniform, such transfers unfailingly improve income distribution irrespective of the size of the transfer. Uniform income transfers, taken as a benchmark, can be used to find out how far the actual transfers have deviated from uniformity, thus indicating the failure of the policy in reducing inequality and poverty in the country.

In this study we have used a decomposable measure[10] of inequality which can be used later for discussing the relationship between growth and distributive justice which has traditionally been hypothesized as a negative one due to the assumed adverse effect of income transfers on savings, investment and, consequently, economic growth. We have derived the conditions under which an economy in which income transfers are uniform can achieve both economic growth and an equitable distribution of income.

A decomposable inequality measure

There are many ways in which economic inequality can be measured and the index of inequality that one uses depends largely on the context. If we are interested in inequality among regions/states of a federal economy, then it is necessary to compare one region's shares in a country's income and population with those of the other regions. If, for instance, it turns out that a single region having only 5 per cent of the country's population accounts for 50 per cent of its income, then regional inequality must be considered rather acute. If, on the other hand, for most regions the share in population and the share in the country's income are close, then inequality is not very large. The entropy measure we have used in this study is based on this principle. Let y_k be the share of the kth region in the country's GNP and p_k its share in the total population of the country. Then an absolute equality in the regional distribution of income is represented by a situation in which the ratio, y_k/p_k is unity for all regions. Any deviation of this ratio from unity indicates inequality. It is, however, not possible to examine all these ratios and come to any conclusions regarding the degree of inequality prevailing in a country. Additionally, an intertemporal or intercountry comparison of inequality becomes impossible if one has to deal with all these ratios between income and population shares. What is required is a summary of the inequality scenario represented by these ratios. Measuring the ratios between income and population shares on a logarithmic scale, the following measure summarizes economic inequality among K regions of a country:

$$T_Y = \sum_{k=1}^{K} y_k \log(y_k/p_k) \tag{1}$$

where K is the total number of states/regions and $\Sigma y_k = \Sigma p_k = 1$. The ratio between the kth state's income share and population share, that is y_k/p_k, is nothing but the ratio between its per capita income and the country's per capita income. We may therefore designate y_k/p_k as the kth state's relative income. The welfare of the kth state is assumed to be a function of its relative income, and let log (y_k/p_k) be the kth state's welfare function. If income share y_k is taken as the probability of achieving the relative income y_k/p_k, then T_r is the expected welfare of the kth state. Any increase in T_Y would indicate an increase in interstate inequality. Theil (1967) has given a proof that $T_Y \geq 0$ and we will not repeat the proof here.

T_Y has a minimum equal to zero which is attained (subject to the condition that the shares add up to unity) when, for all states, the income share and the population share are identical. The situation of maximum interstate inequality arises when, for a given assignment of non-zero population shares to all states, the income share of one state, say the hth state, tends to unity, while the income shares of all other states tend to zero. In this case T_Y tends to $-\log(p_h) > 0$ which is the maximum value of the measure or maximum inequality.

Our choice of the Theil index, T_Y, as a measure of interstate income inequality is based on the consideration that the measure in equation (1) is decomposable and that, as we shall now demonstrate, with uniform income transfers the overall income inequality in a country as well as the interstate and intrastate inequality move in the same direction.

The decomposition of the Theil index is discussed in the context of international income inequality.[11] The model is described as follows. Let n countries in the world economy be grouped into G groups, with the number of countries in the gth group being n_g. Therefore, $n = \sum_{g=1}^{G} n_g$. Let y and p denote income and population shares. Then the decomposition works out as follows:

$$\sum_{i=1}^{n} y_i \log(y_i/p_i) = \sum_{g=1}^{G} y_g \log(y_g/p_g) + \sum_{g=1}^{G} y_g E_g,$$

$$\text{where } E_g = \sum_{k=1}^{n_g} y_{kg} \log(y_{kg}/p_{kg})$$

(2)

The term on the left-hand side is the Theil entropy index of inequality among all countries. This is decomposed as a summation of several entropy measures appearing on the right-hand side. The first term on the right-hand side is the measure of inequality between groups with y_g and p_g denoting the income and population shares of the gth group in the world totals. The first term, therefore, measures intergroup inequality. The second term is the weighted average of inequality levels within groups or intragroup inequality. The inequality within the gth group is measured by the entropy E_g. In the expression for E_g, the terms y_{kg} and p_{kg} are the income and the population shares of the kth country in the totals of the gth group. The first term is referred to as a measure of 'between inequality', whereas the second term stands for 'within inequality'.

We shall now discuss an applications of this decomposition. The model is applied to intercountry data on 94 countries for the period 1979–93. We applied the above decomposition on the World Development Report (WDR) grouping of 94 countries according to per capita income. There are four groups: (i) low-income countries, (ii) middle-income countries, (iii) upper-middle-income countries and (iv) high-income countries. The list of countries are given in WDR tables. The results of the decomposition are given in Table 3.1.

The second column of the table gives the entropy index of inequality among 94 countries; columns (3) to (6) provide the measures of inequality within each of the four groups of countries, and a weighted average of these 'within inequalities' is reported in column (8). The weights used are the shares of the respective groups in world GDP as in the decomposition model presented above. Column (7) gives the index of inequality between the four groups. The decomposition ensures that the sum of columns (7) and (8) is column (2). The values of all entropies are multiplied by 100 for visual convenience. The table shows that 'within inequality' is a small fraction of total inequality. In other words, the levels of inequality within each group are very low and it simply implies the WDR grouping by per capita income creates homogeneous groups of countries. Most of the inequality is between the groups. As the table shows, 'within inequality' has no clear time trend, whereas 'between inequality' has a rising trend along with the 94-country inequality index.

The arithmetic of uniform income transfers

We have already discussed the meaning of uniform income transfer and the forces acting for and against uniformity in the redistribution of income. What remains to be established is the arithmetic of income transfers that cause unidirectional movements in the interpersonal, interstate and intrastate income inequality. Income transfers are uniform if income is transferred from persons with more-than-average incomes to persons with less-than-average incomes. Such transfers can take place at various levels: interpersonal, interregional and interclass. It is a simple arithmetic exercise to show that if the transfers that take place at the interpersonal level are uniform, then the transfers are also uniform at higher degree of aggregation, that is at the interregional and interclass levels.

Let Y_{ijk} be the income earned by the ith person belonging to the jth income class and residing in the kth state, and $\bar{Y}$ is the per capita income. Superscripts are used to date the variables. A uniform redistribution of incomes between time $t-1$ and time t is defined as

$$Y_{ijk}^t = Y_{ijk}^{t-1} - \lambda\left(Y_{ijk}^{t-1} - \bar{Y}^{t-1}\right) \quad 0 < \lambda < 1 \tag{3}$$

Equation (3) shows that income is transferred from persons with more-than-average incomes to persons with less-than-average incomes. It shows that if

Table 3.1 Four-group decomposition

Year (1)	94 countries (2)	Low-income countries (3)	Middle-income countries (4)	Upper-middle-income countries (5)	High-income countries (6)	4-group entropy Between inequality (7)	4-group entropy Within inequality (8)
1979	42.53	2.54	5.49	1.91	1.41	40.85	1.68
1980	44.73	2.74	4.55	17.95	1.59	41.71	3.03
1982	57.04	1.08	3.14	2.14	11.83	46.63	10.41
1983	44.52	0.85	3.26	2.21	3.74	41.10	3.41
1984	45.67	0.92	4.19	2.30	2.39	43.30	2.37
1985	46.76	0.57	2.83	2.34	2.63	44.25	2.51
1986	57.74	0.61	4.52	2.59	9.02	49.59	8.16
1988	49.74	0.93	3.30	2.41	1.42	48.21	1.53
1990	50.00	0.81	4.17	3.35	0.86	48.83	1.17
1991	53.63	8.34	3.42	19.40	1.01	50.91	2.72
1992	51.00	2.33	4.66	6.25	2.84	47.81	3.19
1993	51.22	1.48	6.63	6.24	1.92	48.74	2.48

Source: World Development Reports.

a person's income is higher than average in time $t - 1$, then the person's income decreases between time $t - 1$ and t. It may be checked by aggregating equation (3) with respect to all i, j and k that $Y^t = Y^{t-1}$ with Y representing GNP, so that there is no income growth between the two periods. Also, an increase in λ makes income distribution more equal by raising the size of the transfer. The maximum value of λ is unity in which case everyone has the same income. Aggregating equation (3) with respect to i and k and writing Y_j to represent the total income of the jth income class and n_j to represent the number of people in the jth income class, we get

$$Y_j^t = Y_j^{t-1} - \lambda\left(Y_j^{t-1} - n_j\overline{Y}^{t-1}\right) \tag{4}$$

Equation (4), written in terms of per capita incomes, is

$$\frac{Y_j^t}{n_j} = \frac{Y_j^{t-1}}{n_j} - \lambda\left(\frac{Y_j^{t-1}}{n_j} - \overline{Y}\right) \tag{4a}$$

which shows that an increase in λ improves income distribution by income class.

Now aggregating equation (3) with respect to i and j and writing Y_k for the total income of the kth region and n_k for the number of people located in the kth region, we get the same result for interstate income distribution:

$$\frac{Y_k^t}{n_k} = \frac{Y_k^{t-1}}{n_k} - \lambda\left(\frac{Y_k^{t-1}}{n_k} - \overline{Y}^{t-1}\right) \tag{5}$$

Since the basis of interstate transfer according to the uniformity rule is the difference between a state's per capita income (Y_k/n_k) and the country's per capita income ($\overline{Y}$), the Theil measure of interstate inequality defined in equation (1) will capture the extent to which interstate transfers have deviated from the uniformity rule.

Finally, aggregating equation (3) with respect to i and writing Y_{jk} to denote the aggregate income earned by all earners belonging to the jth income class and residing in the kth state, and n_{jk} to denote the number of persons in the jth income class and residing in the kth state, we get the redistribution rules within each state:

$$\frac{Y_{jk}^t}{n_{jk}} = \frac{Y_{jk}^{t-1}}{n_{jk}} - \lambda\left(\frac{Y_{jk}^{t-1}}{n_{jk}} - \overline{Y}\right) \tag{6}$$

An increase in λ, therefore, is seen to improve personal, class-wise, interstate and intrastate income distributions, provided that the income transfers are uniform.

The decomposition of the Theil measure to capture the effects of uniform income transfers on income distribution at different levels in a federal economy is what remains to be seen. We have shown that the Theil measure is decomposable and total inequality can be broken into components. We have also made one application of the measure to show how international income inequality can be broken up into components so that one can see the trends in 'within-group' and 'between-group' inequalities. If income transfers are uniform, then the trends in total inequality and the trends in the inequality in the components will be similar. However, one cannot expect the income transfers to be always uniform at every level. The Theil index of inequality, therefore, would measure the extent to which income transfers have been uniform.

Growth and distribution

The theoretical relationship between economic growth and income distribution generally turns out to be complex. There has been a great deal of statistical work dealing with this issue and some of it has already been cited. A few more recent studies on the relationship between growth and distribution are Ravallion and Datt (1990)[12] and Jain and Tendulkar (1990).[13] It will be prudent to look at the theoretical models of economic growth to find out if there is any discussion on growth and income distribution. The so-called Cambridge models of Kaldor (1956)[14] and Pasinetti (1974)[15] have discussed the relationship between growth and distribution in the framework of equilibrium growth. Two important parameters in these models are the workers' and the capitalists' propensities to save. In Kaldor's model, equilibrium is attained if the warranted rate of growth of income, which is the ratio between the average of the two savings propensities (s) and the incremental capital output ratio (v), is equal to the natural rate of growth which, in the absence of any technological change, is the exogenously determined rate of population growth.

In a steady state, the per capita income stops growing and its value is determined in such a way that s/v is equal to the rate of growth of the population. If per capita income happens to exceed its steady state value, then the actual growth rate of income ($\Delta Y/Y$) will be less than s/v which also means that $\Delta Y/Y$ is less than the rate of population growth resulting in a fall in per capita income. In the process of income contraction ($v.\Delta Y$) falls short of total savings ($s.Y$) which, under the condition of full employment, will lead to a fall in the price level and a rise in the real wage rate as well as the share of wages in national income. Thus, the decline in per capita income in the adjustment process is associated with an improvement in the income distribution.

Conversely, if per capita income is less than its steady state value, investment will exceed total savings, the price level and the share of profit in national income will rise, as per capita income rises to approach its steady state value. Both Kaldor and Pasinetti, particularly the latter, insisted on the irrelevance of workers' propensity to save.[16] But the overall relationship between the rate of growth and the extent of equality in the distribution of income between wage earners and capitalists is a negative one. Another important aspect of Cambridge growth models as well as the neo-classical growth models is that in the process of income redistribution the real rewards going to the various economic classes do not remain constant.

Both in the Cambridge models and the neo-classical models one finds a relationship between growth and distribution only when the economy is off the steady state path. If one assumes that the economy is always on the steady state path, the rate of growth of income is determined by the exogenously given rate of growth of population with no change in income distribution as neither the factor shares nor the real returns to factors change along the steady state path. An introduction of technological change will however change all this because it may cause a shift in the steady state path of income growth. Technological progress will also change income distribution even if it is of the Hicks-neutral type. The effect of technological progress on growth is unquestionably positive, but its effect on income distribution depends on the nature of the technological progress. For instance, a technological progress occurring in the capital intensive industry may change income distribution in favour of capital.

The subsequent work on income distribution and growth has become a part of development economics with the contribution of Kuznets and Williamson[17] who have built up both the conceptual and empirical basis of the 'inverted-U hypothesis'. According to this hypothesis, during the initial stages of economic development growth of income raises income inequality but reduces it in the later stages. Recently, there has been a revival of interest in the relationship between growth and distribution. Persson and Tabellini (1994) have used an overlapping generation model to show that a reduction of income inequality raises the growth rate of income, assuming that the median income class in the population makes all the political decisions relating to income transfers that are uniform in the sense in which we have defined such transfers in this chapter. They implicitly assume that the median income exceeds the arithmetic mean which implies that the income distribution is negatively skewed with the longer tail falling on the lower range of income. The median class will vote for a transfer if and only if the transfer does not curtail their incentive to accumulate more productive assets. Since by definition a transfer will benefit at least 50 per cent of the population who would accumulate more productive assets, one tautologically gets a positive relationship between growth and equity. The model simply provides an alternative explanation of the forces behind the falling segment of the inverted-U curve, where there is no conflict between growth and reduction of income inequality. However, the most restrictive assumption of this model is the constancy of the rate of return accruing to the asset holders in the process of income transfers.

The framework of analysis we propose to apply in this study is an extension of the model of uniform income transfers where GNP is assumed to remain fixed. We now assume that the people earning below average do not save and those earning incomes above average save a fixed portion of their net incomes and earn interest or profit on their savings. A steady state equilibrium may be disturbed by the government's policy of income transfers from the above-average to the below-average earners. Given the fixed rate of savings, this redistribution of income will reduce total savings, which will fall below the level of investment. Such an excess demand situation in the economy will raise the price level and reduce the real value of the transfers as well as the real incomes. We assume that inflation only cuts down the initially intended size of the transfers. On the other hand, since the real wages fall and the rate of profit rises, the above-average earners recover a part of their lost incomes. In this scenario growth and redistribution may not necessarily be conflicting goals. We present a very simple formalisation of a rather complicated relationship between growth and distribution.

Equation (3) can be changed in the following manner:

$$Y_{ijk}^t = Y_{ijk}^{t-1} - \lambda\left(Y_{ijk}^{t-1} - \overline{Y}^{t-1}\right) + \mu\left[s\left\{Y_{ijk}^t - \lambda\left(Y_{ijk}^{t-1} - \overline{Y}^{t-1}\right)\right\}\right] \tag{7}$$

where s is the rate of savings and

$$\mu > 0 \text{ if } Y_{ijk}^{t-1} \geq \overline{Y}^{t-1}, = 0 \text{ otherwise.}$$

μ is the rate of interest in equilibrium which may be positively related to the distribution parameter λ, as a policy-induced reduction of savings, in the absence of technical progress, may increase its rate of return.

As may be recalled, there was no provision for income growth in equation (3), and the simple transfer mechanism illustrated in equation (3) has been modified in equation (7) to include an income growth component. It is simply assumed that a part of income minus transfer is saved by earners who earn more than the average income and earn a return on this saving in the next time period. It is assumed for the sake of simplicity that the below-average earners do not save. An aggregation of equation (7) will require a distinction to be made between below-average earners and above-average earners because their behaviour is different. After aggregation we get the following equation for income growth:

$$Y^t = Y^{t-1} + \mu s\left[Y_a^{t-1} - \lambda\left(Y_a^{t-1} - n_a\overline{Y}^{t-1}\right)\right] \tag{8}$$

where n_a is the number of people in the above-average income classes and Y_a is the total income of the above-average income earners.

Writing P to denote the total population of the country, the growth rate of GNP derived from equation (8) may be written as:

$$g \equiv \frac{Y^t - Y^{t-1}}{Y^{t-1}} = \mu s \left[(1 - \lambda) \frac{Y_a^{t-1}}{Y^{t-1}} + \lambda \frac{n_a}{P} \right] \tag{9}$$

The expression for the rate of growth in equation (9) shows that it depends on both accumulation and distribution represented by μ and λ respectively. While the former affects g positively, the latter's influence is a negative one if the initial distribution is unequal and the income share of the above-average income class is higher than its population share. The only channel through which a redistribution of income may help income growth is the one in which redistribution assists the accumulation process. We have argued that μ may be positively influenced by λ; in what follows we take μ as a function of λ: $\mu = \mu(\lambda)$, $\mu'(\lambda) > 0$.

Differentiating equation (9) with respect to λ we get:

$$dg/d\lambda = \left[(1 - \lambda) \frac{Y_a^{t-1}}{Y^{t-1}} + \lambda \frac{n_a}{P} \right] \mu'(\lambda) - \mu s \left[\frac{Y_a^{t-1}}{Y^{t-1}} - \frac{n_a}{P} \right] \tag{10}$$

The first term in equation (10) is the accumulation effect of an increase in the intensity of income transfers whose sign is positive. The second term represents the negative effect of redistribution on the rate of growth. One may visualize a situation where the size of the accumulation effect is small due to the low income and population shares of the above-average earners and the second term outweighs the first term. The resulting negative relationship between growth and distribution is typically the case of a country with a small class of entrepreneurs whose command on the economy is relatively low. In this case an increase in the rate of growth requires a fall in λ, that is regressive income transfers. At higher levels of development the accumulation effect is likely to dominate the redistribution effect and an increased intensity of the transfers may lead to a higher growth rate of income. This result may be replicated at various levels of disaggregation, that is interstate and intrastate income distribution. If the below-average earners are also savers, though their savings propensity may be less than that of the above-average earners, the inverted-U relationship between per capita income and the rate of economic growth is strengthened. In this case the below-average earners may acquire upward mobility along the income scale over a period of time exactly the way Kuznets described this process of growth and distribution. One can also imagine a scenario where continuous upward mobility raises the median income above the average and this is the stage from which the relationship between growth and distribution is essentially guided by the factors discussed by Persson and Tabellini.

Inequality and growth: the Indian experience

There is a very large literature on various aspects of economic inequality in the Indian economy.[18] As mentioned by Kuznets (1955), structural changes in the process of growth lie at the heart of the relationship between growth and distribution. It is, therefore, only logical that we follow the growth process of the Indian economy during 1970–92 and see the associated structural changes in terms of the relative positions of the sectors of the Indian economy. Table 3.2 gives the growth rates of the major sectors of the Indian economy for three different periods. It shows, as one may expect, relatively lower rates of growth for the primary activities relative to manufacturing, construction, infrastructure and the services. Growth has, of course, been faster in all sectors in the second period (1982–92) than in the first (1970–82).

We have applied the entropy measure of inequality defined in equation (1) to compute interstate inequality levels relating to the sectors of the economy. The sectors are, however, the components of gross domestic products in national income accounting. This has been done for the period 1970–92 for 23 states and union territories. The Central Statistical Organization (CSO) changed the base year from 1970–71 to 1980–81, but we have made adjustment for this change and the entropies have been calculated at constant prices with 1970–71 as the base year. Table 3.3 shows these inequality measures, denoted by E followed by the subscript indicating the sector.

Table 3.2 Exponential growth rates at 1970–71 prices[19]

	Growth rate (%)		
	1970–92	*1970–82*	*1982–92*
Population	2.17	2.23	2.06
Per capita income	2.46	1.8	3.2
Net domestic product	4.6	4.0	5.1
Agriculture	2.9	2.4	3.2
Manufacturing	6.0	5.5	6.5
Infrastructure I	4.9	2.8	8.1
Infrastructure II	4.8	3.8	6.5
Construction	4.6	4.7	4.7
Primary	3.5	4.1	3.4
Services	6.2	5.8	6.2

Source: Central Statistical Organization, New Delhi.

Table 3.3 Entropy estimates at constant prices (23 states and union territories), 1970–71 = 100

Year	E_Y	E_a	E_q	E_p	E_c	E_i	E_{qr}	E_{qu}
1970	3.19	3.63	18.13	16.1	9.86	7.1	28.55	10.56
1971	3.63	3.52	18.56	17.23	10.47	6.8	28.97	10.8
1972	3.08	3.95	18.72	16.52	10.21	6.7	29.01	11.23
1973	3.74	3.49	17.49	18.1	10.68	7.	26.99	10.83
1974	4.12	4.08	18.61	18.41	10.88	6.9	28.68	11.76
1975	4.01	3.37	18.89	18.06	11.1	6.6	28.41	11.48
1976	4.71	4.01	19.13	18.03	11.64	6.5	27.77	11.54
1977	4.46	3.45	20.59	18.32	11.79	6.2	30.61	12.11
1978	4.89	4.2	21.18	15.58	11.89	6.3	31.59	11.13
1979	6.4	6.04	22.31	16.92	11.45	6.2	31.69	14.99
1980	5.19	4.73	25.49	16.94	11	8.1	38.17	14.41
1981	5.45	5.38	22.51	17.26	11.42	8.4	33.02	13.73
1982	5.55	6.4	19.64	13.74	11.79	8.7	28.95	11.79
1983	5.04	5.27	19.59	12.89	11.2	8.8	27.17	13.32
1984	5.11	5.7	18.32	12.87	10.76	8.5	25.04	13.57
1985	5.41	5.97	19.24	12.2	12.17	8.8	27.2	13.66
1986	5.63	6.37	20.65	11.37	11.71	7.9	30.55	13.35
1987	6.22	7.54	17.34	10.61	11.44	8	23.64	14.14
1988	5.79	6.75	18.33	9.34	11.31	7.7	25.08	13.61
1989	7.1	7.2	19.09	11.42	12.09	8.3	26.05	13.56
1990	6.77	7.04	19.32	11.7	11.38	8.3	28	13.32
1991	7.37	8.89	20.15	11.24	11.65	9.1	27.91	15.16
1992	8.06	8.29	20.88	11.21	11.77	9.6	28.54	16.39

Source: Central Statistical Organization, New Delhi.

Table 3.3 clearly demonstrates that income inequality (E_Y) as well as inequalities in the various components of income except primary sector inequality (E_P) have been increasing over the years. While the manufacturing sector (E_q) as a whole has shown a rising trend, its breakdown into registered (E_{qr}) and unregistered (E_{qu}) manufacturing has given us an interesting picture. While inequality for registered manufacturing has been decreasing, inequality in unregistered manufacturing has been increasing. The other measures of sectoral inequality given in Table 3.3 are E_c and E_i for construction and infrastructure respectively.

A reflection of the divergent growth processes in the different sectors of the Indian economy is found in the time-trend of the sectoral shares calculated as the percentage of net domestic product at 1970–71 prices. These are shown in Table 3.4. So far as the relative shares are concerned, agriculture is the principal loser and manufacturing and services are the principal gainers. These changes in the structure of the Indian economy may be expected to promote upward mobility in manufacturing and services and

Table 3.4 Sectoral shares at 1970–71 prices[20]

Year	Agr.	Cons.	Infra.	Mfg.	Pri.	Ser.	NDP
1970	48.86	5.09	5.69	13.60	2.79	23.98	100.00
1971	47.80	5.18	5.99	13.63	2.87	24.52	100.00
1972	44.89	5.63	6.38	14.69	2.98	25.42	100.00
1973	46.48	5.26	6.09	14.19	2.84	25.13	100.00
1974	45.73	5.16	6.48	14.45	2.95	25.24	100.00
1975	46.83	5.01	6.42	13.93	2.82	24.98	100.00
1976	43.85	5.42	6.74	15.30	2.71	25.98	100.00
1977	45.08	5.31	6.55	14.96	2.54	25.56	100.00
1978	43.75	5.20	6.70	15.64	2.51	26.20	100.00
1979	39.67	5.37	7.40	17.07	2.58	27.91	100.00
1980	40.96	5.82	4.76	15.67	3.10	29.69	100.00
1981	41.22	5.72	4.85	15.52	3.11	29.58	100.00
1982	39.76	5.54	5.15	16.33	2.94	30.28	100.00
1983	40.52	5.24	5.45	16.35	2.72	29.73	100.00
1984	39.90	5.20	5.80	16.11	2.59	30.40	100.00
1985	38.11	5.41	6.10	17.13	2.46	30.80	100.00
1986	36.81	5.46	6.41	17.16	2.37	31.79	100.00
1987	35.25	5.53	6.58	17.82	2.23	32.59	100.00
1988	36.80	5.27	6.17	17.90	2.29	31.57	100.00
1989	35.38	4.98	6.44	18.30	2.36	32.54	100.00
1990	34.65	5.23	6.62	18.55	2.36	32.58	100.00
1991	33.54	5.28	7.06	18.53	2.47	33.11	100.00
1992	34.05	5.23	7.32	17.89	2.38	33.13	100.00

Source: Central Statistical Organization, New Delhi.

downward mobility in agriculture. This brings us straight to the question Kuznets posed: have the growth rates caused by structural changes in the dynamic sectors had adverse effects on the distribution of income?

The relationship between economic growth and income inequality has traditionally been explored in terms of the presence or absence of a U-type relationship between the level of inequality and per capita income. The existence of a U-type relationship in the Indian context has been explored by Mathur (1983)[21] and his study by and large supports the Kuznets–Williamson thesis. Though such a relationship has a relevance in development policy in so far as it prescribes the social safety nets to be used at the levels of high per capita income to check the growth of income inequality in an economy that is becoming increasingly prosperous, it does not really deal with the question of growth versus distribution. The basic question to be answered is *not whether inequality rises with income, but whether inequality rises with the rate of growth of income*.

We have calculated the correlation coefficients between the level of inequality, measured by an entropy, and the annual (year-to-year) growth

Table 3.5 Economic growth and regional inequality (correlation coefficient between inequality and annual growth rates)

Category	1971–92	1971–80	1981–92
Agriculture	−0.847	−0.877	−0.722
	(−7.13)	(−5.77)	(−3.61)
Manufacturing	−0.077	−0.167	0.035
	(−0.35)	(−0.54)	(0.12)
Infrastructure II	−0.682	−0.887	−0.086
	(−4.17)	(−6.07)	(−0.3)
Primary	0.126	−0.062	0.289
	(0.57)	(−0.19)	(1.05)
Services	−0.013	−0.251	0.353
	(−0.06)	(−0.82)	(1.31)
NDP	−0.483	−0.488	−0.441
	(−2.47)	(−1.77)	(−1.7)

Figures in parentheses are *t* values.
Source: Central Statistical Organization, New Delhi.

rates. These are shown in Table 3.5. The correlation between growth and inequality has been found for the entire period (1970–92) as well as for the two sub-periods, 1971–80 and 1981–92. The entropy measures the level of regional inequality and therefore, as the table shows, there does not seem to be any conflict between growth and inequality. This is an alternative approach to the U-hypothesis and the results in the two subperiods do not indicate any turning point in the relationship between growth and inequality at the aggregate as well as at the sectoral levels. In agriculture, growth and inequality are significantly and negatively correlated. In manufacturing, the correlation is negative but not significant. The positive sign of the correlation coefficient in the second period indicates a turning of the relationship between growth and inequality in the manufacturing sector, but since the coefficient is not significant, one cannot draw any conclusion from it. The negative sign of the correlation coefficients is seen in most other cases, but these are not significant except in infrastructure II and NDP.

If we compare Table 3.5 with Table 3.2, it appears that a conflict between growth and inequality may arise in the Indian economy if the rate of growth is sufficiently high. Taking this as our hypothesis, we go back to Table 3.2 which shows that the growth rate in agriculture has been the lowest during the entire period as well as during the two subperiods. *In a sector experiencing a moderate growth rate, no conflict arises between growth and regional distribution.* This has nothing to do with the steadily rising regional inequality in agriculture with respect to time or per capita income. In manufacturing, the growth rates are much higher than in agriculture and a possible conflict between growth and regional distribution may arise, though the correlation result does not show such a conflict in the Indian experience. Infrastructure II shows moderate growth rates and thus the negative correlation between growth and regional inequality turns out to be very significant. The pattern in the service sector is similar to the manufacturing sector, as it shows high growth rates and insignificant correlation between growth and inequality. The only exception to our hypothesis is the primary sector which shows moderate growth rates but insignificant correlation between growth and inequality. Considering the fact that the Indian economy has grown faster during the second period (see Table 3.2), we may be tending towards higher overall as well as sectoral inequality as the economy grows even faster. But as things stand today there is no evidence of a conflict between growth and social justice during the last two decades of Indian economic development.

Summary and conclusions

Dealing with the economic foundations of a welfare state, this chapter has looked into one aspect, namely the achievement of an equitable distribution of income along with maintenance of full employment and price stability. We have pointed out that these goals may be contradictory, as many other writers have discussed as the inner contradiction in the concept of the welfare state. Most developing countries would think that the industrial countries use their welfare state objectives very effectively against imports from the former. But the most interesting aspect of the running of the welfare state is the challenge of securing an equitable distribution of income and at the same time achieving a reasonable rate of growth. It is obvious that without growth, income redistribution is counterproductive in the long run. The issues related to growth and distribution are much more relevant for developing countries than for developed countries because the growth possibilities are not very strong in the latter. We have examined the theoretical relationship between growth and distribution and for this purpose we first looked at the literature on economic growth in the Cambridge as well as the neo-classical tradition. Growth models emphasize equilibrium growth or a steady state and therefore do not directly deal with the effect of growth on income distribution. However, once the economy is off the steady state path and adjustments are taking place to get back to the path, it clearly appears that growth and distribution have a negative relationship. This perhaps is the basis of the hypothesis that in a market economy economic growth would change the income distribution adversely.

In running a welfare state, policy-makers do not entirely depend on markets. The extent of state intervention in market forces varies from country to country and depends crucially on the political systems prevalent in the countries. Many observers would subscribe to the view that the welfare state in Europe is stronger than in North America. In the developing world, state intervention has traditionally been very strong until recently with economic reforms and liberalization of economic policies demanding less of government and more of free enterprise in running the economy. But the government's role in the developing world has been quite different from that in the industrial countries. Governments in developing countries do much more than just redistribute income, as they have been engaged directly in the production processes and performing functions that are normally in the domain of the private sector. At one time it was expected that direct involvement of the government in production would bring about an equitable distribution of income, but there is ample evidence that this has not happened. In the post-liberalization phase, the governments of the developing countries still have to perform their redistributive functions. The crucial question that arises is whether the redistributive functions of the government will come into conflict with the growth process that will now be almost entirely conducted by market forces.

We have taken this question as the main concern of the chapter. Therefore, we have retained the growth mechanism of the traditional growth models in which the market absorbs the savings of accumulators to raise the capital stock leading to growth of aggregate output in the economy. But we have introduced a concept of 'uniform income transfers' by which income is transferred from an above-average earner to a below-average earner with the size of transfer being proportional to the difference between the actual and average incomes. We have shown that a particular measure of inequality, namely Theil's entropy measure, is able to capture deviations from uniform income transfers. We have discussed the tax structure that can achieve such uniform income transfers. Theil's measure happens to be additively decomposable, which means that the measure can break up total inequality into inequality levels among groups of people. In a federal economy like India or the United States, such a measure can present a disaggregated picture in which one can see which sectors or regions are reporting higher inequality even though the total inequality in the country may be under control. In one application of this measure we have decomposed international income inequality into inequality among groups of countries. The result of this exercise shows that there is much more intergroup income inequality than intragroup inequality due to the obvious fact that within each country group governments follow income redistribution policies, whereas in the absence of a world government no such policy can be implemented between country groups. We have then demonstrated that if income transfers are kept at the uniform level, then inequality will fall at every level of disaggregation; that is, there will be an improvement in personal, intergroup and intragroup income distribution.

In the last part of our theoretical analysis we have tried to place uniform income transfers in the context of growth. The ultimate affect of income transfers on growth rates is found to be a combination of two factors: accumulation and redistribution. It is not necessarily true that income transfer will invariably reduce growth rates. The basic intuition is that while income gets transferred from the relatively rich to the relatively poor, the real value of the transfer is eroded by an increase in the price level and the rate of return on investment increases, both of which generate growth. But the ultimate effect of redistribution on growth rates may go either way. There are reasons to believe that in the primary stages the effect of accumulation on growth will remain weak and the negative effect of redistribution will dominate. This implies two things. First, in the primary stages of economic development an attempt to redistribute income will affect growth rates adversely. Second, if growth rates are found to rise, income distribution must be moving in the adverse direction. The second implication agrees with the Kuznets–Williamson thesis that is known as the inverted-U hypothesis. All this puts a great deal of responsibility on welfare-state governments, particularly in developing countries, namely to strike a balance between market-generated growth impulses and the need to achieve an equitable distribution of income at all levels.

Finally, we looked at the experience of the Indian economy during 1970–92 in respect of interregional inequality in GDP as well as in the various sectors or components of GDP. We have not found any evidence to show that India was confronted with a trade-off between growth and interstate inequality during this period. There are, however, some indications that high growth rates may cause adverse movements in income distribution in the Indian economy, though we must grant that the statistical support of this kind of hypothesis is rather weak in our sample.

Notes

1 Daniel Bell, 'The Public Household – On "Fiscal Sociology and the Liberal Society"', *The Public Interest*, Washington DC, Fall 1974, p. 39.

2 J.A. Schumpeter, *History of Economic Analysis*, New York: Oxford University Press, seventh printing 1968, p. 171.

3 M.B. Krauss, *The New Protectionism: The Welfare State and International Trade*, Oxford: Basil Blackwell, 1979.

4 C.P. Kindleberger, *Europe's Postwar Growth*, Cambridge, Mass.: Harvard University Press, 1967.

5 See M.B. Krauss, n. 3.

6 See S. Kuznets, 'Economic Growth and Income Inequality', *American Economic Review*, Nashville, March 1955, and J.G. Williamson, 'Regional Inequality and the Process of National Development: A Description of the Patterns', *Economic Development and Cultural Change*, Chicago, vol. 13, no. 4, part II, July 1965.

7 A uniform income transfer is a transfer from persons with above-average income to persons with below-average income, with the size of the transfer being proportional to the gap between the actual and average income.

8 For an empirical support of this thesis, see N. Kakwani, *Analyzing Redistribution Policies: A Study Using Australian Data*, Cambridge: Cambridge University Press, 1986. Also I.Z. Bhatty, 'Inequality and Poverty in Rural India', in T.N. Srinivasan

and P.K. Bardhan (eds), *Poverty and Income Distribution in India*, Calcutta: Statistical Publishing Society, 1974.

9   For the use of uniform income transfers in theoretical models of growth and distribution see, T. Persson and G. Tabellini, 'Is Inequality Harmful for Growth?', *American Economic Review*, vol. 84, no. 3, 1994.

10 The inequality measure is known as Theil's entropy measure. It is decomposable as interpersonal income inequality can be decomposed into interregional and intraregional inequalities. See H. Theil, *Economics and Information Theory*, Amsterdam: North Holland, 1967.

11 See S. Zandvakili, 'International Comparison of Household Inequalities Based on Microdata with Decomposition', in D.B. Papadimitriou (ed.) *Aspects of Distribution of Wealth and Income*, New York: St Martin's Press, 1994.

12 M. Ravallion and G. Datt, 'Growth and Distribution Components of Changes in Poverty Measures', LSMS Working Paper no. 83, World Bank, Washington DC, 1990.

13 L.R. Jain and S.D. Tendulkar, 'Role of Growth and Distribution in the Observed Change of Headcount Ratio-Measure of Poverty', Technical Report no. 9004, Indian Statistical Institute, Delhi, 1990.

14 N. Kaldor, 'Alternative Theories of Distribution', *Review of Economic Studies*, Oxford, vol. 23, 1956.

15 L.L. Pasinetti, *Growth and Income Distribution: Essays in Economic Theory*, Cambridge: Cambridge University Press, 1974.

16 Later, Samuelson and Modigliani have shown the special character of the Pasinetti Paradox. See P.A. Samuelson and F. Modigliani, 'The Pasinetti Paradox in Neo-Classical and More General Models', *Review of Economic Studies*, October 1966.

17 We have referred to their studies in the section 'Objectives of the Study'.

18 For a survey of this literature see S.K. Das and A. Barua, 'Regional Inequalities, Economic Growth and Liberalization: A Study of the Indian Economy', *Journal of Development Studies*, Sussex, vol. 32, no. 1, 1996.

19 All growth rates are statistically significant. *Infrastructure* I includes electricity, gas and water supply plus transport, storage and communication. *Infrastructure II* is Infrastructure I plus construction. Primary includes forestry and logging, fishing and mining and quarrying. Services include trade, hotels and restaurants plus banking and insurance plus real estate, ownership of dwellings and business services plus public administration and other services. All other income categories are the same as defined by the CSO.

20 Agr. = Agriculture, Cons. = Construction, Infra. = Infrastructure I Mfg. = Manufacturing, Pri. = Primary, Ser. = Services, NDP = Net domestic product.

21 A. Mathur, 'Regional Development and Income Disparities in India: A Sectoral Analysis', *Economic Development and Cultural Change*, vol. 31, no. 3, 1983. Also see A. Mathur, 'Why Growth Rates differ Within India: An Alternative Approach', *Journal of Development Studies*, vol. 23, no. 2, 1987. Das and Barua, n. 18, looking at a different time period, have identified a different pattern of relationship between growth and regional disparity in the Indian economy. According to them the inverted-U may be followed by a rising trend of inequality with growth of per capita income.

4
A World Economy Based on the Welfare State Principle

Hartmut Elsenhans

Introduction

The welfare state is one of the organizing principles at the basis of developing and developed countries, and will play an important role in maintaining a capitalist world system. Its extension to the world economy is not only desirable for social reasons, but is necessary for maintaining an open, 'liberal' and worldwide free-market economy. The welfare state, together with the rule of law and democratic participation, constitutes one of the foundations of a liberal democratic order. Yet the welfare state has come increasingly under fire, threatened by certain developments in the world economy. This is not because the world economy has become increasingly capitalist, but because the world economy is characterized by the integration of non-capitalist economies in the international division of labour and by the capitalist part of the world economy being too weak to transform the rest of the world economy into capitalist systems.

The race to the bottom: déjà vu

Globalization is understood as a massive decrease in the costs of various kinds of transborder economic transactions: trade, services and capital movements. It is said to expose 'expensive' labour in the technically advanced countries of the West to the cut-throat competition of cheap labour in the South, and to contribute to the downfall of the welfare state. It is true that labour in the so-called 'low-wage' countries is able to produce the greater part of low-technology products at unbeatably low prices. Some of these newly industrializing countries even produce a considerable share of high-technology products (however imprecise this term is defined).

Are we to conclude that the welfare state runs the risk of losing its clout in the older, more advanced industrialized countries and being limited to the traditional principles of poor laws and charity?

The threat posed to the bargaining power of labour has been postulated for more than a decade now.[1] The standard view of authors reflecting the attitudes of business merely repeat the arguments alluded to sarcastically by Karl Marx and which have been shown empirically to contradict actual historical developments:

> It has been fashionable amongst English capitalists to describe Belgium as the paradise of labourers because there the freedom of labour and, what amounts to the same, the freedom of capital are neither diminished by the despotism of trade unions nor by factory laws.[2]

It is well-known that Belgium did not remain a low-wage country, so that we can also conclude that the capitalist process will not conform to the predictions of capitalists and academics representing the interests of business regarding today's newly industrializing countries or the not-yet industrialized countries which may engage in similar strategies in the future.

The methodological approach presented in this chapter is a political-economic one which is greatly indebted to Keynesian and post-Keynesian economics. Profit does not depend on the low cost of labour, as claimed by the representatives of new labour, who have taken over the leadership of numerous labour parties in Western Europe. Furthermore, political economy does not primarily deal with international political struggles over the creation of market imperfections in trade and capital movements, as it does in its adulterated form in the Anglo-Saxon world,[3] but focuses on an analysis of the links between the political system, (civil) society and the economy. The level of autonomy of these subsystems depends on the overall structure and condition of the system.[4] With such an approach, the so-called race to the bottom insisted on by the mainstream economics is not inevitable. This type of argument is nothing but a renewed attempt to justify wage repression, just like the argument that labour in industrialized countries has imposed salaries higher than its marginal product.

Neo-classical theory and increasing mass incomes

The argument of the globalization mainstream that globalization makes high-cost labour in the old industrialized countries uncompetitive because of excessively high wages fails to take the theoretical basis of mainstream neo-classical economists into account. In neo-classical economics, the problem of the welfare state's capacity to survive or of its emerging wherever labour is paid its marginal product, and no more, does not exist. The welfare state involves a redistribution between labour, and not a transfer to labour from business. If reduced costs, due to new means of surmounting the problem of space and time, makes new production sites highly competitive, the inevitable consequence is massive investment in these new sites of production followed by rapidly increasing employment. Labour at these new production sites will become scarce and correspondingly expensive, its costs increasing in line with the increase of its marginal product.

In the neo-classical perspective, based on the ideas of Jean-Baptiste Say (1972),[5] capitalists are even forced to exploit the goldmine of cheap labour in the impoverished Third World until the costs of this labour rise to the level of its marginal product due to labour scarcity. The neo-classical view, where the marginal product of labour determines wage levels, maintains that low wages in 'low-wage' countries rapidly reach the levels in the high-wage countries through increasing productivity, independently of demand conditions in the world economy. Wages in high-wage countries can never rise more rapidly than productivity does, as every neo-classical economist has proposed to justify the argument that trade unions are unnecessary.[6] But, ultimately, wages have to rise at that rate because of scarcity of labour. In the neo-classical perspective, full employment is guaranteed at appropriately low wages, but with full employment, any increase in productivity has to lead to rising wages.

In neo-classical economics, a countervailing power to capital is unnecessary, because under perfect competition business cannot refuse further investment, in spite of the unruliness of labour. Business must hire additional labour, provided this labour is cheap enough in relation to the additional product.

No author has described better than Marx how the bourgeoisie develops productivity on the world scale, or has realized more precisely than any culturally oriented approach to economics that productivity will rapidly increase in the not-yet capitalist regions of the world, leading to the worldwide expansion of capitalism. In the neo-classical world, this cheap labour will become scarce irrespective of the development of mass demand and the social structures encountered by capital in the not-yet capitalist world. With full employment, wages have to rise to the level of the marginal product of labour, regardless of whether trade unions exist. Only the existence of slavery would block the process of labour costs rising in low-wage countries to the level of labour costs in high-wage countries in line with productivity developments. Globalization can only pose temporary challenges in a world based on neo-classical economics. The transition will be a short one, as capital accumulation will occur in an explosive manner, at least under the assumptions of neo-classical economics.

The idea of certain socialist and neo-classical theorists of development that economic growth depends on previous accumulation can be considered a fairytale. According to the Bortkiewicz criterion (1907),[7] capitalist entrepreneurs can only apply those technologies which reduce unit costs at constant real wages. As long as banks are willing to supply credit for investment financing, the only limit to the production of investment goods for capital accumulation is a limited supply of labour. But a limited supply of labour does not correspond to the empirical reality of today's low-wage countries. The neo-classical view on the possible limits to explosive growth for the process of globalization in the form of scarcity of capital in end effect leads us to the question of the world banking system's capacity to supply finance. Yet one of the favourite themes of globalization 'theorists' concerns the increasingly ungovernable international financial markets, where capital is traded daily at levels which for most people would seem inconceivable. I have shown elsewhere the exuberant capability of financial markets to create book money, in line with the Keynesian theory of the active role of money.[8] This money is initially fictive, having no real counterpart in the real economy. Liberal authors such as Hayek – a true liberal, clear to his principles, who did not succumb to the material incentives offered to academia by the business world – were quick to sound a note of warning, as the oversupply of money may create the conditions for subsequent economic downturns due to imbalances in the mix of production.[9] According to Hayek, not deregulation but the abolishment of international financial markets based on book money is the necessary solution. Even Hirst and Thompson (1999)[10] have recently discussed a return to the gold standard. It is no accident that the only indicator which justifies considering the current globalization process more intense than globalization before 1913, is short-term capital movements.[11] The process of globalization which characterized the late nineteenth century was, however, linked to an expansion of the welfare state.[12] It is impossible to have Keynesian money creation without Keynesian monetary discipline. This applied to the period at the end of postwar expansion, when politicians undermined the system through a lack of budgetary discipline, but is equally valid for today's stockmarkets.

A globalization of the market for book money is occurring, guaranteed by states who have lost the complementary capacity to reduce this amount of money, so that international liquidity continues to expand. There is no shortage of finances for investment, so a shortage of finances cannot be the reason for the lack of rapid expansion of employment in 'low-wage' countries.[13]

Thus, the problem with the theoretical predictions of neo-classical economics has to be another, as globalization is evidently characterized by a massive growth of technical innovation and the availability of huge amounts of capital and cheap labour worldwide. If the requirements of neo-classical economics for rapid growth are fulfilled and the predictions have still not materialized, it may be appropriate to examine if the previous unsuccessful attempts to explain globalization can be overcome within the framework of a Keynesian model focusing on lack of demand in the wake of globalization.

A convoy model of globalization

In analogy to the conditions of globalization at the end of the nineteenth century in North America and Europe, the point of departure of my argument is the assumption that the world economy consists only of economies which have succeeded in the transition to capitalism. The marginal product of labour rises, so that labour becomes scarce. Real wages follow marginal productivity of labour. Average real wages are on the rise. Economies which do not fulfil these conditions participate in the international division of labour only to a limited degree, namely, where the natural conditions of production (for example raw materials) play an important role, because the price and income elasticity of demand for such products are low in the leading industrialized countries.

Suppose that innovation takes place in a sector producing tradables which increases the competitiveness of one particular economy. The export sector of this economy will hire additional labourers to increase production. As a result, the internal-market-oriented sectors of the innovative economy will experience rising costs, and react by introducing cost-reducing innovations of their own. State-of-the-art production methods will be actively sought in the whole of the economy, and this is rendered more efficient if the economy opens to the world market.

Exports increase following innovation. Non-innovative economies will experience balance-of-payment deficits financed by the outflow of gold or similar assets, such as foreign exchange, which accrue to the innovative economy. The stock of money in the backward economy decreases or its exchange reserves diminish. With a constant velocity of money, that is a steady rate of turnover of money, price levels decrease in the gold-standard economy; with a currency based on book money, exchange rates decrease. The international prices of locally produced goods decrease in both cases. These processes continue until the backward economy becomes competitive in technically backward products which are no longer too expensive on the world market in comparison to backward products from the innovative economy with high costs or a high exchange rate. At the same time, non-innovative products become relatively more expensive in the innovative economy due to scarcity of labour. Obviously, in the non-innovative economy the sector of the economy which becomes competitive earliest is the one whose productivity is relatively less backward here in relation to the innovative economy, because, for example, this sector has a very low productivity in the innovative economy. Thus, the backward economy achieves competitiveness on the basis of backward branches; the less its backwardness in backward branches in relation to more innovative economies, the earlier it becomes competitive and the lower the rates of devaluation. The decline in international innovativeness of the backward economy leads to deteriorating terms of trade, but not to unemployment, because the backward economy is relatively productive in non-innovative branches.

Homogeneity of the convoy type resulting from the empowerment of labour

Relatively high levels of productivity in technically backward sectors of the backward economy are the result of a tendency to full employment in this economy, and not the result of cultural or other similarities. A mechanism operates at the level of the world economy which is similar to the convergence of factor prices at the national level. National economies are characterized by the mobility of labour, which guarantees the convergence of factor prices through the adjustment of price relations between goods and services.

Let us apply this mechanism to the theory of factor-price adjustment at the international level following specialization, according to factor proportions of economies with different factor endowments. Suppose that backward economies achieve full employment by means of (limited) devaluation; labour will be scarce in the non-innovative branches of the backward economy. If there is scarcity of labour in the wake of devaluation and if competitiveness has been achieved on the basis of new exports and new import-substituting products, wages have to rise. Even branches of production where no productivity increase has taken place can continue to employ labour only if they increase wages. Labour in the non-innovative economy receives reasonably high wages for the production of backward products. Currency appreciation will lead to a loss of competitiveness of the technically leading economy, both on the world market and on its own internal market, in branches with below-average productivity increases, forcing these branches to reduce production and employment because of increasing international prices.

These changes in relative prices lead to the convergence of factor incomes at the national level in both types of economies, the innovative and the non-innovative, as factors of production are mobile within national economies. This applies especially to labour. The innovative economy specializes on high-tech products, and upgrades low-tech products to the extent possible. The rest of tradable production has to be given up. Labour in non-tradable sectors migrates to the high-tech sectors until wages also rise in the non-tradable sectors. Even if physical productivity does not increase in non-innovative branches, productivity measured in the earnings of output increases, because prices for products with low productivity increases rise. In the case of labour involving a similar physical or psychological strain or similar costs of training, this convergence takes place within a national framework, as labour is mobile within nations.

In the case of short-term capital, the convergence takes place at the international level within computer networks, because short-term capital is mobile at the international level. To the surprise of globalization theorists, however, in the case of long-term fixed capital in plant and equipment this convergence of factor productivities takes place once more within the national framework, as there are considerable hurdles for long-term capital mobility.[14]

Homogeneity in national differences

Branch-wise factor productivities therefore converge in line with the national average. Due to these processes of factor-price convergence and despite the varying development of branchwise productivities, productivity differentials in particular branches tend to correspond to the difference in average productivity between national economies. Because of these processes of factor-price convergence within national economies, only those enterprises can survive in a particular national economy which are productive enough to be able to pay the necessary costs for factors of production. More productive enterprises will expand until their prices decline due to market saturation, and thus their capacity to pay above-average factor incomes declines. Less productive enterprises will vanish.

Differences in productivity between branches correspond to average differences in productivity between capitalist economies. The difference in average productivity persists because labour markets have not been globalized. Labour is less mobile today than it was at the beginning of the twentieth century.[15] Also, the racial barriers between OECD countries, with their white and *honoris causa* white (Japanese) populations, and the rest of the world which block access to Western labour markets have considerably risen since the beginning of the last century.

Wages which correspond to average productivity differentials are far too high for the backward economy's high-technology branches if productivity in backward branches is high so that full employment is reached at low levels of devaluation. In this case, a backward economy cannot overtake technically more advanced economies in new high-technology branches on the basis of devaluation. This type of international division of labour and its hierarchies is described relatively well by the theory of the product cycle.[16] The technically more advanced economy continually boosts its position *vis-à-vis* the technically backward economies, which, however, with a certain period of delay follow the technically more advanced ones. If a backward economy with low productivity differentials in backward branches were to try increasing its competitiveness in new branches by means of devaluation, its exports from old branches would increase first, so that the economy would experience massive balance-of-trade surpluses.

The convoy model has an inherent tendency towards convergence of productivities. The gradual character of technical progress, together with the relatively large internal markets of the participating economies as well as their tendency to full employment, hence to cost-induced technical imitation, guarantee the rapid diffusion of internationally available technical progress. Technically backward economies are therefore able to catch up without industrial policies. They can avoid the inefficient management of state officials, who intervene in markets and create rents without market control and without the existence of a democratically controlled state. Reliance on the mechanism of devaluation, however, implies relatively low productivity differentials in backward branches and low levels of 'structural' unemployment.

The convoy model and imperialist homogeneity

The basis of the convoy model of globalization is not cultural or social homogeneity, but the capitalist character of all participating economies. Cultural and social convergence are the product of internal structures, and not their condition. The convoy model requires only the following:

- tendential full employment in price and income-elastic products in all economies participating in the international division of labour;
- limits with respect to the scope and, especially, the amount of resources engaged in industrial policy, since enterprises themselves are more efficient in the search for new products and technologies in leading economies;
- the state in catching-up economies can therefore imitate, but cannot overtake on the basis of industrial policies;
- rapid democratization of the consumption of new products via a rapid shift to large-scale production to accommodate rapidly increasing mass consumption, through which productivity increases can be achieved;
- thus, enterprises which depend on rents and market niches (markets for luxury goods) run the permanent risk of losing their profitability with rapid economic growth.

The convoy model of globalization which existed in the last three decades of the nineteenth century did not lead to any major upheavals in Europe. It was basically perceived as a means to improve terms of trade. The theory of imperialism, with its thesis of intensified international conflict, and which argues against the exploitation of the Third World through cheap raw material exports, is not a reflection of globalization linked to the growing economic transactions between industrialized capitalist countries which existed at the time the theory was developed. The delocalization of manufacturing to low-wage countries witnessed today has the very same effect that capital exports had in the late nineteenth and early twentieth centuries: decreasing terms of trade despite the fact that this type of backward economy no longer exclusively specializes on primary products.[17]

Similar to the controversies about imperialism as a 'pioneer of capitalism',[18] export-oriented industrialization has now become the object of controversy, its exploitative character being contrasted with its growth-inducing capacity. Suh[19] has shown, in opposition to Emmanuel,[20] that greater exploitation in branches capable of transforming the economy may have an accelerating effect on overcoming underdevelopment.

The impact of underdeveloped economies

Today's world economy is characterized by the participation of economies in the international division of labour which are sectorally competitive without, however, being able to achieve full employment, neither through export growth (including the implied multiplyer effects) nor by internal-market-oriented growth, possibly combined with export growth. Covering most of the globe, the capitalist system has spread to societies where the condition for the overall transition to capitalism has not been created by pre-capitalist structures, and where the 'capitalist world system' is unable to create this condition simply by offering additional export opportunities.

The condition is a rise in productivity sufficient for marginal product to rise beyond the costs of reproduction of labour, namely, in the areas most remote from capitalist penetration, agriculture and the informal sector. Thus, the conditions for internal-market-oriented growth based on mass demand have not yet emerged. Poor economies are characterized by marginality,[21] and, moreover, average productivity and average household incomes are low so that the share of food in household expenditure and the share of food production in employment are high.

Only labourers who produce at least as much additional food as they consume can be employed in food production. In Third World agriculture, marginal product can be lower than the costs of reproduction of labour (the costs of survival of a worker and his nuclear family). The result is structural unemployment[22] and surplus production, because a substantial share of labour produces a surplus on the limited fertile soils. The model has a series of implications on technical progress.[23] In a closed economy, only agricultural progress which contributes to a rise in marginal product of labour will automatically raise employment via market mechanisms.

The two main social actors in a poor economy, landowners and rural labour, stabilize the system on the basis of self-interested and short-sighted strategies. Labour has to contend with a lottery-type labour market; with each new member of a nuclear family, the number of 'lottery tickets' for this family increases. The process is similar to demographic developments that took place in the phase of protoindustrialization in Europe,[24] where the introduction of market economies was accompanied by the breakdown of restrictive social norms, and led to new reproductive behaviour, particularly among the poor. Nevertheless, the possibility for investment is limited, as markets for mass-consumption goods remain limited. In the absence of dynamically expanding markets, the appropriation of surplus depends on political power. Surplus is appropriated as rent, and not as profit, since capitalist profit – surplus appropriated on competitive markets – depends on the investment spending of capitalists.[25]

Rentiers depend on political power and are therefore inclined to use a part of the surplus for the establishment of systems of clientelism. An obedient part of labour will receive more than necessary for their reproduction in order to help maintain a larger family. The privileges granted to this obedient part of labour depend on their lords; these lords are subject to overlords, who in turn answer to even higher overlords, so that a power structure characterized by vertical clientelistic relations emerges. Economic efficiency is not a criterion for the position of particular lords in this hierarchy.

Rent as the basis of export-led growth

The agricultural surplus can be channelled into investment through state-promoted projects. The development policies based on import-substitution which emerged in the 1940s, as well as the economic variant of the theory of modernization have advocated similar state-promoted strategies against the concept of market incentives. The state classes,[26] the main historical agents of such strategies, ultimately failed because of the inefficient use of a limited supply of resources for investment (with high capital–output ratios, wasteful spending on non-investive activities, and so on). Export-oriented industrialization was inevitable when savings and foreign-exchange gaps widened, especially after the failure of oil-exporting countries to impose a new international economic order or to subsidize the start-up costs for similar cartels in other raw-material exports.

Export-oriented industrialization, however, is also based on rents, but the channelling of these rents into investment projects is more efficient than in the case of import substitution.[27] The rent is used to lower domestic price levels in international currency via devaluation, so that additional export workers become competitive at the price of not being able to buy their wage goods from the world market. Their reproduction is based on goods supplied by local wage-goods production.

The comparative advantage in industry of today's Third World may have emerged relatively early, during the Industrial Revolution in Europe. Indeed, the emergence of comparative advantage depends only on productivity increases occurring in a single branch of one economy. The comparative advantage of the Third World in industry became evident at least by the 1880s, with the rapid growth of the textile industry in the Bombay area. But comparative advantage has to be transformed into cost competitiveness on the world market, and the instrument for this transformation is the adjustment of the exchange rate.

A poor, underdeveloped economy can devalue as long as it is able to supply food and simple industrial consumption goods, produced by the informal factor, to additional export workers. In the wake of the Green Revolution, the capacity of the South and Southeast Asian rice economies to produce agricultural surpluses massively increased, and with it the capacity of these countries to devalue their currencies. Empirical proof for the competitiveness of newly industrializing countries in South and Southeast Asia depending on devaluation is supplied by the complete lack of purchasing power parity of their currencies against Western currencies.[28] The gross national product of mainland China calculated at purchasing power parity is four times higher than the gross national product measured in local currency and converted into dollars at the going exchange rate ($3291 per capita versus $780 per capita).[29] A Chinese household in Beijing can buy nine times as much here with its income than if it were to convert this income into Canadian dollars and go shopping in a typical Canadian city.[30]

Wage differentials between leading industrial economies and catching-up developing economies are normally quoted as 50:1, and real wages in the latter are rarely lower than one-seventh of the real wages in industrialized countries. The more successful among the export-oriented newly industrializing countries such as Taiwan and South Korea have achieved real-wage levels higher than in the poorer regions of the European Union.[31]

Devaluation as the basis of the race to the bottom

There is a new obstacle to the worldwide implementation of the welfare state: the existence of marginality at production sites which have become capable of transforming inevitable and irremovable comparative advantage into price competitiveness through the instrument of devaluation, without this devaluation leading to full employment. Since full employment is not reached, real wages cannot increase in line with productivity increases. A whole set of mainstream proposals for dealing with the problem of job-loss in high-wage economies is therefore not worth further examination. Social standards are inappropriate for protecting high-wage labour in the West, because they will not lead to the removal of the implicit subsidy paid to labour in export-oriented sectors by the internal-market-oriented wage-goods-producing sectors. The truly poor populations of the Third World are not living in the internationally competitive, 'low-wage' countries of Southeast and East Asia, but in sub-Saharan Africa. In Southeast and East Asia, labour was cheap in international currency at the start of their industrialization processes, but nonetheless enjoyed fairly high real wages in comparison to less competitive regions of the underdeveloped world.

Furthermore, measures which only aim at improving the wages of workers who are already employed will inevitably fail, because they will not provide a solution to the massive supplies of cheap (and otherwise unemployed) labour due to the existence of large pockets marginality.

Blocking access to the markets of industrialized countries will only intensify marginality in marginality-ridden countries. The problem of devaluation-driven industrialization emerges once again. It is improbable that poor countries will lose their capacity to produce agricultural surpluses. If access to the markets of industrialized countries is blocked, the marginality-ridden countries will adopt any strategy to raise productivity levels in potential export sectors and overcome tariff barriers through further devaluation. Decreasing agricultural productivity in order to limit further devaluation is likewise not sustainable.

The only option for decreasing marginality is the creation of incentives for increasing productivity and production also in the internal-market-oriented sectors, using the export sector to create multiplier effects in the rest of the economy.

The problem of integrating marginal labour into a market-driven growth process also had to be dealt with during the transition period at the start of the Industrial Revolution in Europe. Marginal labour, that is labour producing less than its costs of reproduction, was employed with the aid of poor laws.[32] The English Poor Laws required the richer classes, especially business and big landowners, to pay the full costs of reproduction of labour. This was paid partly as a salary, and partly as a parish tax to finance charity. The parish tax was paid by the rich whether they employed the poor or not. The salaries paid to poor labour could therefore be lower than the cost of this labour's reproduction. Obviously, the surplus controlled by the richer classes decreased inversely to the level of the poor tax, so that, in end effect, the level of mass consumption was raised by a subsidy to the poor. If profit depends on investment-goods spending, and investment goods are used for the production of simple mass-consumption goods, the shift in purchasing power also had to lead to a reinforcement of profit, despite a decreasing surplus, and this, to the detriment of rent.

Channelling rent and support to marginals in order to promote development

The challenge we are faced with today is to intensify globalization in order to make it socially sustainable. The welfare state has to be globalized to enable the globalization of profit, as opposed to the globalization of rent. Globalization therefore has to be complemented by appropriate development policies for the societies plagued by marginality. In essence, any relevant strategy for overcoming underdevelopment involves the mobilization of surplus in order to increase mass consumption and profit. Increasing industrial production for the benefit of the poor implies that the poor are able to consume an adequate amount of food, either through redistribution or through an increase of the marginal product in agriculture. A redistribution of surplus in favour of the marginalized population can be realized in the form of agrarian reform.[33] Labour time which had not been utilized before land redistribution because of its low marginal product is 'internalized' in the owner-operated farm. The farmer does not have the option of not using his marginal labour time. Not using this marginal labour time will result in a decrease in total production without a decrease in expenses, since marginal labour still contributes to production increases, albeit at a level lower than its own costs. The owner operator cannot avoid these costs, because they are the costs of survival of his family. As long as no alternative possibilities of employment exist, marginal labour is put to work on owner-operated small farms. The new farm-owning families can accept low returns for their marginal labour; because of land redistribution, they receive the rent produced with a limited amount of labour time. The production from these 'first hours of work' contributes more than their share in total labour time to the survival of the respective family.

Agrarian reforms have an important side-effect: owner-operated farms with marginal labour offer labour for rural by-employment at very low prices, since they will prefer non-agricultural by-employment outside the farm if the returns there are higher than the returns of their marginal labour time on the farm.[34]

The promotion of industry in underdeveloped economies has always depended on rents from the highly productive sectors of the Third World, very often raw-material sectors (for example oil), which are invested in not-yet profitable enterprises. These enterprises are expected to contribute to the transformation of the economy by distributing new incomes via employment and by improving the skills of labour, so that new production facilities become profitable from the supply as well as from the demand side.

The contribution of non-governmental organizations (NGOs) to overcoming underdevelopment rests in their capacity to channel financial resources to the truly needy either from the more wealthy local sectors or from abroad. However, their own economic projects are rarely efficient.[35] In most cases NGOs recruit their staff from the middle strata of society, but in spite of their formal education it is unlikely that this staff is more efficient in discovering new and profitable production lines than the entrepreneurs of the informal sector. The large number of bee-keeping projects demonstrates in an impressive manner the limits imposed on NGOs. At least the bees are able to overcome the unequal distribution of land which blocks productivity increases on the part of the human population.

Export-oriented industrialization is itself just one form of mobilizing rent. Workers in the export sector receive wages in local currency which they use to buy locally produced wage goods, because after devaluation they are unable to buy their wage goods from the world market. The only condition for this mobilization of rent from agriculture is either the state regulation of agricultural exports (quite common, even in the market-oriented Asian economies) or high transport costs for food due to its relative bulkiness.

The argument exists that any measure which aims at redistributing surpluses in order to increase mass consumption and profit will face the resistance of the local privileged class. Nevertheless, the industrialized countries of the West would still be able to promote such a reinforcement of mass consumption. One possible strategy would be the creation of an 'artificial' industry producing goods which would be bought up by Western agencies with the same taxpayers' money currently being used for other forms of financial assistance. The products of such an industry would, in essence, be useless, so that they could not be sold on the world market. Their characteristic feature is that they would require the mobilization of unskilled labour in the marginality-ridden economy. The ultimate aim of such an industry would be the removal of marginal labour from the labour market, so that any productivity increase in the economy triggers off the standard mechanism of neo-classical economics; that is, productivity increases leading to the employment of additional labour in turn resulting in an increase in average labour incomes.[36]

Combining instruments in a non-orthodox manner

Any such measure involves a more or less extended non-market element. Such a measure is therefore most likely characterized by decreasing returns, like any administrative activity. State intervention in property rights in the form of agrarian reforms also intimidates producers in the industrial sector, and therefore requires a clear legal framework to make the limits to state intervention credible. Promotion of industries implies moral hazard; either the rules for allocating subsidies are overdetermined, making the process of transferring financial resources clumsy,[37] or local agencies are granted broad discretionary powers so they can benefit from lean government, which also implies the danger of corruptive practices and self-privileging. NGOs are considered superior to government agencies because of the supposed moral commitment of their staff. The initial charismatic leadership of such organizations is, however, not able to implement its programmes without employing non-charismatic and less-ethically-minded subordinates. This is especially so when an organization expands, so that organizations are characterized by 'evolutionary life-cycles'[38] and sometimes end up using authoritarian methods in order to present donors with a model of successful development.[39]

NGOs also try to minimize the ratio between 'output' (the number of poor helped out of marginality) and costs (the subsidies distributed). It was discovered that in Rajasthan NGOs concentrate on the poor living in relatively less poor districts.[40]

Export-oriented industrialization is an instrument for transforming agricultural surplus into consumption on the part of additionally employed workers in the export sector. It does not contribute to an increase in global consumptive capacity like it does for global productive capacity. Thus, imitating this model as an overall strategy for overcoming underdevelopment will function only when a relatively small number of countries make use of it to solve their marginality problems. However, after the large regions of Southeast and East Asia have overcome underdevelopment, the rest of the underdeveloped world will certainly be small enough for its labour surplus to be absorbed by the demand of a much larger developed world than today's.

The proposed measures – industrial policy measures, employment programmes, artificial industries, a redistribution of assets – for transferring welfare-state principles to marginality-ridden economies reflect the necessity of launching the transformation to capitalism of an initially marginality-ridden economy on the basis of support structures from the non-market economy. The non-market support structure can, however, create obstacles to the growth of the market economy. The social groups which have to reach a consensus in order to support such a complex, even eclectic strategy are economically and socially heterogeneous: casual labourers, landless farmers or farmers with too little land, small traders, and so on.

The worldwide implementation of the welfare state depends on the capacity to create synergy effects on the basis of support structures in non-market domains of society, and this, under the conditions of diminishing returns for any type of intervention. The measures used are eclectic, being coherent only in their capacity to increase mass incomes of marginal labour. Agrarian reform, growth of the informal sector, and NGO activities may create synergetic effects even if they are not explicitly coordinated. Rarely have agrarian reforms been implemented with the aim of launching an informal sector, although they have had this effect in most cases.[41] Agrarian reforms are usually implemented on the basis of a political perspective directed against private ownership of the means of production. The political basis of such reforms normally, therefore, did not openly support the informal sector.

With the decline of the bureaucratic development state and its state classes this type of effects through synergetic eclecticism has become more difficult because market radicalism is on the rise. The ascendancy of a narrow focus on the market is all the more greater as the previous failures of state interventionism has led to disillusionment of large strata of society about the possibilities of reform to be engineered either by the state or by the civil society. But not all cultural identity-based movements qualify for such a

negative appreciation. The Welfare State in the West has been also the product of the rise of populist movements and may be so also in Asia, Africa
and Latin America. Low expectations with regard to the feasibility of social
and economic progress has worked to reinforce fundamentalist movements.
These movements reject Enlightenment, a condition for economic and
social progress, as being a Western value, and have replaced it with spiritual
goals where economic progress plays at best a subordinate role.[42]

Postmodernism also blocks welfare-state-oriented capitalism

The real problem facing the political implementation of the welfare state
rests in the low expectations with respect to the feasibility of social progress.
The welfare state has always been regarded as a less-than-ideal solution. In
neo-classical economics, the welfare state is unnecessary; under the condition of full employment the welfare state cannot lead to a redistribution of
income in the interest of labour. The real aim of the welfare state in the eyes
of Keynesian economists is to avoid joblessness due to insufficient levels
of global demand. If the neo-classical argument that economic equilibria
are always full-employment equilibria (provided wages are low enough) is
wrong, redistribution can be regarded as an important instrument of growth.
Those in favour of an extension of the welfare state therefore assume that
market regulation is a good means of managing the economy. As with any
human institution, there is an implicit risk of failure, but this can be kept
with limits, and does not necessarily imply that the system will collapse.
The welfare state is theoretically conceivable in a market economy, if the
market is perceived as an instrument for limiting the influence of the privileged, that is when the working classes have acquired legitimacy in society
with their argument that labour is better suited than the owners of capital
to manage the market economy. Such a situation existed for some time in
the Federal Republic of Germany under the auspices of Karl Schiller, the
former Minister of Trade and Commerce.

The mainstream Left in the discourse on globalization would compromise
its principles with the open acceptance of the market economy as an instrument for realizing the goals which others – such as Marx – had thought to
be the aim of socialism, that is the capacity of society to consciously manage
itself on a democratic basis in the interest of the large majority. Instead of
a focus of this sort, the discourse of the mainstream Left now endeavours
to prove the incapacity of the system to be reformed by society and its
majorities.

In contrast to such attempts to demonize globalization, I maintain the
argument that globalization itself is not the problem, but, rather, the path
it has taken, namely the globalization of rent as opposed to the globalization of profit. The model of the world economy I have presented in this
contribution, which involves combating marginality locally through appro-

priate development policies, offers a perspective for the globalization of profit accompanied by full employment, an autonomous civil society, high levels of competition, and low levels of state interventionism. Complementing export orientation with appropriate development policies in the marginality-ridden underdeveloped economies will allow exports to induce high multiplier effects, enlarging internal-market-oriented production (including local investment-goods production).

This is not the only possible outcome of export orientation. A model is conceivable where developing countries appropriate rents from highly productive export sectors, and use them for diversifying production without achieving full employment. The neo-classical mechanism of rising real wages in line with rising productivity is blocked in this scenario, and increasing surplus is appropriated by rentiers. The Asian crisis of the 1990s demonstrated the potential of this mechanism.[43]

If the integration of marginality-ridden economies into a new convoy model does not succeed, Western industrialized countries will try to protect their labour forces by promoting specialization in branches which are thought to be safeguarded from devaluation-driven exports out of catching-up economies due to high technical requirements. The number of jobs is, however, limited in such branches, so that such a strategy will not create the number of jobs necessary for full employment. The larger social classes will divide themselves along particularistic lines in the struggle over scarce subsidies, ultimately, rents. There is no alternative between globalization and autarky. The only option is between a rentier system and the globalization of the welfare state. A sustainable process of globalization has to promote the welfare state, and can be achieved with a limited bureaucracy if capital fails in its attempt to disempower labour.

Conclusion

Because exchange rates matter more than real wages, there is no theoretical opposition between the welfare state and competitiveness under the conditions of globalization. Globalization is, however, currently being used to attack the welfare state. This involves the risk of creating a worldwide under-conceptionist crisis, which in turn will be followed up by the introduction of nationalist interventionist strategies with the aim of undermining and abolishing a liberal world economy. Regional blocs like the ones that existed during the heyday of colonialism may reemerge around the three centres of capitalist growth. The neo-classical paradigm of self-regulating capitalist economies requires rising mass incomes.

The neo-classical mechanism of bringing about these rising mass incomes is, however, weak and periodically threatened. Capitalist economies reach full employment only in their peak periods; the welfare state is an instrument to empower labour in trough periods.

This cyclical problem which gave rise to the welfare states of the indus-trialized world is complemented today by a structural problem. Due to the green revolution a large number of economies in the South have become capable of accepting any rate of devaluation without achieving full employ-ment. These capacities are subsidizing local labour for employment in export sectors. Cheap wage goods from a rapidly developing agricultural sector allow developing countries to accept nearly any rate of devaluation, at least in the initial period of export-led growth based on labour-intensive products.

As nobody will propose destroying these countries' capacity to produce agricultural surpluses, the only solution is to make use of another factor that limits devaluation, namely a growing level of employment. Eclectic mea-sures can be used to bring about this rise in employment. This requires turning away from the orthodox view about the impossibility of using rents for subsidizing labour; various measures for launching growth by means of rising mass incomes can be grouped under the heading 'welfare state'.

Notes

1   Hartmut Elsenhans: 'Social Consequences of the NIEO. Structural Change in the Periphery as Precondition for Continual Reforms in the Centre', in Egbert Jahn and Yoshikazu Sakamoto (eds), *Elements of World Instability: Armaments, Commu-nication, Food, International Division of Labour: Proceedings of the Eighth International Peace Research Association Conference*, Frankfurt am Main and New York: Campus, 1981, pp. 86–95.

2   Karl Marx, *Das Kapital*. Marx Engels Werke 23, Berlin, Dietz, 1972, p. 701. Trans-lation Hartmut Elsenhans.

3   Hartmut Elsenhans, 'Political Economy or Economic Politics? The Prospects of Civil Society in an Era of Globalization', *Indian Journal of Public Administration*, New Delhi, vol. 46, no. 4, October–December 2000, pp. 567–600.

4   Hartmut Elsenhans, 'Bedingungen des Politischen: Staat, Wirtschaft, Gesellschaft und Politik', in Raban Graf von Westphalen, Volker Neßler (eds), *Parlamentarisches Regierungssystem der Bundesrepublik Deutschland*, München: Oldenbourg, 2001, pp. 55–99. Hartmut Elsenhans, 'Globalization: Neoclassical Endogenous Growth Theory's Appropriation of the Keynesianist Interpretation of Capitalist Growth or Strategic Trade Theory's Attempt to Avoid a Free Market Capitalist World Economy in the Twenty-First Century', in Mary Ann Tetreault (ed.), *New Odysseys in Political Economy*, London and New York: Routledge, 2001.

5   Jean-Baptiste Say, *Traité d'économie politique*, Paris: Calmann-Lévy, 1972, p. 140.

6   For an extreme formulation of the neo-classical argument that any improvement of the conditions of labour is sustainable only if it contributes to productivity increases, cf. Franz, Wolfgang, 'Das Betriebsverfassungsgesetz ist komplett überflüssig', in *Handelsblatt*, Dusseldorf, 6 February 2001, p. 12. Indeed, if any codetermination which creates additional costs for enterprises diminishes com-petitiveness, then only those forms of worker participation are acceptable which reduce costs, and which enlightened business would have introduced anyway. The loss of ideological clout of the German labour movement was illustrated by

trade unions nominating Franz for a seat in the German Council of Economic Advisors in the early 1990s.

7 Ladislaus von Bortkiewicz, 'Wertrechnung und Preisrechnung im Marxschen System', part 3, *Archiv für Sozialwissenschaft und Sozialpolitik*, 25, 2 Tübingen, 1907, pp. 451–9.

8 Hartmut Elsenhans, 'Die Globalisierung der Finanzmärkte und die Entstehung einer neuen Rentenklasse', in Ulrich Menzel (ed.), *Vom Ewigen Frieden und vom Wohlstand der Nationen. Dieter Senghaas zum 60. Geburtstag*, Frankfurt am Main: Suhrkamp, 2000, pp. 538–52.

9 Friedrich A. von Hayek, *The Pure Theory of Capital*, Chicago: University of Chicago Press, 1941, p. 41.

10 Paul Hirst and Grahame Thompson, *Globalization in Question. The International Economy and the Possibilities of Governance*, Cambridge, Mass. and Oxford: Polity Press, 1999, p. 55.

11 Theresia Theurl, 'Globalisierung als Selektionsprozeß ordnungspolitischer Paradigmen', in Hartmut Berg (ed.), *Globalisierung der Wirtschaft: Ursachen-Formen-Konsequenzen. Schriften des Vereins für Socialpolitik 263*, Berlin: Duncker & Humblot, 1999, p. 26. Paul Bairoch, 'Globalization, Myths and Realities: One Century of External Trade and Foreign Investment', in Robert Boyer and Daniel Drache (eds), *States Against Markets. The Limits of Globalization*, London: Routledge, 1996, pp. 173–92.

12 Jens Alber, *Vom Armenhaus zum Wohlfahrtsstaat. Analysen zur Entwicklung der Sozialversicherung in Westeuropa*, Frankfurt am Main and New York: Campus, 1987.

13 The oversupply of capital is described by Hans Mundorf, 'Kein Bündnis für Arbeit kann Arbeitsplätze versprechen', *Handelsblatt*, 9 September 1999, p. 2.

14 Martin Feldstein and Charles Horioka, 'Domestic Saving and International Capital Flows', *Economic Journal*, Oxford, vol. 90, no. 358, June 1980, pp. 314–29. Gerald Epstein and Herbert Gintis, 'International Capital Markets and National Economic Policy', *Review of International Political Economy*, Brighton, vol. 2, no. 4, Autumn 1995, pp. 693–718. Eric Helleiner, 'Explaining the Globalization of Financial Markets: Bringing States Back In', *Review of International Political Economy*, vol. 2, no. 2, 1995, pp. 315–42.

15 Deepak Nayyar, 'Globalisation: The Past is Our Present', *Indian Economic Journal*, vol. 43, no. 3, January–March 1996, pp. 1–18. Carl Strikwerda, 'Tides of Migration Currents of History: The State, Economy and the Transatlantic Movement of Labour in the Nineteenth and Twentieth Centuries', *International Review of Social History*, Amsterdam, vol. 44, no. 3, December 1999, p. 385.

16 Raymond Vernon, 'International Investment and International Trade in the Product Cycle', *Quarterly Journal of Economics*, Cambridge, Mass., vol. 80, no. 1, February 1966, pp. 190–207.

17 Prabirjit Sarkar, 'Long Term Behaviour of Term of Trade of Primary Products vis-à-vis Manufactures: A Critical Review of Recent Debate', *Economic and Political Weekly*, Pune, vol. 29, no. 26, June 1994, pp. 1612–14. Parbirjit Sarkar and Hans Wolfgang Singer, 'Manufactured Export of Developing Countries and their Terms of Trade Since 1965', *World Development*, Oxford, vol. 19, no. 4, April 1991, pp. 333–40.

18 Bill Warren, *Imperialism: Pioneer of Capitalism*, London: New Left Books, 1980.

19 Suk Tai Suh, 'The Theory of Unequal Exchange and the Developing Countries', in Kyong Dong Kim (ed.), *Dependency Issues in Korean Development: Comparative Perspectives*, Seoul: Seoul National University Press, 1987, p. 111.

20   Arghiri Emmanuel, *L'échange inégal. Essai sur les antagonismes dans les rapports économiques internationaux*, Paris: Maspéro, 1969, pp. 109–11.

21   Hartmut Elsenhans, 'Rent, State and the Market: The Political Economy of the Transition to Self-sustained Capitalism', *Pakistan Development Review*, Islamabad, vol. 33, no. 4, December 1994, pp. 393–424. Hartmut Elsenhans, 'Überwindung von Marginalität als Gegenstand der Armutsbekämpfung', Hans Bernd Schäfer (ed.), *Bevölkerungsdynamik und Grundbedürfnisse in Entwicklungsländern. Schriften des Vereins für Socialpolitik 246*, Berlin: Duncker & Humblot, 1995, pp. 193–221.

22   Nicholas Georgescu-Roegen, 'Economic Theory and Agrarian Economics', *Oxford Economic Papers*, vol. 12, no. 1, Oxford, February 1960, p. 32.

23   Hartmut Elsenhans, n. 21, pp. 399–400.

24   Peter Kriedte, Hans Medick and Jürgen Schlumbohm, *Industrialisierung vor der Industrialisierung. Gewerbliche Warenproduktion auf dem Land in der Formationsperiode des Kapitalismus*, Göttingen: Vandenhoeck & Ruprecht, 1977, pp. 41, 170.

25   Michal Kalecki, *Selected Essays on the Dynamics of the Capitalist Economy 1933–1970*, Cambridge: Cambridge University Press, 1971, p. 13.

26   Hartmut Elsenhans, *Abhängiger Kapitalismus oder bürokratische Entwicklungsgesellschaft. Versuch über den Staat in der Dritten Welt*, Frankfurt am Main and New York: Campus, 1981; English translation Hartmut Elsenhans, *State, Class and Development*, New Delhi, London and Columbia, Mo.: Radiant, Sangam, South Asia Books, 1996.

27   Hartmut Elsenhans, 'Rent and Technology Distortion: The Two Cul-de-Sacs of State Correction and Market Orientation in IAC and IBC', *Journal of the Third World Spectrum*, Washington, vol. 6, no. 1, Autumn 1999, pp. 33–56.

28   Pan A Yotopoulos, and Jenu-Yih Lin, 'Purchasing Power Parities for Taiwan: The Basic Data for 1985 and International Comparisons', *Journal of Economic Development*, Seoul, vol. 18, no. 1 June 1993, p. 111. Avanda Weliwita, 'Cointegration Tests and The Long-Run Purchasing Power Parity: Examination of Six Currencies in Asia', *Journal of Economic Development*, 23, 1 June 1998, pp. 103–13. Hans Mundorf, 'Amtliche Wechselkurse dienen oft der Verfälschung der Wirklichkeit', *Handelsblatt*, 28/29 August 1998, p. 2.

29   World Bank, *World Development Report 2000/2001: Attacking Poverty*, Cambridge, Mass., London, New Delhi and Oxford: Oxford University Press, 2000, p. 274.

30   Haichun Chen, M.J Gordon and Zhiming Yan, 'The Real Income and Consumption of an Urban Chinese Family', *Journal of Development Studies*, London, vol. 31, no. 1, October 1994, p. 211.

31   Gérard Lafay, 'Les origines internationales du chômage européen', *Revue d'économie politique*, Paris, vol. 106, no. 6, November–December 1996, pp. 948–63.

32   Hartmut Elsenhans, 'Englisches Poor Law und egalitäre Agrarreform in der Dritten Welt. Einige Aspekte der Theorie, daß Wachstum historisch die Erweiterung des Massenmarktes erforderte und heute die Erweiterung der Massenmarktes erfordert', *Verfassung und Recht in Übersee*, Baden Baden, vol. 13, no. 4, 1980, pp. 283–318; English translation Hartmut Elsenhans, 'English Poor Law and Egalitarian Agrarian Reform in the Third World', in Hartmut Elsenhans, *Equality and Development*, Dhaka: Centre for Social Studies, 1992, pp. 130–62.

33   Hartmut Elsenhans, 'Agrarverfassung, Akkumulationsprozeß, Demokratisierung', in Hartmut Elsenhans (ed.), *Agrarreform in der Dritten Welt*, Frankfurt am Main and New York: Campus, 1979, p. 558.

34   Partha Dasgupta and Debraj Ray, 'Inequality as a Determinant of Malnutrition and Unemployment', *Economic Journal*, Oxford, vol. 97, no. 385, March 1987, pp. 177–80.

35 Hartmut Elsenhans, 'Marginality, Rent and Non-Governmental Organizations', *Indian Journal of Public Administration*, vol. 41, no. 2, April–June 1995, pp. 153–9.

36 Hartmut Elsenhans, 'Reforming the Economic System of Bangladesh: Main Fields of Action', in Hermann Sautter (ed.), *Wirtschaftspolitische Reformen in Entwicklungsländern. Schriften des Vereins für Socialpolitik 209*, Berlin: Duncker & Humblot, 1991, pp. 127–30.

37 Hartmut Elsenhans, Elmar Kleiner and Reinhart Joachim Dreves, *Développement, équité et extension du marché des masses. Une autre alternative. Le cas algérien. L'enjeu des PME industriels*, Paris: Publisud, 2000, p. 59.

38 Jeffrey Avina, 'The Evolutionary Life Cycles of Non-governmental Development Organisations', *Public Administration and Development*, New York, vol. 13, no. 5, December 1993, pp. 453–74.

39 Sara Gordon, 'La cultura política de las organizaciones no gubernamentales en México', *Revista Mexicana de Sociología*, Mexico City, vol. 59, no. 1, January–March 1997, p. 60. Alan Fowler, 'Non-Governmental Organizations as Agents of Democratization: An African Perspective', *Journal of International Development*, Chichester, vol. 5, no. 3 May–June 1993, p. 333.

40 Berthold Kuhn, *Participatory Development and Local Self-Government Reform in Rural India, Case Studies in Rajasthan*, New Delhi: Radiant, 1998, p. 258.

41 Patricia Gray and Hans Wolfgang Singer, 'Trade Policy and Growth of Developing Countries: Some New Data', in *World Development*, Oxford, vol. 16, no. 3 March 1988, pp. 395–403. Servaas Storm, 'On the Role of Agriculture in India's Longer-Term Development Strategy', *Cambridge Journal of Economics*, vol. 19, no. 6, Oxford, December, 1995, p. 773.

42 M. Gadant, 'Réflexions sur les interprétations populaires de l'Islam', in *Naqd – Revue d'études et de critique sociale*, Ben Aknour, October 1991, p. 11.

43 Werner Baer, William R. Miles and Alan B. Moran, 'The End of the Asian Myth: Why Were the Experts Fooled', *World Development*, vol. 27, no. 10, Oxford, October 1999, p. 1743.

5
Globalization and Welfare States
Ramesh Mishra

Introduction

In focusing largely on Western industrial countries recent scholarship on the welfare state has tended to gloss over important implications of globalization for systems of social protection. These include the destabilization of economies through financial liberalization, the influence of international financial institutions on social policy of nations, and the erosion of alternative forms of social protection through global economic integration. This chapter seeks to substantiate this argument by examining the relationship between globalization and social protection in four different groups of countries: less developed, newly industrializing, ex-communist and Western industrial. The nature of the relationship varies in important ways across these groups of countries.

Until recently, the welfare state has been studied almost entirely within a national framework, which is not surprising given that it has developed as, and still remains, very much a *national* enterprise. The basic assumption underlying the welfare state has been that of substantial policy autonomy on the part of the nation state in respect of macroeconomic management and the determination of monetary, fiscal and social policies. Thus it has been possible to study the welfare state with virtually little or no reference to the supranational dimension.[1]

More recently, however, the relative insulation or the 'national embeddedness' of welfare states has been increasingly challenged by a set of developments typically subsumed under the term 'globalization'. In common with many other broad-gauge notions such as modernization and secularization, globalization remains a contested concept.[2] In broad terms it refers to a process through which the nation-state is becoming more open to influences that are supranational. These may be economic, cultural, technological or political in nature. In this chapter the focus will be on economic aspects of globalization understood as (i) economic liberalization, that is freer trade and financial flows across countries; and (ii) the influence of global intergovernmental organizations (IGOs), notably the International Monetary Fund (IMF) and the World Bank (WB), on economic liberalization and social policy of nations.

It is generally recognized that the international context or the 'environment' in which national welfare states operate today is different from the time when the Bretton Woods framework, with fixed exchange rates and capital controls, was firmly in place. But what exactly the new environment means for the welfare state remains contentious.[3] Again, how recent is the global influence on social policy of nations and what forms it takes remain underexplored issues. One problem here is that since the debate has been concerned mainly with the welfare state in advanced industrial societies it has remained confined within somewhat narrow limits. Much of the literature has focused on the impact of global markets and financial openness on the welfare state primarily in terms of curtailment of social programmes or cutbacks in social benefits and expenditures. Framing the issue in this way it has been possible to argue that the consequences of globalization *per se* have not been particularly significant and that current trends and developments can be explained adequately in terms of the influence of other, primarily endogenous variables.[4] The significance of globalization has been played down and marginalized. Even those who start from the premise that globalization matters tend to focus on the diversity of national responses to economic challenges and go on to emphasize the role of national policy choices in shaping social protection.[5] The validity of these approaches and arguments is not at issue here. Rather this chapter is concerned with one of the major limitations of this debate, namely the lack of an international perspective, and its implications.[6]

Thus one of our principal arguments is that in order to understand adequately the nature of globalization and its consequences for the social protection of nations it is necessary to look beyond industrial societies. In short one needs, so to speak, to globalize the globalization and welfare debate. At present it remains compartmentalized with little or no connection between the study of globalization and social protection in different groups of countries. The rest of this chapter will seek to highlight the relationship between the global sphere and social welfare in the four 'worlds' of the less-developed countries (LDCs), the newly industrializing countries (NICs), the former communist countries, and Western industrial countries (WICs). It will then consider the implications of this analysis for the globalization and welfare relationship.

Less-developed countries

The comprehensive system of social protection which we know as the welfare state in industrialized countries does not exist in most developing countries, or exists only in a rudimentary form. Full employment policies, universal healthcare, insurance or assistance-based programmes of income security are often non-existent or only partially developed. However, modes of protection have to be seen in relation to the level of economic development and the institutional setting of nations. Thus it is more appropriate to focus on the *functions* of social protection rather than on specific *structures* or institutional arrangements through which they are met.[7]

While most developing countries share features of social protection with developed countries, for example the provision of education, healthcare and housing, there are other distinctive programmes such as consumer price subsidies, price controls, food rations and the like which play a vital role in sustaining incomes and/or living standards in LDCs. These measures, which constitute alternative forms of social protection, have been the target of drastic cutbacks and restructuring at the behest of the IMF and WB. The stabilization and structural adjustment programmes, initiated by these international financial institutions (IFIs) as a condition for granting or rescheduling loans to LDCs, have been the means for implementing these policies.

The general conditions which led to the 'debt crisis' in the early 1980s are well-known and need be referred to only briefly. Aggressive lending by Western banks, heavy and at times imprudent borrowing by some of the developing countries, a rise in interest rates in the USA and elsewhere, the sharp rise in oil prices in the 1970s, the fall in commodity prices and the recession in the industrialized world – all these conspired to create a situation where many LDCs needed loans while others were unable to service their foreign debts. Although most of the outstanding loans were owed to private banks, the task of managing the debt crisis and ensuring that loans were repaid fell to the IMF. General debt management involved two different measures: stabilization, and structural adjustment. The former was aimed at correcting the balance of payments deficit and involved such action as currency devaluation and a drastic curb on imports. The latter involved a more comprehensive programme of restructuring the economy of the debtor country. It included such measures as a sharp reduction in public spending, the reduction or elimination of consumer subsidies on food and other necessities, the retrenchment of social programmes, privatization of state enterprises and reduction in wages in order to attract foreign companies and make exports more competitive. In place of the import-substitution strategy that many developing countries had followed during the 1970s they were advised to follow a strategy of export-led growth. Stabilization and structural adjustment programmes (SAPs) were a part of the deal struck with the debtor countries in which these changes became a part of the conditions for the rescheduling of loans which ensured that the lenders were repaid interest on their loans.[8]

Thus, between 1978–92 more than 70 LDCs were involved in upwards of 500 programmes under the auspices of the WB and IMF.[9] How far the conditionalities were strictly observed and what were their precise economic and social consequences has been, not unexpectedly, a matter of contention and debate. It must be remembered, too, that in many countries there was a great deal of opposition to these conditionalities and adjustment programmes, indeed the draconian measures required by the IMF and their impact on living standards led to riots and disturbances in not a few countries.[10] Domestic political responses naturally varied and, moreover, circumstances differed from one country to another. Nonetheless, in broad terms conditionalities and SAPs meant the following: first, national autonomy in policy-making was substantially curtailed; second, the economic medicine prescribed by the IMF led to substantial unemployment and reductions in wages, with measures of social protection, notably consumer subsidies, and social development sharply curtailed resulting in a drop – sometimes severe – in living standards and a rise in poverty and deprivation; and third, those countries' economies were opened up to foreign investors and more closely integrated into the global economy, with attendant risks and benefits. For example, the strategy of export-led growth prescribed to these countries resulted in a glut of supply and a sharp fall in export prices. In any case, during the 1980s there was a major reorientation in development policies. Goals of national development were replaced by those of participation in the world market, and the reach of the global economy was extended.[11]

The overall debt burden of LDCs rose by 61 per cent during the 1980s, and from the mid-1980s the annual outflow of funds for debt servicing from the developing to the developed world exceeded the inflow. By 1997 the total debt burden of developing countries had reached almost $2.2 trillion.[12] The hardest hit have been the 40 or so heavily indebted poor countries (HIPCs), mostly in Africa. Since 1980 their debt burden has more than tripled, two-thirds of it the result of earlier loans and arrears unpaid. As the UNDP report sums up, this debt burden 'drains public budgets, absorbs resources needed for human development and inhibits economic growth'.[13] In sum the consequences of structural adjustment and associated policies of the IFIs have been seriously detrimental for social protection and development for many LDCs.

Newly industrializing countries or the emerging market economies

The term emerging market economies generally refers to the NICs of Asia and Latin America which offer opportunities for profitable investment. These countries share with the LDCs the experience of loan conditionalities and austerity policies imposed by IFIs, notably the IMF, with broadly similar implications for the living standards of their populations. However, perhaps what is distinctive about the experience of emerging economies *is the way financial openness can destabilize the national economy* precipitating serious economic crisis and delivering the country into the arms of the IMF which then proceeds to arrange a bail-out with various conditionalities. This is a different situation from that of the LDCs in that here it is essentially the financial openness of national economies and problems of private sector debt, rather than balance of payment difficulties or problems of public debt, that precipitates the crisis.[14] Here the impact of globalization is direct. Moreover, as recent financial crises in Mexico (1994) and South Korea (1997) show, these two NICs – both admitted recently to membership of the Organization for Economic Cooperation and Development (OECD) and the latter boasting a sophisticated industrial economy – have been vulnerable to economic destabilization and the collapse of currency and stockmarkets, with serious consequences for the well-being of the population.[15]

With the opening up of many NICs to foreign investment, in particular portfolio investment, a new chapter seems to have begun in the saga of globalization. As a part of the neo-liberal economic policies promoted by the 'Washington consensus' more and more countries have been under pressure – directly or indirectly – to open up their economies to foreign investment. Down to the 1980s, the NICs of East Asia, for example South Korea, Taiwan and Indonesia, have had a variety of controls and restrictions in place on foreign investment. From about the mid-1980s many of these countries were persuaded to ease or remove these restrictions and to welcome foreign investment.[16] The result was a huge inflow of funds, mainly in the form of portfolio investment in search of substantial returns. Moreover, many companies and businesses in these countries borrowed heavily from foreign lenders in order to finance speculative and other economic activity. Although the principal causes of the financial crisis of Southeast Asia in 1997 remain a matter of contention, given the nature of the financial institutions and limited foreign exchange reserve of many NICs, financial liberalization must be considered an important cause of the crisis. For unlike many of the LDCs discussed above, the Asian NICs, for example, did not have a balance of payment problem, their public sector was relatively small, budgets were not in deficit, and they had been hailed as model developing economies by IFIs such as the IMF.[17] What then went wrong?

In 1997 the perceived weakness of one of the currencies – the Thai baht – and the possibility of its devaluation caused a run on the currency and the 'contagion effect' spread to neighbouring countries. The result was a mass exodus of short-term foreign investment from these countries. The collapse of the currency and the stockmarkets led to economic contraction, massive lay-offs and a sharp drop in living standards.[18] At the same time foreign banks called in their short-term loans (denominated in dollar) which the private borrowers were unable to pay. The resulting shock to the global markets and the possibility of the contagion spreading further afield led the

USA and other G-7 nations to arrange a rescue package. In December 1997 South Korea received a bail-out of $57 billion (the biggest so far, topping the $50 billion Mexican bail-out in 1995). Indonesia received a package of $43 billion. The South Korean rescue package, overseen by the IMF, required the restructuring of the banking system, opening of the economy immediately to foreign imports, raising the limit on foreign ownership of stock, reducing government spending and raising taxes.[19] Moreover, the rescue package had a strong deflationary bias. In the event, the severity of the economic downturn and other factors, including widespread criticism of IMF's policy of 'One size fits all' and strong opposition from within South Korea led the Fund to set aside its austerity policy.[20]

As a result of the economic crisis, production, consumption, employment and incomes all suffered a sharp decline in South Korea, Indonesia and Thailand. The poverty population jumped another 12–20 per cent, and suicide and reported domestic violence increased sharply in, for example, South Korea. In these and other Asian NICs, which had enjoyed conditions of virtually full employment until then, unemployment rose sharply.[21] In South Korea, for example, registered unemployment rose from just over 2 per cent in mid-1997 to over 8 per cent in early 1999.[22] It was the relatively insulated nature of the Asian economies (their 'strategic integration' in the world economy as one economist put it), which was in no small measure responsible for their spectacular economic success and which allowed them to maintain full employment through private sector jobs. Moreover, along with relative job security went some work-related benefits, which is one reason why unemployment insurance and other forms of income support programmes for the unemployed were virtually non-existent or weakly developed in these countries. The sudden and unexpected onset of unemployment therefore had 'disastrous consequences for the unemployed and their families', who 'simultaneously lost their incomes and income-related benefits, such as health insurance'.[23]

In a sense the East Asian crisis was nothing new. In 1994–95 Mexico had been hit by a not dissimilar crisis which illustrates very well the perils of financial openness for emerging market economies. By 1994 Mexico had not only joined the North American Free Trade Association (NAFTA), but also the OECD thus symbolizing its coming of age as a relatively stable and maturing economy. These developments led to a large inflow of foreign portfolio investment in the early 1990s, and rising stockmarket prices and high interest rates on short-term bonds made the country very attractive for higher returns. However, the bubble was to burst soon. During 1994 the stockmarket fell by about a third in value, and in December 1994 the peso was devalued by 30 per cent, but in fact fell further. Confidence in the functioning of the 'borderless' global economy as well as in NAFTA was at stake. A bailout package of some $50 billion (the biggest ever) was arranged hastily by the G-7 nations under US leadership to stabilize the peso and to restore investor confidence. Once again the task of setting the conditionalities and supervising the loan fell on the IMF.[24]

The result of the economic crisis, high interest rates and the austerity policies demanded by the IMF was a massive inflation, a sharp contraction in consumer demand, rising unemployment and falling wages. True, within a couple of years the Mexican economy improved, growth picked up and investor confidence had been restored, but it was a different story for the large majority of the people. During 1993–98, for example, average wages *fell* at a rate of 1.6 per cent per annum while prices *rose* by an annual rate of 19.7 per cent.[25] In the late 1990s, four-fifths of the country's population was still worse off than in 1982.[26] Moreover, membership of NAFTA and the conditionalities attached to the loan means that the economy is now more open than before to global investors and thus at a higher risk for the repetition of the 1994–95 crisis through the sudden exit of portfolio capital.

In sum, financial liberalization has introduced a serious risk of destabilization of the economies of NICs through the sudden outflow of portfolio capital and other forms of 'hot money'. Financial bailouts are aimed primarily at protecting investors' and creditors' interests and the associated conditionalities seem to add to the diswelfare of the general population resulting from the crises. Moreover, the resolution of the problem within the framework of financial openness increases the risk of recurrent crises and diswelfare for the population, likely to be followed by further bailouts. Thus a vicious cycle is set in motion. The consequences for systems of social protection are contradictory. On the one hand exposure to the global economy increases insecurity, undermines existing forms of social protection and thus underlines the need for an adequate social safety net. On the other hand, the disruption of the economy, resource constraints and fiscal austerity and the ideology of privatization militate against developing programmes of social welfare. How nation-states come to terms with this problem depends on a host of economic and political factors. Thus Korea and Mexico present clear contrasts. Following the economic crisis Korea made a commitment to protect minimum social standards and to strengthen and extend its social welfare system. Mexico has followed a policy of 'targeting', that is providing some assistance to the low-income and deprived sections of the population, while restricting social spending generally.[27]

The former communist countries

As far as transnational influence on welfare is concerned, the ex-communist countries share a number of features with the LDCs and emerging economies – economic vulnerability due to financial openness, the influence of IFIs on social policy, the erosion of 'social protection by other means' – but within a context that differs in important respects from that of the other two groups of countries. For one, the former communist countries have been in a difficult process of transition from state socialism towards a market economy and open society. For another, all this is taking place against the backdrop of a well-developed system of social protection, and the impact of supranational forces needs to be seen in this context.

With the collapse of communism in the USSR and Eastern Europe in the late 1980s the former communist countries were faced with the task of reconstructing their economies and societies. In broad terms this meant a transition from state socialism to some form of liberal economic and political order, a transition that had no historical precedents and thus no blueprints or models as a guide. At any rate it was also evident that these countries would need economic assistance to make the transition (a different model of economic transition is being followed by China and Vietnam), an assistance that could only come from the West. It came packaged with the dominant Western economic ideology of neo-liberalism. These countries were advised to go for an all-out radical reform and to integrate their economies within the world economy. This meant moving away from a relatively closed economy and society to one completely open to global capitalism in terms of trade and financial flows. This approach to transition, which came to be known as 'shock therapy' (ST), involved such things as trade and financial liberalization, currency convertibility and the unleashing of market forces in the domestic economy.[28]

The transition was expected to create some economic dislocation and problems of adjustment in the short run. In fact the policy of ST, combined with weaknesses inherited from state socialism, proved disastrous for many of these countries resulting in a huge drop in production, large-scale unemployment, a sharp decline in wages, large increases in poverty and deprivation and in economic inequality. This was accompanied with massive inflation, balance-of-payments problems and a serious lack of revenue for governments.[29]

The system of social protection these countries inherited was a part of the old order of state socialism with its ideological commitment to economic security and collective consumption. Its three major bases were (i) full employment for both men and women, (ii) a system of consumer price subsidies which held down the cost of living very substantially ('social protection by other means'), and (iii) a set of universal, if low-quality, services such as health, education and childcare, and a range of income transfer programmes, for example pensions and child allowances, again at a low level of benefits. Employment-related benefits were also important and in fact overlapped with state programmes.

The decollectivization of the economy and its marketization under the ST approach meant the end of full employment and a drastic reduction, if not elimination, of subsidies. Each of these had a considerable negative impact on living standards and the sense of economic security of the population.

The third base of social protection – the social programmes – has also been restructured resulting, in broad terms, in greater selectivity and residualism. Some income-transfer programmes, for example pensions, have seen a good deal of privatization. Given the policy of compulsory full employment (an aspect of state socialism), these countries did not have unemployment insurance or similar measures; these had to be put in place as a part of the transition.[30]

With balance-of-payments and other economic problems resulting from the transition these countries needed financial aid. This involved IFIs such as IMF and WB and, as in the case of the LDCs, the task of arranging and supervising loans provided these IFIs with the leverage for influencing economic and social policy.[31] In general, fiscal austerity, the reduction of public expenditure and greater use of selectivity in social programmes have been the guiding principles of the IMF's policy for these countries. With the ST approach and associated adjustment policies the social costs of transition – varying in degree from one country to another – have been heavy in terms of impoverishment and destitution, inequality, falling life expectations and other quality-of-life indicators.[32]

Although the economies of some of the former communist countries, for example Poland and Hungary, have recovered well since the mid-1990s the legacy of the transition and adjustment policies for social protection would appear to be more long lasting while the burden of foreign debt continues to weigh heavily on many of these countries.[33] In sum, supranational influences – working through global investors as well as IFIs – have been prominent in shaping economic and social policies with serious consequences for the living standards of the people. Moreover, forms of social protection specific to state socialism – notably compulsory full employment and consumer subsidies – have been substantially dismantled making for a marked structural convergence towards Western forms of social protection.[34]

Western industrial countries

At first sight the situation of the WICs seems to be very different from that of the other group of countries discussed above. *First*, as we have seen, in all three groups of countries the role of the IFIs – primarily IMF but also the WB – in curtailing policy autonomy of nations and in restructuring social policy in a neo-liberal direction has been quite prominent. In the WICs, by contrast, IFIs have played no such role, and these countries have not had their policy-making autonomy impaired in this way. *Second*, in many emerging market economies financial liberalization has brought a large measure of volatility through the ebb and flow of short-term foreign investment resulting in the destabilization of economies, falls in output, rises in unemployment, drops in living standards and rises in poverty. The loans and conditionalities that have usually followed under the auspices of the IMF contain a bias towards a deflationary policy and fiscal austerity. The 'social protection by other means' that has characterized the emerging Asian economies, in conditions where state welfare remains little developed, has been weakened as a result. In the WICs, by contrast, financial liberalization and the free flow of investment across borders has not meant the destabilization of economies or serious currency crises – problems that a country's own economic and financial resources (including borrowing on the market) cannot cope with. In short, the kind of impact of globalization on economic and social welfare of nations seen in East Asia and elsewhere recently has no counterpart as far as WICs are concerned. These differences are not unimportant. Does it mean, then, that the WICs are immune to the destabilization of their economies and free from the influence of IGOs?

Let us begin with the influence of IGOs. The WB has little to do with WICs, while the IMF has not been involved in bailing out any WICs for over two decades. Thus it has not had a direct say in the fiscal and social policy of these countries. On the other hand the indirect influence of the IMF on WICs – by way of the surveillance of monetary and fiscal management, offers of expert advice, regular meetings and consultations with finance ministers and other government officials of member countries – is not to be underestimated.[35] And, by and large, this influence has been strongly monetarist and liberal in orientation. The OECD, which acts more as a think-tank for the WICs, also seeks to influence the economic and social policy of member countries. Although more eclectic and less orthodox in its approach than the IMF, the OECD also favours financial liberalization, greater market-orientation of economies and a smaller role for the social state.[36]

In sum, although IGOs such as the IMF and OECD do not exercise direct control over social policy of the WICs indirectly they influence policy options and choices of these countries. True, the pro-market liberal policies recommended by these institutions are not an easy sell within member states. WICs are democracies and therefore government policies are subject to challenge by interest groups and opposition parties. In short, democracy acts as a counterweight to global neo-liberalism. Here again the WICs may be in a somewhat different position than the LDCs, the NICs and ex-communist countries where democracy and civil society are not so well-developed and institutionalized.

Although the WICs have not so far experienced any destabilization of their economies it would be wrong to conclude that they are immune to such a development. Thus the Asian crisis of 1997 which was followed by financial crises in Brazil and Russia in 1998 did pose a threat to the stability of the global economy as a whole. The bailouts organized by the G-7 governments (led by the USA) during the 1990s were, in part, meant to contain and defuse the crises and stop the contagion from spreading more widely. An example of a direct threat to Western financial institutions was the prospect of the collapse in 1998 of Long-Term Capital Management, a leading American hedge fund which was highly leveraged. The domino effect on stockmarkets and other financial institutions and through them on the US economy could apparently have been serious, and a rescue package for the fund was put together hastily by Western banks at the initiative of the President of the Federal Reserve Bank of New York.[37] Clearly the increased integration of the global economy itself together with financial openness means that the WICs are also potentially at risk.

Compared to the stable financial regime under the Bretton Woods dispensation, the current regime of financial openness and flexible exchange rates increases the risk of large-scale economic destabilization, making national welfare states vulnerable. Indeed, as the experience of a number of Nordic countries in the early 1990s shows, the currencies of WICs have at times come under severe pressure resulting in significant shifts in social policy.[38]

Despite these commonalities between the WICs and other countries, the impact of globalization on WICs takes a somewhat different form. It is more indirect and diffuse in nature although broadly in the same neo-liberal direction. We shall look briefly at three broad areas of social concern: full employment, social security, and taxation and inequality. Keeping in mind that conditions vary from one country to another and that global pressures are mediated through the political economy of the nation-state the following generalizations seek to capture the broad trend. *First*, financial openness and mobility of capital together with flexible exchange rates means that Keynesian macroeconomic management in order to create full employment and stable economic growth is not feasible – or at least not effective – in an open economy. *Second*, heightened international competition and associated changes in market conditions demand greater labour-market flexibility and the acceptance of low-wage employment. Governments are under pressure to cut back unemployment benefits and social assistance to the able-bodied. *Third*, conditions of openness and capital mobility are exerting a downward pressure on taxation and social spending as nations are placed in a competitive situation in order to attract or retain private investment and create a business-friendly environment. Bond markets are influencing the fiscal policies of nations through the credit rating of governments. Taxation is becoming more regressive as top income tax rates plummet and there is a marked shift from income and corporate taxes to insurance contributions and consumption taxes. Both pre-tax and post-tax inequality of incomes has increased markedly in many OECD countries.[39] In sum global capitalism, with the support of IGOs such as the IMF and OECD, is exerting a good deal of pressure, directly or indirectly, to scale down the post-Second World War welfare state, with its full employment and social citizenship built within a more stable international framework of finance and relatively closed national economies.[40]

However, counter pressures in the form of democratic opposition, long-standing national commitment to social partnership and social market approach, for example in Continental Europe, are moderating the neoliberal thrust of global capitalism. Hence, overall, we find that WICs have not so far travelled far down the road of shrinking the social state and reducing social protection.[41]

Summary and conclusions

Evidence from the world outside of the WICs suggests that an exclusive focus on the latter in terms of the effect of globalization is limiting in a number of ways. For one it ignores almost entirely the role of IGOs in curtailing the policy-making autonomy of nations, one of the key issues in the relationship between globalization and social protection. This role has been direct and pronounced in the case of a large number of countries around the world and needs to be brought into focus. This is important for a number of reasons. *First*, it draws attention to the fact that globalization involves more than just pressure from markets and private enterprises; IGOs are also involved. *Second*, it highlights the fact that IGOs are also influencing the social policy of WICs and that the nature of this influence has yet to be examined systematically. *Third*, a focus on the IGOs, notably the IMF, the OECD but also the World Trade Organization, underlines the fact that globalization is a *process* – rather than a finished state. This is important in that a good deal of complacency in the literature about the durability of the welfare state stems from treating globalization as though it was a finished state. A related point is that these IGOs are closely involved in the process of extending the reach of globalization. The Multilateral Agreement on Investment (MAI), a measure which was piloted through the OECD in near secrecy for about three years before being shelved, is a case in point.[42] *Fourth*, a focus on the role of these IGOs raises the issue of legitimate governance in the area of global policy-making. For IFIs such as IMF and the WB are not democratic bodies but reflect the economic power of donor nations. Yet their decisions have direct implications for the welfare policies of nations. Other IGOs, for example the OECD, also suffer from a lack of transparency and accountability (witness, for example, the secrecy surrounding the MAI).

We turn next to the implications of financial openness and cross-border flow of capital for nations. Here again an exclusive focus on WICs tends to miss out almost entirely on the role of financial openness in destabilizing economies. In Mexico (1994–95), in East Asian countries (1997–98), and in Brazil and Russia (1998) the sudden exodus of foreign capital has had a major impact on their economies resulting in loss of output, bankruptcies, unemployment, a fall in living standards and poverty. Moreover, these crises required bailout loans which generally involve further belt-tightening and public expenditure cuts. In the case of East Asian countries economic destabilization has disrupted, if not substantially weakened, the bases of their economic success and 'social protection by other means'; that is, rapid economic growth and private-sector full employment. Systems of social protection have also been undergoing a transformation in former communist countries bringing them closer, at least in form, to the Western welfare state model. Thus globalization is leading to an institutional convergence in systems of social protection, a development that is missed out if the focus is exclusively on WICs.[43]

No doubt, financial openness and the flow of foreign investment has also brought economic benefits for countries outside the WICs. However the question must be asked at what cost? And what kind of benefits and for whom? For as the case of Mexico, for example, shows economic growth can resume within a short time following the crisis, stockmarkets surge and foreign investors return. But it is a different story as far as the majority of people are concerned. They may have to pay for the cost of adjustment in terms of a fall in living standards and retarded social development for a long time. Whereas the bailouts protect the interests of foreign and domestic investors there may not be any kind of bailout for the people of the country concerned. Moreover, bailouts generally curtail the policy-making autonomy of the countries, at least in the short run, leaving their economic and social policies a hostage to IFIs and foreign creditors. True, national responses vary and, as the example of Korea shows, may extend social protection. Nonetheless they have to contend with globalization pressures.

More generally, the devastating effect of financial openness raises the question of the need to regulate financial flows in order to prevent economic destabilization. Recent studies by UNCTAD, for example, show that the rising frequency of financial crises is associated with the growth of international capital flows in the 1990s.[44] Needless to say an adequate system of national social protection requires a measure of economic stability that cannot be provided by a highly volatile globalized economy subject to 'shocks'. A look at countries outside the WICs underlines the serious consequences that can result from financial openness. So far the WICs have been spared the kind of dramatic destabilization we have seen elsewhere, but this does not mean that Western economies are immune to the virus of instability – they too are potentially at risk in a global economy.

In sum, there is a case for bringing an international and global perspective to bear on the study of the relationship between globalization and social welfare. At present it tends to be compartmentalized in terms of different groups of countries due to academic specialization and the important differences that exist among countries. This specialized approach needs to be *complemented* by a wider and more unifying international perspective. This could provide the common ground for the study of globalization and welfare relationship across major types of society; namely developed, developing and transitional (ex-communist), and offer a more adequate basis for understanding this complex relationship.

Notes

1. This is not to say that exogenous variables have not received some attention. For example, the thesis that international vulnerability of small trade-dependent countries leads to cooperation among social partners, in short corporatism, and results in a more developed system of social protection has been advanced by Peter Katzenstein, *Small States in World Markets*, Ithaca: Cornell University Press, 1985. F. Castles, 'Social Protection by Other Means', in F.G. Castles (ed.), *The Comparative History of Public Policy*, New York: Oxford University Press, 1989 has argued that high tariffs and restriction on immigration enabled Australia and New Zealand to develop a 'Wage-earners' welfare state' as a part of a system of social protection by 'other means'.

2. The literature on globalization is immense. D. Held *et al.*, *Global Transformations*, Stanford: Stanford University Press, 1999 provides an encyclopedic overview.

3. The last six or seven years have seen a burgeoning literature concerned with economic internationalization and its implications for social protection. See for example, M. Rhodes, 'Globalisation and West European Welfare States; A Critical Review of Recent Debates', *Journal of European Social Policy*, London, vol. 6, no. 4, 1996; Ramesh Mishra, *Globalization and the Welfare State*, Cheltenham: Edward Elgar, 1999; J.D. Stephens, E. Huber and L. Ray, 'The Welfare State in Hard Times', in H. Kitschelt *et al.* (eds), *Continuity and Change in Contemporary Capitalism*, Cambridge: Cambridge University Press, 1999; Fritz Scharpf and Vivien Schmidt (eds), *Welfare and Work in the Open Economy*, Vols I and II, Oxford: Oxford University Press, 2000; Paul Pierson (ed.), *The New Politics of the Welfare State*, Oxford: Oxford University Press, 2001; Duane Swank, *Global Capital, Political Institutions, and Policy Change in Developed Welfare States*, Cambridge: Cambridge University Press, 2002.

4. See for example, P. Pierson, 'Post-Industrial Pressures on the Mature Welfare States', in Pierson, n. 3; F.G. Castles, 'On the Political Economy of Recent Public Sector Development', *Journal of European Social Policy*, vol. 6, no. 3, 2001; Stein Kuhnle (ed.), *Survival of the European Welfare State*, London: Routledge, 2000.

5. See for example, Robert Sykes *et al.* (eds), *Globalization and European Welfare States*, Basingstoke: Palgrave Macmillan, 2001; Swank, n. 3.

6. Bob Deacon *et al.*, *Global Social Policy*, London: Sage, 1997, and Vic George and Paul Wilding, *Globalization and Human Welfare*, Basingstoke: Palgrave Macmillan, 2002, go some way towards extending the perspective beyond Western industrial societies. The journal *Global Social Policy* provides a useful forum for debating the issue of globalization from a variety of regional perspectives. See for example, 'GSP Forum: A North–South Dialogue on the Prospects for a Socially Progressive Globalization', *Global Social Policy*, vol. 1, no. 2, 2001.

7. Castles, n. 1.

8. Susan George, *A Fate Worse Than Debt*, Harmondsworth: Penguin, 1988; Philip McMichael, *Development and Social Change*, Thousand Oaks, Cal.: Pine Forge Press, 1996.

9. McMichael, n. 8, p. 132.

10. *Ibid.*, p. 203.

11. *Ibid.*, p. 153.

12 UNDP (United Nations Development Programme), *Human Development Report 1999*, Oxford: Oxford University Press, 1999, p. 107; see also International Monetary Fund (IMF), *World Economic Outlook*, Washington, DC, 2001, p. 220, for more recent figures.

13 UNDP, n. 12; see also UNDP, *Human Development Report 2002*, p. 30 on various initiatives, including the Jubilee 2000 movement, on debt cancellation for poor countries.

14 A. Singh, '"Asian Capitalism" and the Financial Crisis', in J. Michie and J. Grieve Smith (eds), *Global Instability*, London: Routledge, 1999.

15 Singh, n. 14; I. Grabel, 'Rejecting Exceptionalism: Reinterpreting the Asian Financial Crises' in Michie and Grieve Smith, n. 14.

16 Singh, n. 14, p. 28.

17 D. Felix, 'Asia and the Crisis of Financial Globalization', in D. Baker *et al.* (eds), *Globalization and Progressive Economic Policy*, Cambridge: Cambridge University Press, 1998; Singh, n. 14.

18 ILR (International Labour Review), 'Social Aspects of the Follow-up to the Asian Financial Crisis', *International Labour Review*, vol. 138, no. 2, 1999; UNDP, n. 12, p. 40; OECD (Organization for Economic Cooperation and Development), *Economic Surveys 1998–1999: Korea*, Paris, 1999.

19 Grabel, n. 15, p. 37.

20 T.J. Palley, 'International Finance and Global Deflation', in Michie and Grieve Smith, n. 14, p. 107; Singh, n. 14, p. 33.

21 ILR, n. 18, p. 195; UNDP, n. 12, p. 40.

22 OECD, n. 18, p. 20.

23 ILR, n. 18, p. 195.

24 Grabel, n. 15.

25 OECD, n. 18, 'Basic Statistics, International Comparisons'.

26 U. Pieper and L. Taylor, 'The Revival of the Liberal Creed: The IMF, the World Bank, and Inequality in a Globalized Economy', in Baker *et al.*, n. 17, p. 50.

27 On Korea, see for example K. Yeon-Myung, 'Welfare State or Social Safety Nets?', *Korea Journal*, vol. 41, no. 2, 2001; H.K. Lee, 'Globalization and the Emerging Welfare State; The Experience of South Korea', *International Journal of Social Welfare*, vol. 8, no. 1, 1999. On Mexico, see for example Enrique Peters, *Polarizing Mexico: The Impact of Liberalization Strategy*, Boulder: Lynne Rienner, 2000, pp. 148–50.

28 P. Gowan, 'Neo-Liberal Theory and Practice for Eastern Europe', *New Left Review*, no. 213, 1995; G. Standing, 'Social Protection in Central and Eastern Europe', in G. Esping-Andersen (ed.), *Welfare States in Transition*, London: Sage, 1996.

29 Standing, n. 28; WB (The World Bank), *Making Transition Work for Everyone: Poverty and Inequality in Europe and Central Asia*, Washington, DC, 2000; Joseph Stiglitz, *Globalization and Its Discontents*, New York: W.W. Norton, 2002, pp. 133–65.

30 Standing, n. 28; G.W. Kolodko, 'Equity Issues in Policymaking in Transition Economies', in V. Tanzi *et al.* (eds), *Economic Policy and Equity*, Washington, DC: International Monetary Fund, 1999.

31 IMF, *World Economic Outlook October 2000: Focus on Transition Economies*, Washington, DC, 2000, pp. 85–91; Z. Ferge, 'Welfare and "Ill-Fare" Systems in Central-Eastern Europe', in R. Sykes *et al.* (eds), *Globalization and European Welfare States*, Basingstoke: Palgrave Macmillan, 2001, pp. 131–35.

32 WB, n. 29; Stiglitz, n. 29, Ferge, n. 31.

33 Ferge, n. 31; WB, n. 29; S. Strange, 'The New World of Debt,' *New Left Review*, no. 230, 1998; IMF, n. 12, p. 220 for the debt burden of Transition countries.

34 It is important to distinguish between convergence of policy and convergence of structure or the institutional form of social protection. It is the latter form of convergence that is being claimed here. Arguably, in some respects, the former also seems to be occurring. See Ferge, n. 31 for a perceptive commentary on the 'Westernization' of East European welfare systems.

35 R. O'Brien *et al.*, *Contesting Global Governance*, Cambridge: Cambridge University Press, 2000, pp. 161–2; IMF, *Annual Report* (various years).

36 Deacon, n. 6, pp. 70–3; Mishra, n. 3, pp. 8–11; S. McBride and R. Williams, 'Globalization, the Restructuring of Labour Markets and Policy Convergence: The OECD "Jobs Strategy,"' *Global Social Policy*, vol. 1, n. 3, 2001: Nicola Yeates, *Globalization and Social Policy*, London: Sage, 2001, pp. 28–30.

37 I. Warde, 'LTCM, a hedge fund above suspicion', *Le Monde Diplomatique*, Paris, English internet edition, 1998. As Stiglitz writes, 'The New York Federal Reserve Bank engineered a private bailout of one of the nation's largest hedge funds, Long Term Capital Management, since the Fed feared its failure could precipitate a global financial crisis', see n. 29, p. 150.

38 J. Crotty *et al.*, 'Multinational Corporations in the Neo-Liberal Regime', in Baker *et al.*, n. 17, pp. 137–40; P. Kosonen, 'Globalization and the Nordic Welfare States', in Sykes *et al.*, n. 31, pp. 164–67, 171.

39 OECD, *Economic Outlook 63*, Paris, 1998, pp. 159–62; OECD, *Economic Outlook 69*, Paris, 2001, pp. 173–5; R. Clayton and J. Pontusson, 'Welfare State Revisited', *World Politics*, vol. 51, n. 1, 1998; Mishra, n. 3, pp. 41–4; Scharpf and Schmidt, n. 3, vol. I, table 3.1, p. 143.

40 Mishra, n. 3; Swank, n. 3; Evelyne Huber and John Stephens, *Development and Crisis of Welfare States*, Chicago: Chicago University Press, 2001.

41 The literature on the resilience and durability of Western welfare States is quite substantial; see for example, Pierson, n. 3; Stein Kuhnle (ed.), *Survival of the European Welfare State*, London: Routledge, 2000.

42 Tony Clarke and Maude Barlow, *MAI: Multilateral Agreement on Investment and the Threat to Canadian Sovereignty*, Toronto: Stoddart, 1997; E. Braunstein and G. Epstein, 'Creating International Credit Rules and the Multilateral Agreement on Investment', in Michie and Grieve Smith, n. 14.

43 As mentioned earlier (n. 34), it is important to distinguish policy convergence from institutional or structural convergence. Much of the debate on whether welfare states are converging as a result of globalization pressures has been about policy or the substance of social provision. Very little attention has been paid to institutional convergence. This is not surprising considering that the focus of attention has been on Western industrialized nations. On these points see R. Mishra, 'Social Protection by Other Means: Can it Survive Globalization?', in P. Kennett (ed.), *A Handbook of Comparative Social Policy*, Cheltenham: Edward Elgar, 2003.

44 UNDP, n. 12, p. 40.

6

The British Welfare State: Development and Challenges

Tom Burden

Introduction

In this chapter I examine key phases in the development of social policy and look at their impact on the subsequent establishment of the welfare state. The phases considered are the Tudor Poor Law, the Poor Law Amendment Act of 1834, the new liberalism of the Edwardian period, and the Second World War. The Keynesian welfare state was subsequently challenged by welfare pluralism, communitarianism, Marxism, feminism and environmentalism, as well as by neo-liberalism. The subsequent rise of New Labour involved strong neo-liberal elements in its policies on work, education and training for work, managerialism, and poverty, inequality and social exclusion. The Third Way is shown as resting on fragile foundations and as lacking ideological coherence. It is argued that this weakness might be resolved through a scheme of basic income, and it will be seen that the approach of New Labour is likely to create a 'wage earners welfare state' in which minorities of various kinds are marginalized. Some of the arguments in this chapter have been developed at more length elsewhere.[1]

Key phases of social policy development

This section will identify the legacy of key phases in the development of social policy in Britain up until the mid-1970s.

The Tudor Poor Law

The Tudor Poor Law was established in a period in which the transition to capitalist relations of production was taking place.[2] Many features of the present system of state income support can be traced back to the Poor Law Act 1601, which set up a national system of social regulation at an early stage in the development of capitalism. The legislation provided for separate treatment for each of three categories unable to maintain themselves. The able-bodied were to be set to work with materials provided by the parish, usually in a workhouse. Those deemed unwilling to support themselves would be subject to a disciplinary regime in a house of correction. The 'impotent' poor, unable to maintain themselves, would be maintained by income supplements or the provision of almshouses. Important legacies of the scheme were the classification of the poor according to their adjudged ability to perform wage labour, the use of a combination of income support and institutional provision, and the denial of any relief to the working poor.[3]

Significant developments occurred after 1794 when provision was first made for the 'working poor'. A meeting of magistrates agreed to pay poor relief in cash or kind whenever the price of bread reached a threshold level. The relief was paid whether or not the applicants were in paid work. This system was established at a time when wages in many areas were falling below subsistence level due to the inflation caused by the Napoleonic War and to a series of bad harvests. In addition, the authorities were concerned to minimize the growth of radicalism in the aftermath of the French Revolution. This early form of index-linked benefit was known as the 'Speenhamland system' after the place where the magistrates had met.

This Speenhamland system was an attempt to reestablish a degree of economic security for the rural working class. It led to increases in expenditure on poor relief, and thus to higher rates (local property taxes), that provoked the opposition of ratepayers. It led to low wages, since employers could pay them in the knowledge that they would be supplemented from the parish rates. The system also offended the tenets of classical political economy by interfering with the free determination of wages. The key legacy of this period was a willingness to consider non-punitive measures to relieve poverty, particularly in response to strong pressure from below where social order was threatened.

Reform of the Poor Law 1834 and the consolidation of liberal doctrine and policy

The industrial revolution in Britain led to new pressures to reconstruct the state apparatus. Reformers felt that urbanization and industrialization created new conditions which required a more disciplined and orderly society – people needed to be made to adjust to the new demands of a competitive market economy. From around 1800, major changes in the state were introduced. The reformers wished to establish a modern state apparatus run on bureaucratic lines that would support the consolidation of the capitalist free market economy. The rationalistic statism of Benthamism[4] was combined with an acceptance of the arguments of classical political economy that the removal of restrictions on private property and the market would normally secure efficiency in the economic sphere. State intervention was seen as justified only to protect individual freedom and free exchange between individuals, for instance through law and order measures.

The Poor Law (Amendment) Act 1834 embodied the ethos of the reformers. Its two main authors were Chadwick, a leading Benthamite, and the
classical economist Nassau Senior.[5] The Act transferred the responsibility for
the poor to some 600 Poor Law Unions, run by Guardians elected by the
ratepayers. The Poor Law Board was an early example of bureaucratic organization in the state. The Board exercised control through instructions to
local Guardians, and through an Inspectorate. It laid down detailed rules
governing every aspect of the internal organization of the workhouses. The
basic principle of the amended or 'new' Poor Law was that as far as
possible no cash payments ('outdoor relief') would be made, and the only
assistance for the poor would be the offer of a place in the workhouse. This
was a 'total' institution run on authoritarian lines.[6] Conditions in this institution were designed to deter any but the most desperate from accepting
the offer. The Act incorporated the notion that individual failings were the
cause of destitution.

Legacies of the Act included a centralized system of poor relief, a punitive
approach towards the poor, a concern to minimize state expenditure on the
poor, the provision of benefits at a level of bare subsistence and the degradation of the status of recipients of poor relief, who lost the right to vote.

The 'new liberalism'

The 'new liberalism' was a reforming tendency within the British Liberal
Party that developed in the early part of the twentieth century. It exercised
an influence over policy in the Liberal governments of 1906–14, and more
broadly over welfare reforms throughout the first half of the twentieth
century.[7] Some leading Liberals felt that the party could no longer continue
to support Victorian *laissez-faire* principles as a result of growing evidence
of deep-seated poverty and other social problems that seemed to result from
an uncontrolled market. Rowntree, a progressive industrialist, demonstrated
that wage levels were so low that they were insufficient to maintain a normal
level of health and working efficiency for many workers.[8] He established the
modern study of poverty using a 'scientifically' calculated poverty line.
While the new liberalism is the ideological current most closely associated
with reform in this period, other organizations and currents of opinion also
played an important part. These included the 'national efficiency movement', Fabianism and eugenics.

The national efficiency movement was a broad coalition in favour of
improvements in welfare policies. It united progressive industrialists, social
reformers and those concerned about Britain's military strength, particularly
in the aftermath of the military failures in the Boer war. It campaigned for
policies to improve the health and strength of British workers in order to
enhance industrial productivity and military strength.[9]

Fabianism has been the principle source of reformist plans and ideas
within the British Labour Party. From the beginning, the strategy of the

Fabians was 'rationalist', 'élitist' and 'gradualist'. They were rationalist in that they believed that research and discussion could produce solutions to all social and economic problems. They were élitist in that they believed that a small number of dedicated intellectuals could alone create effective pressures for reform. They were gradualist in that they sought a steady progress towards socialism rather than a sudden revolutionary shift.

Eugenics portrayed social problems as caused by people who were biologically inferior; an important feature of the general intellectual climate of the time was a belief in the hereditary character of social problems. This was closely related to 'social Darwinism', the application to society of ideas on the role of 'natural selection' and competition between species in ensuring the 'survival of the fittest'.[10] For example, the Mental Deficiency Act 1913 viewed 'feeble-mindedness' as hereditary. It was seen as the main cause of poverty, unemployment, crime, prostitution, promiscuity, alcoholism and vagrancy. Under the Act, the feeble-minded could be, and often were, compulsorily detained.[11]

A major innovation introduced by the new liberals was National Insurance. This employs compulsory personal saving to provide a fund to supplement income when it is interrupted. National Insurance was first used in Germany in the late nineteenth century. It was devised as a right-wing strategy to divert support away from the socialist movement and to attach the working class to the existing conservative order. It works by redistributing income within an income group – healthy workers support the sick, those in work support the unemployed. In Britain the National Insurance Act 1911 introduced means-tested health insurance and a scheme of unemployment insurance.[12]

The legacy of the new liberalism was central to the eventual development of the postwar Keynesian welfare state. The concerns of the national efficiency movement in relation to military efficiency and economic productivity remained a key concern of reformers. The ideas of the eugenics movement also remained influential particularly on the right, although in a modified form they played a part in the development of an authoritarian strand in social democratic reformism which viewed compulsion as necessary to secure social improvement. The invention of the poverty line provided a scientific basis for setting the level of social benefits.

The insurance schemes represented a move away from the punitive approach of the Poor Law although some elements of continuity were maintained. The schemes were designed to restrict benefits to a category of 'deserving' individuals. The division between 'deserving' recipients of insurance benefits, and the 'undeserving' who were only given assistance subject to means tests or other conditions, has continued. Key features of the scheme were consistent with the values of capitalism. National Insurance benefits had to be 'earned' by contributions. The insurance principle would reinforce self-help. Rules on the number of contributions necessary before benefits could be drawn would prevent abuse by malingerers. Contributions from the employer and the state would symbolize a concern for employee welfare and contribute to a sense of citizenship. Benefits set at subsistence level would keep costs low, maintain work incentives and encourage the private provision of insurance.

The war and the Keynesian welfare state

During the Second World War (1939–45) there were major shifts in ideology and policy. Under the pressure of war and of the growth of popular radicalism, the rhetoric of moderate reformism was widely adopted across the political spectrum. There was a considerable increase in the power and influence of the working class and its industrial and political organizations.[13] A key role was played by the Beveridge Report of 1942 in the formulation of plans for a welfare state.[14] This proposed a comprehensive system of national insurance based on a single weekly contribution that would finance a broad range of benefits set at subsistence level. It excluded those unable to work, such as the handicapped, and offered lesser benefits to women.[15]

The major legacy of the Beveridge scheme was the idea of a comprehensive welfare state. Another key feature was the focus on workers as the principal recipients of benefits and on work as a central qualifying condition. Another more radical legacy of the wartime reforms was universalism. This was the name given to the principle that social benefits should be made available to everyone in an eligible category. Family allowances were paid to all families with two or more children, regardless of income. The proposed health service, available free to all in need, was another universal benefit.

The term 'Keynesian welfare state' refers to the kind of policies established in many western capitalist countries after the Second World War. It involved a system of managed capitalism and extensive welfare provision. The adoption of these policies has been seen as part of a 'postwar settlement' which was able to resolve social antagonisms and form the basis for a period of social harmony.[16] The two key new liberal thinkers whose ideas underpinned the postwar settlement were Keynes and Beveridge. Keynes' theories involved a system of government intervention to increase spending in order to create jobs, whilst preserving the market and individual economic and political freedom. Beveridge was linked to the idea of a welfare state covering all needs 'from cradle-to-the-grave'. During the long postwar boom, the Keynesian welfare state became viewed as an established and essential feature of society with considerable support across the political spectrum.

The Keynesian welfare state has been identified as a key characteristic of all Western-liberal democracies at similar stages of economic development.[17] The welfare state was a particular model of social protection designed to ensure a fit and healthy population, echoing concerns earlier in the century. The model citizen was depicted in a particular way; as Powell (1999) states:

The Beveridgean citizen was the fully employed (and insured) married, white, able-bodied, male worker, with other categories of people – including women, ethnic minorities, disabled people, children and elderly people – experiencing highly conditional forms of welfare exclusion outside the 'normal' universalism.[18]

The end of the Keynesian welfare state

Our discussion of key phases in the development of social policy illustrates the importance of the legacy of these formative periods. Parts of the welfare state apparatus retain significant characteristics that were present at a time when they were founded, and reflect the particular balance of social interests that underlay their establishment. The apparatus of administration, the procedures employed in dealing with social issues, the occupational groups established, the networks and contacts with existing social interests, have all helped to sustain these organizations and their characteristic mode of operation over long periods.

Developments on the Left

Towards the end of the long boom a range of critiques of the Keynesian welfare state emerged. One response was an attempt to revive and rework the social democratic approach to the welfare state, which involved a partial rejection of the statism characteristic of much Fabian thought. Instead, there was an emphasis on partnership between a range of agencies. The state has a role not as an exclusive provider, but as a partner with other agencies in building welfare services in a system of 'welfare pluralism'. Welfare pluralism is concerned to reduce the role of the state in the provision of welfare – it is also sometimes known as the 'mixed economy of welfare'.[19] Welfare provision is seen as resulting from the combination of activities undertaken in the statutory sector, the voluntary sector, the private sector and the informal sector, which consists mainly of families.

Another new development was 'communitarianism'. This is critical of liberal individualism, although it retains a strong attachment to traditional morality.[20] The main idea of communitarianism is to balance individual rights and community responsibilities. Unrestrained individualism is seen as having undermined family and community relationships. The goal of communitarians is to promote community rather than equality. Communitarianism has become a key idea in those versions of reformism that downplay economic egalitarianism and emphasize moral improvement. For communitarians like Etzioni, a strong community requires traditional nuclear family structures, providing strong parenting. It also requires members of communities to accept their duties and responsibilities in the form of service to others.

Some critiques developed from a more radical direction. Marxism reemerged as a significant voice in the study of social policy. However, other radical viewpoints were also important, including feminism, environmentalist anti-industrialism associated with Illich, and the radical pluralism associated with 'new social movements'.

Marxism had developed a view of state welfare provision as a means by which ruling groups stifle dissent and reinforce their own dominance, whilst failing to make any substantial reductions in inequality. It sees capitalist society as based on exploitation, inequality and class conflict.[21] Radical critiques of modern society have in recent years moved away from the exclusive emphasis on class inequality characteristic of Marxism and developed a focus on the issue of identity. This is evident in the radical literature which rejects industrialism.[22] This viewpoint is commonly a feature of the environmentalist or green political perspectives that are becoming significant in the study of social policy. Identity is also an important factor in the ongoing feminist critique of conventional social policies and the social policy literature.[23] The issue of identity is also at the forefront of the literature on new social movements.[24] Identity also figures in those versions of the postmodernist critique which adopt a radical perspective.[25]

Taken together, these strands of critical opinion constitute a comprehensive critique of the idea of the welfare state. They form part of a broad range of alternatives offered to the growing dominance of the neo-liberal perspective. However, these alternatives have remained politically weak because of the strength of the new right which gained power in several countries and employed the revived ideology of liberalism as a means of legitimating their appeal and as the basis for designing their policies.

Neo-liberalism

The right-wing economic critique of the Keynesian welfare state was founded on 'monetarism'. Monetarism was a revival of classical political economy, and monetarists argued that only 'supply-side' economic policies were viable. They focused on promoting economic efficiency by controlling inflation, which involved the control of the 'money-supply' by manipulating interest rates, ensuring wage restraint and cutting back on state borrowing.[26]

Following Hayek, neo-liberals promoted the idea that state intervention was generally harmful to society.[27] They developed a critique of the welfare state administration and of the role of the welfare state professions. The liberal theory of motivation that focuses on the rational pursuit of self-interest was used to develop a 'rational choice' model of bureaucracy.[28] This viewed the expansion of welfare spending as driven by the self-expanding welfare state bureaucracy. In this model civil servants running public sector organizations seek to expand their departments; a higher budget will provide more jobs and improve career prospects for bureaucrats.

Pressure for increased expenditure also comes from professionals who provide services, such as doctors, teachers and social workers.

The economic and social policy implications of Hayek's perspective were most clearly worked out by Friedman.[29] In principle, he argued, all services should be provided by the market since then people can express their preferences freely in terms of what they are willing to pay for. This implied privatization; competition between providers in a free market will ensure that services will be produced efficiently. However, if for practical or historical reasons state social provision exists and cannot be privatized, it must be run on lines which are consistent with market principles. This implied marketization and the use of 'provider markets' or 'quasi markets'. Consumers must be able to choose between providers who must compete with one another. The recipients of services are seen as consumers (buying a product) rather than clients (receiving a professional service).

Neo-liberalism also had a moral critique of the welfare state. Hayek believed that state planning held inherent moral dangers. It led to a reduction of independence and of the sense of personal responsibility. A perceived breakdown in traditional moral values came to be seen as having led to the emergence of an 'underclass', characterized by illegitimacy, violent crime and drop-out from the labour force.[30]

Neo-liberal welfare policies attained a dominant position in the West in the 1980s. A major restructuring of the state apparatus took place, which could partly be seen as a reversion to the Gladstonian policies of minimizing public expenditure and pursuing the goal of a balanced budget. Policies are now aimed at removing barriers to the free operation of the market. By the end of the twentieth century, therefore, there was again an element of political consensus around the nature of welfare and the role of the state:

> In one country after another the majority of voters give their support to parties that explicitly demand the curtailment of welfare provisions, or promise more benign taxation of individual incomes. . . . The astounding unanimity on this point among the parties across the political spectrum served some analysts as a main argument to assert the advent of a new 'solidarity' of sorts; of a new political consensus 'beyond left and right'.[31]

The political debate on welfare was now focused on how to reduce expenditure on welfare, categorize welfare applicants for purposes of new eligibility criteria, manage welfare markets more efficiently and eliminate welfare 'dependency'.

New Labour and the Third Way

In Britain in 1997, New Labour was elected after 18 years of Conservative rule. New Labour claims to herald new times, beyond social democracy and neo-liberalism, and it has stated its attachment to the 'Third Way'. Echoing communitarianism, New Labour makes an appeal to 'community values', civic responsibility, family solidarity and respect for the law, executed in the name of social inclusion and economic efficiency. However, the key idea is that the Third Way is believed to be best suited to confront the single most important force shaping our world – globalization. The International Monetary Fund (IMF) defined globalization as 'the growing economic interdependence of countries worldwide through the volume of cross-border transactions in goods and services and of international capital flows, and through the more rapid and widespread diffusion of technology'.[32]

The idea of globalization certainly lent support to the case for the free market and reduced public expenditure, and the concept of globalization has been adopted by both right and centre-left parties. For the political right it has confirmed the need to create competitive and flexible markets, and to attack collectivism and labour union rights. For the political centre-left, like New Labour, it has served to justify setting strict limits to state intervention.

Globalization is the key idea in the Third Way. According to Giddens, globalization means the era of the nation-state is over as states have lost most of the sovereignty they once had.[33] Public policy at the national level can no longer control market forces and these have to be accommodated. There is a shift in power from the nation and communities to transnational companies and global capital.

Work

Paid work is central to the social policy strategy of the Third Way. New Labour refers to its employment, training and benefit policies as based on 'welfare-to-work'. As Dahrendorf (1999) argues: 'Third Way reforms of the welfare state [involve] above all the strict insistence on everyone, including the disabled and single mothers, working. Where normal employment – let alone desired employment – is not available, people have to be made to work by the withdrawal of benefits.'[34]

However, finding permanent paid employment for everyone appears increasingly difficult in modern industrial societies. The obvious solution to this might be to share out the existing work perhaps by limiting working hours as has been done in France. However, New Labour opposes this policy seemingly on the grounds that a great deal of current unemployment is 'voluntary' and that the unemployed must be persuaded or required to take up the work which is available.

The characterization of work as the most important form of social partic-ipation through which citizenship status and social inclusion can be earned, is itself potentially exclusionary.[35] The absence of sufficiently secure, well-paid work, together with inadequate social protection for people outside paid work, has been argued to lie at the heart of the process of social exclusion. As Gorz argues: '. . . because social production in contemporary society demands less and less work and distributes less and less in wages, it is becoming increasingly difficult to obtain a sufficient, regular income from paid work'.[36]

The stress on work is a problem for groups such as disabled people and lone parents, for whom existing work opportunities will not necessarily lead to improvements in their circumstances. The depiction of work as a moral obligation and as a necessary part of self-esteem is also problematic when opportunities are scarce in particular occupations and geographical locations. As Levitas[37] has pointed out, in a climate of high unemployment, the strengthening of associations between self-esteem, work and social status may be particularly damaging for young men, who are less likely than young women to gain a positive sense of identity through other means, such as caring responsibilities.

The emphasis on work is problematic for other reasons. It can be argued that in very wealthy countries like Britain, on the assumption of a fairer distribution of the existing social product, increased output and productivity is hardly necessary and that more emphasis might be put on enriching life outside of work rather than on expanding and giving priority to work itself. New Labour has made a few improvements in trade union rights. However, it has no proposals to reduce the pressures created by work. It has done little to reduce hours of work, and its embrace of globalization and the principle of flexibility are likely, if anything, to increase pressures at work, and the economic insecurity of employees at all levels.

Education and training for work

To facilitate their programme of 'work-friendly' reform, New Labour has focused on the concept of developing the human capital of the nation. It believes that people are trapped in poverty because they lack the skills or motivation to find 'paid work'. The solution is to make job opportunities available for everyone through education or training, which is increasingly likely to be compulsory, and through having 'work' linked to welfare benefits, in practice, a form of 'workfare'.

The emphasis on paid 'work' as a way out of poverty fails to take account of the structural and institutional barriers to employment. Dual labour markets continue to be an important feature with a minority of securely employed and relatively well-paid workers, and a growing number of poorly paid and insecurely employed, often part-time workers.[38]

New Labour policies assume that improvements in education will lead to a reduction in poverty and inequality. However, inequalities in education, and the unequal distribution of access to formal and elaborated knowledge that this involves, closely reflect inequalities in income and wealth.[39] It appears from this research that it is still true to say that it is the structure of social inequality in society which is the main cause of educational inequality, rather than the lack of opportunities for people to learn.[40]

A relatively new element in this debate is the belief that education needs to focus on the 'basic skills' of numeracy, literacy and information technology if it is to contribute to economic success. This is related to an emphasis on vocationalism in education and a belief that training will increase employment. However, it is far from certain that an entirely utilitarian curriculum will contribute to economic progress. A major tendency in modern employment is for a reduction in the level of skills and knowledge required of many members of the workforce. Many of the jobs which are undertaken by the lower occupational groups have very low skill requirements and these can easily be met by the present workforce.[41]

Managerialism

A key part in the overall approach of New Labour is played by its attachment to managerialist solutions.[42] There is a strong assumption that service improvements can be made without increasing costs, through the use of targets, monitoring and evaluation, performance management, community and social 'auditing' and the widespread adoption of what can be identified as 'best practice'.

Another aspect of managerialism is the emphasis given to 'modernization'.[43] A general feature of modernization is the idea that social improvement should not be held back by the power of vested interests. Modernization also involves the idea that the most up-to-date knowledge should form the basis of social provision and that the work of agencies and professionals should be monitored to ensure that it is undertaken in line with this knowledge.

Managerialism is central to the attack on professionalism along with an antagonism towards the traditional ethic of public service, and the replacement of these by an individualistic, market-oriented approach. Critics fear that this will further reinforce the cultural shift towards possessive individualism and the aggressive pursuit of self-interest.

A line of criticism which has been addressed at the social policies of New Labour concerns the complexity of the system which they are constructing. The range of benefits for families with children is extremely complex, which means that the proposed beneficiaries will have great difficulty in understanding the level and types of benefits to which they may be entitled given their family circumstances. Similarly, the proposed arrangements for pensions, or for benefits for the disabled, could hardly be described as simple.

The emphasis on managerialism involves considerable costs in terms of increased expenditure on management, and continued downgrading of professional competence and judgement. Management consultants and their public sector equivalents, the Audit Commission, seem to have become the 'organic intellectuals' of the Third Way.

Poverty, inequality and social exclusion

The approach taken by New Labour to improving the living standards of the poor involves the use of tax credits, based partly on the model employed by the Democratic administration of President Clinton in the USA. Tax credits (referred to as 'negative income tax' in an earlier era of social policy debate) are being used as a means of establishing a minimum level of income for various categories of recipient. Tax credits are being employed for single parents, childcare, working families, people with disabilities, carers and old people. However, these benefits are based on the use of means tests and they have to be applied for. This is justified as a form of 'targeting', that is ensuring that public money is only given to those who need it. However, means tests often limit the distribution of benefits due to the complexity of the procedures involved in claiming, ignorance of the benefits available, the humiliation and invasion of privacy involved in means-testing, the stigma associated with the status of claimant and the low level of many of the benefits. Means tests often also create a 'poverty-trap' for those in work. As a result, additional wage income can be reduced substantially leaving many lower-paid workers trapped at a disposable income level only just above the poverty line.

New Labour tends to avoid the use of the term redistribution. The government also prefers to talk of social exclusion rather than social inequality. Levitas has discussed how the New Labour social exclusion agenda has keyed into elements of three competing discourses around social exclusion which she names: RED, the Redistributionist Discourse, historically a key component of Labour policy but largely set aside by New Labour; SID, the Social Integrationist Discourse which emphasizes the primacy of work; MUD, the Moral Underclass Discourse which includes a focus on the behaviour of the poor and their presentation as culturally and morally distinct from the 'mainstream', with a focus on dependence on state benefits and on 'idle, criminal young men and single mothers'.[44]

An important element in the government's overall approach to social inclusion involves the expansion of opportunity through educational reform. The government has gone so far as to describe its aims in this area as the achievement of 'an equal chance for all young people'. These policies may succeed although the experience of the last 50 years of education reform indicate that educational reform has not so far been an effective route to reducing poverty let alone decreasing inequality. Throughout the twentieth century class inequalities in education have remained remarkably constant despite a series of education reforms justified with reference to improving equality of opportunity.[45]

New Labour appears determined to do little to modify the existing level of inequality in Britain.[46] However, it is this level of inequality that has always formed the main barrier to the success of schemes designed to reduce poverty.[47] New Labour's policies to raise the living standards of the poorest people are relatively modest; for example the time period it has set itself for the abolition of child poverty is 20 years. Where changes are being made by New Labour, as with the minimum wage and the use of tax credits to raise the income of various groups, the new target levels of income are often low.

Research evidence now overwhelmingly points to the links between violence, crime, low self-esteem, high levels of mortality and morbidity, and the scale of income inequality in society. There are strong links between trends in ill-health and insecurity in the labour market, the lack of control we feel over our work environment, the fears and effects of unemployment, and low social status.

> The crucial determinants of population health and health inequalities turn out to be less a matter of medical care or the direct effects of exposure to hazardous material circumstances, as of the effects of the social environment as structured by social hierarchy. . . . Societies which were unusually egalitarian and unusually healthy were also unusually cohesive. . . . [T]he index of civic community is closely correlated with income distribution.[48]

These factors contribute to chronic anxiety and poor immunity. Healthy societies have a more equal distribution of wealth. Increases in social inequality fragment society into competing groupings and encouraging more aggressive social interaction.[49] Low self-esteem can increase hostility between groups and individuals as they attempt to ward off feelings of ineptitude and lack of power.

Concepts such as poverty and social exclusion depict the unacceptable face of inequality in terms of the experience of those who are most disadvantaged by them. This removes attention from the other side of the scale of inequality, the massive and growing incomes and wealth enjoyed by a minority of the population. Significantly, there is no government discussion at all of inequalities in the distribution of wealth and their social implications. The issue of income inequalities is addressed solely by considering income at the bottom end of the scale. New Labour is pledged to retain the existing levels of the income tax and has announced that it will not increase the maximum rate of tax levied on the highest incomes beyond the current level of 40 per cent.

The government appears to believe that the existing level of inequality has to be maintained as the basis for economic efficiency. It can be argued, however, that economic advance would be encouraged by shifting the control of social resources so that poor people had more access to them. It is certainly the case, as the experience of the Second World War showed, that egalitarian policies are an essential element in strategies designed to secure social inclusion.[50]

The unresolved dilemmas of the Third Way

It can be argued that New Labour's Third Way rests on fragile foundations. Unlike previous great coalitions in UK politics, such as Thatcherism or 'Old' Labour, New Labour has not, after several years in government, created a coherent political project or a hegemonic political ideology. Rather:

> In place of an ideology or myth it has a rhetoric [that] implies that there is no rational alternative to the policies it favours. But it lacks emotional and moral resonance. . . . The underlying message is curiously apologetic. The world is changing, we are told. We may not like the changes; we may think them harmful or even wicked, but we can't stop them. All we can do is to adapt to them as gracefully as possible. It is the rhetoric of a management consultant, advising a company to redesign its products, not of a political leader, mobilizing his followers for a rendezvous with destiny.[51]

The overall approach of New Labour appears to rest on a number of questionable articles of faith about the nature of the economic process and about the economic capabilities of government. The globalization thesis is not an immutable truth. The belief that the global economy will remain free of systemic crises may be over-optimistic. It may be that the economic cycle of boom and bust will return. Centring economic management on the manipulation of the interest rate by the central bank may prove inadequate. Increasing employment by raising the skill levels of the labour force may prove a failure.

New Labour social polices have much in common with neo-liberalism, and there would appear to be little reason to dispute Hall's (1998) claim that:

> The framing strategy of New Labour's economic repertoire remains essentially the neo-liberal one: the deregulation of markets, the wholesale refashioning of the public sector by the New Managerialism, the continued privatization of public assets, low taxation, breaking the 'inhibitions' to market flexibility, institutionalizing the culture of private provision and personal risk, and privileging in its moral discourse the values of self-sufficiency, competitiveness and entrepreneurial dynamism.[52]

Any attempt to shift policies away from an approach based on the principles of the new right has to reckon with the impact of the state apparatus. The restructuring of the state undertaken along with the adoption of neo-liberal policies has reduced its capacity to operate as an effective means of implementing an expansive welfare policy. This restructuring has been so successful, that when New Labour attempted to expand public spending in 2000, it was unable to reach its new spending targets because of resistance within the state to increasing expenditure.

The citizen's income: a possible way forward

In this final section we consider an alternative welfare strategy founded largely on a single social policy initiative – the 'Citizen's Income' (or 'Basic Income'). A guaranteed Citizen's Income, would be distributed irrespective of social status and set at an amount deemed necessary to meet subsistence needs. Each citizen would receive the same basic amount, with extra-supplements paid in line with higher living costs due to, for instance, child-care responsibilities or disability. Paid work would be taxable, at a rate sufficient to sustain expenditure on Citizen's Income and other public spending.[53] A Citizen's Income would replace all other forms of income maintenance and be administratively simple and cost-effective.

Citizen's Income offers possible solutions to some of the key problems associated with Third Way social policies. In particular, it deals with the difficulties associated with the priority given to work, it can be used to expand employment, it has the potential to reduce social inequality, it is an effective means to the elimination of poverty, and removes excessive complexity from the benefits system. It would avoid the poverty trap in which many people find themselves. It would encourage more people to save by being non-means-tested. It would also target need in a non-stigmatizing way.[54]

Citizen's Income has been the subject of significant academic debate and growing political interest. It was supported, for example, in the manifesto of the Green Party in the UK general election of 2001. Lipietz's treatment of Citizen's Income links it to radical work strategies and the development of a 'third sector'. This refers to a permanently subsidized new employment sector offering jobs that are stable, dignified and socially recognized. This might include neighbourhood and environmental services managed by community enterprises and co-operatives.[55] This third sector is also emphasized in Third Way writing on economic and social regeneration. Beck supports the argument for a Citizen's Income and an alternative labour market similar to Lipietz's 'third sector', embracing such activities as parenting, working with children, and artistic, cultural and community work.[56]

There are, no doubt, difficulties in getting a Citizen's Income policy accepted as part of an alternative political programme. As Jordan acknowledges: 'the moral argument against this approach – that it rewards laziness, and gives no real encouragement to any social virtue – seems as stubbornly persuasive as ever'.[57]

Opponents of a Citizen's Income thus argue that it would be economically and socially damaging by generating a disincentive to work. However, winning the comfortable middle classes over to a Citizen's Income may be politically problematic, but not impossible. Citizen's Income is based on universalist principles, and universality is crucial to social inclusion which is itself a key theme in Third way thought. As Hall observes:

> William Beveridge understood that: 'universalism', despite its costs, was essential to binding the richer sections of society into collective forms of welfare. . . . [T]he whole system would be in danger as soon as the rich could willingly exclude themselves from collective provision by buying themselves out. Why should they go on paying for a service they had ceased to use?[58]

Existing universal benefits such as family allowances, free healthcare and free education have wide support, and many of the economic and social arguments which were used effectively in the long campaign in favour of establishing family allowances are also relevant to citizens income.[59]

Conclusion

It may be asked, finally, what sort of society does New Labour intend to create. One possible finishing point is what has been described as a 'wage-earners welfare state', which would be consistent with the emphasis which has been put on welfare to work and on the use of means tests and tax credits which limit benefits to those with incomes which the state judges to be deficient. In Australia and New Zealand, policies of this kind are familiar. In these countries benefits act as a safety net rather than an enhancement of the living standards of all.[60] However, this approach marginalizes the poor, the unemployed, single parents and ethnic minorities. Whether this is the destination towards which Britain is travelling remains to be seen.

The continuation of policies giving a central place to paid work and the failure to deal effectively with poverty and social inequality may well have serious negative implications. The cost in terms of ill-health, crime, social conflict and social distress create the possibility of opening up a debate of a more radical kind about the sort of society which people might wish to live in. If this debate takes hold, then the Citizen's Income may prove an important strategic idea which could take forward the historic concern of the Left to create a more equal and just society.

Notes

1 See T. Burden, C. Cooper and S. Petrie, *Modernising Social Policy: Unravelling New Labour's Welfare Reforms*, Aldershot: Ashgate, 2000.
2 See V. George, *Social Security and Society*, London: Routledge & Kegan Paul, 1973, chap. 1.
3 P. Golding and S. Middleton, *Images of Welfare*, London: Martin Robertson, 1982, chap. 1.

4   L.J. Hume, *Bentham and Bureaucracy*, Cambridge: Cambridge University Press, 1981, chap. 2.
5   S.G. Checkland and E.O.A. Checkland (eds), *The Poor Law of 1834*, Harmondsworth: Penguin, 1974, Introduction.
6   See I. Goffman, *Asylums*, Harmondsworth: Penguin, 1961, pp. 13–116.
7   T. Burden, *Social Policy and Welfare*, London: Pluto, 1998, section 1.19, and P. Weiler *The New Liberalism*, New York: Garland, 1982.
8   S. Rowntree, *Poverty: A Study of Town Life*, London: Macmillan, 1901.
9   G.R. Searle, *The Quest for National Efficiency*, Berkeley: University of California Press, 1971.
10   G. Jones, *Social Darwinism and English Thought*, Sussex: Harvester, 1980.
11   Burden, n. 7, section 1.16.
12   P. Hennock, 'The Origins of British National Insurance and the German Precedent 1880–1914', in W.J. Mommsen (ed.), *The Emergence of the Welfare State in Britain and Germany*, London: Croom Helm, 1981, chap. 5.
13   A. Davies, *Where did the Forties go?*, London: Pluto, 1984, chap. 3.
14   W. Beveridge, *Social Insurance and Allied Services*, London: HMSO, 1942.
15   L. Bland, T. McCabe and F. Mort, 'Sexuality and Reproduction: Three "Official" Instances', in M. Barrett, P. Corrigan, A. Kuhn and J. Wolff (eds), *Ideology and Cultural Production*, London: Croom Helm, 1979, chap. 4.
16   J. Krieger, *Reagan, Thatcher and the Politics of Decline*, Cambridge: Polity Press, 1986, chap. 2.
17   C. Kerr, J.T. Dunlop, F.H. Hall and C.A. Myas, *Industrialism and Industrial Man*, 2nd edn, London: Pelican, 1973.
18   M. Powell, *New Labour, New Welfare State? The 'third way' in British Social Policy*, Bristol: The Policy Press, 1999, p. 2.
19   Burden n. 7, section 1.23.
20   *Ibid.*, section 1.24.
21   See T. Burden and M. Campbell, *Capitalism and Public Policy in the UK*, London: Croom Helm, 1985; chap. 1.
22   Burden n. 7., section 1.29.
23   J. Dale and P. Foster, *Feminists and State Welfare*, London: Routledge & Kegan Paul, 1986, and F. Williams, *Social Policy, A. Critical Introduction*, Cambridge and London: Polity Press and Basil Blackwell, 1989.
24   Burden, n. 7, section 3.10, and A. Scott, *Ideology and the New Social Movements*, London: Unwin Hyman, 1990.
25   See P. Leonard, *Postmodern Welfare: Reconstructing an Emancipatory Project*, London: Sage, 1997, chaps. 1 and 2.
26   Burden, n. 7, sections 4.2 and 4.3.
27   F. Hayek, 'The Principles of a Liberal Social Order', in A. de Crespigny and J. Cronin (eds), *Ideologies of Politics*, Capetown: Oxford University Press, 1975.
28   Burden, n. 7, section 3.3.
29   M. Friedman, *Capitalism and Freedom*, Chicago: University of Chicago Press, 1962, and M. Friedman and R. Friedman, *Free to Choose*, Harmondsworth: Penguin, 1980.
30   C. Murray, *The Emerging British Underclass*, London, IEA Health & Welfare Unit, 1990.
31   Z. Bauman, *Work, Consumerism and the New Poor*, Buckingham: Open University Press, 1998, p. 5.
32   Quoted in M. Mullard, and P. Spicker, *Social Policy in a Changing Society*, London: Routledge, 1998, p. 120.

33 A. Giddens, *The Third Way: The Renewal of Social Democracy*, Cambridge: Polity Press, 1998.
34 R. Dahrendorf, 'Whatever Happened to liberty?', *New Statesman*, London, 6 September 1999, p. 27.
35 R. Walker, 'Does Work Work?', *Journal of Social Policy*, Cambridge, vol. 27, 1998, no. 4, pp. 533–42.
36 A. Gorz, *Reclaiming Work: Beyond the Wage-Based Society*, Cambridge: Polity Press, 1999, p. 72.
37 R. Levitas, *The Inclusive Society? Social Exclusion and New Labour*, Basingstoke: Palgrave Macmillan, 1998.
38 B. Jordan, *The New Politics of Welfare*, London: Sage, 1998, chap. 2.
39 S. Gorard, *Patterns of Participation in Adult Education and Training*, ESRC-funded Learning Society project; Working Paper no. 13, Cardiff, Cardiff University School of Education, 1998.
40 A. Goodman, P. Johnson, and S. Webb, *Inequality in the UK*, Oxford: Oxford University Press, 1997.
41 See H. Braverman, *Labour and Monopoly Capital*, London: Monthly Review Press, 1974, and R. Sennett, *The Corrosion of Character*, London: W.W Norton, 1998, p. 156, table 9.
42 See J. Clarke, A. Cochrane and E. McLaughlin, *Managing Social Policy*, London: Sage, 1994, chap. 1.
43 See DoH (Department of Health), *The New NHS – Modern and Dependable*, London: The Stationery Office, 1997; Cabinet Office, *Public Services for the Future: Modernization, Reform, Accountability*, Cmd. 4181, London: HMSO, 1999; Cabinet Office, *Modernising Government*, Cmd. 4310, London: HMSO, 1999.
44 R. Levitas, *The Inclusive Society? Social Exclusion and New Labour*, Basingstoke: Palgrave Macmillan, 1998, p. 21.
45 See D.V.Glass (ed.), *Social Mobility in Britain*, London: Routledge & Kegan Paul, 1954; A.H. Halsey, A.F. Heath and J.M. Ridge, *Origins and Destinations*, London: Clarendon Press, 1980; A.F. Heath and J.M. Ridge, 'Schools, Examinations and Occupational Attainment', in J. Purvis, M. Hales *et al.*, *Achievement and Inequality in Education*, London: Routledge & Kegan Paul, 1983.
46 P. Townsend, *Will Poverty Get Worse Under Labour?*, Edinburgh: University of Edinburgh Press, 1998.
47 C. Howarth, P. Kenway, G. Palmer, and C. Street, *Monitoring Poverty and Social Exclusion: Labour's Inheritance*, York: Joseph Rowntree Foundation, 1998.
48 R. Wilkinson, 'Why Inequality Is Bad For You', *Marxism Today*, London, November/December 1998, p. 38
49 B. Jordan, *The New Politics of Welfare*, London: Sage, 1998.
50 A. Calder, *The People's War*, London: Cape, 1969.
51 D. Marquand, 'Can Labour Kick the Winning Habit?', *New Statesman*, 23 October 1998, p. 26.
52 S. Hall, 'The Great Moving Nowhere Show', *Marxism Today*, November/December, 1998, p. 11.
53 H. Breitenbach, T. Burden and D. Coates, *Features of a Viable Socialism*, Hemel Hempstead: Harvester Wheatsheaf, 1990, chap. 2.
54 B. Jordan, *The New Politics of Welfare*, London: Sage, 1998.
55 M. Dunford, 'The Hour-Glass Society: The Sharing of Work versus the Disintegration of Society', *City*, Abingdon, No. 8, December 1997, pp. 171–87.
56 U. Beck, 'Goodbye to All That Wage Slavery', *New Statesman*, 5 March 1999, pp. 25–7.

57   B. Jordan, *The New Politics of Welfare*, London: Sage, 1998, p. 159.
58   S. Hall, 'The Great Moving Nowhere Show', *Marxism Today*, November/December, 1998, p. 12.
59   P. Hall, H. Land, R. Parker and A. Webb, *Change, Choice and Conflict in Social Policy*, London: Heinemann, 1975, chap. 9.
60   B. Easton, *Social Policy and the Welfare State in New Zealand*, Auckland: Allen & Unwin, 1980.

7
The Welfare State System in France

Sophie Nadal

Introduction

In the aftermath of the Second World War, France followed an egalitarian welfare state model based on the principles of equality, fraternity and solidarity and established a well-developed social security system. Under the system, anyone born or resident in France is entitled to social security benefits. The key components of the system are a well-developed healthcare, unemployment and pension schemes. The Rocard reforms of 1992 made it explicit that 'any person who because of his or her age or physical or mental status or economic situation is unable to work has the right to obtain from the society, decent means to live'. A law enacted in 1999 entitles French people to healthcare without any contribution as a prerequisite. On the whole, the system is directed to fight poverty and social exclusion on the one hand, and to guarantee a minimum standard of living to everybody on the other. It operates on a basic General Insurance Scheme, complemented by additional schemes managed by mutual or private insurances. The decision of the European Court of Justice on 12 September 2000 to allow free competition in the additional schemes has the potential to weaken the French welfare state system since free competition and welfare privatization can dilute people's commitment to social solidarity. The European Union's mercantile ideology which gives supremacy to the economy over social values, the ongoing ageing process, growing unemployment and the neoliberals' advocacy of the state's non-intervention role are among the emerging challenges to the French welfare state system.

When mentioning the welfare state, jurists refer to the right to social welfare, and to a further extent to benefits as well as to health and social services. The term 'social policies' in its full meaning refers to all the instances regarding the rights of people enduring difficult living conditions, suffering from joblessness or precariousness, as well as those victims of social risks – due to happy or unhappy events, such as maternity or illness. The influence of William Beveridge's ideas on the French system is recognized.

Nowadays France enjoys a fairly developed social welfare system, but, nevertheless, social welfare continues to be a very controversial issue. Too many state interventions for some, not enough for others. To begin with, it is worth focusing on what the so-called welfare state refers to. From a legal angle, the concept of social security must be specified as well as that of social risks. The risks covered by social security due to its very nature need to be defined. They should be referred to as social risks, that is to say risks that run within the society. However, such a definition is not satisfying. On the one hand, there are risks obviously linked to social life which are not covered by social security – for example car accidents. On the other hand there are risks which are covered by the social security which are not linked to collective social life. As Dupeyroux and Ruellan (1998) noted, Robinson Crusoe was himself threatened by illnesses and old age.[1] A more accurate definition was therefore suggested – social risks should be defined by their consequences. They should either entail a decrease of income (unemployment, disability) or an increase of expenses (family events). Finally, William Beveridge suggested that social security should consist in abolishing the state of need by ensuring citizens a sufficient income to provide for their needs and charges. In a nutshell, the right to social security should eradicate economic precariousness, and thus any public measure could be considered as welfare. More precisely, on theoretical grounds social security can be defined as all those measures which aim to fight social exclusion.

This, however, is not the concept held by the French legal tradition,[2] where the right to social security is defined as the right to a new deal aiming at guaranteeing the economic security of individuals facing some specific problems. The general organization of French social security reflects this concept. However, some recent changes in French law which are meant to fight exclusion – result in a questioning of the classical legal definition of the French social security system.[3]

The crux of this chapter is mainly synthetical. It aims at pointing out the specific features of the French welfare system, then at emphasizing the changes which are currently being undertaken. Thus it will be possible to highlight the problems the system now has to face, which actually put at stake the notion of a welfare state in itself.

The French social welfare policies

Historical background

The creation of the contemporary French social security system dates back to 1945, and before defining its general organization and the main welfare schemes, a brief historical background would be appropriate.

Based mainly on P. Laroque's report, who is considered in France as the founding father of social security, the Edict of 4 October 1945 is regarded as the cornerstone of the French welfare state system.[4] William Beveridge's ideas, especially the importance of global and universal concepts (according to which the whole population should be entitled to the right to welfare) deeply influenced the conception of the French social security system in 1945. Thus the Edict of 1945, by establishing in its first article an organization of social security aimed at providing protection to the working population (it is in this respect a professional concept of social security), planned the eventual extension of welfare to all citizens. It is in this respect that the law of 12 May 1946 – called the generalizing social scheme – stipulated the compulsory liability to welfare. However, this endeavour failed and it is only recently, thanks to the universal health scheme (law of 27 July 1999), that the French system can be considered as universalist.[5] In reality, from 1945 onwards the French system was to expand, little by little, the provision of some benefits (the health scheme in particular) to include some other categories beyond the working population, for example students. But this expansion lacked cohesion. As it was criticized, the system underwent its first reform in 1967, called 'Jeanneney', which focused on three general principles: the harmonization of basic schemes, financial compensation between legal schemes, and a generalizing scheme. On this final point, the generalization was operated risk by risk. The goals of harmonization and compensation, which illustrate the principles of equality and national solidarity, were achieved progressively, but this evolution was to be challenged by the first oil shock of 1973.

The growing unemployment rate led to widening financial discrepancies, and thus all subsequent reforms were committed to strive for reducing costs. To this phenomenon we may add the growing demographic discrepancies which tended to worsen the problem of pension schemes. To respond to this, the opening requirements of entitlement to pension schemes were made more difficult for the private sector (40 years of contributions instead of 37.5), and new taxes were created (tobacco, alcohol). A move towards capitalization rather than allotment has also been suggested, a system which would do away with the ideal of solidarity, which lies at the roots of the French concept of social security. These are the reasons why a reform was launched in 1994 to face up to these issues. It is worth noting that ever since, all the succeeding governments have been preoccupied with rebalancing the financial system. Some symbolic social measures had been taken in the socialist decade (1981–92), viz. the age of retirement was brought down to 60, creation of the minimum wage, and so on,[6] but, the recurrent financial difficulties led to a new reform in 1995, named after Prime Minister Juppé. One of its main characteristics has been the power given to parliament, allowing it to vote a yearly financial law. To deal with the financial crisis, *contribution au remboursement de la dette sociale* (a contribution to the social debt) was enforced and a regulation policy of health expenses was launched along with harsh sanctions in case of non-compliance.[7] Above all, a reform of specific schemes was considered, in particular pension schemes which is very beneficial to the recipients, but very costly. This last part of the reform triggered a five-week strike, which eventually led to the abolition of the reform. Still, today, financial difficulties remain.

Social security

Social security involves several statutory bodies defined by law.[8] French-born or French residents must register for the social security scheme under their corresponding professional status; they are called people liable to social security and are said to be affiliated.

The *Régime Général des Travailleurs Salariés* (the general payrolls insurance scheme) protects payrolls in the industrial and trading sectors as well as people belonging to no other scheme. This scheme allows welfare for several professional or non-professional risks as follows. The health insurance scheme provides daily cash benefits to compensate the wage loss that a sick leave entails. They are delivered to the person who is physically handicapped, as certified by a doctor. The payments become due on the fourth day following the beginning of the sick leave. This rule aims to deter absenteeism. These benefits are not considered wages, but they are, however, subject to taxation. The health insurance scheme includes benefits for paying back all or part of the medical fees incurred by the afflicted person or family (husband, wife or children). The benefits are therefore family-based, relying on three basic principles. First is the principle of a free choice of doctor. Theoretically, the freedom is total but in practice things are different insofar as there are large discrepancies in doctor's fees depending on whether the doctor is linked to the state health scheme. The medical health record stipulated in 1994 aims at restricting the patient's choices since it supposes a medical follow-up. The second principle is that of pay first then to get reimbursed. Finally is the principle of the moderating coupon, which implies that some of the expenses are to be paid by the contributor to the social security scheme. However, there are some possible exemptions linked to the social situation of the contributor or to the nature (seriousness) of the health services required.

Persons benefitting from the health insurance scheme may also benefit from the maternity scheme. This scheme includes benefits in kind, taking care of medical expenses, hospital fees and payments. The disablement scheme allows for a pension aimed at compensating the wage loss as well as supporting the necessary medical assistance. The whole-life scheme guarantees the rights of any contributor's beneficiaries the rights to the payment of a subsidy. The widowhood scheme aims to help a married couple to overcome financial debts after the spouse's death. The professional (accidents or illnesses linked to work) scheme offers insurance cover for any accident or mishap at work. The pensions paid on account of the pension scheme, however, are very weak. At best they are equivalent to the minimum wage rate, which is why they are complemented by additional schemes. This latter is arousing raging debates over the age of retirement with full pension (today 60). In the case of particularly weak subsidies, additional benefits are made possible through a minimum pension scheme which allows a minimum wage.

Besides the general scheme, there are some specific schemes which often allow more substantial benefits for the risks mentioned previously. These apply to some specific professional groups such as miners or railwaymen. The specific benefits they are allowed, however, are currently at stake, especially because of existing discrepancies between lengths of contributions to the pension scheme. Such discrepancies create a feeling of inequality as regards welfare. The agricultural scheme allows welfare benefits to those who are on the agricultural payrolls, tenants and smallholders.

Added to these legal schemes are also additional scheme that complement the general, specific and agricultural schemes; they allow more substantial welfare (mainly as regards illness, death or retirement). The basic benefits alone do not provide the contributor with minimum required benefits, which is why some schemes have been established with collective agreement. Among them some are compulsory, for instance in the case of pensions. In addition, many risks which are covered by the insurance policy can be covered by companies or various professional branches. For example, the contingency funds are covered by mutual insurance companies or private insurance companies, and are very competitive.

Currently the system is undergoing a crisis and several changes appear to be necessary. Two questions arise in the debate: (a) the amount of health-care expenditure which threatens the financial stability of the whole system; and (b) demographic evolution which challenges the current pension scheme system.

Healthcare[9]

French health expenditure has increased substantially. If one considers France's position in a decreasing order regarding health expenses in GDP, France ranked 8th in 1960, 7th in 1980 and 4th in 1993. It is worth noting that there are no links between the substantial expenses and the medical service and its efficiency on the overall health of the population. If, on the whole, French people seem to be in fairly good health according to various indicators, the reality appears to be far more diversified: the mortality rate of premature babies is still high, a great deal of illnesses are poorly covered, and social as well as geographical inequalities exist. Among the reasons for the increase of expenses, is the growing commercialization of medical services. Health and medical services are gradually becoming consumer goods and thus new reactions to death or illnesses have developed. This is why checks on medical expenses have been enforced by two laws, in 1993 and 1994, based on:

- Forecasting, required of doctors to estimate the amount of fees and prescriptions.
- The creation of tools to identify medical practices, to codify medical services and files on follow-ups.
- The targeted prohibition of medical actions considered as useless.
- A system of penalties in case of exceeding forecasts.

Of course this regulating policy limits the freedom of the contributor as well as of the doctor.

Pensions[10]

The financing of pensions is undoubtedly today's most burning issue in the French welfare state system. On the whole, it is the imbalance in the ratio of employed and unemployed people which is likely to worsen considerably because of the ageing baby-boomers that raises a major problem of financing social security.

The working population contributes to the elderly's pensions based on the principle of generation solidarity, which is at the root of the idea of social solidarity. However, not all workers contribute to the pension scheme at the same level, depending on their age of entrance to the labour market (increasingly late these days); unemployment and illnesses are also taken into account. Thus the total wage bill is declining, which entails a slackening of provisions. The French system is based on allotment or sharing; that is to say, in such a system the working population pays a contribution which is given back immediately in the form of benefits. Thus, the profitability of such a system is based on the ratio of contributors. Today, a radical change which would mean resorting to capitalization, which implies individual saving, is out of the question, although some advocate a system which would combine both trends to respond to the problem.

It seems quite obvious today that longer contributions are likely to be required to entitle citizens to full pension benefits (40 years in the private sector), which in turn implies a lengthening of the working life delaying the age of retirement to over 60.[11] Moreover, the idea of introducing a degree of capitalization, through the promotion of pension funds mainly, is becoming increasingly popular. Pension funds appeared in the French system in 1997, with the creation of saving retirement funds that grant a life annuity. Such a system is often criticized for excluding social solidarity, and foreign experiments have shown that executives are the only group likely to be involved. The development of such practices would imply a long-term institutionalization of inequalities. A wide part of the population would then only benefit from minimum welfare through the general scheme. This issue is being fiercely debated since it would mean radically reforming the concept of the French welfare state, in which only the better placed and the more competitive would benefit from social cover while a mass of the population would have to live on state welfare.

Targeted forms of social solidarity

The unemployment scheme is a central element in the French system. Those on a payroll who experience dismissal benefit from a substitute wage, but are required to show proof of a minimum length of affiliation. Indeed the insurance system requires a minimum contribution, and this excludes some temps who are nevertheless potential jobseekers and, of course, seasonal workers. Unemployment benefits require jobseekers to be registered at a job centre (the French ANPE) and to actually be searching for a job, which is checked by an external department of the labour ministry. The payment of subsidies may be stopped. A system of retraining is provided to beneficiaries, to ease retraining and to provide them with extra benefits.

The above system is based on a compulsory tax on wages and is based on the principle of *professional solidarity*. It appears quite striking that the growing unemployment rate has shaken the system chronically as number of people on payrolls declines.[12]

When the jobless no longer, or simply do not, depend on professional solidarity, either because they have used up their rights or because they were not entitled to the rights to social security, *national solidarity* provides them with subsidies. Some specific solidarity benefits are aimed at long-term jobseekers who cannot benefit from the full pension scheme, and amount to FF84.07 daily. The *insertion subsidy* targets jobseekers who have not contributed long enough; its daily amount is FF59.22, and it is paid for a maximum one-year term and gives entitlement to a health insurance scheme. Nevertheless, the system is today threatened and changes are underway.

A draft agreement was signed in September 2000 between the social partners in charge of managing the system.[13] This agreement envisages numerous new schemes aimed at helping jobseekers to get back to work, but it is harshly criticized. According to the agreement, all jobseekers must be enrolled on a 'back-to-work' plan in order to be entitled to the subsidies. Violation of the terms of the agreement or plan by the jobseeker, or an illegitimate job offer refusal, entails sanctions which may result in stopping the subsidies.

The measures are actually quite relevant to today's conflict between the working population and the unemployed. In French society it is acknowledged that only 40 per cent of the population of working age actually has a job, while they support the whole population. Thus for each worker the charges are considerable, while at the other end of the social scale meagre amounts reach the unemployed. The unemployed who benefit from these payment aspire to the same living conditions as the working population, but quite obviously the working population does not accept their complaints which would imply even greater charges. This leads to slogans and myths. On the theme of fraud: too many jobseekers are seen as couch potatoes. On the theme of lies: some unemployed are seen as not needing any help and are moonlighting. No matter what the reality is, one must acknowledge that these themes are finding echoes in the system. The collective attachment to the ideal of solidarity is crumbling, while the idea of individual responsibility is beginning to prevail.[14]

Aimed at people in great distress, social benefits convey a *social solidarity* duty towards the poor. They do not take into account insurance, and their logic is only to help individuals make a living. Today expenses on people in distress keep on rising (over 2.8 million people currently). Entitlement to those social benefits is based on earnings, and generally speaking the benefits consist of:

- Medical aid; all health expenses are paid by the state.
- Aid for the elderly; housework aid consists in helping the elderly to stay at home and assists with household chores.
- Nurses' services may be provided at home.
- Accommodation fees may also be paid.

More generally speaking, the ageing of the population requires new forms of benefits to help the elderly and their relatives to face up to the expenses of their growing dependency. These benefits are called autonomy help to support the elderly as well as to compensate the family splits and to help reduce the consequences of non-affiliation. Without any family protection, the elderly tend to become loners. In France, the number of people living alone is estimated to be around 6.6 million, of which 65 per cent are over 55. Loneliness and poverty often get intertwined. Two-thirds of the people depending on the minimum pension scheme are effectively outcasts. Finally, among social benefits there are specific aids for the handicapped and aid for the poorest. The minimum welfare payment is given to those who are not entitled to employment benefits (income support).

A great advance made by Rocard's government was the legislations passed on 1 December 1988 (*loi n° 88–1088: dite 'Revenu Minimum d'Insertion'*) and 29 July 1992, (*loi n° 92–722: adaptation de la loi du 1/12/88 relativ au revenu minimum d'insertion et à la lutte contre la pauvrete' et l'exclusion sociale et professionnelle*) which legitimate a constitutional principle that the right to live entails living decently. According to Article 1 of the 1992 law: 'any person who because of his or her age or physical or mental status or economic situation is unable to work has the right to obtain from society decent means to live.' This benefit is therefore above all a means to fight poverty and guarantees a minimum living standard to any citizen. However, this system not only guarantees minimum resources to anybody in distress, but is also meant to fight social exclusion.[15] The aim is to lead beneficiaries toward reintegration into society. This measure is still under debate since one can question the legitimacy of a measure regulating a fundamental right and making it depend on social integration. Integration in this case means attending retraining programmes or similar activities. If on the whole the system seems to work against poverty, one can allow mixed feelings regarding exclusion. The poor are still denied access to accommodation and medical care, and professional integration seems to be a failure.

Present challenges

Fighting exclusion and European integration

Obviously the major problem with the French welfare state system is financial, and the periodic efforts made by succeeding governments have generally consisted of modifying and readjusting devices of the financial system creating an impression of a patchwork. Today, deeper reflection is needed. At the national level, the system, whose organization appears to be very complex and confusing, happens to be inefficient in eradicating poverty and social exclusion. Moreover, European integration which implies the supremacy of economy over social values puts at stake the already weakened national mechanisms. From an external point of view (in other words at the European scale mainly) the French system must face up to the mercantile ideology prevailing even in the social field.

Inner challenges

More than five and a half decades have passed since the Edict of 1945. Yet, the success of the institution is undeniable. For the great majority of French people, social security stands as a fundamental right, but all the social institutions are undergoing a legitimacy crisis. The social security bodies have been subject to greater bureaucratization, which has impeded their efficiency and ability to adequately respond to social risks. The principle of state welfare is undeniable, and it is in accordance with the idea of public service. Nevertheless, philosophical debates about the place of man in society (on allottments to the state in society) have yielded to economic ones (on financing the rising expenses), which actually puts at stake the managing efficiency of the state. It is actually its existence and its intervention which are being questioned.[16]

Traditionally, the administrative organization of the French social security system has relied on equality. Relevant to the ideal of social democracy, equality implies that an important place should be allotted to insured individuals, employers and trade unions. Thus, the management of various schemes is the responsibility of the said social partners, under the gaze of the state. Nevertheless, social security must face up to a liberal assault which advocates the concept of non-intervention on the part of the state. Employers mainly protest the high costs of social contributions and call for radical changes. They wish for a more flexible management and criticize the financial grip of the state over several schemes. According to them, excessive state control is bound to jeopardize the system. In 2000, employers' criticisms grew fiercer within the conflict aroused by the reform of the unemployment scheme. Dissatisfied with the control and censorship operated by the Ministry of Employment over the reforms of schemes negotiated with the unions, MEDEF, the most important employers' union, threatened to resign from joint social security institutions. Such a resignation would of course block the whole system. This threat is aimed at forcing the government to allow greater autonomy to joint institutions that would fix their legal, economic and managing framework within the overall social security system. The debate is still raging, and the issue is important since state intervention responds to a key requirement: national solidarity. And, it is actually on behalf of this key idea that the fight against exclusion has been started again. Genuine solidarity implies that the poorest have access to welfare, but it is in this respect that the government has only recently tried to tackle the issue on a durable basis.

The concept of equality lies at the roots of the French Republican ideal. Since 1945, it has been one of the pillars of the welfare state along with the principle of fraternity. In this respect France has developed a fairly simple egalitarian model. The point is to increase social rights, reduce wage gaps and develop social benefits. Even if some changes in the French model of social policy have appeared necessary because of the evolution of the social and economic context, the general pattern of the social security system has not changed much.

In the 1990s, the need to reevaluate the concept was highlighted by promoting the notion of equal chances for all. The notion of equality no longer refers to wages alone, it must also take into account each individual's ties to the state. Indeed, when there are no ties, equality becomes merely theoretical. If welfare is able to fight poverty rather efficiently, then exclusion must decline. Therefore the point is to reach equal chances for all in real life. In the last decade, the substantial widening of inequalities has aroused great concern, and it is this concern that has triggered some affirmative action policies regarding specific needs in the general interest.

In other words, if each citizen under the law has the right to benefit from welfare, this must actually be seen to be the case in reality. To put this differently, every citizen must be entitled to welfare benefits on an equal basis, and this each citizen, on account of these welfare benefits, should be able to enjoy the same chances of personal fulfilment and of developing his or her potential.[17]

Each citizen's individual situation should be taken into account when considering welfare, and as early as 1995, within the national development scheme, some measures were taken to narrow regional discrepancies. Emergency development zones were set up and reinforced by tax exemptions to boost economic development. In addition, counties' interdependence has been encouraged, in both the educational and cultural fields.

Recognizing that universal policies may not be efficient, emergency education zones (areas targeted for special help in education, called ZEPs) were set up, reinforcing educational services in these sectors. The 29 July 1998 law, *loi n° 98–657 du 29 Juillet 1998 d'orientation relativ à la lutte contre les exclusions*, reflecting the fight against exclusion, was real progress. It reinforced existing laws mainly on the tutoring and advising of staff in schools of those areas while expanding the state's field of action. Thus several concepts have been marked as national targets: for example equal access for all to culture, sports, holidays and leisure during their lifetimes. More generally, the 1998 law considers all facets of exclusion: facilitating access to the labour market, to legal help, to accommodation and in preventing overindebtedness. Where classical social welfare has failed in its fight against exclusion, because of its supportive trend (*Revenu Minimum d'Insertion*), this new form of welfare appeals to the concept of citizenship.

The question arises as to whether such a system should entail any obligations on the part of those who will benefit from it. Should any reciprocity be assigned?[18] Some think so, arguing that social solidarity to the poor should be reciprocal. This idea can be rejected in so far as the state's intervention should not be conditional as long as the issue is how to guarantee fundamental rights. But, on the more specific question of providing health schemes to the poorest, certain measures have been taken recently. The 27 July 1999 law, *loi n° 99–641 portant création d'une couverture maladie universelle*, relevant to the comprehensive welfare scheme, is part of the fight against exclusion adopted by the 1998 law. Article 1 stipulates 'a comprehensive health scheme, which guarantees total support of healthcare to all, and to people whose incomes are the lowest the right to additional benefits is granted as well as fees exemption.' This law guarantees access to existing rights without any new ones.

The right to healthcare is part of the fundamental rights mentioned in the foreword of the Constitution of 1946. This law thus extends the ambit of the health scheme. In France in 1999 about 150,000 people had no social security, but now rights are open without any contribution prerequisite. Up to that point, people who did not earn enough to afford the moderating coupon could be supported through regional Medicare. Now, the state through comprehensive health insurance has now returned to its role of a welfare state by supporting additional benefits to those people without any income limits. This means that effective access to heath benefits is now provided and the effectiveness of the principle of health insurance is established. By combining the additional insurance schemes with the system, lawmakers have underlined that the health insurance field is primarily not a commercial market like others, and that all health insurance agents will have to struggle for the real achievement of the national solidarity objectives. This is worth mentioning if we consider the evolution of social insurance policies resulting from European integration.

Challenges from outside: European Union laws

Free movement of people

Free movement of people in the European Union has major consequences for welfare. Indeed, no European worker can be considered, in this respect, as a foreigner in a EU member state, but discrepancies in the European welfare systems impede this freedom. That is why the EC Commission has tried to reconcile different welfare systems of various EU member states. As early as 1971, a legislation marked the main lines of coordination, but its application is limited to legal and compulsory insurance schemes. Thus, the minimum pension insurance schemes or *Revenu Minimum d'Insertion* which guarantee minimum income supports are not included.

Furthermore, the payment of unemployment benefits in a host country is limited to three months. In order to ensure that a worker is not subject to several legislations and does not run the risk of being denied any welfare, the EU legislation stipulates that only one law, namely the law of the place of work, can apply to workers who circulate around the Union. Therefore, if a payroll pays his or her contributions in the country where they work, the state where they are resident cannot require any contributions. Nevertheless, some ambiguous administrative practices deny the right to welfare to some citizens on the basis of affiliation in their home country. Thus, all European governments do not always cooperate. Recently, in a Banks affair, the Belgian government was condemned by the European Court of Justice on similar grounds. This lack of close collaboration between member states can be further criticized on the basis of the Fundamental Rights Charter, adopted in December 2000 by the European governments, which mentions the right to social security and the right to welfare as fundamental rights. However, the right to a minimum wage is not mentioned. Indeed, some member states fear that in developing welfare, economic growth will be slowed down because of the social expenses it would entail.

A last point must be dealt with: the exportation of non-contributory welfare within the Union.[19] Indeed, it is worth making a distinction between two types of welfare. Some benefits are paid on behalf of professional contributions paid during working life, others from social risks paid on behalf of legal criteria without taking into account former payments. A European Union ruling, adopted in 1992, considered that these non-contributory benefits conceived by the different member states should be paid exclusively to people living in the concerned member state.[20] This ruling had an important consequence; those Europeans benefiting from such a benefit within a member state were likely to lose their rights to free circulation inside the

Union. Therefore, to sojourn in a member state, the ruling requires the person to have a sufficient income. Thus a European whose income mainly consists of non-contributory benefits cannot be allowed to travel since he cannot bring his income along.

Through this technical problem, one can understand the extent to which the economic logic of the European Union deeply affects the social rights and liberties of people. The Union's Court of Justice, in the Jauch case decided on 8 March 2001, has recently recognized the dependency allowance transfer.[21] This polemical decision has disturbed Union law, but it has to be approved if one considers that European integration implies solidarity between member states in matters of social protection.

Free movement of services

Another essential principle of European Union laws – the free movement of services – is bound to have considerable consequences on the very concept of social security. The entire evolution of the French system proceeds from two main values: solidarity, and the absence of a mercantile logic in the field of social matters. Still, growing costs have triggered a liberal assault which wishes to entrust part of the public system's responsibilites to the private sector. Thus, some member states have started privatizing social benefits by increasing contributions of the private sector in the organization, and functioning of healthcare and in the management of health insurance schemes. The objective is to limit public expenses. Actually, this trend is quite relevant to the harsh criticisms of the welfare state. Privatization, in developing competition between services, is considered to increase their efficiency. Besides, individuals would become more responsible for their own social cover. Though many European states have taken the route to privatization, France remains attached to its republican model. Equality and fraternity imply that welfare should depend on public funds and services since they are the only ones assigned with a duty of general interest. Market rules cannot meet the requirements of solidarity and social cohesion.[22]

The Union laws do not question the state monopoly of social security. The European Court of Justice, for example, has conceded that European laws on competition, and on the principle of free circulation of services, are not obstacles to the state monopoly of social security and basic welfare. This is a key notion. The French system is founded on a basic scheme (called the general insurance scheme) complemented by additional schemes managed by mutual or private insurances. Without these additional schemes, payments derived from the basic scheme would be totally inadequate. Now the Union's jurisprudence remains ambiguous on whether, for the additional benefits, the principles of free circulation of services and free competition can apply, through which competition might lead to a decline of the welfare state in the French model. The liberal model is attracting growing attention.

In its judgement on 12 September 2000, the Court of Justice has conceded free competition to additional pension schemes,[23] and this decision jeopardizes the French additional scheme system. To a considerable extent it contradicts the European social model in which welfare cannot be regarded as part of a regular market. One of the distinguishing features of welfare benefits in Europe is their efficiency in the fight against poverty and exclusion, and such aims, excluding any sense of economic profitability, may in the near future become secondary if the logic of welfare privatization is confirmed. In such a system the individual would no longer be the target. Imperialist market rules could only lead to widening social inequalities.

The commitment to the principle social solidarity is thus challenged by the forces of free competition. In addition, the prevailing market ideology over social values is a phenomenon which greatly extends the Union's framework, and the globalization of exchanges raises the problem of competition between countries where social protection is developed and others where it is not.[24] The coordination of international trade rules and basic social norms has been debated since the end of the nineteenth century, and the adoption of social clauses in international treaties has long been demanded by the French. This question has been shelved within the WTO but it has aroused great hostility on the part of low-wage countries which consider it as an attempt on the part of developed countries to remain competitive while protecting their markets.

France is steadily accumulating profits from its commercial ventures whereas the real value of wages in the country keeps on decreasing. Thus wages rise at a lower pace than productivity, which is actually the configuration of those countries where a social clause is resisted. In the defence of essential social values over market logic, developed countries would certainly be more credible if they demonstrated their willingness to apply social clauses to themselves. At a time when Europe has moved to the single monetary unit, one may hope that it will more bluntly commit itself to debate on a needed worldwide social regulation.

Conclusion

Presently, the French social security system is passing through a critical phase of transformation, and, certainly, safeguarding the system would require a new approach towards funding pensions in France. A viable solution would be to follow a uniform pattern, for both public and private sectors, regarding the length of pension contributions. However, in the health sector, to find the means to finance the health insurance scheme would prove more difficult. The government has resorted to sparingly but surely restricting access to benefits, for example recently with respect to foreigners. But this has created a new situation which threatens the role of health insurance in the country as a fundamental social right. In a general sense, the role of private insurance seems to be increasing in the French system of social solidarity. If this tendency gains ground it may erode the position of social security in France as a public service.

Notes

1 J.J. Dupeyroux and R. Ruellan, *Droit de la Sécurite Sociale*, Paris: Précis Dalloz, 1998, 13th edn, p. 8, note 2.

2 P. Rosanvallon, *La crise de l'Etat-Providence*, Paris: Éditions du Seuil, 1981, pp. 143–6.

3 M. Borgetto, 'Minimas sociaux et revenus d'activité: éléments d'une problématique générale', *Droit social*, Paris, 2000, p. 693.

4 P. Laroque, 'De l'assurance sociale à la sécurité sociale: l'expérience française', *Revue internationale du travail*, Genève, 1948, no. 6, p. 621.

5 M. Borgetto, 'Logique assistantielle et logique assurantielle dans le système français de sécurite sociale', *Droit social*, Paris, 2003, p. 115.

6 About the evolution of the French system during this period, see J.J. Dupeyroux, R. Lafore, M. Borgetto and R. Ruellan, *Droit de la Sécurité Sociale*, Paris: Précis Dalloz, 2001, 14th edn, pp. 300–33.

7 'Le plan Juppé', *Droit social*, Paris, 1996, p. 227.

8 A. Barjot, 'La sécurité sociale: son histoire à travers les textes', Vol. III, Paris, *Ass. pour l'étude de l'histoire de la sécurité sociale*, 1988.

9 D. Tabuteau, 'Les nouveaux mécanismes de maîtrise de l'évolution des dépenses de santé', *Droit social*, Paris, Novembre 1991.

10 R. Ruellan, 'Retraites: l'impossible réforme est-elle achevée?', *Droit social*, Paris, 1993, p. 911.

11 A.M. Guillemard, 'Equité et redistribution entre générations: un défi pour l'avenir des retraites et de l'ensemble des systèmes de sécurite sociale', *Revue internationale de la sécurité sociale*, Genève, vol. 52, no. 3, 1999, p. 81.

12 EC Commission, 'Problèmes de marginalisation', *Droit social*, Paris, 1987, p. 79.

13 R. Lafore, 'Le contrat dans la protection sociale', *Droit social*, Paris, 2003, p. 105.

14 J.P. Chauchard, 'La notion de risque social', *Travail et Protection Sociale*, Paris, June 2000, p. 4; M. Blondel, 'L'étatisation: antichambre de la privatisation', *Droit social*, Paris, 1996, p. 241.

15 A. Baschenis, 'Le droit au travail face à la revendication d'une allocation universelle', *Droit ouvrier*, Montreuil, 1999, p. 148; R. Bergham, 'Résurgence de la pauvreté et lutte contre l'exclusion: un nouveau défi pour la sécurite sociale', *Revue internationale de la sécurité sociale*, Genève, no. 1, 1997.

16 P. Rosanvallon, *La nouvelle question sociale; repenser l'État-Providence*, Paris: Édtions du Seuil, 1995; J. Commaille, *Les nouveaux enjeux de la question sociale*, Paris: Hachette, 1997; D. Kessler, 'L'avenir de la protection sociale', *Commentaires*, Paris, no. 87, 1999, p. 199; M. Borgetto and R. Lafore, 'La République sociale: contribution à l'étude de la question démocratique en France', *Coll. La Politique éclatée*, Paris, PUF, 2000.

17 P.Y. Greber, *Les Principes fondamentaux du droit international de la sécurité sociale*, Lausanne, Reálités Sociales, 1984, p. 109.

18 M. Burdillat and J.L. Outin, 'Les liens entre l'emploi et la protection sociale: portée et limites des aménagements successifs', *Revue française des affaires sociales*, Paris, nos 3–4, 2000, p. 147.

19 J.P. Lhernould, 'Exportation des prestations sociales non contributives dans l'espace européen', *Revue de jurisprudence sociale*, Paris, no. 5, 2001, p. 387.

20 *Ch. Soc. de la Cour de cassation*, 13 December 1979; *Bulletin* V, no. 976; *Ch. Soc. de la Cour de cassation*, 14 December 2002; *Revue de jurisprudence sociale*, Paris, 2003, no. 89.

21 *Cour de justice des Communautés européennes*, 8 March 2001; *Revue de jurisprudence sociale*, Paris, May 2001, no. 691.

22 A.M. Brocas and P. Hadolph, 'Monopole ou concurrence en matière de protection sociale', *Droit social*, Paris, 1995, p. 748; D. Lenoir, 'Protection complémentaire: les dangers du développement concurrentiel', *Droit social*, Paris, 1995, p. 753; J.P. Lhernoud, 'La place des entreprises d'assurances dans les régimes de base d'assurance maladie', *Revue de droit sanitaire et social*, Paris, 1998, p. 223.

23 J.P. Lhernoud, 'Nouvelles dérives libérales de la Cour de Justice des Communautés Européennes en matière de retraites complémentaires', observations sous Cour de justice des Communautés européennes, 12 September 2000, *Droit social*, Paris, 2000, p. 1114.

24 S. Amin, *Les défis de la mondialisation*, Paris, l'Harmattan, 1996; A. Brender, 'L'impératif de la solidarité: la France face à la mondialisation', *La Découverte*, Paris, 1996; P. Chalmin and M. Albert, 'Quel avenir pour le modèle social européen?', *Societal*, Paris, 1997, no. 12.

8
The Welfare State in Postwar Germany

*Lutz Leisering**

Introduction

In this chapter I shall deal with the Federal Republic of Germany (1949–2003). Germany pioneered modern state welfare through the introduction of social insurance by Chancellor Bismarck in the 1880s, and as in other countries the German welfare state grew massively during the postwar decades and has been in crisis since the mid-1990s. The characteristics of the German welfare state include a broad political consensus; a 'social market economy' as a key integrative formula; corporatism and intermediate actors rather than the state proper as key actors; a federal system with a strong local government; little scope for private welfare provision; and with security rather than equality as its overarching aim. In this chapter I shall advance two theses: (1) that the socially fragmented systems of social insurance have developed into a quasi-universalist system of social security, amounting to a 'centrist' rather than a 'conservative' welfare regime (Esping-Andersen); and (2) that the German welfare state has changed considerably during the postwar decades, but in an evolutionary way rather than by radical reforms.

Germany came late to industrialization, but pioneered modern state welfare in the nineteenth century. Before depicting the historical phases of the rise of social policy in Germany, we have to explain what 'Germany' means, because since the late nineteenth century, Germany has undergone more drastic changes, both of political regime and territory, than most other Western countries. During four decades after the Second World War there were two diametrically opposed regimes coexisting within Germany. Imperial Germany, the Reich (1871–1918), was followed by the Weimar

* This chapter is an updated version of 'Germany: Reform from Within', in Pete Alcock and Gary Craig (eds), *International Social Policy: Welfare Regimes in the Developed World*. Basingstoke/New York: Palgrave Macmillan 2001, pp. 161–82. I thank Pete Alcock and Gary Craig for their helpful comments and encouragement.

Republic, the first German democracy (1919–33), and by National Socialism, the Third Reich (1933–45). After a period of occupation, a democratic and capitalist West Germany, the Federal Republic of Germany (FRG), and a totalitarian and communist East Germany, the German Democratic Republic (GDR), were founded in 1949 and only reunited in 1990. These historical periods have left their marks on social policy as on other areas of policy. Yet, despite the changes, there were considerable institutional continuities across political regimes. Unification in 1990 was a takeover of the GDR by the FRG. On one day, all FRG legal and social institutions were imposed on the eastern part, including the basic institutional arrangements of social policy.

Since its foundation as a national state in 1871, Germany has been a federal state consisting of (currently) 16 states (Länder); federalism was abandoned only during National Socialist and communist rule. This diversity stems from pre-1871 traditions when 'Germany' was split into numerous small states and principalities. The federal structure of the German polity is laid down in the 1949 Constitution in article 20 which cannot be changed even by a 100 per cent majority in parliament. A major aspect of German federalism is that education almost exclusively falls within the competence of the Länder. Unlike other countries, education is therefore not normally considered to be part of 'social policy' and, for example, does not figure in the social budget.

The historical background

Several historical phases of the emergence of social policy in Germany can be distinguished:

- *Laying the foundations (1880–1918).* In the 1880s, Chancellor Bismarck introduced social insurance systems to protect workers – and from 1911 white-collar workers also – against the risks of sickness, industrial injury and old age. These were paternalist and authoritarian reforms with a double edge both against the economic liberals of the day and the socialist workers' movement which were seen as a threat to the imperial regime. While Britons think of the late 1940s as the founding years of 'the welfare state', Germans think of Bismarck as the founding father of their social insurance state. Primary education had already been made compulsory in Prussia (the largest pre-1871 German state) in 1825. During the First World War, foundations were laid for modern industrial relations between trade unions and employers.
- *Democracy and economic crisis (1918/1933).* The first years of mass democracy gave rise to substantial departures in social policy such as the introduction of social rights in the new Constitution, the creation of a new branch – unemployment insurance – of social insurance, and social democratic policies in the municipalities, for example in the field of

health and family services. However, massive economic and social problems and political confrontation led to societal breakdown and the emergence of National Socialism.

- *The National Socialist 'welfare state' (1933–45)*. One of the original promises of the regime was to replace mass unemployment and misery by new welfare. The racist and authoritarian ideology left its mark on social policy, by orienting health, family and education policies towards eugenic aims, replacing trade unions and the labour party by a fascist organization of industrial relations, the principle of self-government of social insurance by authoritarian rule, and by expelling Jews and critics of the system from the civil and welfare services. However, much of the basic institutional structure of social insurance remained intact or was even extended.
- *Establishing the postwar welfare state (1949–66)*. After the Allied occupation, the two Germanies were founded in 1949. In the FRG, the major focus of this chapter, debates about a new, more egalitarian welfare state along the lines of Beveridge or the ideas of the German labour movement soon subsided. Instead, ingrained social policy institutions were restored by a centre/centre-right government led by the Christian Democratic Party (CDP), increasingly backed by the social democratic (SDP) opposition. Economic reconstruction, promoting house-building, and integrating millions of migrants were the main social policy tasks of the early years, followed by a gradual expansion and reform of social security and the 1949 Constitution introduced the welfare state (or rather the 'social state') as an unalterable principle of the FRG. The major 1957 old-age pensions reform act became the legitimating cornerstone of postwar welfare.
- *Modernizing the welfare state (1966–75)*. With the Social Democrats in government, an unprecedented expansion of social policy unfolded, provoking high hopes of social planning and active policies directed to enhancing 'the quality of life' for all groups in society, and not only for workers, as in traditional industrial social policy. Education boomed and a wide range of new or extended benefits and services was introduced, for example housing benefit, means-tested grants for students and active labour market policies. Keynesian economic policy and neo-corporatist systems of negotiation between state, employers and employees were also introduced. It was also the formative period of social work as a semi-profession.
- *Consolidation and new expansion (1975–95)*. Economic crisis and political challenges terminated the era of expansion. Fiscal constraints began to dominate policy-making, and social security systems were restructured rather than extended. Unlike Margaret Thatcher, however, Chancellor Helmut Kohl's neo-conservatism largely remained rhetorical during his 16 years of office (1982–98). Benefits were cut repeatedly but key

structures remained intact. There were even new departures, especially benefits and social rights for families and mothers and, above all, the explosion of social spending triggered by the unique historical event of unification with the economically run-down East Germany in 1990. In 1996 social spending (not including education) reached an all-time peak of 35 per cent of GDP. After unification, social expenditure reached an historic scale of about two-thirds of the (East German) regional GDP. Without this effort, mainly flowing from annual transfers of some DM 150 billion from west to east, the enormous problems of mass unemployment and social upheaval could not have been handled in a politically safe manner.

- *The socialist 'welfare state' – the GDR (1949–90).* The GDR, too, was a welfare state but counterposed to the Western variety. It claimed to deliver more social security than West Germany. Rather than redistributing wealth produced in a market as in western states, the GDR model aimed to abolish the market altogether and establish a command economy oriented towards 'social' aims, for example by securing jobs for everybody, by massive subsidies of basic consumer goods and by tying housing, social services and pension entitlements to the workplace. The design of social services and benefits broke with the Bismarckian tradition even more than had the National Socialists. Centralized and uniform benefit schemes prevailed. In the early years, active discrimination policies against children from bourgeois families achieved higher equality of opportunity in higher education than in West Germany. However, social security benefits were low, social services, for example old-people's homes, were in poor condition and there was collective as well as individual (relative) poverty. In the late 1980s, the GDR became the first welfare state to collapse under the burden of its social services.

Bismarck's initial policies have left their mark till the present day, basic principles and forms of organization having survived. However, the widespread notion of continuity needs qualification. In an evolutionary process of gradual change, especially in the years after the Second World War, German social policy has been substantially transformed. What started as social insurance for limited groups of workers and with low benefits, gradually grew into a comprehensive, quasi-universalist network of social services for the entire population. Only after 1949 did Germany become a fully mixed society, representing a third-way between economic liberalism and a residual welfare state on the one hand, and a socialist or communist system of totalitarian and authoritarian provision of goods by the state on the other. When Germans prefer the term 'social state', as entwined in the postwar Constitution, to the term 'welfare state', they want to draw a dividing line between social policy that respects the freedom of the individual and the

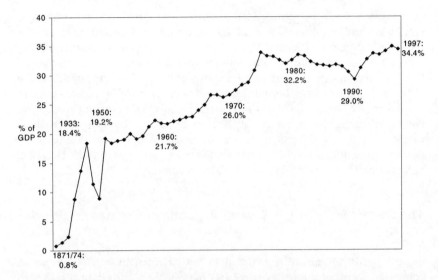

Figure 8.1 Social spending as a percentage of GDP, 1871–1997 (excluding education)

Note: Years before 1950: 1871/74, 1885/89, 1900/04, 1925/29, 1930/32; 1933 peak due to low GNP at time of depression.

Source: Compiled from Heinz Lampert, *Lehrbuch der Sozialpolitik*, 5th edn, Berlin *et al.*, Springer, 1998, p. 293; Manfred G. Schmidt, *Sozialpolitik in Deutschland. Historische Entwicklung und internationaler Vergleich*, 2nd rev. edn, Opladen, Leske & Budrich, 1998, p. 154; Federal Ministry of Labour and Social Affairs (Bundesministerium für Arbeit und Sozialordnung, BMA), *Sozialbericht 1997*, Bonn, 1998, p. 278.

market as a general principle ('social state'), and a hypertrophied system of state provision and control ('welfare state').

Nevertheless, the West German welfare state expanded considerably during the postwar decades, with social spending almost doubling its share in gross net product to around one-third (see Figure 8.1). In 1950 the FRG started with the highest level of social spending among Western countries, although in later decades some countries spent even more. At the same time the numbers of social services clients as well as of staff providing and delivering services have increased drastically. Currently, more than a third of the population derive most of their income from the welfare state, either as clients or as staff. Social law has expanded equally, with more complex legal regulations than in most other welfare states.

Continuity still remains a key feature of German social policy development. It can be seen, first, in the survival of the principle of social insurance which in Germany has the specific meaning of a 'pay-as-you-go' system financed not primarily by taxes but by contributions of employers and employees and run by semi-autonomous non-state bodies administered by employers and employees; second, in the deeply-entrenched federal struc-ture of government with each of the three levels – central government, states (*Länder*) and municipalities – having their own domains of social policy; and third, in the informal great welfare state coalition that has shaped social policy since 1948. Both big parties alternately leading the federal govern-ment – the CDP and the SDP – have been welfare state parties throughout, equally fostering the expansion of the welfare state and joining forces in all major social policy reforms in postwar Germany. Since the mid-1990s, some of these principles are being questioned. Are we nearing the end of a model of social policy that started almost 120 years ago?

The welfare state in the Federal Republic of Germany, 1949–95

Consensus

German political culture is oriented towards consensus and compromise; compared to other countries there has been little confrontation either in politics or industrial relations. The expansion of state social policy has been able to draw on relatively homogenous pro-welfare state beliefs and values backed by all political parties. Policy-making has been dominated by a centre/centre-right party (the CDP) which led the government during two-thirds of the FRG's first half century, mostly supported in an informal socio-political coalition by the non-socialist SDP, itself open to compromise in postwar reconstruction. In this sense the FRG has been a 'centrist' welfare state.[1]

Economic liberalism among the Christian Democrats has been tempered by a pronounced conservatism with regard to family and social relation-ships, the social element being tangible in the strong and well-organized labour wing of the party. The Social Democrats, even whilst upholding the flag of socialism in the 1950s, supported legislation that restored the ingrained fabric of the welfare state. The small liberal party, the Free Demo-cratic Party (FDP), in government for most of the postwar years alternating between coalitions with the Christian Democrats and the Social Democrats, was generally more critical of the welfare state but joined the general con-sensus in practical politics. The Green Party, founded in 1980 and, since 1998, in a government coalition with the Social Democrats, is an innova-tive, less dogmatic, pro-welfare-state party. Radical liberal critics of the welfare state have always had a voice in the debate but only from the mid-1990s did their views gain weight.

The relationship between labour and capital is equally geared to social integration and consensus. Their cooperation as 'industrial partners' (*Tarif-partner*) is also based on compromise, reflected in the very low level of industrial conflict. The German model of industrial democracy, enacted in

1951 and 1976, with a strong representation of trade unions on the executive boards of private companies (*Mitbestimmung*), has received attention worldwide. Social insurance as the core of the German welfare state expresses a normative compromise and consensus between collective and individualist values, through compulsory membership and earnings-related benefits.

Ludwig Erhard and the 'social market economy'

The term 'Social Market Economy', coined in 1946 and explicitly designed as a 'third' or middle way, has been the hallmark of West German democratic welfare capitalism since the Second World War. The concept originated from the German school of economics called 'ordo-liberalism', developed in the 1930s and 1940s against both unfettered liberalism and the experience of totalitarian rule and command economy under fascism and Stalinism. Although 'social state' also became a key term of the political language in Germany, it was not a founding formula of postwar Germany; as noted earlier, the late 1940s/early 1950s witnessed a restoration of the Bismarckian tradition rather than innovation as in Britain.

'Social market economy', with its promise of regaining wealth and welfare in a free society, won the CDP the first (1949) election. Its main protagonist, Ludwig Erhard, Minister for Economic Affairs 1949–63, became the 'father of the economic miracle' in postwar Germany. Erhard had a narrow conception of social market economy, a kind of people's capitalism,[2] geared to increases in wages, consumption and property for all strata of society, rather than substantial social services provided by the state. He advocated measures like anti-inflation, currency and anti-trust policies to strengthen, not contain, the operation of the market. It was not a variety of, but an antidote to, the welfare state. Erhard saw the 'welfare state' – a negative term in his view – as a 'modern paranoia'.

The great 1957 old-age pensions reforms which Chancellor Adenauer had to fight through against Erhard, were the first political defeat for Erhard's perspective and a major step towards interpreting 'social market economy' in a pro-, not anti-welfare-state way. By the early 1960s, it had become the widespread term signifying consensus and social peace in the middle ground. On the occasion of a (small) economic recession in 1967, elements of Keynesianism were officially adopted by policy-makers, thereby broadening the role of economic policy in welfare provision.

Intermediate agencies and corporatism

Dating back to the absolutist, militarist Prussian tradition and idealistic Hegelian social philosophy, a strong belief in the 'state' – an essentialist term preferred to the more pragmatic Anglo-Saxon term 'government' – is deeply entrenched in German social thought although the German politico-administrative system, especially in respect of social policy, is less centralized, less 'statist' than many other welfare states. This is reflected in the social budget, the budget not of any government agency or body but a sum of elements from a variety of scattered budgets of mainly non-governmental institutions. Most is spent in the five branches of social insurance, by para-state bodies, mainly funded and administered by its members and employers, the two largest branches, health and old-age pensions, accounting for half. However, social insurance, like other non-state bodies, is subject to legal regulation, to some financial support and to political control by the state: Old-age pensions insurance receives an annual state subsidy of some DM 100 billion.

The corporatist structure, the variegated web of semi-autonomous actors, groups and institutions, has been typical of German social policy since its inception. Social welfare is produced by a broad range of intermediate agencies which are neither purely governmental (such as a national health service) nor entirely independent (such as occupational pensions and private insurance). These agencies have been granted privileged status as providers or coordinators of welfare services, adding up to a tightly regulated structure of society. Liberal critics claim this accounts for much of Germany's inflexibility in adapting to the new global economy.

The key elements of German corporatism are:

- The five branches of social insurance – accident, old-age, health, unemployment, and long-term care: these systems are differentiated by occupational groups. For example, for many years, members of the white-collar branch of old-age pensions enjoyed better conditions than members of the blue-collar branch;
- Social professions, above all medical doctors: they have higher socio-legal status and incomes than doctors in most other countries. From 1955, doctors who have signed in with Health Insurance have a monopoly. Treatment by private doctors is not reimbursed by health insurance so that they have remained marginal in the health sector. Contractual doctors are paid on a fee-for-service fixed-price basis.
- 'Social partners' – associations of employers and trade unions in industrial relations;
- Systems of coordination, negotiation and bargaining between corporate actors: between the 'social partners' – their autonomy being guaranteed by the Constitution – and between the sickness funds and the associations of medical doctors; and
- Voluntary welfare organizations, which need to be described in more detail since they occupy a central position in the organization of personal social services.

Subsidiarity, a key principle of the German welfare mix, laid down in the Social Assistance Act and in the Children and Youth Welfare Act, means that small units have priority over larger units, especially over the state, whenever appropriate. Help by bureaucratic organizations is subsidiary to support relationships within the family, and state aid is second to aid by voluntary welfare associations. This principle pertains to the entire range of personal social services directed to age groups (youth and elderly), to families, and to 'problem groups' (the poor, people with disabilities). The welfare associations employ over one million waged employees (1996) and large numbers of unpaid (voluntary) helpers.

Major umbrella organizations of voluntary welfare include *Caritas* (Roman Catholic) and *Diakonie* (Protestant), mirroring the bi-confessional structure of German Christianity; the Non-Denominational Workers and Central Jewish Welfare Associations, and the Red Cross. These associations act as service providers in service centres, hospitals, residential homes and care for elderly and people with disabilities and sheltered employment. In addition, they are political actors – in the field of children and youth services they have a formal say in the administrative board. Besides their welfare associations, the churches also play a direct part, for example by running social work schools. After many years of privileged symbiosis with the state and a high degree of bureaucratization, the associations now find themselves under pressure to improve efficiency to survive in competition with commercial providers in the social services market developing under the new Long-Term Care Insurance. In social policy debates, they have subsequently moved from conformism with official policies to sustained criticism of benefit cuts and lobbying for the poor.

National and local

The German political system has a three-tier structure, with each tier – central government, the States (*Länder*) and the municipalities – having distinct legislative, fiscal and administrative powers. Domains are demarcated in detail in the Constitution which also gives to the municipalities the right to self-governance (Article 28). Conflicts between the three levels often cut across party lines. Since the 1980s, for example, the federal government has repeatedly cut unemployment benefits to shift burdens to Social Assistance which is regulated by central law in a fairly standardized way but financed by the *Länder* and the municipalities. Even after the growth of national social spending had ended, social spending's share of municipalities' budgets still almost doubled from 12 per cent in 1980 to 22 per cent in 1996.

Although social assistance funding and administration is less centralized than in Britain, provisions do not vary as much between regions and communes as in Italy. The emphasis of local social policy is on personal social services and social work: social planning for youth, elderly and the poor, arranging a local mix of voluntary and municipal welfare agencies, and securing quality of services. Health activities are limited because the centralized system of sickness funds and contractual doctors has tended to absorb the entire health service. In their predominant field, education, the states have not, however, lived up to the expectation to raise quality through competition and their role in financing and planning hospitals has been a major obstacle in the reform of health insurance.

The welfare mix: public and private

As in other countries the welfare state is only one segment of the social production of welfare. There is a mix of public and private services and, even within the comprehensive German version of this mix, a pronounced mix within the public welfare domain. As noted, most of the institutions of the German welfare state are not 'state' proper but 'intermediate' agencies. This is reflected in the financing of the social budget which is shared by the three levels of government and by employers and employees who pay contributions to social insurance.[3]

Thus, even in the comprehensive German welfare state, there has always been a mix of provision:

- Security in old age rests on the 'three-pillars model' of state pensions, occupational pensions and private pensions, with, however, a strong emphasis on the state pillar.
- In the field of health insurance, the long-standing 'peace boundary' between public and private insurance – the income threshold where compulsory membership of public health insurance ends – has remained undisputed to the present day. Due to the high quality of public services, the publicly-insured are not driven to take up a (more than supplementary) private insurance. For civil servants (*Beamte*), there is a special state-run (non-insurance) scheme which covers half of medical bills, leaving the other half to private insurance.
- The complex institutional arrangement of health insurance includes links to semi-markets: to pharmaceutical industries and producers of medical technology, and to the doctors who are not employees of the state or of any sickness fund but business-like monopolistic providers with special privileged contractual relationships with health insurance. This corporatist welfare mix is, however, regulated by government.
- The German 'dual system' of vocational training for youth, which is considered a model by other countries, combines state schooling during part of the week with company-based work and practical qualification. This system has led to higher qualification levels and less youth unemployment than in many other countries.
- German 'social housing' involves a public–private partnership. Private landlords get state subsidies for building flats if they agree to let them to low income people at a modest rent fixed by government.

The macro-welfare mix is mirrored in the micro-welfare mix that each citizen makes up for him or herself. Most people derive their income and personal social services from more than one source, for example they top up a state pension by occupational and private pensions. However, in most cases there is a source of income that dominates the individual income package: market wages (earned income), intra-household transfers (for example from male earner to his wife) and social wage (cash benefits by the state). Looking back over the last four decades, the state's share in social welfare production has not only increased on the aggregate level (see Figure 8.1 above) but also on the individual level: compared to market wages and income derived from one's family (including transfers from earners to their spouses and children) the social wage has gained weight. The data also show that this pertains mainly to young and old people, that is to age groups. Moreover, the growth of state provisions is not a zero-sum game: the extension of higher education has simultaneously prolonged the time young people are cared for by their families. Female labour-market participation is increasing, though still on a lower scale than in many other countries.

Social insurance: the road to quasi-universalism

Given the variety of intermediate and corporatist agencies, a picture of a highly fragmented system emerges. Social insurance, in particular, is fragmented by occupational groups, with three main branches of old-age insurance, and 475 sickness funds, and with schemes for occupational groups outside social insurance, primarily for civil servants, farmers and some professional groups. However, changes since the 1950s have gradually transformed the system. The social insurance state has been increasingly integrated and extended, and with regard to benefits, funding and institutional structure this 'fragmented' system has given way to a tightly interwoven quasi-universalism:

- *Integration.* The difference between the white-collar and the blue-collar branch of old-age pension insurance has been steadily removed. Sickness funds nowadays offer virtually identical services to their members and a system of financial compensation established to account for different distributions of risks among the clientele, especially between West and East German funds.
- *Extension of coverage and benefits.* Non-waged groups, for example the self-employed, students, housewives and artists, were admitted to insurance. Aspects of family policy were introduced 1985 and have been increasingly extended since, thus acknowledging family work, that is raising a child, as an independent source of entitlement to benefits in addition to paid work ('natural contribution'). Under the 2001 act, raising one child equals three years of paying contributions. In health insurance, non-waged (house)wives and children of an employed father have always been entitled to full services without paying contributions.
- *Extension of bargaining systems* ('corporatization'). Hospitals and, to some degree, the pharmaceutical industry, have been included in corporatist

bargaining and planning, originally confined to medical doctors who run private surgeries outside the hospital system.

The system is thus nearing universality. More than 90 per cent of the population are currently covered by social insurance for old age and health. By contrast, truly universal citizenship-based schemes are rare in the German system. The most important universal scheme is Child Benefit, repeatedly reformed since the foundation of the FRG. Since the 1990s there has been a strong pressure from all parties to raise it.

There is also a substantial range of selective benefits, particularly Social Assistance. Due to the strength of social insurance schemes, the number of social assistance recipients is much lower than in many other countries, although unemployment, growing numbers of lone mothers, and immigration have led to the number of social assistance recipients (basic income support, not special needs support) more than quadrupling since 1970 to 5 per cent. Non-take-up amounts roughly to 50 per cent of those entitled. However, most claims are short[4] and German social assistance is more 'universal' than related schemes in many other countries. Everybody below a certain income level, including wage-earners and foreigners, are entitled to benefits. Unemployment Assistance, the lower echelon of unemployment benefit, is half-way between means-testing and social insurance.

Security first, equality second

Although people often associate the concept of welfare state with egalitarian values, many welfare states and Germany's in particular are geared more to achieving security than equality. Security is an objective of social policy in two ways:

- Some transfers and services aim to guarantee basic or minimum incomes and minimum provisions. The 1961 Social Assistance Act introduced the right to assistance, establishing a socio-cultural (not just physical) minimum, including full coverage by health services.
- Security can also mean safeguarding a status attained earlier in life, and this is mainly achieved by social insurance. Pensions, industrial injury insurance and unemployment benefit are earnings-related. The bulk of the German welfare state, therefore, is not directed to the poor but to the broad middle mass. This is redistribution over the individual life course, not between rich and poor.

However, the system also has egalitarian components:

- Health insurance and (long-term) care insurance not only redistribute between the sick and the non-sick but also between rich and poor, since services are not earnings-related whilst contributions are.

- In addition, there is massive redistribution in favour of married couples and families with children because they pay the same contributions as singles unless the spouse is in full-time employment.
- Survivors' pensions for old age create entitlements for people who have not paid contributions, thereby enhancing equality.
- There is a strong commitment to equality between age groups.
- Health insurance does not ration services for the elderly.
- Higher education is free.

By and large, social security policies have been effective; poverty rates are below the European average; and numbers of recipients even in East Germany are surprisingly low and not growing fast (although the stigma of social assistance is higher there). One reason is the enormous amount of money paid for labour-market measures such as job-creation schemes. Another reason is the extension of the West German system of old-age pensions to the east which turned the East German elderly into unification 'winners'. Despite unprecedented social upheaval, therefore, the east has not, as some predicted, led to mass misery.[5]

The German welfare state and German society at large are more gender-biased than other countries. The insurance system is geared to the male breadwinner based on contributions paid out of wages. The welfare state sets strong incentives to stay in the family and stay out of the labour market. Labour-market participation among women, especially among married women, is rising but still low. One of the reasons, besides the conservative ideology of the CDP, is the scarcity of social services allowing women to delegate housework and childcare and, at the same time, creating job opportunities for women. Only since 1996 is there a (formal) guarantee of a place in a nursery school for each child from the age of three. Germany thus generally lags behind in the move towards a service society. There are relatively few service jobs and few part-time jobs.

Germany: a conservative welfare regime?

In Esping-Andersen's *Three Worlds of Welfare Capitalism* (1990),[6] Germany is seen as the epitome of the conservative welfare state regime: achieving a medium degree of decommodification (of enabling people to live independently of the market), grading benefits and entitlements by occupation and social status, and upholding a conservative concept of society that emphasizes family, traditional gender roles and intermediate social bodies such as churches, voluntary welfare associations and occupational status groups.

Esping-Andersen rightly depicts Germany as a welfare regime of the middle ground, between individualism (liberal regime, epitomized by the USA) and 'statism' (social democratic regime, Sweden). But the label 'conservative' is also a simplification, and it tends to overrate differences to other countries, both with regard to institutional structure and politico-ideological background.

First, the German welfare state is more egalitarian and universalist than it looks. Apart from the civil servants, coverage by social insurance has become quasi-universal in all its branches. In old-age pensions the differentiation by occupational groups has in practice become irrelevant. The health system, although formally organized as an insurance, is strongly egalitarian and near-universal – missed by Esping-Andersen because he only looked at cash benefits. Moreover, social insurance is a hybrid system that mixes elements of all three worlds of welfare capitalism: contributions by employees are combined with contributions by employers and with state subsidies; and earnings-related benefits (mirroring market principles) go together with compulsory membership (contradicting the freedom of the market).

Second, the political tendency of the German regime is 'centrist' rather than conservative:[7] it is shaped by a reformist centre/centre-right party joint by a pragmatic social democratic party which was strong though mostly in opposition. Re-analysing Esping-Andersen's data, Obinger and Wagschal (1998)[8] found that his conservative type actually falls into two types, a 'centrist European social insurance state' (including Germany) and a type which really meets Esping-Andersen's criteria of conservativism (found in France, Italy and Austria). The Kohl government (1982–98) has further tempered the conservative outlook of German social policy.

Groping in the dark: at the threshold of a new welfare state? (1995–2003)

Between the mid-1970s and the mid-1990s, the welfare state was under considerable pressure, both economically and politically; there was much talk about crisis, about dismantling the welfare state and, when Chancellor Kohl of the Christian Democratic Party took office in 1982, a call for a moral change in social policy and society at large. However, the ingrained structure of social security systems survived and even took up the historical challenge of German unification in 1990, an event somewhat obscuring Kohl's lack of strategic vision. But from the mid-1990s the crisis has become more real, and several changes point to transformation of the postwar welfare state.

For a start, political consensus among the major parties and the social partners (the trade unions and the employers' associations) characterizing the postwar period has become brittle. The Social Democratic Party (SDP) now acknowledges that the welfare state not only solves but creates problems. It has adopted the view that unemployment is partially caused by excessive rates of contributions, raising the price of labour.

Globalization also exerts particular pressures on the competitiveness of the German economy, the world's second biggest export economy. Financing social benefits mostly by contributions rather than taxes makes the German benefit systems particularly vulnerable to the crisis in employment – and to competition by low-wage countries – because half of the contributions are paid by the employers as part of labour costs. Similarly, the design of social insurance as pay-as-you-go-systems rather than capital funding, in conjunction with high replacement rates, makes the system more vulnerable to the effects of the ageing of the population, especially in the context of one of the world's lowest birth rates.

There are further problems unique to Germany. Since the Second World War, German society has been more homogeneous than other societies, as revealed by data on beliefs and attitudes; the quest for social harmony between social groups was overwhelming. The 1990s, however, have confronted the Germans with a new – or newly perceived – world of social heterogeneity and social cleavage.

Firstly, there is the East/West divide since national unification in 1990. Many of the support measures for East Germans were financed from social insurance funds (rather than general taxes), thus adding to pressures on social insurance. Unemployment in the east is still very high (*c*. 20 per cent), and economic growth too slow, temporarily slightly above but mostly below Western rates; eastern tax revenues continue to be low; and high transfers from the west will be needed for many years to come. Nearly fifteen years after unification, there remains divisive resentment between east and west.

Secondly, there is a problem of immigration and ethnic conflict. Germany has one of the highest proportions of foreigners in Europe (8.5 per cent in 1993), and politicians have been slow in facing this fact. Between 1988–96, 2.3 million 'settlers' (persons of German descent from Russia and East Europe) and *c*. 2 million asylum-seekers from all over the world came to Germany. Poverty rates among foreigners are twice that of native citizens; and some of the settlers are becoming marginalized.

The changing composition of the social budget over the last decades[9] indicates some of the new challenges of the welfare state. Health insurance is a cost factor as can be seen from its growing share in the budget, currently nearing 20 per cent. The ageing of the population is not yet reflected in the budget because its peak lies ahead, but the vast German system of old-age pensions already accounts for more than 30 per cent of the overall social budget. All in all, the share of social insurance has grown from below to well-above half social spending (including the 'labour market' item which largely flows from unemployment insurance). At the same time, social assistance and local personal services expenditures have more than doubled (to more than 8 per cent), indicating the increase in social risks not covered by the standard systems of social insurance.

Conclusion: evolutionary change

Despite the new challenges, and a weakening of political support for welfare, there is no sign of a fundamental break with the ingrained institutions of the welfare state. Most reform does not aim at new institutions or at privatizing social services, as evident in neo-liberal regimes. It is rather a reform from within, especially a mobilization of the existing intermediate institutions – non-state and non-market institutions like social insurance – so characteristic of German social policy. Moreover, there are few instances of straightforward privatization – shifting provisions to market and family – but rather new links between public and private. Changing the welfare mix need not be a zero-sum game – more private, less public – but extending private welfare production may require increased state regulatory control – just as a more active role of the (non-state) social insurance agencies requires more government regulation.

One example is the changing role of intermediate agencies: Social Insurance (in the specific German meaning of a non-state and employment-based way of organizing social security), corporate actors in the health sector (sickness funds and monopolistic doctors' associations) and local governments are revitalized as social policy agents, especially in health and social assistance. Another is the new links to private provisions and agencies (rather than mere 'privatization'), especially in the field of long-term care (introduced as a new branch of social insurance in 1994), old-age pensions and again social assistance. Comparing welfare states we therefore have to bear in mind that in some countries change may be smoother and less visible but not necessarily smaller than in countries where visible institutional breaks are more common and where a rhetoric of change prevails. As described earlier, health insurance has been thoroughly transformed over the years to near universality while formally it is still 'social insurance'. More recently, old-age pension insurance, though particularly vulnerable to the ageing of the population, has been successfully adapted to demographic change, including a new public–private mix with a larger share for private pensions, strongly regulated and subsidized by government in the major reform act of 2001.

All in all, true to its tradition of evolutionary adaptation to social change, the German welfare state since the 1990s has been undergoing considerable change within the framework of old institutions and without rhetoric of grand reform. Old and new, continuity and discontinuity, are intertwined. In a new situation – the return of political conflict, economic and demographic challenges, the decline of social harmony – old institutions are reformed from within: they change substantially but retain basic characteristics and continue to be viewed as the same institutions.

By the time the Social Democratic Party won the 1998 election, after 16 years of the Conservative Kohl government, Germany had come to be considered a laggard in adapting to the new exigencies of a globalizing economy. Politicians pointed to the Netherlands, to Denmark, to Britain or the USA as models of reducing unemployment, of deregulating the economy and of successfully restructuring welfare. German unemployment rose, whilst it fell elsewhere. The economic growth rate is currently the lowest among EU countries. In 2001, in the international study of educational achievement of 15-year-old schoolchildren, PISA, Germany ranked at the very bottom, even below transitional countries like Korea.

The German political system makes it truly difficult to induce changes, and political immobility seems to prevail. Germany is highly fragmented with many 'veto players':[10] the Constitutional Court interferes massively with social policy; in the second chamber of the federal parliament, the *Bundesrat*, where the states are represented, the government party is often in a minority; and the states and the municipalities have a say in finance, taxation and hospital planning.

The new Social Democratic Chancellor, Gerhard Schröder, in his first term (1998–2002) took up the challenge of improving Germany's competitiveness, in particular through reforms of taxation and old-age pensions and by tackling the public debt. But he failed to reduce unemployment. Attempts at reforming health insurance equally came to nothing. In the fields of education and ethnic conflict, more far-reaching changes may be necessary; here there is much public controversy little determined action, despite some departures in higher education. For the federal election in September 2002, no political party had offered clear-cut models for change. The Social Democratic Party, together with the Green Party, again won the election to form a coalition government. With the heightening economic and mental crisis the pressure for change became overwhelming in early 2003. The key areas of reform include the labour market (as before), industrial relations, old-age pensions (taking the 2001 reform further) and, more than before, health insurance. The year 2003 could mark the beginning of the most far-reaching transformation of the German welfare state in the postwar era.

It remains to be seen if social cleavages will challenge the German model of social integration; if there will be a shift from the 'transfer state' to a 'social investment state' with more emphasis on education and employment, and less on paying for time off employment; and if there will be revolutionary breaks or, as before, a smooth and evolutionary adaptation. It is also open as to whether ongoing administrative modernization will successfully transform the welfare state from within (and from below, by reform of local government). The future of the German welfare state is more uncertain than for many years, although Germany's history suggests that the end of the welfare state is not near. In 1999, the German Chancellor, Gerhard Schröder, and the British Prime Minister, Tony Blair, collaborated in a programmatic paper on the 'Third Way'. In principle, this is what the German 'social state' has always been about.

Notes

1 Manfred G. Schmidt, *Sozialpolitik in Deutschland. Historische Entwicklung und internationaler Vergleich*, 2nd revd edn, Opladen: Leske & Budrich, 1998 (the authoritative, most comprehensive and up-to-date analysis of German social policy, including history, theory and cross-national comparison, from the point of view of political science), p. 220.

2 Werner Abelshauser, 'Erhard oder Bismarck? Die Richtungsentscheidung der deutschen Sozialpolitik am Beispiel der Reform der Sozialversicherung in den Fünfziger Jahren', *Geschichte und Gesellschaft*. vol. 22, 1996, no. 3, pp. 376–92.

3 Federal Ministry of Labour and Social Affairs (Bundesministerium für Arbeit und Sozialordnung, BMA), 1998, Sozialbericht 1997, Bonn, 1998, p. 295.

4 Lutz Leisering and Stephan Leibfried, *Time and Poverty in Western Welfare States. United Germany in Perspective*, Cambridge: Cambridge University Press, 2001.

5 *Ibid.*

6 Gøsta Esping-Andersen, *The Three Worlds of Welfare Capitalism*, Cambridge et al.: Polity Press, 1990.

7 Manfred G. Schmidt, n. 1, p. 220.

8 Herbert Obinger and Uwe Wagschal, 'Drei Welten des Wohlfahrtsstaats? Das Stratifizierungskonzept in der clusteranalytischen Überprüfung', in Stephan Lessenich and Ilona Ostner (eds), *Welten des Wohlfahrtskapitalismus*, Frankfurt/ New York: Campus, 1998.

9 Federal Ministry of Labour and Social Affairs, n. 3, p. 289.

10 Manfred G. Schmidt, n. 1.

9
The Welfare State in Austria

Emmerich Talos and Marcel Fink*

Introduction

The changes which have taken place in the welfare state systems of highly industrialized Western states over the two last decades have been described in different terms and theoretically explained by various commentators after applying different methods.[1] In comparative analysis, a break with the preceding decades, described as the end of 'the golden age of the European welfare state'[2] or even the emergence of a 'neo-conservative turning-point' have been detected.[3] At the same time there has been repeated discussion on the endogenously and exogenously caused 'structural problems' of modern welfare states.[4] These problems are reflected – according to the general findings – not only in financial and governance problems, but also in contributions to the duration and intensification of the stated legitimation crisis of modern welfare states. In connection with this, Jessop explains the corelationship of the economic crisis and the disintegration of social consensus on the 'Fordist' growth model, which had shaped the decades after the Second World War. At the same time he describes the 'erosion of the nation state' and the gradual displacement of the 'Keynesian welfare state' by a model that he describes as 'Schumpeterian workfare regime'.[5] What it means is that as national full employment no longer has priority over international competitiveness, and that redistributive social policy loses its importance against the background of a 'productivistic' supply-side-based reorganization of social and economic policy, as a result the hitherto predominant role of nation-state-controlled political governance (at any rate in specific political fields) is increasingly 'replaced' by novel forms of 'gov-

* We wish to thank in particular Petra Wetzel. A sizeable part of the socio-statistical data is due to her research undertaken in another context; see P. Wetzel, 'Armutsgefährdungen trotz Erwerbsarbeit und sozialstaatlicher Sicherung', in E. Tálos (ed.), *Bedarfsorientierte Grundsicherung*, Wien: Mandelbaum, 2003, pp. 27–63.

ernance' on varying political levels. What comes along with these changes, according to Jessop, is a 'denationalizing of the state'.

On the other hand, international comparative research still underlines the substantial stability of the welfare state, and that earlier growth has given way to stagnation of a relatively high level of social security.[6] Moreover, various forms of realization of the welfare state can be observed, which again feature diverse structures, deficits, weak points and perspectives for the future. The current reorganization occurs – according to the findings – in extremely varying modes 'as these . . . welfare states today seek to adapt, they do so very differently'.[7] A major reason for this has to do with institutional legacies, inherited system characteristics, and the vested interests that they cultivate.[8]

This chapter aims to focus on Austria's current social policy against the background of its historical roots. The first part explains the high path-dependency, till recently, in the configuration of social policy in Austria and the fundamental features of the Austrian welfare state. The second part focuses on the current problems and challenges the system is confronted by presently. The politics of the last decade has responded to these problems in the form of a (defensive) 'policy of adaptation'. The relevant measures, which were of an increasingly restrictive character during the second half of the 1990s, found room for manoeuvre only within the framework of established programmes and contained hardly any components capable of substantially changing the fundamental principles of the system. However, under a new constellation of government (centre-right coalition government of ÖVP and FPÖ) as from spring 2000, far reaching structural measures, most of which leading to considerable welfare state retrenchment, have been decided. Notably, this neo-liberal/conservative policy reversal, which has advanced at a considerable pace, pertains not only to the nature of its content, but also to its effects on the ability of the Austrian welfare state to achieve social integration. Furthermore, we also analyse the prevalent explanations concerning the power to assert political control, and general questions about the activities of the Austrian state.

Historical background and the founding principles of the Austrian welfare state

Just as in other European countries, considerable expansion of social policy in Austria is a post-Second World War phenomenon.[9] Social policy has gained importance in the context of the configuration of living conditions of more and more people. To understand Austrian social policy in the Second Republic, it is important to note that the expansion of the country's social policy took place in conformity with the mould that was established towards the end of the nineteenth century: the model of a conservative-corporatist welfare state.[10]

At first, in the latter half of the nineteenth century, it was the problem of poverty that was the focus of social and security policy for Austrians. In differentiation to poor relief, the introduction of a state-wide social policy was carried out by the government of Taaffe (1879–93).[11] These measures were part of arrangements made to settle the 'labour question' and to obtain the alignment of manpower with capitalist conditions of working and production. With the introduction of national health and work accident insurance (1888/89) Austria laid the bedrock of a social insurance system that links social protection and employment participation. While the phase of the First World War was characterized by regressive tendencies, the First Republic was characterized by a remarkable extension of social policy. After the introduction of unemployment insurance in 1920, a further expansion of social insurance occurred with specific laws concerning employees as well as farm and forest workers. A discontinuity in the social policy development process started to show up early in the 1930s, and is clearly manifest in the major regress in social policy development of the First Republic during the phases of Austro fascism (1934–38) and the Nazi regime (1938–45).[12]

All in all, social policy was the crux of divergent political options from the end of the nineteenth century up to 1945. Its process of development was determined by conflicting political and social interests and their relative strengths, which is reflected in the various advancements, stagnations and setbacks that took place.

Social policy during the Second Republic does not show comparable discontinuities, at least until the end of the 1980s. Further development was marked by a considerable expansion from the 1950s well into the 1970s, and the term 'golden age of the welfare state',[13] which was used for West European countries, holds good for Austria as well. Despite differences in its content and conflicts between relevant political and social protagonists, social policy after 1945 was characterized by the continuation of those central principles that had been laid down in the nineteenth century. In the years after the Second World War a universal insurance for the entire resident population, similar to the Swedish system, was only rarely discussed, and the decision was taken, with the creation of the 'Universal National Security Law' (*Allgemeines Sozialversicherungsgesetz*; ASVG) in 1955, for a traditional social insurance of the Bismarck-type, closely linked to employment category and earnings, as well as family status.

According to the principle of the linkage of social security with employment participation in Austria, integration into the labour market/employment is a basic requirement for social insurance benefits. As a result, many women were and still are excluded from independent social insurance, many being only included in the system as 'co-insured' or as 'surviving dependants', whereby the social protection depends substantially on the stability of marriage. At the same time, other forms of cohabitation are not equated with marriage (for example in old-age pension insurance). It is only in sub-areas (family allowance, preventive health check-ups, long-term care benefit) that the entire population is covered; at the same time, the system is partially open for everybody, by offering the possibility of voluntary insurance (*de facto* especially in the domain of health insurance).

As a principle, the requirement of employment participation correlates with the principle of equivalence between level and/or duration of contribution and level of social benefits. The social insurance system reproduces income disparities and variations in the occupation records of employed people – and with it, especially, gender-specific economic and social inequalities. As distinct from the Scandinavian and other countries, little importance was attached in Austria, in the configuration of social security systems, to the concept of a minimum income in the form of minimum standards (minimum or basic amounts). Only in the public pension scheme does there exist a (means-tested) so-called 'equalization supplement', which is applied to raise the level of very small pensions to a standard rate. Besides, maternity allowance is also paid as a lump-sum, although it is in fact an insurance benefit.

As mentioned earlier, the Austrian welfare state experienced a considerable expansion up to the 1970s, but since the 1980s signs of change have been apparent. These modifications up to now have not changed the basic principles, but rather the extent and the range of coverage of social policy: selective measures for a further expansion of the welfare state have been accompanied by a reduction of services and a deterioration of access to social benefits, whereby the latter evidently gained ascendancy during the 1990s. Indeed, with the establishment of a middle-right government of the ÖVP (Austrian Peoples Party, *Österreichische Volkspartei*) and the FPÖ (Austrian Freedom Party, *Freiheitliche Partei Österreichs*) in February 2000, this process has not only accelerated, but Austria, with a mix of neo-liberal and conservative bias propagated and effected by this government, follows but also surpasses the mainstream development of increasingly restrictive social policies in EU Europe (which of course shows variations of degree from state to state in international comparisons[14]). Moreover, the increasingly expressed request to explicitly reconstruct diverse insurance-based welfare programmes in the mould of means- and income-tested benefits or national assistance, is a fundamentally new development in the welfare state system of the Austrian Second Republic.

Changes of basic conditions and context: challenges for the welfare state

For more than a decade the contextual conditions for the welfare state in Austria – as in many other highly developed Western countries – have been changing.[15] Industrial growth has lower expansion rates, and internationalization and the EU alignment of the economy has not only restricted the

Table 9.1 Population forecast and age cohorts

Year	Age		Ratio of over 65s to those between 15 and 65
	15 to 65	65 and older	
1998	5,450,860	1,247,785	1:4.37
2000	5,478,118	1,258,992	1:4.35
2002	5,504,925	1,268,052	1:4.34
2004	5,504,347	1,303,367	1:4.22
2006	5,453,877	1,390,110	1:3.92
2008	5,431,847	1,453,003	1:3.74
2010	5,433,837	1,487,462	1:3.65
2015	5,389,729	1,588,389	1:3.39
2020	5,298,432	1,701,585	1:3.11
2025	5,116,344	1,884,911	1:2.71
2030	4,855,101	2,138,846	1:2.27
2035	4,613,541	2,355,465	1:1.96
2040	4,487,890	2,422,841	1:1.85
2045	4,433,488	2,375,113	1:1.87
2050	4,334,083	2,325,200	1:1.86

Source: ÖSTAT,[16] population projection (forecast), middle variant.

scope for national politics but has also exerted political pressure on the fallback systems of the welfare state, while problems and challenges keep growing. In the long run, demographic change marked by the ageing of the population (Table 9.1) is one of these challenges. This is the result of rising life expectancy on the one hand, and a declining birthrate on the other, with the consequence of a remarkable transformation in the proportions of economically active and non-active persons, associated with rising expenditures for the preservation of the old-age pension system.

Of similar significance are diversifications of employment and occupational structure. This is explicit at two levels: (1) in increasing unemployment, and (2) in the increase of so-called atypical employment. Unemployment rates by sex, and total levels, are shown in Table 9.2.

Unemployment has affected the Austrian labour market since the early 1980s and showed a continuous upward trend until the year 1998. Recently, the unemployment rate was three times as high as in 1980/81 (1981: 2.4 per cent; 1998: 7.2 per cent). The number of persons who have been affected by unemployment at least once a year has increased threefold: in 1980 all in all about 240,000 people were affected by unemployment at least once a year, whilst in recent years the number has been more than 700,000 (see Table 9.3). The labour market situation improved in 1999, and even more in 2000, which can be observed in the rise of jobholders as well as from the reduction of the number of unemployed persons. However, it is evident that

Table 9.2 Development of unemployment rates by sex, and unemployment levels in the 1980s and 1990s

	Unemployment rate (%)			Unemployment level*		
	Women	*Men*	*Total*	*Women*	*Men*	*Total*
1981	2.7	2.2	2.4	31,286	38,008	69,295
1982	3.5	3.8	3.7	40,220	65,126	105,346
1984	4.3	4.7	4.5	49,870	80,599	130,469
1986	5.2	5.1	5.2	63,116	88,856	151,972
1988	5.6	5.1	5.3	68,800	89,829	158,631
1990	6.0	4.9	5.4	76,762	89,032	165,795
1992	6.2	5.7	5.9	85,896	107,202	193,098
1994	6.7	6.4	6.5	94,374	120,567	214,941
1996	7.3	6.9	7.0	102,482	128,025	230,507
1998	7.5	6.9	7.2	108,365	129,429	237,794
1999	6.9	6.5	6.7	100,225	121,519	221,744
2000	5.9	5.8	5.8	86,804	107,506	194,314
2001	5.9	6.2	6.1	88,560	115,324	203,883

*Annual average level.
Source: HV, AMS.[17]

the positive trend during 1999 and 2000 is over now, and since mid-2001 unemployment has been rising again.

Of no less relevance, especially because of its long-term impact, is the increase of so-called atypical forms of employment, meaning those forms of employment that diverge from standardized, full-time, continual occupation that are secure under labour and social law.[18] Such non-standard forms of employment include part-time employment, marginal part-time employment, fixed-term employment, temporary employment, work on call, telework, and so-called quasi-freelance occupation or quasi self-employment.[19]

This growth trend is still advancing slowly in Austria in comparison to other countries, as can be seen in Table 9.4. However, in general all of the signs pointing to a long-term growth trend of such forms of employment also apply to Austria. The largest expansion can be found in part-time occupation (more than 15 per cent), and the sex-specific differences are most strongly marked for this form of occupation. The proportion of women among part-time workers was around 85 per cent in 2003. The number of male and female employees with fixed-term contracts is also growing, its proportion in the whole dependent working population being around 7.5 per cent. The number of temporary employees has been continually growing since its first legal regulation in 1988, although this proportion is still rather small (about 0.7 per cent). A considerable growth has also been noticed in marginal part-time jobs, that is occupations below a certain level of income

Table 9.3 Unemployment rates, affectedness, rate of affectedness according to sex and age cohort, 1988–2001

Age cohort	Unemployment rate (%)				Affectedness (000s)*				Affectedness ratio (%)**			
	1988	1999	2000	2001	1988	1999	2000	2001	1988	1999	2000	2001
15–18	2.8	2.7	2.6	2.9	31	23	23	24	14.7	15.2	15.3	16.7
19–24	6.7	6.9	6.3	7.0	155	125	119	126	28.7	31.3	31.2	33.1
25–29	6.2	6.3	5.5	5.9	96	106	97	96	21.2	23.3	22.2	22.9
30–39	5.3	6.2	5.4	5.7	121	213	206	209	16.7	20.4	19.5	19.8
40–49	4.7	5.9	5.2	4.5	91	138	137	146	13.6	17.5	16.9	17.2
50–59	5.2	10.6	8.9	9.7	47	105	101	99	14.3	22.7	21.7	20.8
60+	2.6	6.5	7.4	10.6	2	5	5	6	7.1	19.9	23.5	21.9
Women	5.6	6.9	5.9	6.1	224	305	292	299	18.3	21.0	19.9	20.1
Men	5.1	6.5	5.8	6.2	319	412	397	407	18.3	21.9	21.3	21.9
Total	5.3	6.7	5.8	5.9	543	717	689	706	18.3	21.5	20.7	21.1

*Affectedness: all persons who were noted as being unemployed for at least one day; in thousands. **Affectedness ratio: affectedness as a per cent of non-self-employed persons plus unemployed persons in their age cohort.
Source: AMS; own calculations.

Table 9.4   Details of atypical employment in international comparison

	Part-time employment (% of total labour force)			Fixed-term employment (% of all employees)		Temporary employment (% of total labour force)
	1973	2000	Women's share 2000	1983	2000	1999
Belgium	3.8	15.7[c]	89.5[c]	5.4	9.0	1.6
Denmark	22.7[d]	21.7	75.6	12.5	10.2	0.2
Germany	10.1	19.4	85.5	10.0	12.7	0.7
Greece	6.5[e]	4.6	64.8	16.3	13.1	–
Spain	n.a.	8.2	78.2	15.6	32.1	0.8
France	5.9	16.9	69.8	3.3	15.0	2.7
Ireland	5.1[d]	16.6	74.9	6.1	4.6	0.2
Italy	6.4	8.8	72.8	6.6	10.1	–
Luxembourg	5.8	11.3	90.3	2.3	3.4	–
Netherlands	16.6[d]	41.2	73.4	5.8	14.0	4.0
Austria	6.4	17.0	85.5	6.0[a]	7.9	0.7
Portugal	7.8[d]	10.7	69.2	14.4	20.4	1.0
Finland	6.7[d]	12.2	65.7	11.1	17.7	–
Sweden	23.6[d]	22.8	76.3	12.0	14.7	0.8
UK	16.0	24.9	80.1	5.5	6.7	2.1
USA	15.6	13.3	68.4	–	2.2[b]	1.8[b]

[a]Dates Austria are for 1995; [b]1994 for fixed-term employment, 1995 for temporary employment; [c]1998; [d]1979; [e]1983.
Sources: OECD *Employment Outlook* (1973 for part-time, and 1983 for fixed term employment as for the USA in general); Eurostat Labour Force Survey and Panorama of EU Industry, Brussels 1997, 25/76 for temporary employment in the USA.

(in 2001: ATS[20] 4076 per month), which, consequently, are treated differently for the purpose of social security (selective integration since 1996). In the past, this form of employment was completely excluded from social insurance schemes (with the exception of work-accident insurance). In 2003 there were more than 200,000 persons registered as carrying out 'marginal part-time jobs'.

In many cases atypical employment is not only connected with low and/or unsteady income, but also provides only selective admittance to social security schemes. This applies especially for those occupations which are on the border between dependent and self-employed occupation (the so-called 'free service contracts', 'new self-employed' and 'quasi-self-employed', respectively) as well as for marginal part-time employment.

Altogether, it is certainly true that in Austria the predominant majority of all forms of employment are still so-called 'standard working contracts', or 'regular forms of employment', and presumably great changes will not occur in this regard within the next few years. However, it is quite evident that the number of occupations that deviate from this norm, with regard to continuity and full-time status, and that offer sufficient material and social security, is steadily increasing. These changes in the environment of the welfare state affect the welfare state itself, a fact clearly seen in the various problems arising.

Unemployment which has been steadily increasing up to 1999, a strong rise in the number of claimants (e.g. for early retirement), growing life expectancy, slow wage growth and the occurrence of atypical forms of employment (especially part-time employment), as well as strategies aimed at budget consolidation, have all intensified *financial problems*. It is evident that these changes have a stronger impact on systems mainly funded by social insurance fees, which are based upon wages, than on systems that to a larger degree are financed on the basis of general taxes. The disparity between insurance contribution receipts and expenditures in Austria is steadily growing, especially in the area of statutory pension schemes. But financial problems are discernible in the sphere of health insurance as well.

Beside these quantitative problems, there are others of a *qualitative* nature, as for example exclusion from the social security system where part of the unemployed (according to AMS data, about 10 per cent) are not entitled to unemployment benefits or unemployment assistance as they do not meet the eligibility criteria. As these data include only unemployed persons registered at an employment office, the number of unemployed persons who receive neither unemployment benefits nor unemployment assistance is often underestimated. According to the *Labour Market Survey* carried out for Eurostat[21] each year in the form of a random sample survey, almost 30 per cent of all unemployed in Austria in 1998 (36 per cent of all women, 25 per cent of all men) did not get any insurance benefits.[22]

At the same time, the employment- and earnings-orientation of the Austrian old-age social security system also gives rise to considerable problems, particularly for women. Estimates of the Federation of Austrian Social Security Institutions[23] from 1998 show that the number of women over 65, residing in Austria, who had no claim to an own or derived old-age pension was about 150,000, which is in fact almost one-fifth of the whole resident female population of this age group.[24] Likewise, in the mid-1990s, about 410,000 women aged 60 or over, which corresponds to 41 per cent of the whole female population of this age group, had no claim to an *own* old-age pension.[25]

In the context of lingering labour market problems, an increase of unemployment and the proliferation of atypical forms of employment, it becomes evident that social security facilities at this stage cannot rule out impoverishment of individuals, even in cases where there is eligibility for benefits. The available data on unemployment benefits and unemployment assistance show that for a considerable proportion of all persons concerned – of

Table 9.5   (Danger of) poverty level among various population groups, 1999

Population groups	Endangered persons (%) within group	Poor** persons (%)	Poor persons***
Employees	5	2	89,000
Self-employed	15	4*	19,000
Short-term unemployed	10	6	39,000
Long-term unemployed	30	13	48,000
Retired persons	22	7	102,000
Single parents	13	7	30,000
MPH +1****	5	0*	5,000*
MPH +2	7	3	67,000
MPH +3	17	4	43,000
Foreign workers (non-EU)	18	4*	15,000*
Total Population	11	4	296,000

*Low absolute composition of group; ** Poor person: low income together with other relevant restrictions; *** In absolute figures 296,000 persons count as being poor. As persons may belong to more than one group, the sum of the column is not 296,000; **** Households with more than one person plus 1 child etc.
Source: ECHP.[26]

which females are in the majority – the benefits are from low to extremely low. If we use the means-tested equalization supplement reference rate for pension insurance as our 'starting point' – €705 (converted on a monthly basis) in 2000 – which is generally regarded as the poverty level, we have to concede that about half of all unemployment benefits are below this level, and that as much as 70 per cent of all female claimants fall below this threshold. Even more serious is the situation regarding unemployment assistance. In 2000, more than 70 per cent of all men and about 90 per cent of all women drew benefits below the equalization supplement reference rate.

At the same time, a comparison of data bifurcated on the basis of sex clearly shows significant variations in old-age pension standards and that they are very low for many recipients. Even with new entrants, the median direct pension of women in 2002 was not even half the male median direct pension. At the same time almost half of all old-age pensions paid to women were below the equalization supplement reference rate, whereas this was true in the case of less than 10 per cent of men.

Poverty reports of recent years show that even a rich country such as Austria is confronted with the problem of the imminent danger of pauperization and risks of destitution (see Table 9.5). The conclusion is that about 11 per cent of the population have a weighted per capita income of less than

60 per cent of the median per capita income of the resident population. These persons are considered as being endangered by poverty. If other conditions, for example substandard living conditions or debts with regular payments occur in addition to low income, people can be regarded as poor according to general definitions: this is true for about 4 per cent of the whole population.

Clearly, despite its expansion and relatively high risk coverage, the Austrian welfare state is confronted with a multitude of problems. Most of them are the result of changing basic framework conditions (like a diminished economic growth rate, ageing of society, spreading of atypical employment, rising unemployment rate) on the one hand, and the problem that most of the welfare programmes and systems are strongly linked to employment and marital status on the other. Offe (1995) suggests that systems of this kind, for which a tight coupling between gainful occupation and the social security system is characteristic, show a 'constructional defect' in several respects.[27] Although we do not want to follow this judgement outright, still we assume that against the background of changed framework conditions, social security systems that are mainly related to employment and family status ought to be supplemented by adding instruments of basic and minimum social benefits and/or guaranteed minimum income. However, till now this topic has not been put onto the current political agenda in Austria. However, this is just one aspect. In view of the changed constellation of political power since early 2000, we can expect alterations that point in the direction of a significant reorientation or turnaround concerning social policy in Austria. This transition, however, mainly shows signs of being a restrictive reorientation and thus does not seem to aim at a problem-orientated solution whose principal intention would be to solve social (and not predominantly budgetary) problems. Recent measures focus primarily on the quantitative problems of the Austrian welfare state system (that is, financing problems) while ignoring qualitative aspects that deal with the capability of specific welfare programmes to solve social problems. Nevertheless, these restrictive tendencies in the development of social policy in Austria did not begin just with the above-mentioned political change, they had already become apparent – albeit to lesser extent – during the 1990s.

Key developments of the 1990s

While the trend to the beginning of the 1990s comprised expansions as well as restrictions with regard to existing welfare programmes, from the mid-1990s the development became rather one-way and became fixed upon the option of a clearly restrictive policy of (defensive) 'adaptation'. The result of this trend is a number of measures in the area of social insurance and family benefits, which 'led to restrictions or even a rescinding of previous regulatives'.[28] In addition, these politics of adaptation also had an impact on the sphere of employment law (for example regarding the enforcement of increased labour market flexibility). Besides, EEA and EU membership[29] directly required some new arrangements, while others were indirectly linked with Austria's accession, for example the obligation to uphold budget discipline.[30]

As already mentioned, development up to the 1990s was not marked solely by restrictive options, as was evident in the labour legislation[31] and also in a set of arrangements in social insurance programmes – for example the introduction of an own retirement pension insurance for unpaid partners in agriculture (1991), the possibility for joining the public retirement pension insurance system voluntarily, independent of gainful occupation (1992), or the implementation of long-term care benefit (1993). So far as unemployment assistance is concerned, since 1988 women whose partners are full-time employees are also entitled to benefit, and since 1989 foreigners (under certain conditions). Furthermore, in the unemployment insurance scheme a uniform net compensation rate was introduced, which had a beneficial effect on low income recipients.

At the same time, we find increasingly restrictive arrangements on unemployment benefits – for example, the repeated reduction of the net compensation rate of unemployment benefit for higher income brackets (1993, 1995) and the extension of the calculation period for unemployment benefit to one year (1996). These measures have also had a potentially negative impact on a possible subsequent period of unemployment assistance. In addition, the requirements for access to unemployment benefits were repeatedly tightened (1991, 1993, 1995), as were the sanctions against abuse in terms of the Unemployment Insurance Act (1996). Likewise, restrictive tendencies can be noticed in retirement pension and family benefits schemes. In the course of the 1990s, for example, regulations on reduced payment for early retirement were tightened (1996) and the required waiting period was lengthened (1996). As far as family benefits are concerned, the 'policy of adaptation' of the 1990s led to a reduction of family allowances, the elimination of birth-allowance, the reduction in parental leave benefits, and the tightening of eligibility for special unemployment assistance. As far as health insurance is concerned, the retained amount (of non-reimbursed benefit) was raised and a prescription fee was introduced in the middle of the 1990s.

The effects of Austria's membership of the European Union have not been uniform. Although the modified general settings forced the expansion of social regulation and provisions in some areas, the requirements for budget discipline (that is the Maastricht criteria for EMU[32]), however, had and still have negative effects on social benefits in their respective national implementation.

Regarding the expansion of social regulations, a series of adaptations in industrial law were necessary. In this area, EU Directives pertaining to employees' protection, protection of employees in cases of mass-dismissal and takeover of a firm, employees' information about their contracts of employment, equal treatment of sexes, maternity protection, and application of national social systems to migrant workers, all had to be transformed into national law. Relatively high significance is attributed to the adjustment of Austrian law to Community law regarding sexual discrimination.[33] In the realm of active labour market policies, the consequence of joining the European Union is an expanding radius of activity. After having traditionally played a relatively unimportant role in Austria, active labour market policy was allocated higher resources in the 1990s. Enhancement of expenditure on active labour market programmes (up to 0.52 per cent of GDP in 1999; OECD 2000: 249) can be traced back to the resources that were conceded from the ESF,[34] as well as to the additional resources used from a transformation of 'passive funds' into such active measures, as suggested in the 'Employment Guidelines' of the EU.

All in all, it is obvious that Austria's accession to the EU has led to an extension of the welfare state in some areas. Otherwise, the financial restrictions which accompanied the decision to participate in the first wave of the monetary union had a negative impact on social security systems. However, the decision for budget consolidation, which was made by the government, seems to represent the most obvious impact of EU membership on the Austrian social system.[35] EU membership, plans to join EMU, and the prospect of the country's budget coming increasingly under the spotlight of international assessment and evaluation, have cumulatively placed Austria's government under political pressure to push through radical budget cuts and have provided the justification for doing so. Pertinently, the restrictive measures introduced in the areas of unemployment insurance, family benefits, health insurance and retirement pensions go back to the mid-1990s, and form part of the 'austerity packages' of 1995 and 1996.

The new turn: alignment of social policy to the neo-liberal conservative mainstream

Certainly during the last decades, neither stagnancy nor a clear-cut break has occurred in Austria's social policy.[36] Still, a clear shift in social policy plans and measures can be perceived under the first term of the centre-right coalition government of ÖVP and FPÖ in office between February 2000 and November 2002. The programme of this government – as expressed in governmental conventions, budget speeches and statements of representatives of the government coalition – has focused on central issues of neo-liberal social and welfare policy.[37] A core element has been the 'slimming down' of state-controlled tasks pertaining to 'more self-responsibility'. This plea for a 'slim state' correlates with the plea for a substantial change in the traditional system of social security. 'New Social Security' has – as indicated in the wording of the government programme – a fundamentally different approach.

This new approach implies a new prioritization of social policy in two respects: first, the alignment of the welfare state to individual distress and need. This alignment of social policy with the need for assistance if entirely implemented would amount to a reorientation of the present welfare state, which is concentrated on the provision for risk for the economically active population on the one hand *and* help for needy persons on the other, towards a 'social assistance state' *à la* Thatcherism.[38] Secondly, this reorientation would entail the subordination of social policy to budget, economic and competitiveness priorities, which together would mean a massive reduction of protective social policy measures and programmes.

Socio-politically, conservative concepts have continuously influenced the Austrian welfare state leading to compromises between the divergent options of the relevant actors. Crucial aspects in this connection are specific notions on marriage (legally fixed as a heterosexual couple), on family (as a form of cohabitation of both parents with their children), and on the specific form of derived provision for women in public social insurance – in short: man as the breadwinner, woman as responsible for family reproduction.[39] The coalition government of ÖVP and FPÖ intended to maintain and in specific fields even to reinforce these conservative traditions, as programme statements about family, child allowance and compatibility of job and family show.

Soon after assuming office in February 2000, the first coalition government of ÖVP and FPÖ took initiatives to bring about extensive changes (for example, 150 Days of Austria's New Government) in all areas of social policy[40] – even against substantial public opposition and in avoidance of the involvement of social partners.

In the sphere of old-age pensions, the policy of the former SPÖ/ÖVP-coalition,[41] which had started restrictive arrangements with its 'austerity packages' (1995/96) and the reform of old-age pensions (1997), has been intensified. The age for early retirement was raised by 1.5 years within a very short transitional period. The deduction of 2 per cent in cases of early retirement before the age of 60 (for women) and 65 (for men) respectively was raised to 3 per cent, and a reduction of widow's and widower's pensions was introduced.

Under cover of an 'increase of social targeting accuracy', a number of benefit reductions were carried out with the aim of achieving budget consolidation and zero deficit: non-contributory co-insurance for childless spouses or long-time companions, for example, has been abolished – with only few exceptions. The additional revenue will not be used for health insurance but for the budget. The taxation of benefits (due to an accident at work or an occupational disease) is an innovation, just as the intensification of sanctions in case of termination of a working contract by the employee. At the same time, unemployment benefits have been reduced, the net compensation rate has been decreased (from 57 per cent to 55 per cent), the family supplement has been considerably reduced, and controls and sanctions regarding persons entitled to obtain unemployment benefits have been intensified. Furthermore, regulations concerning the health system include the raising of prescription charges and the introduction of a co-payment for out-patient visits.

In tune with the neo-liberal and conservative intentions of the first coalition government of the ÖVP and FPÖ have been further plans to modify Austria's social policy. Examples are the envisaged introduction of a legal obligation to take out *a* health insurance instead of the present compulsory statutory health insurance (that is, promoting the opting-out of the statutory insurance scheme), and the plans for a radical transformation of the pension system into a three-pillar model.

In autumn 2002 the first coalition government of ÖVP and FPÖ resigned on the background of growing inner-party tensions within the FPÖ. In the following election of November 2002 the FPÖ lost heavily, where as ÖVP came off as the strongest party for the first time since 1966. Together, ÖVP and FPÖ gained a majority for a second period and took office in February 2003 after lengthy negotiations. This second coalition government of ÖVP and FPÖ, probably misinterpreting the outcome of the 2002 election as a general vote for welfare state retrenchment, is now about to implement large-scale structural reforms in the unemployment and pension systems. The latter will bring benefit reductions of up to 20 per cent (and in specific cases even more) in the long run. At the same time signs of occurrence of legitimacy problems are evident, as surveys and regional elections show that support for the ÖVP-FPÖ coalition is shrinking to a large degree.

It appears that the performance objectives and measures of the current social policy underline that Austria now follows a certain developmental pattern in the direction of a 'neo-liberal-conservative about-turn', contrived for many highly industrialized countries of the Western world much earlier.[42] The thesis that in Austria fast political change could hardly be realized due to the relatively high importance of so-called 'vetoplayers',[43] might have to be reconsidered against the background of the speed of recent reforms.[44] However, the enforcement of reforms has been made easier by the fact that the vast majority of the administrations of the provinces (*Bundesländer*) are dominated by the federal governmental parties. At the same time, the weakening of the social partners,[45] which had already started a few years ago, made it easier to exclude them from decision-making to an even wider extent and to decide measures against their (mainly the trade unions') will.

At the same time, developments of the last decade and the changes in social policy apparent under the ÖVP–FPÖ-government show that purely functional attempts alone cannot deal with the whole problem: international changes in political options and strategies in the area of social policy cannot simply be explained as the consequence of changed economic conditions or industrial globalization, and thus be reduced merely to 'practical constraints'. It is evident that even under the condition of internationalization of business relations and integration into an institution such as the EU, the nation-state's policies still have a relevant role to play. During recent years Austrian development has moved in the direction of reinforced neoliberal and neo-conservative strategies. The acceleration and amplification of this trend, which has been done through political change, shows that it does make a difference, which societal objectives are pursued by a national government (or not) and how much power other interest groups can display.

Conclusion: alternatives to current policy

A progressive enforcement of the individualization and privatization of social risks, as has already been carried out by the ÖVP-FPÖ government between 2000 and 2002, will not be able to remove the deficiencies in modern societies' abilities to solve social problems. Far from it. The general and extensive reduction of the welfare state would have precarious consequences even in a rich country like Austria. As far as the primary distribution of incomes is concerned, more than 40 per cent of the whole population are situated – according to the European Household Panel Survey (1999) – below the level of a weighted per capita income of ATS 130,667 per year.[46] All these persons can be regarded as being at risk from poverty. In view of diverse social benefits the proportion of persons who are actually below this level, becomes reduced to about 11 per cent of the entire population. The poverty gap, the difference between the poverty level and the average equivalence income of poor persons, amounts to 68 per cent before drawing of social benefits, and becomes reduced to 17 per cent after availing of social benefits.

However, against this background, not only that a general reduction of social benefits can prove critical, there is a need for the extension of specific programmes. As soon as it becomes clear that the trend towards atypical employment, the diversification of family structures and so on is progressing, reforms of a strongly employment-related social system are essential – but somewhat different from the political measures which are planned, or that have been executed lately, in Austria.

Important measures in this context would be to accord equal status for both atypical employment and normal labour contracts at all levels of association (in law, collective negotiations and contracts within the company) – together with equal status as far as qualification, advancement and company social benefits are concerned. Even though such measures might appear hard to carry through and their actual impact may be doubtful,[47] activities in this area are essential because of their importance for shaping political awareness. An alternative to a policy of reinforcing the interdependence of employment and social security, and of transforming the welfare state system towards means-tested benefits, is to supplement the existing social systems. Such supplements could be provided (i) by introducing a means-tested basic protection to enlarge the existing institutions of social insurance by introducing minimum standards (this would involve tax-financed instruments within the existing system with the aim of preventing poverty in case of unemployment, invalidity, old age or single-parent status);[48] and (ii) by introducing a basic retirement pension for all, which could supplement the employment and earnings-related pension scheme and which would be free from labour market and family status constraints.

There is scope for further social reforms in Austria in areas like employment and (primary) income and social transfers. But, in order to justify appropriate measures in the area of social security, it is not necessary to go for further deregulation of employment relationships, as is occasionally suggested in connection with governance options such as the so-called 'flexicurity'.[49] The present size and distribution of atypical forms of employment throughout Europe, and the growing variation and unsteadiness in employment, indicate that no further strategies of labour-market deregulation are necessary in order to justify an adaptation of instruments of social security which is not driven primarily by budget concerns but which is motivated by the aim of solving the problems of social inequality and exclusion.

Notes

1 G. Esping-Andersen, 'Towards a Post-industrial Welfare State', *Internationale Politik und Gesellschaft*, Bonn, no. 3, 1997, pp. 237–45; P. Pierson (ed.), *The New Politics of the Welfare State*, Oxford & New York: Oxford University Press, 2001; P. Taylor-Gooby (ed.), *Welfare States under Pressure*, London *et al.*: Sage, 2001.

2 J. Alber, *Vom Armenhaus zum Wohlfahrtsstaat*, Frankfurt/New York: Campus, 1982; P. Flora, 'Introduction', in P. Flora (ed.), *Growth to Limits*, Vol. 1, Berlin and New York: de Gruyter, 1986, p. xii; R. Mishra, *The Welfare State in Capitalist Society*, Hertfordshire: Harvester Wheatsheaf, 1990, p. 12.

3 J. Schmid, *Wohlfahrts-Staaten im Vergleich*, Opladen: Leske & Budrich, 2002, p. 47. See also, for example, A. Cochrane and J. Clarke (eds), *Comparing Welfare States: Britain in International Context*, London: Sage, 1993, chapter 9.

4 C. Offe 'Schock, Fehlkonstrukt oder Droge? Über drei Lesarten der Sozialstaatskrise', in W. Fricke (ed.), *Zukunft des Sozialstaates, Jahrbuch für Arbeit und Technik*, Bonn: Dietz, 1995, pp. 31–41; E. Tálos and H. Obinger 'Sozialstaaten nach dem "goldenen Zeitalter", Eine Einleitung', in E. Tálos (ed.), *Soziale Sicherung im Wandel, Österreich und seine Nachbarstaaten im Vergleich*, Wien *et al.*: Böhlau, 1998, pp. 7–30.

5 B. Jessop, 'Towards a Schumpeterian Workfare State? Preliminary Remarks on post-Fordist Political Economy', *Studies in Political Economy*, Ottawa, no. 40, 1993, pp. 7–39; B. Jessop, 'Post-Fordism and the State', in A. Amin (ed.), *Post-Fordism, A Reader*, Oxford *et al.*: Blackwell, 1994, pp. 251–79; B. Jessop, *Narrating the Future*

of the National Economy and the National State? Department of Sociology, Lancaster University 1999, at http://www.comp.lancaster.ac.uk/sociology/soc014rj.html

6   J. Schmid and R. Niketta, 'Wohlfahrtsstaat: Krise und Reform im Vergleich, Einführung in die Thematik und in den Band', in J. Schmid and R. Niketta (eds), *Wohlfahrtsstaat: Krise und Reform im Vergleich*, Marburg: Metropolis, 1998, p. 18ff.

7   G. Esping-Andersen, 'After the Golden Age? Welfare State Dilemmas in a Global Economy', in G. Esping-Andersen (ed.), *Welfare States in Transition*, London *et al.*: Sage, 1996, p. 6.

8   G. Esping-Andersen, *ibid.*, p. 6; J.D. Stephens, E. Huber and R. Leonard, 'The Welfare State in Hard Times', in H. Kitschelt *et al.* (eds), *Convergence and Divergence in Contemporary Capitalism*, Cambridge: Cambridge University Press, pp. 192–3; D. Swank, 'Political Institutions and Welfare State restructuring: The Impact of Institutions on Social Policy Change in Developed Democracies, in P. Pierson (ed.), *The New Politics of the Welfare State*, Oxford and New York: Oxford University Press, 2001, pp. 197–237.

9   J. Alber, *Vom Armenhaus zum Wohlfahrtsstaat*, Frankfurt/New York: Campus, 1982; M.G. Schmidt, *Sozialpolitik in Deutschland, historische Entwicklung und internationaler Vergleich*, 2nd edn, Opladen: Leske & Budrich, 1998.

10 G. Esping-Andersen, *The Three Worlds of Welfare Capitalism*, Cambridge: Polity Press, 1990; St Leibfried 'Sozialstaat Europa?', *Nachrichtendienst des deutschen Vereins für öffentliche und private Fürsorge*, Frankfurt/Main, no. 70, 1990, pp. 295–305.

11 E. Tálos, *Staatliche Sozialpolitik in Österreich*, Wien: Verlag für Gesellschaftskritik, 1981; H. Hofmeister, 'Ein Jahrhundert Sozialversicherung in Österreich', in A. Köhler and H.F. Zacher (eds), *Ein Jahrhundert Sozialversicherung*, Berlin: Duncker & Humboldt, 1981, pp. 445–721.

12 E. Tálos, 'Sozialpolitik im Austrofaschismus', in E. Tálos and W. Neugebauer (eds), '*Austrofaschismus*', Wien: Verlag für Gesellschaftskritik, 1988, pp. 161–78; E. Tálos, 'Sozialpolitik in der "Ostmark", Angleichung und Konsequenzen', in E. Tálos, E. Hanisch, W. Neugebauer and R. Sieder (eds), *NS-Herrschaft in Österreich: Ein Handbuch*, Wien, ÖBV and HPT, 2000, pp. 376–408.

13 P. Flora, 'Introduction', in P. Flora (ed.), *Growth to Limits*, Vol. 1, Berlin and New York: de Gruyter, 1986, pp. xi–xxxvi.

14 See e.g. G. Esping-Andersen, 'After the Golden Age? Welfare State Dilemmas in a Global Economy', in G. Esping-Andersen (ed.), *Welfare States in Transition*, London *et al.*: Sage, 1996, pp. 1–31; G. Esping-Andersen, 'Towards a Post-industrial Welfare State', *Internationale Politik und Gesellschaft*, Bonn, no. 3, 1997, pp. 237–45; D. Swank, 'Political Institutions and Welfare State Restructuring: The Impact of Institutions on Social Policy Change in Developed Democracies', in P. Pierson (ed.), *The New Politics of the Welfare State*, Oxford and New York: Oxford University Press, 2001, pp. 197–237.

15 G. Esping-Andersen, 'After the Golden Age? Welfare State Dilemmas in a Global Economy', in G. Esping-Andersen (ed.), *Welfare States in Transition*, London *et al.*: Sage, 1996, pp. 1–31; St Leibfried and P. Pierson, 'Halbsouveräne Wohlfahrtsstaaten: Der Sozialstaat in der Europäischen Mehrebenen-Politik', in St Leibfried and P. Pierson (eds), *Standort Europa, Sozialpolitik zwischen Nationalstaat und Europäischer Integration*, Frankfurt/Main: Suhrkamp, 1995, pp. 83–5; J. Schmid and R. Niketta, 'Wohlfahrtsstaat: Krise und Reform im Vergleich, Einführung in die Thematik und in den Band', in J. Schmid and R. Niketta (eds), *Wohlfahrtsstaat: Krise und Reform im Vergleich*, Marburg: Metropolis, 1998, pp.

17–19; R.G. Heinze, J. Schmid and Chr. Stünck, *Vom Wohlfahrtsstaat zum Wettbewerbsstaat, Arbeitsmarkt- und Sozialpolitik in den 90er Jahren,* Opladen: Leske & Budrich, 1999, pp. 23–5.

16 ÖSTAT = Statistical Office of Austria (*Österreichisches Statistisches Zentralamt*).

17 HV = Federation of Austrian Social Security Institutions (*Hauptverband der Österreichischen Sozialversicherungsträger*). AMS = Austrian Labour Market Service (*Arbeitsmarktservice Österreich*).

18 U. Mückenberger, 'Die Krise des Normalarbeitsverhältnisses', *Zeitschrift für Sozialreform,* Wiesbaden, no. 31, 1985, pp. 415–34.

19 M. Fink, 'Atypische Beschäftigung und deren politische Steuerung im internationalen Vergleich', *Österreichische Zeitschrift für Politikwissenschaft,* Wien, no. 4/2000, pp. 401–15; E. Tálos (ed.), *Atypische Beschäftigung. Internationale Trends und sozialstaatliche Regelungen,* Wien: Manz, 1999.

20 ATS = Austrian schillings (13,7603 ATS = 1 euro = 1,07084 US$).

21 Eurostat = Statistical Office of the European Union.

22 Eurostat, *Erhebung über Arbeitskräfte, Ergebnisse 1998,* Brussels: Eurostat, 1999.

23 That is, that recipients of civil servants' pensions are not included.

24 H. Stefanits *et al.,* Vom Leistungsbezieher zum Pensionisten, Soziale Sicherheit, Wien, no. 4/1999, pp. 299–301.

25 *Weibuch der SPÖ-Frauenvorsitzenden, Eigenständige Alterssicherung für Frauen,* Wien: SPÖ, 1997, p. 6.

26 ECHP = European Community Household Panel Survey.

27 C. Offe, 'Schock, Fehlkonstrukt oder Droge? Über drei Lesarten der Sozialstaatskrise', in W. Fricke (ed.), *Zukunft des Sozialstaates, Jahrbuch für Arbeit und Technik,* Bonn: Dietz, 1995, pp. 31–41.

28 M. Hörndler and K. Wörister, *Soziales Österreich: Sicherungssysteme im Überblick,* Wien: Bundesministerium für Arbeit, Gesundheit und Soziales, 1998, p. 112. See also: E. Tálos and K. Wörister, 'Soziale Sicherung in Österreich', in E. Tálos (ed.), *Soziale Sicherung im Wandel, Österreich und seine Nachbarstaaten im Vergleich,* Wien *et al.*: Böhlau, 1998, pp. 209–88.

29 EEA = European Economic Area.

30 E. Tálos and Chr Badelt, 'The Welfare State between New Stimuli and New Pressures: Austrian Social Policy and the EU', *Journal of European Social Policy,* Thousand Oaks, vol. 9(4), 1999, p. 353.

31 E. Tálos and B. Kittel, 'Sozialpartnerschaft und Sozialpolitik', in F. Karlhofer and E. Tálos (eds), *Zukunft der Sozialpartnerschaft, Veränderungsdynamik und Reformbedarf,* Wien: Signum, 1999, p. 141.

32 EMU = European Monetary Union.

33 G. Falkner, 'Österreichische Gleichbehandlungspolitik und das EU-Recht', *Bericht über die Situation der Frauen in Österreich,* Wien: Bundesministerin für Frauenangelegenheiten and Bundeskanzleramt, 1995, pp. 416–28; E. Tálos and Chr Badelt, 'The Welfare State between New Stimuli and New Pressures: Austrian Social Policy and the EU', *Journal of European Social Policy,* Thousand Oaks, vol. 9(4), 1999, p. 353.

34 ESF = European Social Fund.

35 E. Tálos and Chr Badelt, n. 34, p. 353.

36 E. Tálos and K. Wörister, 'Soziale Sicherung in Österreich', in E. Tálos (ed.), *Soziale Sicherung im Wandel, Österreich und seine Nachbarstaaten im Vergleich,* Wien *et al.*: Böhlau, 1998, p. 282.

37 See e.g. Austrian Federal Government, *150 Days of Austria's New Government (150 Tage Österreich neu regieren. Ein parlamentarische Bilanz),* Wien, 10 July 2000.

38 B. Jessop, 'Thatcherismus und die Neustrukturierung der, Sozialpolitik –
    Neoliberalismus und die Zukunft des Wohlfahrtsstaates, *Zeitschrift für Sozialreform*,
    Wiesbaden, no. 11/12 , 1992, pp. 709–34.
39 S. Leitner, *Frauen und Männer im Wohlfahrtsstaat*, Frankfurt *et al.*: Lang, 1999. I.
    Mairhuber, *Die Regulierung des Geschlechterverhältnisses im Sozialstaat Österreich*,
    Frankfurt *et al.*: Lang, 1999.
40 *Documents of the AK 2000 (Unterlagen der AK Wien)*, Das Arbeitsrecht-Paket,
    Arbeitsmarktpolitische Begleitmaßnahmen zum Pensionspaket, Berufsausbil-
    dungspaket, Das Pensionspaket, Das 'Treffsicherheits'-Paket, Wien, 2000; J.
    Wöss, 'Sozialabbau treffsicher. Eine Bestandsaufnahme der Sozialpolitik der neuen Bun-
    desregierung', *Arbeit und Wirtschaft*, Wien, no. 12, 2000, pp. 12–17.
41 Coalition between the Austrian Social Democratic Party (*Sozialdemokratische Partei
    Österreichs, SPÖ*) and the Austrian Peoples Party (*Österreichische Volkspartei, ÖVP*).
42 J. Schmid, *Wohlfahrts-Staaten im Vergleich*, Opladen: Leske & Budrich, 2002, p. 47.
    See also e.g.: A. Cochrane and J. Clarke (eds), *Comparing Welfare States: Britain in
    International Context*, London: Sage, 1993, chapter 9.
43 G. Tsebelis, 'Decision Making in Political Systems: Veto Players in Presidential-
    ism, Parliamentarism, Multicameralism and Multipartyism', *British Journal of Polit-
    ical Science*, Essex, vol. 25, 1995, pp. 289–325.
44 Austria is allocated a relatively high to very high 'vetoplayer-index', see e.g. U.
    Wagschal, 'Besonderheiten der gezügelten Sozialstaaten', in H. Obinger and U.
    Wagschal (eds), *Der gezügelte Wohlfahrtsstaat, Sozialpolitik in reichen Industrienatio-
    nen*, Frankfurt/New York: Campus, 2000, p. 58; H. Obinger on the background of
    the actual development comes to the conclusion that the power of vetoplayers
    in Austria is overestimated by such indexes or that it has at least declined
    significantly in recent years; see H. Obinger, 'Vetospieler und Staatätigkeit in
    Österreich, Sozial- und wirtschaftspolitische Reformchancen für die neue Mitte-
    Rechts-Regierung', *Zeitschrift für Parlamentsfragen*, vol. 32, 2001, pp. 360–86.
45 These are not regarded as 'Side-government' in a classical sense, because their
    importance in the process of decision-making is not legally accepted or is only
    very limited (assessment procedure etc.). That is why the Social Partners have
    been called 'informal vetoplayers'; see H. Obinger, *ibid*.
46 Traditional OECD scale (ECHP, 2000). Evaluation according to modified scale is
    not available.
47 M. Fink, 'Atypische Beschäftigung und deren politische Steuerung im interna-
    tionalen Vergleich', *Österreichische Zeitschrift für Politikwissenschaft*, Wien, no.
    4/2000, pp. 401–15.
48 G. Bäcker-Breil, 'Das Reformkonzept der bedarfsorientierten Grundsicherung.
    Begründing – Grundelement – Rahmenbedingungen', in Österreichisches Netzw-
    erk gegen Armut und soziale Ausgrenzung (ed.), *Dokumentation: Zweite Österre-
    ichische Armutskonferenz 20–21 Jänner 1997*, Thema: Soziale Grundsicherung,
    Salzburg, Österreichisches Netzwerk gegen Armut und soziale Ausgrenzung,
    p. 38; G. Bäcker and W. Hanesch, *Arbeitnehmer und Arbeitnehmerhaushalte
    mit Niedrigeinkommen*, NRW Landessozialbericht Band 7, Ministerium für Arbeit,
    Gesundheit und Soziales des Landes Nordrhein-Westfalen, 1998, p. 397; E. Tálos
    (ed.), *Bedarfsorientiert Grundsicherung*, Wien: Mandelbaum, 2003.
49 B. Keller and H. Seifert, 'Flexicurity – das Konzept für mehr soziale Sicherheit flex-
    ibler Beschäftigung', WSI-Mitteilungen, Frankfurt/Main, no. 5, 2000, pp.
    291–300; T. Wilthagen, *Flexicurity: A New Paradigm for Labour Market Policy Reform*,
    WZB Discussion Paper FS, I pp. 98–202, Berlin: WZB, 1998.

10
The Swedish Welfare State and New Challenges

Nimmi Kurian

Introduction

The Swedish welfare state system has come to be regarded as a model worthy of emulation across the world. Sweden has built an advanced cradle-to-grave welfare state system around Per Albin Hansson's concept of *Folkhemmet* (People's Home), because of its extensive service orientation in which benefits are based on people's needs and are distributed universally without discrimination. The Swedish model has also been called the 'Middle Way', as it presents a viable third approach between the two poles symbolized by a free market economy and a centrally planned economy. The Swedish model presents a viable mix, wherein competitive allocation of resources and private ownership of the means of production coexists with the deep ideological commitment towards a welfare state.

This chapter looks at the crisis of the 1990s when Sweden experienced a severe recession, and its impact on the welfare state system. We shall argue that the welfare state was not the cause of the recession, and that the downturn can be traced to the tax reforms undertaken in 1991. The system has shown resilience and steered through the crisis by making some marginal modifications – largely by tightening benefits and by providing space for privatization of service delivery. The modifications thus brought about in the 1990s do not constitute a rollback or dismantling of the welfare state system, rather the response has shown the system's adaptability to meet new challenges and social needs.

While all modern welfare states profess to strive towards a fair distribution of well-being to their citizens, there exists pronounced differences between them on various counts, be they of form or of content. Thus, welfare states will differ from one another as far as their goals, organization or the levels of social spending are concerned. As a result, there have emerged different expressions of the same idea in different countries, each with its own national flavour, reflecting distinct national priorities, circumstances and identities. At the core is a crucial dilemma which each welfare state seeks to resolve in its characteristic fashion: Is welfare a public or a private good?[1] If for instance, social insurance, health and education are defined as public goods, it then implies that these goods will be available to all without exclusion. Gösta Esping-Andersen has identified 'three worlds' of welfare capitalism, namely the corporate welfare model, the liberal welfare model and the social democratic model.[2]

The Swedish welfare model

The Swedish welfare state system is interchangeably referred to as the Social Democratic model owing to the dominant role played by the Social Democratic Parties of the region in developing a highly advanced, cradle-to-the-grave welfare state system. Universalism and non-discrimination are the hallmarks of this model with extensive social rights. The distinctive feature of the system is that all citizens are entitled to social rights as a matter of right which is decided by an individual's needs and not by his/her performance in the market. Since it offers universal benefits, the system also enjoys high public support. Such an extensive service orientation of optimal quality has ensured that the role of the market as a co-provider remains minimal. The system is also credited with whittling down social cleavages and can boast of an impressive degree of decommodification. Unlike the liberal welfare state system, the Scandinavian model concerns itself not merely with the alleviation of the lot of the poor, but provides a vast array of services universally.

Such a dense social service network has high maintenance costs and is complex to administer with a high tax burden. But while the maintenance of such a system entails heavy costs, it manages to lower the costs of unproductive expenditure such as unemployment benefits, which the other regimes incur. A productivistic social policy based on an employment-maximization strategy increases the number of taxpayers whereas other regimes reduce them.

A full-employment strategy constitutes a cornerstone of this model, since employment is the *sine qua non* of an individual's welfare. The rationale on which a full-employment strategy rests is the conviction that provision of employment opportunities yields benefits that far outweigh the granting of unemployment benefits. According to Esping-Andersen, the Swedish model

> is unique in its bias towards a 'productivistic' and preventive social policy; it spends relatively little on unemployment benefits but invests heavily in employment, training, job mobility, adult education, the prevention of illness and accidents and family services. It is a welfare state both designed for and dependent upon the minimization of social need and the maximization of employment. The philosophy is that, money spent here creates greater savings elsewhere.[3]

This strategy enables the state to maximize tax revenues and curtail unproductive public expenditure. The state is thus required to provide income security only to a small minority, which may be temporarily displaced from work. This is in contrast to residual welfare states, which frame their social policies towards paying compensation for social problems. Institutional welfare states such as the Nordic countries pursue preventive social policies, and hence the importance accorded to the expansion of employment opportunities. The state thus devotes a substantial portion of welfare expenditure as investments to spur economic growth, which helps to sustain the system. Resource mobilization is sourced by way of a steeply progressive income-tax system. A positivist welfare state presupposes a strong central state both as a regulator and also as a provider of welfare.

The Swedish welfare state model is synonymous with social democracy which was the dominant political force credited with developing this universalistic system of welfare entitlements. Truly, Sweden's success has a great deal to do with policies pursued by the Social Democratic Party (SDP). According to Esping-Andersen, the Swedish welfare state has been endowed with a dual identity: both as a model of a highly advanced welfare state and as a flagship of the achievements of the social democrats.[4] The institutionalization of welfare proceeded simultaneously with the uninterrupted political domination of the Social Democrats for over four decades from 1932 to 1976. This vital fact has enabled the party to realize and implement its welfare state agenda. The SDP has continued to enjoy strong and stable popular support to this day. The party first came to power in the shadow of the Great Depression and geared its policies towards restructuring Swedish society on egalitarian lines. There was a strong ideological commitment to the principle of equal pay for men and women and solidarity wages for lower income groups.

Under the Social Democrats, Sweden built up a highly advanced cradle-to-the-grave welfare state system, successfully combining high economic growth with strong welfare entitlements over a long period. Economic growth in Sweden took off in the last quarter of the nineteenth century when the country changed course from being an exporter of raw materials to developed-country status. It experienced very high rates of growth between 1870 to 1970 with per capita rates among the best in the world. For instance, Sweden's per capita growth was 2.3 per cent between 1870–1913; 1.6 per cent between 1913–50; and 3.3 per cent between 1950–70.[5]

The Swedish model assigned to the state a very active role, which was to concern itself not merely with the alleviation of poverty but to provide optimal and differentiated services to cater to the needs of the influential middle class. This fact necessitated a large public sector and a steeply progressive income tax, the two features which represent an integral part of Sweden's identity. The size of Sweden's public sector has grown steadily and is among the largest in the West, with public expenditure levels close to 65 per cent of its gross national product,[6] compared to 45 per cent in other OECD countries.[7]

A large public sector also created the need for high tax levels. Sweden has a high tax ratio by international standards, with taxes making up close to 51 per cent of GDP in 2003. High tax levels constitute a regular feature of Scandinavian countries. By contrast, in liberal welfare states such as the United Kingdom, Australia and New Zealand, the tax burden is substantially lower. Taxes and social security contributions amounted to 30.4 per cent in Australia, 36.4 per cent in New Zealand and 35.3 per cent in the UK.

The Swedish welfare state model has been anchored in a full employment strategy and marked by a high level of labour-force participation The Swedish model created its distinctive identity by following active labour-market policies, an extensive service orientation and gender equalization measures. Sweden has the largest proportion of women in the workforce; the labour force participation rate is 82.7 per cent for men and 78.7 per cent for women. The large public sector is also a big employer in Sweden. In 1993, the public sector made up 32.4 per cent of total employment.[8] Gender equal-ization policies have been followed and the provision of facilities such as daycare, para-maternity and parental leave have seen a very high participa-tion rate by women. Daycare facilities attract heavy subsidies, amounting to $12,000 per child in a year.[9] State subsidies are also available to private coop-eratives or institutions engaged in the provision of day-care services. But while the state thus allows private providers to operate, it imposes very strin-gent quality and quantity standards under its role as a regulator. And as more and more women enter the workforce, the differentials in men's and women's earnings have shown a declining trend. The availability of gener-ous childcare facilities has also impacted favourably on fertility rates, which have registered a healthy growth. The municipalities have, since the mid-1990s, been directed by law to offer subsidized day-care facilities to all chil-dren, and the expansion of day-care and pre-school facilities has facilitated the entry of women into the workforce. Two-thirds of all children in Sweden (in the age group of one-and-a-half and six years) are entrusted to these day-care centres.

Another important feature of the Swedish system is that the bulk of social services is provided by local government institutions. The central govern-ment has increasingly limited itself to the role of a regulator while public institutions at the local level are entrusted with the responsibility of pro-viding the lion's share of social services. The state as a service provider is limited to only a few services which are national in nature; namely the police, the military and treatment homes for addicts. In its regulatory capac-ity, the state exercises strict control over the quantity and quality of services.

The municipalities are granted enough freedom to enable them to effec-tively meet their obligations. The options available to them include utilizing the services of private organizations or providers as long as they clearly meet laid-down guidelines. Once approved, a private provider can receive subsidies from the municipalities for the services to be rendered. Thus, the local-level institution in Sweden provides the maximum extent of services as well as generates the largest number of jobs. Gun-Britt Andersson has appropriately referred to local government as the place 'where the heart of the much referred to Swedish welfare state is found'.[10]

New challenges

The crisis of the 1990s, when Sweden experienced one of the most severe economic depressions since the 1930s, has been widely viewed as a major challenge to the country's welfare state. The economic difficulties that Sweden has experienced since the 1990s has been cited as stemming from the retarding effects of its active welfare state. There is no arguing that Sweden experienced a severe economic downturn during the last decade. Between 1991 and 1993, the GDP growth rate was negative and over the period 1990–95 it averaged only 0.4 per cent. There was a dramatic rise in unemployment from 1.6 per cent in 1990 to 7.7 per cent in 1993. If one includes those in active labour-market programmes, the respective figures would be 2.1 per cent and 12.5 per cent.

There was also a sharp rise in total government expenditure, as a percentage of GDP from 60 per cent in 1989 to 74.1 per cent in 1993.[11] Sweden's per capita income rank (PPP) slid by 10 per cent during this period to 17 which was poorer than its rank a century ago.[12] There was also a marked deterioration in the position of central government finances; from posting a healthy budget surplus before the crisis struck, the budget turned to a deficit of spectacular proportions. For example, in 1989 the budget surplus was a comfortable Skr 30 billion, but by 1993 it had regressed into a deficit of around Skr 200 billion.

It may be noted that Sweden's economic performance had swung dramatically and became a race to the bottom, all in a span of four years. A country which had a consistently healthy economic performance for over 40 years, had turned, as it were, on its heels and gone under. A crisis of such proportions at once initiates a debate as to what caused such a spectacular decline. Sweden's welfare state has come under siege and critics have attempted to make a quick correlation between the welfare state with its increasing tax burdens and social benefits and economic decline. Based on the 1990s crisis in the Swedish economy, a case has been made that the Swedish welfare state has become far too expensive to uphold and maintain.

There is a persuasive case against such doomsday prophets, however – Walter Korpi and Sten Ljurggren, among others, have provided very convincing alternative interpretations of the post-1990 decline of the Swedish economy. The huge budget deficit which Sweden experienced in the early 1990s came about a direct consequence of the far-reaching tax reforms of 1991. The new tax regime granted substantial tax breaks to high-income earners and did away with the structure of progressive tax rates, which had been the hallmark of the Swedish system. Corporate taxes were axed from 52 per cent to 30 per cent. The adverse effects these measures had on the government's fiscal position was inevitable; between 1990 and 1992, government revenues shrank by Skr 120 billion, due entirely to the liberal tax breaks.[13]

Another factor which intensified the severity of the 1990s crisis was the shifting of the priority of economic policy from maintaining full employment to fighting inflation. Full employment has traditionally formed the cornerstone of the Swedish welfare state, but close on the heels of Sweden's decision to gain entry into the European Union, it decided to align its policies with those followed in the European Union. With Sweden's entry on 1 January 1995, there was increasing demand for 'harmonization' and 'convergence' with the rest of Europe for enhanced economic cooperation. Thus, the long-standing tenet of full employment was jettisoned and Sweden's unemployment insurance programmes were ill-equipped to deal with soaring levels of unemployment.

Today, Sweden has successfully put the crisis behind it and the economy is once again on the growth track.[14] The government remains committed to the goal of full employment and has largely succeeded in meeting the targets set in 1996 to halve unemployment from 8 per cent and to increase the proportion of people in regular employment to 80 per cent.

Impact of the 1990s crisis on social policy

It is important to examine the impact of the crisis on Sweden's social policies. Although Sweden has overcome the economic crisis and returned to a high growth path, has it been able to insulate the welfare state system from it? It is clear that the welfare state has not been immune to the recession, and certain measures taken by the government attest to this fact. There have been marginal adjustments to social entitlements, aimed basically at curbing free-riding tendencies and to shore up individual responsibility. Thus, for instance, waiting days for sickness benefits have been introduced, replacement rates for sickness have been pegged at a lower ceiling of 75 per cent of the wage, as well as a moderate reduction in unemployment benefits and parental leave.

A more important change is being effected in Sweden's pension policy. Together with unemployment benefits, the pension system has formed the edifice of the Scandinavian welfare state. Traditionally, pensions were based on a two-tiered universal system. The first tier of public pensions guarantees a fixed amount as a pension to all who have resided in Sweden for over three years and are 65 and above. Pensions in the second tier include the national supplementary pension that relates pension payment to previous income. In the 1990s, certain radical changes were brought about in the pension system, with a move towards integrating both the basic and additional pensions into one. A contributions-based system is being introduced for the first time with employee contributions to be used to finance pensions. Service for entitlement to full pensions has been raised to 40 years, and efforts are also being made to develop a privately financed pension scheme.

Another important change was the introduction of the voucher system in Sweden's education system in 1992 whereby the government allocates public money to enable students to study at private schools. The programme of voucher implementation marked an important departure in Sweden's educational system that had, for decades, placed overriding emphasis on the principle of equality. The country has traditionally been a big spender on education, spending nearly $7000 a year per student, making up 7.7 per cent of GDP in 1990.[15] Private schools are subject to a high degree of regulation and are required to obtain approvals from the National Agency for Education. Public schools have had near total monopoly with all but 0.6 per cent of school-going children attending private schools. Public schools continue to have a predominant position in the country's educational system, notwithstanding the voucher experiment. The introduction of the voucher system was an initiative undertaken by Carl Bildt's government in 1992 which saw its victory after six decades of SDP rule to be an indication that 'collectivism and socialism have been thrown on the scrap heap of history'. The decision was taken to decentralize the educational system under which educational funding and management was to be devolved from the central nodal agency to the municipalities. The measures were aimed at relaxing the state's monopoly on education and to give Sweden's children more choice. As a result, the National Board was abolished, block grants were made available to the municipalities and grades were reintroduced. Under the new experiment, parents were provided with vouchers of 85 per cent of the cost of educating a child in a public school. The SDP government reduced the funding amount from 85 per cent to 75 per cent but has retained the programme.

On the whole, the voucher experiment has brought important changes in Sweden's education system. Besides providing more choice, it has introduced an element of competition in the system that has secured high public support. Although the rate of participation in private schools has gone up only marginally, interestingly, the voucher experiment in Sweden's education system has touched off a debate on the need for choice in other areas such as welfare, health, childcare and the whole gamut of social services.

Another notable trend is the move towards decentralization and privatization of services delivery. Alternative operational forms in social services are becoming increasingly common. While the ultimate responsibility for the provision of services lies with the municipalities through public funding, the service itself may be provided by others. This trend which began in a strong way in the early 1990s has shown a steady rise. In order to better meet the needs of new target groups, and to boost efficiency and productivity, certain social service activities run by the municipalities have been opened to competition. Thus the bulk of the institutional care for children and young people comes under private management. Stress is also being laid on both cooperation and competition between the public and private providers of services. An example of this has been the ending of the state monopoly on placement services in 1993; private placement agencies have since made a modest entry into the labour market. There is also evidence of increasing specialization within social services with special initiatives being designed to meet the specific requirements of different groups of claimants.

Conclusion

Thus the Swedish welfare state has undergone certain changes and a degree of transformation is under way. But important as these changes may be, it is far more important to interpret recent spending cuts and welfare reforms. It is this crucial interpretation that is open to debate. Critics have seen, in these changes, the beginning of the end of the welfare state and have pronounced that the day of big government spending is long past. Do these changes represent a rollback and a dismantling of the welfare state in Sweden? Hardly. It is important to see these changes and reforms in perspective and resist the temptation to view any change as a systemic crisis. It is hasty and premature to attempt a connection between the economic downturn of the 1990s and a collapse of the welfare state. The 1990s crisis was not a welfare state crisis and the quick correlation between the two, which many have done, is faulty. It is also important to define what one means by a 'crisis' of the welfare state. If 'crisis' is defined in the sense of a systemic breakdown and a dismantling of the welfare system, as is often the case, then clearly the Swedish welfare state is not in 'crisis' mode. These measures have basically affected monetary transfers and have not had an adverse impact on social services.

But this is not to imply at all that the system is problem-free, and there is little doubt that the Swedish welfare state is confronted with a host of strains and problems. When Sweden broadened the notion of full employment in the late 1970s to encompass women, the handicapped and others, it had the negative fallout of resulting in a high degree of gender segregation. Women have, by and large, tended to be concentrated in public-sector jobs with men in the private sector. Sweden is also confronted with a high level of absenteeism and also a high share of low-skilled but well-paid jobs. There are also severe cost problems. Pressure on costs further rise with an ageing population, which has meant that scarce resources have to be set aside for pensions and sickness insurance. The rising incidence of individualism in society also consigns the elderly and the sick to greater dependence on the state. Ageing populations constitute a phenomenon common to a graying Europe, which is undergoing a significant shift in its demographic structure. Another related issue of concern is the high rate of early retirement in society, which has, by reducing contributory revenue, increased social security expenditure. One must remember, though, that these problems are not exclusive to Sweden, most advanced capitalist welfare states face a host of similar challenges. The present 'crisis' is also not a new one in the debate over the survival of the European welfare state, which has waxed and waned over the decades. Cutbacks in benefit levels which have taken place in the Swedish welfare state in no way represent a paradigm shift away from the universal, egalitarian system.

But, although there is still a strong commitment to universalism and egalitarianism, there is also a demand for a range of differentiated services to meet the needs of an increasingly heterogeneous population structure. The system needs to strike a fine balance between these two elements or face erosion of support from the higher social strata, which will seek exit options. It is the structural factors such as demographic profile, unemployment and income levels which determine trends in social security benefits. For the system to remain viable in the long run, it has to constantly evolve and upgrade the range and quality of its services to meet the needs of its populace. Another such challenge being faced by Sweden is the integration of immigrants into the social fabric; little specialized attention is being paid to this problem and failure to recognize this heterogeneity at once raises complex problems of social exclusion.

In the long run, the Swedish welfare state's vulnerability will arise from the difficulties in financially sustaining an active welfare state. As a result of the internationalization of capital markets, high capital mobility is a condition Sweden has to contend with. The Swedish system's near total reliance on tax revenues to meet the social services requirements has to grapple with not just internationalization, but also moves towards European integration. Together, these have created increased pressures for a leaner tax system. Given that public-sector employment has fallen from 26.1 per cent in 1989 to 21.9 per cent in 1997,[16] there is also an increasing need to expand private-sector employment.

These challenges notwithstanding, the fundamental tenets of the Swedish welfare state with its active social service orientation remain intact. Total social expenditure continues to be impressive and substantially higher than the average in OECD countries. Although there has been some increase in income inequality, by and large Sweden still boasts of a very even income distribution by international standards. Sweden continues to have one of the highest levels of female participation in the labour market, and holds first place in the gender-adjusted Human Development Index as well as the gender empowerment measure. Trade union density in Sweden, one of the highest in the world, is also particularly strong among women at 85.7 per cent. There continues to be a strong accent on ensuring equality between men and women in the workplace, as evidenced by new legislation passed on 1 January 2001, where amendments were carried out in the 1991 Act dealing with equality between men and women. Universal welfare state programmes also continue to enjoy widespread public support. Universality assures that benefits are shared by the entire population and are firmly rooted in the principle of social inclusion.

These are definitely not the symptoms of a system in crisis, but are more a proof of a resilient welfare state.[17] Owing to the changing requirements of each period it is but natural that social policies will undergo change, but such changes do not indicate a collapse of the system, rather they are a measure of its adaptability.

Notes

1   B. Rothstein, 'The Universal Welfare State as a Social Dilemma', April 1998, at www.nsd.uib.no.
2   See Gösta Esping-Andersen, *The Three Worlds of Welfare Capitalism*, Cambridge: Polity Press, 1990.
3   Gosta Esping-Andersen, 'The Making of a Social Democratic Welfare State', in Klaus Misgeld, Karl Molin and Klas Amark (eds), *Creating Social Democracy: A Century of the Social Democratic Labour Party in Sweden*, Pennsylvania: Pennsylvania University Press, 1992, p. 26.
4   *Ibid.*, p. 35.
5   Lennart Jorberg, *Swedish Economy in a Hundred Years*, Stockholm, Swedish Economy, 1982, p. 23, cited in Peter Stein, n. 7.
6   Gun-Britt Andersson, 'Role of State as Provider and Regulatior: A Swedish Perspective', in B. Vivekanandan (ed.), *Building on Solidarity: Social Democracy and the New Millennium*, New Delhi: Lancer's Books, 2000, p. 103.
7   Peter Stein, 'Sweden: From Capitalist Success to Welfare State Sclerosis', *Policy Analysis*, Washington DC, no. 160, 10 September 1991, at www.cato.org.
8   Gun-Britt Andersson, n. 6, p. 110.
9   Peter Stein, n. 7.
10 Gun-Britt Andersson, n. 6, p. 110.
11 Paul Hirst, 'Can the European Welfare State Survive Globalisation? Sweden, Denmark and the Netherlands in Comparative Perspective', at www.polyglot.lss.wisc.edu.
12 'The Rise and Fall of the Swedish Welfare Model', at www.undp.org.
13 'Undermining the Welfare State in Sweden', at www.lbbs.org.
14 See OECD, *Economic Survey of Sweden*, Paris, 2001.
15 'Sweden's Voucher Experiment', at www.edexcellence.net.
16 Paul F. Scharpf, 'The Viability of Advanced Welfare States in the International Economy: Vulnerabilities and Options', at www.mpi-fg-koeln.mpg.de.
17 See Paul Pierson, 'The New Politics of the Welfare State', *World Politics*, Princeton, vol. 48, no. 2, 1996, pp, 143–73.

11
Political Economy of the Finnish Welfare State

Jukka Pekkarinen

Introduction

In its basic outline, the Finnish welfare state meets the broad characteristics of a Nordic type of welfare state: an emphasis on public services and reliance on relatively autonomous local administration for their provision, as well as, in social security, a combination of universal flat rate benefits and earnings-related social insurance. Yet the Finnish case has certain salient features of its own; the system is subject to tight economic constraints, and welfare expenditure has been constrained to the dividend left over by economic growth. Even in a cyclical context, the balanced budget constraint has made welfare expenditure clearly pro-cyclical.

On a more positive side, the viability of the Finnish welfare state structure is enhanced by the fact that it is supported by the main political parties from the right to the far left; it also has the backing of the labour market organizations. This broad support influences the dynamics of the Finnish system. While under normal circumstance adjustments are often delayed by distributive struggle on some minor details, the Finnish welfare state has proved itself capable of deep structural reforms in times of serious economic or social crisis. We shall see that this capacity to make rapid adjustments in difficult times adds to the sustainability of the welfare state system in Finland.

Accounts of the emergence, scope and performance of welfare states in different industrial societies are understandably diverse. Following loosely the tradition of the *Great Transformation* by Karl Polanyi, many studies interpret the role of the welfare state in functionalist terms, as society's self-defence against the disruptive influences of the market economy. From this angle, much stress in the explanations for the rise of the modern welfare state is given to the level of development of the market system in each society. Differences in the structure of various national social protection systems are in turn accounted for in terms of such structural prerequisites of the economy as its industrial structure and its exposure to foreign trade.

There are also studies whose starting points are more 'voluntarist' in the sense of assigning a central role to factors like historical heritage, ideologies and political power balance of each society. Finally, an economist is inclined to account for both functionalist and voluntarist viewpoints by assuming that different types of welfare states represent different sorts of socio-economic equilibrium. These all meet the constraints imposed by the structural characteristics of the economy and society in question, but can be sustained, under these constraints, by different sets of choices determined by interaction, conflict and coordination between firms, employers, employees and their organizations, political parties and government.

The interpretation of the rise and scope of the welfare state in Finland given in this chapter largely follows the economist's approach just described. It proposes that there exists, at a general level, a Nordic model of a welfare state, which differs from its Continental European, Anglo-Saxon as well as Asian counterparts and reflects the specific structural characteristics of the Nordic countries. Yet, at a more specific level, there are clear differences among different versions of the Nordic welfare state. This divergence of the Nordic experience is exemplified by concentrating on the Finnish case, which supposedly is the least well-known to foreign scholars. Its divergence is indicated mostly by comparing it with the Swedish welfare state, which outside the Nordic countries is often understood as *the* Nordic model.

What is being argued is, first, that both the similarity at a general level as well as the divergence at a more specific level reflect different structural, ideological and political preconditions of each welfare model. Sweden and Finland share much in common as far as their economic structure is concerned, yet differences in the geo-political exposure and foreign trade structure of the two countries as well as differences in their ideological traditions and political power structures have given rise to salient differences between the Swedish and the Finnish varieties of the Nordic model.

Second, differences between the two versions of the Nordic model are in the first instance not that much reflected in the structure, not even in the socio-economic outcome of the two welfare models, as in the *politics* by which they are managed and adjusted to changes in economic circumstances. The Swedish model is generally interpreted as a social democratic creation and is laden with a high degree of *conflict* between the left and the right. The Finnish welfare state model, on the other hand, is more broadly based on a *consensus* between the main political forces from the moderate right to the far left as far as the basic scope and framework of the welfare system is concerned. The welfare state in Finland does not have as strong a social democratic image as its Swedish counterpart – or, as some observers have put it, all main political forces in Finland are social democratic to the extent that they share the basic values and priorities of a welfare state.

This difference in the politics of the welfare state accounts, third, to certain differences in the *dynamics* of the two types of the Nordic model. In the Swedish model, change in the policy priorities often takes place as a result of a thorough and intellectually explicit reevaluation of the inherited policy paradigm. The new version of the model leaves the basic goals of the model intact but may imply a fundamental reconsideration of the policy mix by which these aims are pursued.

In the Finnish case, the change of the model is normally more incremental in nature. Reflecting the peripheral economic and geo-political position of the country, the budget constraint of the welfare state is usually adjusted tightly to the general economic conditions prevailing in the country. On the other hand, as far as the structure of the welfare state is concerned, adjustment is often more complicated in Finland. It results from political conflicts and compromises between different parties and interest groups, and most often the thrust of the adjustment is not that much on the basic outline of the inherited welfare policy package as on its various distributive and allocative details. Yet under certain circumstances, the consensus backing the Finnish model has also proved capable of sustaining a fundamental revaluation of both the objectives and the means of economic and social policies. Such fundamental reorientation of the model has typically been connected with a big change in the external economic environment, which may have called national survival as a whole into question.

In what follows, I first summarize the common features of the Nordic welfare state and indicate the specific characteristics of the point of reference, that is the Swedish case. After this, the analysis will concentrate on Finland by discussing the historical background, specific characteristics and the working of the Finnish model.

Nordic welfare states: common characteristics

Historical background

The Nordic or, more properly, Swedish model is often regarded as *the* model of the welfare state. As far as the ideological anchoring and theoretical clarity of the welfare system are concerned, it is unquestionable that Sweden rightly occupies a pioneering role in forming the 'third way' of the reformist left in the interwar period. The rise of the Swedish ideas of the welfare state exemplifies an exciting combination of professional analysis on the one hand, and ideological and political campaigning on the other. In this endeavour, Swedish economists, Gunnar Myrdal and other members of the Stockholm School anticipated the Keynesian ideas of economic policy and also laid down the foundations for a new theory of social policy as a way to enhance economic stability and efficiency.[1] On the political front, the leaders of Swedish social democrats further developed the Austrian and Danish ideas of active reformism as a substitute for the traditional Kautskian socialism devoid of any clear recipe for active intervention in the capitalist economy.[2]

Among politicians, there were also intermediaries, like Ernst Wiggfors, who were able to utilize new economic theories for building up a political strategy. In their writings, a three-stage transfer to democratic socialism was envisaged. In the first stage, active demand management and income equalization through social policy reforms were to be used to stabilize the market economy. This was to be followed, in the second stage, by comprehensive economic planning as a means to enhance growth and structural change in the framework of a market economy. Finally, in the third stage, economic democracy was to be widened and redistribution of wealth achieved by relying on various collective saving schemes (later wage-earner funds). As a matter of fact, the Swedish social democrats pursued this three-stage strategy for democratic socialism until the failure of the plan for wage-earner funds in the 1980s.[3]

Apart from the strategy of the democratic left, certain qualifications should be imposed on the factual primacy of the Swedish, or more generally of the Nordic, model of the welfare state. In the Nordic countries, the welfare state aspect of new economic policies did not come to play a major role until the postwar period from the 1950s onwards, that is after the debate on active stabilization policies and the actual failure of the strive for effective economic planning in the late 1940s. In fact, the Nordic countries were to some extent delayed in their development of the welfare system. In several European countries, the GDP share of social expenditure exceeded the Nordic figures in the first decade after the Second World War, but it was in the 1950s and 1960s when the real take-off of the Nordic model, as measured by the extent of social expenditure, took place and the Nordic model consequently became largely assimilated with its welfare state dimension.[4]

In their relatively delayed build-up of the welfare model in the postwar period, the Nordic countries were able to learn from the experience of the European predecessors. In addition to this, in all Nordic countries an effort was made to accommodate the welfare state to the structural characteristics and economic policy prerequisites of each country. While designing welfare reforms, much attention was paid to contributing, through them, positively also to economic growth and structural change.

This national linkage between the welfare state and the structural prerequisites and economic policy agenda of each country in turn led to differences in the details of welfare state policies of different Nordic countries. Yet the divergence does not exclude strong similarities in the basic set-up. Before taking account of the specificity of the Finnish case, I shall point out some common features in the background and basic framework of the welfare states of different Nordic countries:

Role of the state and public vesus private responsibility for welfare

Before the rise of the modern welfare state, that is in the traditional peasant society already, public responsibility for the care of the elderly, disabled and the poor gradually increased. It was increasingly accepted that individuals might, through no fault of their own, be captured by poverty and become incapable of helping themselves. From early on, responsibility of the family for the material welfare of its members was considered in the Nordic countries as more restricted than elsewhere. Furthermore, the social role of the church as well as various religious charity associations became smaller than elsewhere in Europe. These attitudes were partly a reflection of the Lutheran religion of the Nordic countries, that conceived the relation of man to God as a discrete private issue, which did not depend on the social status of the individual and which could not be facilitated by private charity. These religiously based attitudes paved the way for a type of society where the government gradually occupied a primary role in the provision of welfare services and social security, and where individuals, not the family, were taken as the basic unit of the social security system.

Local provision of public services

Emphasis on public responsibility in taking care of the disfavoured from early on found expression in the initiatives of local communities for various types of welfare services. This reliance on the public sector at the local level reflected an old tradition of local democracy in the Nordic countries, which it in turn further strengthened. Increasing need for education, health and social services, which became evident in the early stages of an industrial society, led to a reorganization of local administration and removal of the remaining social responsibilities of the parish to secular local authority. Later on, during the first steps towards the modern welfare state at the beginning of the twentieth century, it was characteristic of the Nordic countries that initiatives for new public services were taken by local communities.[5] It was not until a new form of service had become relatively widespread as a voluntary, locally financed provision that it was legislated as a mandatory responsibility of the municipalities and allocated state subsidies for that purpose.

Involvement of labour market organizations

A further characteristic of the industrial societies of the Nordic countries is a high degree of organization and a consensual approach to labour-market bargaining. While creating a generally peaceful atmosphere in the labour markets took somewhat longer, in the case of Finland a considerably longer time, national confederations of employers and employees were formed in all Nordic countries in the early twentieth century. As noted by Göran Therborn (1992), in 'Germanic' countries, covering in this context all Nordic countries, the rise of well-organized mass parties of the left occurred simultaneously with the formation of trade unions, as mutually reinforcing parts of the same effort of class organization.[6] Moreover, in the Nordic case, as distinct from many continental European countries, employers adopted the same type of organization pattern for their own interest associations out-side the state structure. Groundwork for a tripartite negotiation structure between employees' and employers' confederations and the state was thus created. In the postwar period, this was developed to a Nordic type of social corporatism by which coordination between nationwide wage settlements, taxation as well as other economic and social policies was sought, with dif-ferent degrees of explicitness in different countries. This has also had its impact on the development of the welfare state.

The welfare state as a class compromise

An effective class organization on the left found its counterpart, apart from employers, among farmers, from early on. Like workers, farmers were also organized simultaneously, both politically as agrarian parties, and industri-ally as farmers' associations. A relatively even distribution of land property and a high frequency of independent small or medium-sized farmers facili-tated this agrarian class organization. As on the left, the parties came to have the upper hand in pursuing an agrarian class strategy.

Generally, the cultural and ethnical homogeneity of the Nordic socie-ties contributed to a rise of encompassing interest organizations.[7] Given the parallel between political and industrial interest-group organization, an overlapping class-based organization cutting through both political and industrial interest groups thus came to characterize all Nordic countries in the twentieth century. It was on this groundwork that the welfare state was also built. As the left was not capable of pursuing social reforms on its own before the Second World War, it sought alliance with the farmers. 'Cow deals' between workers and farmers were concluded, as first steps towards the modern welfare state in the 1930s. Later, the significance of this particular type of class compromise became diluted; yet in Finland it has remained more important than elsewhere in the Nordic countries, and in all Nordic countries it is still reflected in the basic structure of the welfare state.[8]

Targeting a welfare state conducive to growth and structural change

In all Nordic countries, industrialization has taken place relatively late and partly coincided with the rise of the welfare state. Moreover, in these small countries, industrialization has been export-led. This has resulted in an experience of periphery and external dependence that in turn has shaped the Nordic welfare systems. On the one hand, the perceived increase in inse-curity resulting from higher exposure to foreign trade has intensified the claims by workers for a more effective social safety net as a precondition for submitting the economy to increasing foreign competition. On the other hand, the benefits attached to access to wider markets have made employ-ers more ready to agree to employees' demands for better social security. Furthermore, both the employers and the representatives of the state have observed the requirement that the build-up of the welfare state is as conducive to growth and structural change as possible. This has been reflected, for example, in attempts to internalize changes in the tax wedge in nominal wage settlements by coordinating wage policies and tax policies; in an emphasis on active labour market policies as well as in attempts to synchronize social benefits; and taxation to reduce the risk of 'poverty traps'.[9] Again, however, notice should be taken of national specificity in this combination of economic, social and labour market policies in different Nordic countries. This is the viewpoint we shall now turn to more closely in the Finnish context.

Special features of the Finnish case

How does the Finnish case figure in the above general Nordic scheme? The scope and structure of the Finnish welfare state broadly compares with the common Nordic model,[10] despite the fact that it is somewhat leaner and of later vintage than the welfare states of other Nordic countries. Its present shape and reception also reflect the impact of the severe recession of the early 1990s that hit Finland more heavily than, for example, Sweden. Output fell by about 13 per cent from the preceding peak to a trough and unemployment rose dramatically, from 3.5 per cent in 1990 to 17 per cent in 1993. Although unemployment has now fallen back close to the EU average, it is, at about 9 per cent, still much higher than in other Nordic countries and by far exceeds the level previously characteristic of Finland up to the beginning of the 1990s. The recession also swept state finances into a state of disarray, which in turn led to a series of cuts in public expenditure in the 1990s. Yet the basic structure of the welfare state was preserved. Expenditure cuts consisted of across-the-board belt-tightening and did not lead to total termination of any major welfare programmes. Inequality and poverty have increased substantially in recent years, yet Finland still has a relatively even distribution of income and a low poverty rate compared to other industrialized countries.

A special feature in the structure of the Finnish welfare state that should be mentioned at the outset is the high degree of participation of women in the labour force. Extensive full-time employment of women has characterized Finland since the Second World War, and even earlier. Although female employment has more recently increased in other industrial countries as well, it is still among the highest in Finland, especially if counted on a full-time basis. It is particularly the jobs offered by the welfare state, that is health, education and social services, that are dominated by the female labour force. On the other hand, women's extensive participation in the labour force has increased the need for new types of welfare services like day-care. There is also a fairly high level of income support to families with children.

As far as the above list of common characteristics of the Nordic welfare states is concerned, Finland shares the same historical background of a relatively homogenous society dominated by an independent small and medium-sized peasantry as in other Nordic countries. Together with the impact of the Lutheran religion, this historical heritage has contributed to a trust-based public order and uncorrupted public administration as well as a strong government state with a relatively broad set of responsibilities. This historical background is also reflected in the structure of the country's welfare state. Social security is individually, not family, based in Finland. There is a dual system of social security, consisting on the one hand of universal flat-rate basic benefits independent of the labour market status of the individual, and of earnings-related mandatory social insurance on the other. An extensive network of public services also characterizes Finland, as does the dominance of local provision of all types of welfare services. In fact, in Finland the thrust on the local level in the provision of services is still more noteworthy, as the country lacks an intermediate level of government with its own taxation right. Municipalities, in some cases with less than 1000 inhabitants, provide most of education, health and social services. As the supply of these services has gradually expanded to more comprehensive forms, like higher occupational education and special healthcare, an effective organization of which requires a relatively large population, cooperation between municipalities has been increasingly needed in the provision of these services. Apart from guiding legislation, the state's participation primarily consists of financing a share (presently about 20 per cent on average) of the costs of these services through block transfers to local government.

A high degree of organization characterizes Finnish labour markets, as does an active participation by employers' and employees' organizations in the management of the social security system. As in other Nordic countries, the Finnish welfare state is historically based on an even broader class compromise where the agrarians have also actively participated. As we shall see, these special features related to class compromise have been preserved in the Finnish case even better than in other Nordic countries.

Finland also demonstrates certain interrelated special features that have shaped the structure, resource constraints and, in particular, the political economy of its welfare state. In what follows, I discuss in more detail two such characteristics of the Finnish case, which are closely interrelated:

- the connection of welfare state building to the economic development pattern and to economic policies followed in the country; and
- the politics of the Finnish welfare state.

Tight economic constraints

Relative backwardness and instability

Finnish industrialization is late even by Nordic standards, with half of the active population still working in agriculture and forestry in the early 1950s, despite the relatively rapid rate of growth from the late nineteenth century onwards. Rapid structural change continued throughout the postwar period, as reflected by the fact that the increase in employment in manufacturing, and later on to a more dominating extent in services, has decreased the share of primary industries in the labour force to less than 5 per cent.

As a matter of fact, Finland launched its process of industrialization in the middle of the latter part of the nineteenth century from a position that bears resemblance with that of the present-day developing countries. In the latter part of the nineteenth century, the real per capita GDP of the country amounted to less than one-fourth of that of the richest nations of the time; then, at the end of the 1860s, Finland experienced the latest large-scale peacetime famine in Western Europe. Since then, growth of GDP in Finland has exceeded the average of the industrial countries, and as a consequence her GDP per capita now slightly exceeds that of the average of EU and OECD countries.

In addition to a relatively rapid average growth rate, a further salient feature of economic growth in Finland has been its cyclical volatility. Apart from the depression of the early 1990s, marking the deepest recession of Western industrial countries in the postwar period, economic cycles had been more prevalent in Finland than elsewhere in Western Europe. This experience of relative backwardness and instability has moulded economic and social policies in the country. Closing the standard of living gap vis-à-vis the richer Western neighbours has been given a high priority. Combined with Finland's exposed geopolitical status as a small neighbour to an expansionist superpower in the East, the relative economic backwardness has resulted in a particularly strong experience of *periphery* in setting national policy priorities.

The target of getting out of the periphery and safeguarding national sovereignty has been reflected in the prominence given to national security considerations in the foreign trade and integration policy of the country. In the postwar period, Finland struck a balance in her foreign policy between paying notice to the security interests of the Soviet Union and deepening her own economic and cultural linkages with the West. Finland used the options provided by the European economic integration to approach the West and to expand her own room of manoeuvre. This is shown, for example, by the country's association with EFTA in the 1960s, by its support for the plan for the European Economic Area, and finally Finland's entry into the EU together with Sweden and Austria in 1995. The latest manifestation of Finland's security policy-based approach to integration is her access, as the only Nordic country, in the third stage of EMU in 1999.

Experience of periphery has also had a deep impact on the economic policy approach of the country. The 'Gerschenkronian' hypothesis of a connection between the power of the state and the degree of backwardness applies particularly well to the Finnish case. During autonomy under Russian rule in the nineteenth century, the state was already active in promoting early industrialization.[11] Connections between civil servants, the independent role of which has since then been prominent in formulating economic policies in Finland, and domestic industrialists were close. The state actively promoted industrial initiatives through legislation, investments in communications, higher education and other investments in infrastructure as well as by directly providing finance from its own savings. After Finland gained independence in the aftermath of the First World War, the state actively promoted economic diversification; and several state-owned companies were created for this purpose in mining, engineering and paper industries. Industrial policy activism, exercised with the consent of private industry, continued in the postwar period.[12] It is not until the very recent past that the state, in reaction to closer integration and a more sophisticated industrial structure of the economy, retreated from this kind of direct intervention in the supply side of the economy.

A constrained welfare state

State activism on the supply side of the economy has had consequences that are directly relevant for the shape and constraints of the welfare state. It has been a main aim of economic policy to provide room for industrial investment and growth, and to this end, state finances have traditionally been kept in surplus and public savings have been channelled through various routes to investment, both public and private. Welfare expenses have been regarded rather as a way to consume the 'surplus' provided by industry, and care has been taken in adjusting promptly to the room for manoeuvre determined by the state of industrial strength of the country.

Apart from this striving for a financial surplus in the public sector for the sake of facilitating economic growth, the fiscal constraints on the growth of welfare expenditure have been shaped by a perception of the cyclical *volatility* of the economy and of the related fragility of its growth process. Connected with the exposed geopolitical location of the country, this has led to a high priority given in Finnish policy-making for preserving fiscal autonomy and the state's capacity to act. This has been reflected in a high degree of aversion against debt finance of government expenditure.

As a consequence of this resistance against public indebtedness, public expenditure, including expenses on the welfare state, have been submitted to a cyclically changing cash constraint (like current tax revenue). Thus

Finland has until recently rejected the Keynesian attempts to 'lean against the wind' in fiscal policies.[13]

The fact that counter-cyclical reactions in government surplus have been curtailed and a tight fiscal constraint has been imposed on welfare expenditure has shaped the dynamics of the welfare state in Finland. Periods of a rapid increase in welfare expenditure have typically coincided with long cyclical upswings, as in the early 1970s and in the 1980s. Recession years in turn have rather witnessed a retreat of the welfare state, as in the late 1950s, late 1960s, mid-1970s and again in the aftermath of the recession of the early 1990s. Occasional overshooting notwithstanding, welfare expenditure has been kept tightly within the limits imposed by the growth potential of the economy.

On the other hand, the procyclical nature of the execution of welfare programmes has contributed to the economy's cyclical instability, which in Finland has been more salient than in other Nordic countries. In a sense, economic policies in Finland have aimed at a higher long-term growth potential at the cost of greater cyclical instability.

Political background

Broad consensus

The politics of the Finnish welfare state is also different from other Nordic countries, especially Sweden. As mentioned above, the welfare state in Sweden is heavily associated with social democracy, in the eyes of both its defenders and opponents. This strong political anchoring to social democracy differentiates the Swedish ideology of the welfare state from the Finnish case. While the roots of the modern welfare state in Finland also date back to a 'cow deal' (called a 'red ochre coalition' in Finland) between the social democrats and the agrarian party in the late 1930s, the later political dynamics of the Finnish welfare model has been quite different.

In Finland, the social democrats have not had an exclusive right to the welfare model. From early on, the agrarian party developed its own approach to welfare policies, pursuing farmers' interests, by far the biggest industrial group in Finland until the 1950s. Partly as a result of this active approach of the agrarian party to welfare reforms, the support of the party among farmers was stabilized at a high level (20–25 per cent of the votes). This paved the way for a prevalence of coalitions in postwar Finland, where there was a broad consensus on the welfare state developed as a compromise between the farmers, represented by agrarian party, and industrial workers, represented by social democrats. The influence of the two parties was rather evenly divided.

The much stronger positions of the social democrats in the interwar period were weakened mainly by two developments in the postwar era. First, the progress of the agrarian party dented the support for the social democrats among small farmers, which had been considerable in the first half of the twentieth century. Second, the rise of the communists and their left socialist allies after the war meant a tightening competition for the votes of industrial workers as well as erosion in the support for the social democrats among the landless population in the countryside. On the whole, the social democrats have remained as the biggest party in the country most of the time in the postwar period (on average around 25 per cent of the votes).

All three main parties of the left and the centre – that is the social democrats, agrarians and communists – and their allies shared, with their own emphasis reflecting the interests of each party's supporters, the broad ideology of the welfare state. Both the centre and the far left have stressed the role of universal flat-rate benefits, while the social democrats have typically given a higher priority to earnings-related social insurance. As a compromise, the Finnish social security system has developed as a combination of universal flat-rate benefits and earnings-related social insurance. A well-developed system of public services in the areas of education, health and social services has been in the interests of all three parties.

These three parties also dominated government coalitions in Finland until the 1980s, although there were long interruptions in the participation of the communists.[14] This broad consensus on the welfare state paved the way for its even wider acceptance in Finnish politics. The broad ideology of the welfare state also became accepted by the main party in opposition, the Conservatives, certainly by the 1980s. This in turn has led to a situation where all three types of pair-wise coalitions between the left,[15] the centre (former agrarians) and the conservatives are possible and capable of finding a common approach to the welfare state.[16] It is an indication of the strength of the consensus surrounding the welfare state that neither a populist anti-tax party nor any neo-liberal party has found significant support in the country so far. Indeed, one of the new parties that has found strongest support, that is the greens, has joined the Finnish consensus on the welfare state, admittedly again with its own ingredients (like, say, devotion to ideas of 'citizen's income' or negative income tax). Support for the welfare state is also strong in opinion polls directly addressed to the issue.

Such a broad support across the political spectrum enhances the legitimacy of the Finnish welfare state. On the other hand, as is shown more closely below, the 'common property' nature of the welfare state affects its dynamics and its mode of change in a peculiar way.

Corporatist ingredients

The political economy of the welfare state in Finland is also shaped by certain features of the traditions of *industrial organization* in the country. In comparison to other Nordic countries, trade unions remained weak in Finland until the aftermath of the Second World War. Collective agreements were firmly resisted by employers, who themselves were effectively organized, and the influence of the unions was eroded by a persistent power struggle on the control of the unions between social democrats and communists.

A rapid increase in union enrolment took place in the aftermath of the Second World War. Yet a set-back was caused by a split of the unions, with an accompanying division of the social democratic party, from the late 1950s to the late 1960s. After reunification, union enrolment rapidly increased and has since then stabilized at a high level of around 80–90 per cent without significant differences between blue-collar workers and salaried employees.

The late stabilization of the role of the trade unions meant that the relation between the parties of the left and trade unions took a somewhat different shape in Finland than in other Nordic countries. The interwar strategy of the Finnish social democrats had not been based on such a close cooperation between the party and the unions as in Scandinavia. Cooperation gradually increased from the 1930s, and especially after the war with the rapid increase in trade union enrolment, yet a fully tight cooperation between the parties of the left and the unions was still prevented by a continuous power struggle between social democrats and communists on leadership in the trade union movement. In Finland, social democrats and communists remained organized in the same trade unions. To preserve this unity, itself in the long-term interest of the union movement, the trade union leaders, most of them social democrats, were careful not to make the cooperation with the party too close.

The relatively loose ties, as compared to other Nordic countries, between the social democratic party and the trade unions in turn influenced the relationship between the state apparatus and trade unions. As a matter of fact, during the war state authorities had already encouraged a more effective labour market organization in order to acquire more means for the management of the war economy. In the postwar period, government occupied an active role in voluntary incomes policies carried through by tripartite negotiations between government, trade unions and employer confederations. This incomes policy framework was not built up smoothly. First, incomes policy experiments after the war collapsed with the split of the trade union movement in the 1950s, and it was not until the late 1960s that voluntary incomes policies became an established element of the economic policy tradition in Finland that has been withheld, short interruptions notwithstanding, until the present.

The incomes policy tradition in Finland is different, for example, from Sweden, where in wage settlements the government has been careful not to impose incomes policies 'from above'. While the Finnish case cannot be described as a state-centred corporatism such as, for example, in Austria, the role of the government in it is nevertheless central in facilitating the passing through of centralized wage settlements. The government keeps a keen eye on the negotiations; it provides information and arbitration, and it is also usual that the government makes settlements in taxation, social expenditure and labour market legislation conditional on the outcome of wage negotiations.[17]

Through centralized wage settlements, trade unions have become a central player in the political economy of growth in Finland. Wage settlements have been targeted at controlling inflation and maintaining the relative unit labour costs at levels compatible with the targets on functional income shares, growth and investment. Failures in settling this distributive conflict have every now and then been reflected in outbursts of inflation, deteriorating competitiveness, falling employment and, ultimately, a depreciating currency. This has resulted in a kind of a political business cycle called a 'devaluation cycle' in the Finnish context, where inflation, functional distribution of income, growth and employment interact. This growth cycle notwithstanding, the overall record of incomes policies in Finland has been positive. They have been conducive to growth, facilitated consensus on taxation and welfare state expenditure, and at the same time enhanced a responsible role for the trade unions.

Trade unions have also shaped the Finnish welfare state directly. The design of the social security system has not been left to parties and the government alone, but the participation of the labour market partners, as well as the farmers' confederation, has been highly visible. This has kept up the tension, mentioned above, between universal flat-rate benefits on the one hand and earnings-related social insurance on the other. The labour market partners have traditionally prioritized, together with social democrats, earnings-related social insurance against flat-rate benefits, which in turn have found their support, apart from the Centre Party, from the farmers' confederation. The dispute has shaped, for example, the design of the Finnish pension system in the postwar period. First, in the 1950s, the mandatory pension scheme originally created as a funded scheme in the 1930s, was made a flat-rate universal 'people's pension' based on a pay-as-you-go system. As a reaction to this, employers and employees negotiated a partly funded occupational pension scheme in the early 1960s. This mandatory scheme is administered by private insurance companies, but both the government and the labour-market partners closely participate in its management. Furthermore, the trade unions themselves operate the earnings-related unemployment compensation system, financed by mandatory, wage-based contributions by employers and employees, whereas the government runs the system of flat-rate, means-tested unemployment assistance.

Dynamics of the Finnish welfare state

The consensual participation by government, parties and labour-market organizations shapes the dynamics of the welfare state. The broad consensus gives it a firm legitimacy, and the existence of the welfare state is not questioned. On the other hand, as far as attempts to adjust the welfare state in a planned way to changes in the environment, and so on, are concerned, the multitude of vested interests often results in conflicts over various distributive details of the system. This may inhibit adjustment and tends to dissolve the debate on structural reforms to partial arguments about various subparts of the system. Repetitive, unresolved distributive conflict over various details of the system can also undermine peoples' attachment within the welfare state and pave the way for a sort of alienation from politics.

On the other hand, the fact that the welfare state has wide public support and is sustained by encompassing organizations can on certain occasions increase the readiness to also accept, apart from adjustments to moves in the budget constraint discussed above, major changes in the system. If large, thorough-going structural adjustments to changes, for example in the external environment, are conceived necessary for the viability of the welfare system, they may be agreed on as a comprehensive package. On these occasions, consensus on the basic elements of the system helps to bring about the necessary intervention to reshape it. The adjustment of Finnish society to new political and external conditions after the Second World War exemplifies such a major reform. One can also see some elements of such corporatist management of the adjustment of the welfare state in the way the Finnish system was trimmed after the recession of the early 1990s, through across-the-board cuts while keeping the basic skeleton of the system intact.

Conclusions

The argument over the sustainability of the Finnish-type of welfare state is out. What is unquestionable is that, for example, the forthcoming demographic change, which in Finland will be among the sharpest in Europe in the next two decades, makes the welfare state's capacity to adjust more important than ever for its sustainability. The same applies to the increasing external pressures attached to globalization, that is intensification of worldwide competition in product markets and increasing international mobility of both financial capital and real investments. A necessary condition for a successful adjustment to such large changes in the framework of a consensus-based welfare state, is that while the fairness of the welfare system is maintained, conflicts on its distributive details are not allowed to inhibit structural adjustments of the system necessary for its efficiency. Engagement of encompassing organizations is a potential asset in safeguarding the sustainability of the system as a whole. It remains to be seen whether the Finnish welfare state, which has successfully met several deep challenges so far, may even in future find the means to deploy this asset in a conducive way.

Recent developments give some ground for optimism. According to several recent surveys of competitiveness, Finland tops the list as far as the readiness of both the private and the public sectors to progress towards the new economy is concerned. In the reform of the welfare state to meet the challenge of an ageing population, the piecemeal adjustments that have taken place in, for example, in the Finnish pension system so far, can be singled out in the European context as an outstanding example of the method to thin out the future benefits provided by the 'first pillar' of the mandatory pension system across the board, while maintaining the coverage of the public pension system intact. In many other European countries, in contrast, leeway has been sought to cut the benefits attached to the public pension system by opening access and providing tax subsidies to private voluntary pension schemes. While the Finnish method of maintaining coverage of the public pension system may require more effort to reach consensus on reforms, it may prove more viable as far as the legitimacy and distributive acceptability of the reforms is concerned.

Notes

1 Actually a Finnish social theorist, Pekka Kuusi, did some pioneering work on the positive linkages between economic growth and welfare state policies in the early 1960s. His ideas had a profound effect on social policies in Finland.

2 The excitement for this new vision of the third way is vividly demonstrated, for example, by the memoirs of both Tage Erlander, a long-time Swedish prime minister, and by Ernst Wiggfors, the Swedish minister of finance during the build-up years of the Swedish model.

3 This ideological background partly explains why the debate on the wage-earner funds was so hot in Sweden in the 1980s.

4 See Peter Flora and Arnold J. Heidenheimer, *The Development of Welfare States in Europe and America*, New Brunswick and London: Transaction, 1981.

5 Jorgen Lotz, 'Local Government Reforms in the Nordic Countries – Theory and Practice', in Rattso, Jorn (ed.), *Fiscal Federalism and State-Local Finance – The Scandinavian Perspective*, Cheltenham: Edward Elgar, 1998, pp. 19–28. Lotz refers to Kjeld Philips' earlier writings on this aspect.

6 Göran Therborn, 'Lessons from "Corporatist" Theorizations', in J. Pekkarinen, M. Pohjola and B. Rowthorn (eds), *Social Corporatism*, Oxford: Clarendon Press, 1992, pp. 24–44.

7 Mancur Olson, *The Rise and Fall of Nations*, New Haven, Conn.: Yale University Press, 1982.

8 It is still to be seen, for example, in the institutionalized combination of a universal flat-rate benefits and earnings-related social insurance, which Esping-Andersen and others regard as characteristic at Nordic welfare states. Gösta Esping-Andersen, *The Three Worlds of Welfare Capitalism*, Cambridge: Polity Press, 1989.

9 Thus, for example, it is a common practice in the Nordic countries that means-tested social security benefits are individually, not family based. The benefits are also subject to tax, and 'tax expenditure' on social security (i.e. tax deductability of private expenditure on e.g. health, education) is in the Nordic countries of

minor significance compared to most other industrialized countries. As far as the role of active labour-market policies is concerned, special reference should be made to the Rehn–Meidner model, originally presented to the LO Congress in Sweden in 1951. Later developments of the model are described in Andrew Martin, 'Trade Unions in Sweden: Strategic Responses to Change and Crisis', in P. Gourevitch *et al.* (eds), *Unions and Economic Crisis*, London: Allen & Unwin, 1984.

10 For a description of the Finnish welfare state, see Reino Hjerppe, Seija Ilmakunnas and Iikko B. Voipio (eds), *The Finnish Welfare State at the Turn of the Millennium*, Helsinki: Government Institute for Economic Research, 2000.

11 Sakari Heikkinen, Visa Heinonen, Antti Kuusterä and Jukka Pekkarinen, *The History of Finnish Economic Thought 1809–1917, The History of Learning and Science in Finland 1828–1918*, Helsinki: Societas Scientiarum Fennica, 2000.

12 Juhana Vartiainen, 'The Economics of Successful Intervention in Industrial Transformation', in M. Woo-Cumings (ed.), *Developmental State*, Ithaca and London: Cornell University Press, 1999, pp. 200–34.

13 For a comparison of the fiscal policy tradition of the Nordic countries, see Jukka Pekkarinen, 'Keynesianism and the Scandinavian Models of Economic Policy', in P.A. Hall (ed.), *Political Power of Economic Ideas*, Princeton NJ: Princeton University Press, 1989, pp. 311–46.

14 The communists were in opposition from the late 1940s to the late 1960s, and on several occasions also in the 1970s and 1980s.

15 The left alliance, as the offspring of the former communist party, is now closely allied with the social democrats in its policies towards participating in government.

16 In the first part of the 1990s there was a coalition between the centre and the conservatives, which since 1995 has been substituted by a broad 'rainbow coalition' between the left, the conservatives and the greens.

17 See Jukka Pekkarinen, 'Corporatism and Economic Performance in Sweden, Norway, and Finland', in J. Pekkarinen, M. Pohjola and B. Rowthorn (eds.), *Social Corporatism*, Oxford: Clarendon Press, 1992, pp. 298–337.

12
Challenges Facing the Danish Welfare State

Jørn Henrik Petersen

Introduction

Setting the stage

After outlining concerns about the basic objectives of the welfare state as suggested by the international literature, this chapter will briefly present data on the attitudes of the Danes regarding 'their' welfare state, suggest the causes underlying the change from a social security state towards a welfare state, introduce a number of indicators illustrating the rapid growth of the welfare state, and describe the Danish welfare state as nationally delimited by nature. I will show that this prototype of the welfare state faces a number of challenges: partly from an increasing openness of the economy; partly from a rising demand for leisure; partly from an unfavourable demographic development; and partly from the assumed reliability of bureaucratized humanitarianism. The contribution concludes that Danish politicians seem to be caught in a deadlock caused on the one hand by the need to ensure a sustainable fiscal policy, and on the other hand by the acknowledgement that the Danish population seem to react strongly against restrictions on time-honoured 'rights'.

In the developed world, uneasiness is growing about continuing rises in government social welfare spending and the behaviour that it seems to encourage.[1] After the postwar period of growth and expansion, welfare states are now suffering from budget and legitimacy pressures. Expansion has slowed, and concern about the basic objectives and purposes of social policy is increasing.[2] There is now a worldwide debate about the scope, the level and the structure of social security.[3] Since the economic problems of stagflation first surfaced in the early 1970s the state of the welfare state, its present condition and future prospects, has been a matter of almost continuous speculation and dispute. When looking for the causes of a lagging economic performance mirrored by a persistently high rate of unemployment it is understandable that many have asked whether Europe's welfare state, in particular, is a burden on the economy.

Underlying the discussion are issues of *affordability*,[4] *taxable capacity*,[5] *sustainability*,[6] *restructuring*,[7] *retrenchment* and *dismantling*.[8] Even though some of these concepts are embarrassingly nebulous, they appear time and again in the literature and in the public debate. And yet the general verdict is that the welfare state has remained more or less intact.[9] Despite the rhetoric of dismantling and retrenching the welfare state, major social programmes and levels of social expenditures in almost all developed countries remain largely unaffected. There is no empirical signs of crisis and emphasis should rather be directed at analysing the welfare states' capacity to adapt to changed circumstances, some argue.[10]

Preservation of time-honoured programmes and unchanged levels of expenditures, however, do not necessarily ensure the continuous existence of the very same welfare state. Imagine that the welfare state is not seen as the independent variable, but as a dependent variable. In that case one might argue that even if changes in the wake of efforts to cut spending and to shore up the legitimacy of the welfare state appear to be small and not to challenge the basic principles of social policy, when seen in a longer perspective their cumulative effects might be more dramatic. Analysing in particular Denmark – described as a country in which the ideals of the welfare state are well-entrenched – Cox (1997) acknowledged trends towards a change of the idea of welfare entitlements from a *social right of citizenship* to a more *discursive right*.[11]

Because welfare spending continues to grow in Denmark, these changes are often overlooked by scholars who examine the spending effects of retrenchment. But growth in spending has much to do with increasing demand on welfare programmes. A greying population and high unemployment are two of the more pronounced engines of growth. To accommodate the growing demand and keeping spending from rising even higher, Danish governments have instituted small changes in programmes over the years. Research that employs quantitative measures of welfare spending fails to capture how these small changes have shifted the categories of eligibility and altered the conception of entitlement.[12]

Discussions on 'affordability', the 'critical level of taxation' and 'taxable capacity' frequently degenerate into rhetoric, and the idea of the welfare state as a burden to the economy remains controversial. Fifty-nine years ago Clark[13] argued that, once a government's share in national income exceeds 25 per cent, strong inflationary pressures emerge. Much of the ensuing critical debate concentrated on his stipulation of a specified limit. Lost amid the ridicule Clark was subjected to, as the share of taxation in national income skyrocketed, was his general principle that there exists a positive relation between the relative size of government and the strength of inflationary pressures. Without specifying any 'limit', Johnson (1975)[14] endorsed Clark's thinking by emphasizing that deficit spending and the resulting inflation, by alleviating the intensity of taxpayer resistance, are important factors having made possible the increase of the relative size of the public sector. Buchanan and Wagner (1977)[15] did point to the implications for individual liberty arguing that Keynesian norms, rightly or wrongly, may suggest an increase in aggregate public spending. But an expansion in overall budget size is reflected, they argued, in increases in particular spending programmes, each one of which will quickly come to develop its own *beneficiary constituency*, within both the bureaucracy itself and the clientele groups being served.

A related problem has to do with the possible connection between the level of taxation and individuals' willingness to comply with the *rules of the game* set by the political system in general and the mode of being implied by the comprehensive welfare state in particular. Lindbeck (1981)[16] underlined that the corollary to increased marginal tax rates – apart from their possible effects on incentives – is a rising price on honesty. This in turn means that loyalty to society may be weakened. The welfare state's *mode of being*, that is the cultural preconditions of a sustainable welfare state, requires that the present contributors show generosity towards their less lucky fellow countrymen and that the behaviour of these are characterized by modesty and restraint in collecting benefits – both groups acknowledging the reversibility of roles over time.[17] The continued expansion of the welfare state may be a threat to this mode of being. Coined under the headline 'eurosclerosis', some Swedish economists have criticized the Swedish welfare state,[18] while the sociologist Korpi (1988)[19] did not find evidence in favour of the argument that the welfare state is necessarily economically inefficient.

Many Nordic sociologists and political scientists (and fewer economists) think that everything in the garden of the Nordic welfare state is lovely. This view is a corollary to their understanding of the Nordic welfare state from a labourist approach and an ethnocentric perspective. I myself feel more comfortable by endorsing Lindbeck's (1995) dictum:

> it is easy to visualize how welfare-state policies, under favourable circumstances, may generate virtuous circles of reduced poverty, better neighbourhoods, less street crimes, improved health among low-income groups, the accumulation of widely distributed human capital, increased labour productivity, and higher labour force participation rates for women and various ethnic minorities; and all this contributes to an expanded tax base, which facilitates the financing of the welfare-state programs in the first place. We may also speculate that welfare-state policies contribute to improved social coherence, and perhaps even to greater tolerance in the population for the continual reallocation of resources that characterizes a dynamic market economy, and that this reinforces the legitimacy, and hence the support of the welfare state among those who do not perceive much direct benefit to themselves . . . indeed, it is

largely because of various virtuous long-term consequences of welfare-state arrangements that I have often described the modern welfare state as 'a triumph of western civilization'. But if we do not watch out for hazardous dynamics, there is a risk that the welfare state will destroy its own economic foundations.[20]

The attitudes of the Danes regarding 'their' welfare state

Compared to previous decades, the public dispute on social policies has turned away from emphasizing gaps in social protection towards urging concerns about 'affordability', 'globalization' and 'incentives'. A restructuring of the welfare state has loomed large on the political agenda. How does this compare with the attitudes of the Danes?

Survey data suggest a widespread support for the welfare state in the late 1960s. In 1973 a sudden 'welfare backlash' occurred, witnessed by the electoral success of a newly formed anti-tax party.[21] Following this event welfare state support gradually recovered to peak in 1987. The development does not support the thesis that the electoral backing of the welfare state will decline in the long run due to income increases and accompanying middle-class lifestyles, and it does not disclaim the alternative idea that an institutional welfare state in which almost everybody is a potential welfare user is less exposed to this risk. Institutionalization, so the argument runs, weakens reasoning in terms of self-interests. This view is to some extent confirmed by the fact that universal programmes are supported to a greater extent than are selective/targeted/means-tested ones.[22]

Table 12.1 similarly demonstrates that Danes are strongly in favour of 'their' welfare society. It has to be 'defended at any price'. Their support, however, is a bit ambiguous in the sense that many Danes believe that it has grown too expensive and that too many citizens without genuine 'needs' take advantage of the benefits offered. The strong support of the view that

Table 12.1 Share of respondents (%) completely or partly agreeing to the following statements

• The welfare society is an accomplished success which must be defended in any case	79%
• The welfare society is a good society; but it is too expensive to society	76%
• The welfare society has expanded too much in the sense that many take advantage of public benefits even though they could easily manage without	78%
• People ought to contribute before they can benefit	91%

Source: Juul (1996).[23]

contributions (obligations in one sense or another) have priority to the collection of benefits runs to some extent counter to the basic principles of the Danish welfare state, as we shall see below.

Following a heated debate on the pressure of taxation, an investigation by SONAR[24] recently showed that 63 per cent of the Danes responded in the positive to the assertion, 'I do pay too much in taxation', while 36 per cent thought that they paid a reasonable amount. No-one responded that the tax payments were too small. In response to the question: 'Are you personally willing to accept an increased taxation in order to improve social benefits', only 17 per cent responded in the positive, 69 per cent in the negative with 14 per cent declaring 'don't know'. These figures suggest that the Danes are sceptical regarding further tax increases.

From a social security state towards a welfare state

Denmark introduced old-age relief separate from the Poor Law in 1891, voluntary insurance against sickness subsidized by the state in 1892, and in 1898 a scheme of employers' liability for accidents at work which rapidly developed into an insurance system financed by the employers. In 1907 a state-subsidized voluntary insurance against unemployment was introduced.

The 'welfare diamond' shown in Figure 12.1 suggests that the market, the voluntary sector and the family (together constituting civil society), as well as the state/government, are institutions promoting individual welfare. During the twentieth century the weight has gradually been shifted towards the state or the public sector as the primary institution, in particular in the Danish model originating from the 1891 Act on Old Age Relief.[25] By this Act:

- The state/government was adopted as the *decision-making* authority and the municipalities/counties as the *implementing/managing* units;
- *Universal coverage* was introduced;
- *General taxation* within a *pay-as-you-go* financing method was adopted;
- Any *linkages* between benefits and financial contributions were rejected;
- *Institutional services* provided by the public authorities were given great emphasis;
- *Generous benefits for low-income individuals* and modest ones for the better-off were implemented; and
- *Reduction of poverty and inequalities in income distribution* were adopted as the basic objectives.

The epoch from the early 1890s up to the 1950s may be called the phase of the *social security state*, as well-defined functional welfare measures were taken over by the public sector. The *criteria of entitlement* followed a

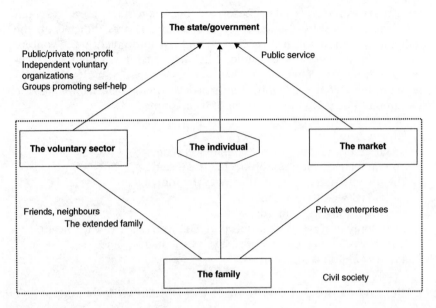

Figure 12.1 The welfare diamond
Source: Fridberg (1997).[26]

casuistic principle; the events provoking benefits were perceived as imputable to, but unbearable by the individual.

Subsequent to the Second World War, the scope of imputable acts was more and more narrowly defined and eventually almost denied. Motives of individual acts were removed from the individual and attributed to external or previous factors. Three phenomena were decisive: The *'demostrategy'*,[27] a related *extended understanding of democracy*[28] and a *'scientification' of social policy*.[29] Another more pedestrian but important factor was the *increasing labour force participation of women*.

However, it may be these factors – mirroring *der Zeitgeist* – caused fundamental societal changes during the 1950s and 1960s. The social security state was replaced by the welfare state almost representing a myth of the golden age; the founding fathers saw a paradise in this life, a blessed and faultless society. The welfare state was understood almost religiously as the redeemer of the people from the competitive capitalism and the centrally planned society both embodying the devil. The corollary to this understanding of society is the idea of the individual as a victim of external factors meaning that he or she is basically irresponsible for his or her life. This perspective implies an extension of the themes and interests begging for the good graces of the politicians. The suggested revocation of the imputable to be replaced by the role of the victim means the gradual self-disintegration of the social security state to be replaced by the logic of the welfare state: it revolves about compensation for all disadvantages and inconveniences inflicted on the individual by life itself. If it is accepted and put into practice, the concept of compensation causes a dynamic of its own which turns the social security state into a welfare state.[30] These remarks suggest some of the weaknesses of the welfare state while simultaneously urging that the welfare state has much to be placed to the credit of its account:

- Poverty is reduced or alleviated;
- Social exclusion and polarization are weakened;
- An equitable distribution of income is ensured;
- The income stream is smoothed over the individual's lifecycle;
- Individual security is provided;
- Social tensions are reduced;
- The supply of services like education, childcare, old-age care, healthcare is increased compared to a provision by the market; and
- Social cohesion is safeguarded.

Indicators of the development of the Danish welfare state

Despite a strongly fluctuating rate of unemployment (see Figure 12.2) – generally lying below the rate of the OECD-Europe countries – the number of

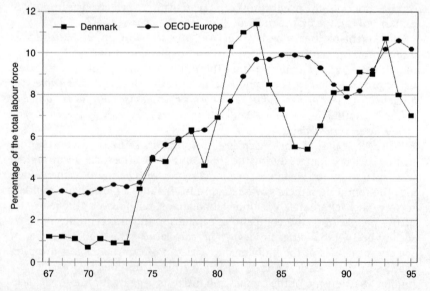

Figure 12.2   Rate of unemployment
Source: OECD (1997).[31]

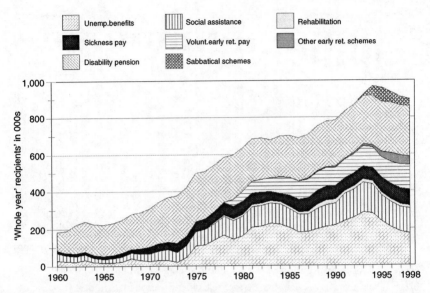

Figure 12.3 Recipients of transfer payments in the age group 15–66
Source: Finansministeriet 1997, Statistisk Tiårsoversigt 2000.[32]

recipients collecting transfer payments has been persistently growing from 6.2 per cent of the group of age 15–66 in 1960 to a peak of 26.3 per cent in 1994 (Figure 12.3). Following several legislative initiatives, the number was doubled during the period 1960–73 despite a historically unusually low rate of unemployment. In the wake of the first oil crisis the development mirrored a dramatic increase in the number of 'whole-year-recipients' from 1973 until 1975. The phase 1975–95 shows another doubling partly due to the higher average level of unemployment and partly due to the introduction of a number of schemes offering benefits to people who in principle might have worked.

Another characteristic of the era has been a generally constant frequency of employment. The reflected image is a constant share of the 15–66-years-old cohort either collecting transfer incomes or being provided for in other ways. Within the group of the employed, the period is characterized by a declining share being privately employed and an increasing proportion of publicly employed persons. The change in the composition of the unemployed group is the more spectacular. As illustrated by Figure 12.4, the part of the group living on the basis of publicly provided transfer incomes has been persistently growing, while the share provided for in other ways has been in decline over the 30 years illustrated. This reflects that public provision has replaced provision by the family (Figure 12.1). The byproduct has

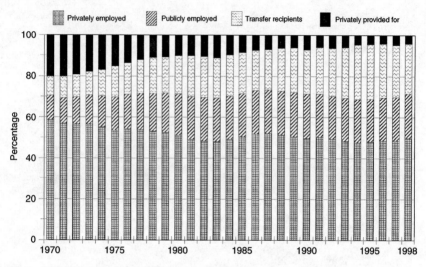

Figure 12.4   The distribution of the population of age 15 to 66
Source: Danmarks Statistik: Statistisk Tiårsoversigt, different years.

been a remarkable increase in current government disbursements and receipts as witnessed by Table 12.2. In 1960, Denmark was 6 percentage points below current disbursements' share of GDP in the OECD-Europe countries, while being 11 points above in 1995. Most of the increase took place in the two decades from 1960 to 1980. The table suggests, too, that the Danish welfare state is very service-intensive, while there is not much difference between the Danish model and other European welfare states regarding transfer payments.

The hallmarks of the Danish welfare state

The Danish welfare model is founded on the assumption that people live their entire life in the country in which they are born and that their mutual solidarity is nationally delimited, so that people managing well are willing to finance welfare benefits to their less lucky fellow men – being convinced that they themselves will be similarly treated if or when they get ill, old, unemployed or handicapped.

The Danish, the Bismarckian and the Beveridgean welfare state models all rely on the pay-as-you-go procedure regarding the mode of financing. The two latter rely on the principles of *social insurance*, while the former is based on a *tax-transfer mechanism*. The Bismarckian model applies wage-differentiated contributions and the benefits are dependent on previous contributory payments, previous income and previous employment records,

Table 12.2 Development indicators for the Danish welfare state

		1960 (percentage)	1960–70	1970–80	1980–90	1990–95	1960–95	1995 (percentage)
					(percentage points)			
Current government disbursements as a percentage of GDP	Denmark	21.4	+13.2	+17.6	+4.6	+2.9	+38.3	59.7
	OECD-Europe	27.1	+4.8	+10.5	+1.8	+4.5	+21.6	48.7
Government final consumption as a percentage of GDP	Denmark	13.3	+6.4	+6.7	−1.4	−0.1	+11.9	25.2
	OECD-Europe	13.4	+1.6	+3.2	−0.1	+0.2	+4.9	18.3
Social security transfers as a percentage of GDP	Denmark	7.4	+4.2	+5.0	+1.8	+3.1	+14.1	21.5
	OECD-Europe	9.5	+2.7	+4.9	−0.1	−3.2	+10.7	20.2
Current government receipts as a percentage of GDP	Denmark	27.3	+14.0	+10.5	+4.0	+1.9	+30.8	58.1
	OECD-Europe	30.9	+6.0	+6.0	+0.8	+2.4	+15.1	46.0

Source: OECD (1997).

	1970	1970–80	1980–90	1990–99	1970–99	1999
Number of public employees, Denmark	384,000	+307,000	+81,000	+38,000	+424,000	808,000

Source: Danmarks Statistik, Statistisk Tiårsoversigt, different years.

while the Beveridgean model makes use of equal contributions and equal benefits. They are both market-like arrangements in the sense that they – contrary to the tax-transfer mechanism – presuppose a *quid-pro-quo relation*.

The German and the British basic principles are derived from a perspective of reciprocity from the generational as well as the individual point of view. The Danish model, however, relies primarily on the idea of *role reversability*: the reversability of roles means that one imagines what help one would have appreciated if one were in 'the other's' place, and that one actually provides 'the other' with a similar benefit. The pay-as-you-go procedure ensures a principle of reciprocity as far as generations are concerned, but the tax-transfer mechanism implies reliance on a *norm of beneficence* at the individual level.[33]

The future sustainability of the Danish welfare model

Globalization and internationalization

The Danish welfare model is exposed to a number of challenges, the first of which has to do with the *internationalization* and *globalization* of the economy. The growth potential of most modern economies is conditioned by the openness of the economy and an extended economic integration. This is the positive side of the Janus-head of globalization. The individual economies on the other hand are made extremely interdependent and vulnerable; their independent decision-making regarding fiscal and monetary policies is constrained.

Mobility of capital may cause a political tax competition among countries endeavouring to attract capital. This may erode the national tax bases and may be a challenge in particular to a social security system that relies to a large extent on general taxation as its instrument of financing. Greater mobility of the most productive persons in a global labour market also tends to create increased inequalities and to put a brake on the progressiveness of the income tax system.

The development of *global workplaces* raises basic issues concerning rights and responsibilities. The more mobile the population, the greater is the risk that the implicit social contract of the nation state will be eroded. The implication is that financing from general taxation will meet greater difficulties implying that the problem of setting priorities will be intensified. There may then develop an increased pressure to make the 'contract' explicit, that is to introduce a more explicit linkage between contributory payments and 'rights' – a *quid-pro-quo relation* at the individual level in one way or another. The experiences of the United States suggest that mobility does not necessarily imply a harmonization of the welfare levels across countries, but there will be a strengthened competition among countries to appear attractive to the most valuable members of the labour force as well as to capital.

A high level of social security spending triggers a high level of contributory payments and/or a high level of general taxation. Heavy social contributions and taxes, high and rigid wages, and extensive job rights make the hiring of additional workers prohibitively costly and the labour market inflexible. The implied high labour costs inevitably reduce the economic viability of enterprises in a world of global competition, forcing them to shift towards more capital-intensive production technologies or to relocate into low-cost regions, thus negatively affecting the demand for labour. One of the most pressing problems the old welfare states have to face is that *the market for unskilled labour has become international.*

The problem is enhanced by the development of the so-called 'knowledge- and information society' as a corollary to the rapid introduction of new technology. This development – intensified by a more extensive international division of labour – calls for a well-educated and flexible labour force causing problems not only for immigrants, cf. below, but for all unskilled workers without vocational education. The result might be *new forms of marginalization and social exclusion* concentrated on a more or less well-defined subgroup of the population. To the extent that a more or less permanent dependency is concentrated on a subgroup, this is a challenge to the idea of role reversability forming the ethical basis of the Danish welfare state model. Secondly, the problem is intensified because of the compressed income structure of Denmark.

A more heterogeneous population

A second challenge is caused by the development of a more heterogeneous population.[34] Immigration of refugees and asylum-seekers has increased the share of immigrants and descendants of immigrants from 2.7 per cent of the population in the mid-1980s to 7 per cent in early 2000.

Immigrants are difficult to integrate into the Danish labour market, and the OECD[35] has demonstrated that Denmark has the largest additional unemployment level among immigrants. In 1997 their unemployment amounted to three times the unemployment among the Danes. The generous transfer incomes for low-income individuals mean that minimum wages are relatively high compared to many other countries. The structure of wages is strongly compressed. The corollary is difficulties for immigrants in finding jobs.

For 1998 it has been estimated that 64 per cent of non-Western immigrants are collecting temporary benefits compared to 36 per cent among the Danes.[36] If minority groups become long-term dependent on social benefits this will be a threat to national solidarity and might give rise to a demand for more individual rights. In addition, it will provoke reasoning in terms of *'them'* and *'us'*, contrary to the basis of the Danish welfare model, and the principle of *role reversability* will be eroded.

Societal cohesion, the reliance on the idea of role reversability, the legitimacy of a comprehensive redistribution of incomes and the acceptance of

Table 12.3   Contributions to the number of working hours, 1960–98 (%)

	1960–70	1970–80	1980–90	1990–98	1960–98
Change in the number of working hours	–3.9	–6.0	0.5	2.6	–7
Contributions from:					
• labour force participation	0.3	5.0	3.3	–2.2	7
• unemployment	0.5	–5.9	–2.8	3.3	–5
• average working hours	–12.8	–10.1	–4.4	–0.8	–28
• demography	8.0	4.7	4.3	2.3	19

Source: Finansministeriet, *Danmark som foregangsland. Arbejde og Service*, København, 1999.

a high level of taxation seem to be anchored in the remarkable homogeneity of the Danish population. The homogeneity itself, however, seems to make integration more difficult. Observers sometimes speak about the Danes as a tribe. In my definition of the Danish welfare state (p. 186) I urged the fact that it is assumed that people live their entire life in the country in which they are born and that their mutual solidarity is nationally defined. This makes it difficult to cope with non-tribe members and to sustain a welfare state model relying on a tax-transfer mechanism and based on universalism. Such a model, obviously, is more vulnerable compared to the continental European model based on accumulating rights.

No doubt the coherence of society is a basic Danish value. Globalization and a more heterogeneous population raise the issue of keeping control of the embedded values defining national identity. The challenge is that growing heterogeneity may transgress the limits ensuring societal sustainability of the structure of values.

Demographic development

The sustainability is, thirdly, threatened by demographic development. Since the mid-1960s, the growing welfare state has been easier to finance because of a favourable demographic development implying an increase in the number of people of working age and in particular because of the entrance of women into the labour market (see Table 12.3). This development has come to an end. The number of young people entering working age is declining and the female labour force participation rate of today is by and large similar to that of men. There is *no more easy money for social security*, and on top of this we know that the groups set to retire in the future are large compared to those entering the labour market. The number of old people will grow relative to the number of people engaged in gainful employment (Figure 12.5) which will put pressure on the financing of the welfare state.

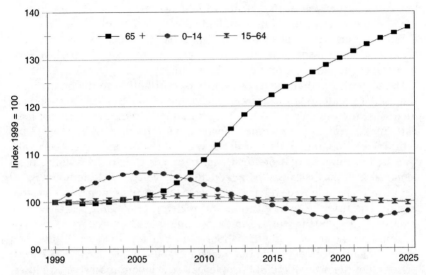

Figure 12.5 The number of children, old and potentially active, 1999–2025
Source: Danmarks Statistik, Befolkningsfremskrivning.

Rising expectations

A fourth factor has to do with rising expectations. Future generations of old people have grown up as children of the welfare state and they are not moderate in their demands compared to the present generation of pensioners representing the children of the 1930s marked by the depression.

Increasing demand for leisure

The welfare state has, fifthly, to cope with an increasing demand for leisure. Increasing family incomes have given rise to an increased demand for leisure, enhanced by the progressive income tax. Increased leisure means a decline in gross income, but the higher the marginal tax rate is, the lower is the reduction of the net income. To the extent that families voluntarily reduce their labour supply either by individual decisions or by supporting the endeavours of trade unions bargaining about working hours their welfare increases. But two corollaries are involved. The first is that *the non-active population does not share in the welfare-enhancing effects*, and the second is that *the tax basis is eroded* implying a need for higher tax rates and/or a reduction of public expenditure: this the financial basis of the welfare state is undermined. Most Danes support the welfare state in opinion surveys and in their political acts, but simultaneously they demand more leisure. Individually and on a family basis the increased leisure means a gain of welfare, because the value of the extra leisure exceeds the value of the income loss net of taxation. Individually it appears rational to demand additional leisure, but it erodes the basis of the celebrated welfare society. The sustainability of the welfare state demands that individual acts do not run counter to the common desires. Here, individual and collective rationality seem to be contradictory. Some of the contributions and changes to the number of working hours over the period 1960–98 are shown in Table 12.3.

The table shows that the largest positive contribution to the financing of the welfare state is caused by a favourable demographic development increasing the number of working hours by 19 per cent. Rising labour force participation (mainly by women) increased the number by another 7 per cent. Increasing unemployment in the wake of the oil crises meant a reduction in the number of working hours by 5 per cent only, but the most remarkable impact is caused by a reduction of average working hours by 28 per cent. Increasing wealth has to a large extent been coined into increased leisure. The rising level of taxation and increasing marginal tax rates have intensified the pressure towards a descending labour supply.

Young people are entering the labour market at a higher age, either delaying their entrance to the labour market or because of long educational periods. On the other hand old people leave the labour market at still lower ages – a trend provoked by the introduction in 1979 of a favourable pre-retirement scheme. And the gainfully employed have reduced their numbers of working hours on a yearly basis by reducing working hours per week and by bargaining in favour of longer holidays.

Extended individualization

Whether the trend towards a greater reliance on individualization has to be understood as a challenge to the welfare state as such is an open question. But it is a fact that recent years have witnessed a shift of the Danish welfare system as a welfare state prototype towards another trajectory.

Unilateral transfer payments were among the hallmarks of the Danish model from the early days, but the basic change of the pension system reflected in the development of *labour market pensions based on a capital-reserve system* and void of most redistributional measures illustrates that the principle of *reciprocity* is gaining ground. The same is true regarding voluntary, early retirement pay. The scheme was reformed in 1999, among other things increasing the contributory payments and letting the contributions have the status of private property, thus increasing individual decision-making and weakening the solidaristic elements. Another new trend has been the development of private sickness insurance arrangements at the company level, reflecting a scepticism concerning the working of the Danish healthcare sector. The 1990s witnessed a changed labour market policy implying that the time-honoured rights were replaced by a set of rights conditioned by obligations. Unilateral transfers – something for nothing – were replaced by quid-pro-quo based transfers – something for something. The responsibility of civil society was given greater emphasis.

If these trends are intensified, we have to face a crowding-out of a number of traditional welfare state arrangements. Whether this will weaken the welfare state/society or not is an open question, but the adopted principles of the Danish welfare state are at stake.

Concerns about incentives

A seventh group of concerns refer to *incentives*. A higher contribution and/or tax rate will, *ceteris paribus*, increase labour costs and reduce net earnings, thus enhancing the problems regarding 'tax wedges'. And, in addition, one has to acknowledge the complicated interplay between tax rates and targeted benefits causing – at least in some countries – an effective trap in the sense that it is impossible to change one's position, because the effective marginal tax rate (that is, the sum of the marginal tax rate itself and the rates applied in targeting different benefits) is close to – and in extreme cases even exceeds – a hundred per cent.

Disincentives in this sense mean the existence of a wedge between the social and the private returns on individual activities caused by the institutional design of social protection systems and the implied financing. They may reduce the supply of labour and saving, increase the amount of 'do-it-yourself-work', promote a barter economy, weaken job-mobility and geographical mobility, enlarge the return on tax evasion, encourage the underground economy, urge moral hazard behaviour and so on.

There is no systematic and non-controversial empirical evidence on the extent of these effects, and to some extent the impact may be mitigated by non-financial incentives, for instance by efficient work enforcement rules.

On the other hand it seems reasonable to assume that the impact of disincentives grows with the tax and transfer level. This is all the more important if we take account of the hypothesis[37] that the disincentive effects of welfare state arrangements on economic behaviour and the implied economic distortions are often delayed because *habits and social norms* constrain economic behaviour. The assumptions of the hypothesis are (i) that today's habits and social norms are influenced by institutions, including economic incentives and government control systems of the past; (ii) that an individual is more likely to conform to certain habits and social norms, the more other individuals in society do so; (iii) that earlier acquired habits and social norms tend to survive after the incentive or control system have changed; (iv) that a sufficiently large increase in economic disincentives, or a sufficiently large softening of government control, creates a tension between habits and social norms on the one hand, and economic incentives and government control on the other, and that this will induce some individuals to stop following earlier obeyed habits and norms, with others following suit; and (v) that major macro-economic shocks to the national economy may speed up the process by which earlier obeyed habits and norms are abandoned. Factors (i)–(iii) ensure that the national economy is encapsulated for a while from the effects of a deterioration in economic incentives, while (iv) means that sufficiently large deteriorations in economic incentives may gradually overcome the inertia generated by initially existing habits and norms.

The corollary to high effective marginal tax rates is a higher financial reward from *freeriding*, *moral hazard* and *outright cheating*, that is a high tax on honesty eventually leading to a weakening of loyalty towards society – not only among those who are hurt by the combined effect of high marginal tax rates and the transfer reductions with rising earnings, but also among those who notice that others are engaging themselves in freeriding, moral-hazard, cheating or in general being excessively 'smart' with tax-transfer-motivated transactions:

> Thus, the Nordic welfare systems are vulnerable in that their very aim for universal coverage, flexibility, and internal rationality have removed characteristics that could service as reminders that the provisions are not paid out of a bottomless well, but by the citizen himself in his capacity as taxpayer. That factors which belong together economically, and which should thus also be psychologically connected, are systematically kept apart by the Nordic welfare system itself exacerbates the problem of the 'free rider' – who is, after all, not an immoral abuser of the system, but rather a rational, sensible economic man.[38]

The implications of systemic responsibility

The responsibility of 'the system' may as an eighth factor contribute to a weakening of individual responsibility. If the responsibility is collectivized by rules of taxation and transfers, personal responsibility becomes abstract, depersonalized and alienated:

> Welfare ideology seeks rational, predictable solutions to man's tribulations. To meet the demands for justice and equality of that ideology, rational humanitarianism must be meted out on a predetermined impersonal basis.
>
> But while humanitarianism may become more evenly distributed through the logic of rationalism, in the process it loses its heart. The conscience of the average citizen is soothed by the assumed reliability of bureaucratized humanitarianism, and he begins to believe that his fellows will be taken care of by the system without any effort on his part. The milk of human kindness therefore flows less frequently from one human being to another; instead it is dispensed in homogeneous form through regulations and institutions. It is this dualism in moral outlook – this preoccupation with formalized humanitarianism coexistent with a dearth of spontaneous humanity – that makes Swedes seem so paradoxical.[39]

The same observation applies in the Danish case.

The changing nature of demand and the changing nature of politics

Historically, the 'needs' of a population have had to do with *'external welfare'*, that is the material terms of life to be satisfied by provision of cash and services. This demand is easily met by the welfare state representing the systemic world. But to a growing extent people's 'needs' – in the rich part of the world – now concern *'internal welfare'*, the feeling of 'belonging', the feeling of identity and acceptability, self-esteem and so on. This demand has much more to do with immediate face-to-face relations between men and women, and calls for 'proper answers' in the real-life world. It calls for measures originating within the welfare *society*, and cannot be met by the usual remedies of the welfare *state*.

Simultaneously, the concept of politics is becoming transformed. Years ago labourers would vote for the Social Democratic Party, farmers for the Liberals, academics for the left wing parties or the Social Liberals, and so on. The parties represented ideologies and the ideologies had repercussions concerning the basic economic structure. The correspondence between one's place in the social structure and one's political attitudes did to some extent predispose for the development of a welfare state in one manner or another. But today it seems that this frame for policy has been replaced by a much more individualized 'policy' based on a personal, moral, reflective approach. The 'old politics' was more in line with the idea of a welfare state, while the 'new politics' to a greater extent complies with the welfare society.

The schizophrenic man

It appears to me that the modern man of the Nordic welfare state is to a great extent schizophrenic in the sense that he praises solidarity in principle but acts in a self-centred manner in practice. One may speak about *solidaristic egocentrism*. Similarly, there are indications of risk-willingness in personal life running parallel to a demand for full security ensured by the collectivity. One may speak about *risk-bearing security addicts*.

The *responsible citizen* of previous days appears to be replaced by men *victimized* by external circumstances.

A final observation

Anticipating future fiscal problems caused by future demographic developments, the Danish government has set up a so-called Plan 2010 implying that the labour force has to be increased and that the growth rates of public expenditures have to be curtailed in order to ensure a sustainable fiscal policy. So far the results achieved have not been very positive. The problem is that the Danish population by and large can be divided into two groups: members of the labour force, and those who receive income-transfer payments. Taking the demographic development into account, this means that a rising labour force can be achieved only by stimulating or forcing recipients of transfer incomes into gainful employment, or by weakening the incentives to an early withdrawal from the labour market. The modest political changes of the criteria for collecting voluntary, early retirement pay introduced in 1998/99 met with extreme criticism from the population, and this has more or less paralysed the politicians. The former Social Democratic government – responsible for implementing the changes – was turned down at the subsequent election and the new bourgeois government declared that it did not have the objective of implementing basic changes to the social security arrangements. The new government has concentrated efforts on adopting measures to restrict immigration. One has to acknowledge, however, that the problems in the wake of rising immigration mirror some problems internal to the Danish welfare model as traditionally understood. The increased openness of the economy demands serious reflection concerning the time-honoured characteristics of the Danish welfare state. The basic issue is how to cope with the challenges discussed above without changing the basic hallmarks deeply embedded in Danish values.

However it may be, the sustainability of the Danish welfare state and the uniqueness attributed to the implied welfare state prototype cannot be taken for granted. And it has to be acknowledged that at least some of the challenges are corollaries to the 'hereditary' characteristics of the developmental trajectory of the Danish model – Lindbeck's hazardous dynamics – while others follow independently from the implied path dependency. There is hardly any doubt, however, that in order to sustain itself, the welfare state has to be transformed. Whether the future society will be better or worse no-one knows, but it will be different from the society we have known up to the present.

Notes

1   See, for example, D.J. Besharov, J. Ehrle, and K.N. Gardiner', 'Social Welfare's Twin Dilemma: Universalism versus Targeting and Support versus Dependency', International Social Security Association, 2nd International Research Conference on Social Security, Conference Volume, Geneva, ISSA, 1998, pp. 1–41.
2   See, for example, R.H. Cox, 'The Consequences of Welfare Retrenchment in Denmark', *Politics and Society*, London, vol. 25, 1997, pp. 303–26.
3   See, for example, W. Schmähl, 'Financing of Social Security, Two papers on the Instruments and Methods of Financing Social Insurance Schemes', Zentrum für Sozialpolitik, Universität Bremen, Arbeitspapier, Bremen, no. 21, 1997.
4   See, for example, V. George and S. Miller, 'The Welfare Circle towards 2000. General Trends', in V. George and S. Miller (eds), *Social Policy towards 2000: Squaring the Welfare Circle*, London: Routledge, 1994.
5   See, for example, A. de Jasay, *The State*, Oxford: Blackwell, 1985.
6   See, for example, F. Cairncross, 'Is the British Welfare System Sustainable?', in P. Koslowski and A. Føllesdal (eds), *Restructuring the Welfare State, Theory and Reform of Social Policy*, Berlin: Springer, 1997, pp. 9–20; D. Döhring, 'Is the German Welfare State Sustainable?', in P. Koslowski and A. Føllesdal (eds), *Restructuring the*

Welfare State, Theory and Reform of Social Policy, Berlin: Springer, 1997, pp. 38–64; and K. Schuyt, 'Is the Welfare System of the Netherlands Sustainable?', in P. Koslowski and A. Føllesdal (eds), *Restructuring the Welfare State, Theory and Reform of Social Policy*, Berlin: Springer, 1997, pp. 21–37.

7   See, for example, P. Koslowski, 'Restructuring the Welfare State: Introduction', in P. Koslowski and A. Føllesdal (eds), *Restructuring the Welfare State, Theory and Reform of Social Policy*, Berlin: Springer, 1997, pp. 1–8.

8   See, for example, P. Pierson, *Dismantling the Welfare State: Reagan, Thatcher and the Politics of Retrenchment*, Cambridge: Cambridge University Press, 1994; and P. Pierson, 'The New Politics of the Welfare State', *World Politics*, Vol. 48, Princeton, Johns Hopkins University Press, 1996, pp. 143–79.

9   See, for example, J. Alber, 'Is There a Crisis of the Welfare State ? Cross-National Evidence from Europe, North America and Japan, *European Sociological Review*, 4(3), 1988, Oxford, pp. 181–207; S. Marklund, *Paradise Lost? The Nordic Welfare States and the Recession 1975–1985*, Lund: Arkiv, 1988; and R. Mishra, 'Social Policy in the Post-modern World', in C. Jones (ed.), *New Perspectives on the Welfare State in Europe*, London and New York: Routledge, 1993, pp. 18–42.

10 See, for example, R. Klein, 'O'Goffe's Tale, or What Can we Learn from the Success of the Capitalist Welfare States?', in C. Jones (ed.), *New Perspectives on the Welfare State in Europe*, London and New York: Routledge, 1993, pp. 7–18.

11 R. Cox, n. 2, p. 309.

12 *Ibid.*, p. 320.

13 C. Clark, 'Public Finance and Changes in the Value of Money', *Economic Journal*, Oxford, 55, 1945, pp. 371–89.

14 H.G. Johnson, 'Living with Inflation', *Banker*, London, vol. 125, 1975, pp. 863–4.

15 J.M. Buchanan and R.E. Wagner, *Democracy in Deficit. The Political Legacy of Lord Keynes*, New York, San Francisco and London: Academic Press, 1977.

16 A. Lindbeck, 'Disincentive Problems in Developed Countries', *Institute for International Economic Studies*, Stockholm, Reprint Series, no. 171, 1981.

17 J.H. Petersen, 'Vandringer i Velfærdsstaten. 11 bidrag om Velfærdsstatens Legitimitet', Odense: Odense Universitetsforlag, 1996; J.H. Petersen, 'Moralske Epistler. Umiddelbare Betragtninger over Velfærdsstatens Grundproblemer', Odense: Odense Universitetsforlag, 1999; and J.H. Petersen, 'Socialøkonomi og -politik', Odense: Odense Universitetsforlag, 2000.

18 A. Lindbeck, P. Molander, M. Persson, A. Sandmo, B. Swedenborg and N. Thygesen, *Turning Sweden Around*, Cambridge MA: MIT Press, 1995; J. Agell, 'Why Sweden's Welfare State Needed reform', *Economic Journal*, Blackwell Publishers, vol. 106, 1996, pp. 1760–71; and M. Henrekson, 'Sweden's Relative Economic Performance: Lagging Behind or Staging on Top?', *Economic Journal*, Blackwell Publishers, vol. 106, 1996, pp. 1747–59.

19 W. Korpi, 'Economic Growth and the Welfare State – Leaky Bucket or Irrigation System?', *European Sociological Review*, Oxford University Press, vol. 1(2), 1988, pp. 97–112; and W. Korpi, 'Eurosclerosis and the Sclerosis of Objectivity: On the Role of Values among Economic Policy Experts', *Economic Journal*, vol. 106, 1996, pp. 1727–46.

20 A. Lindbeck, 'Hazardous Welfare State Dynamics', *American Economic Review*, Princeton, 1995, vol. 85(2), pp. 9–15.

21 The reason for the welfare backlash was probably the extreme growth of public expenditures and taxes during the period 1968–71, in which a majority bourgeois government held office.

22 J. Goul Andersen, P.A. Pettersen, S. Svallforss and H. Uusitalo, 'The Legitimacy of the Nordic Welfare States, Trends, Variations and Cleavages', in M. Kautto, M. Heikkilä, B. Hvinden, S. Marklund and N. Ploug (eds), *Nordic Social Policy, Changing Welfare States*, London and New York: Routledge, 1999, pp. 235–61.

23 S. Juul, 'Befolkningens holdninger til velfærdssamfundet', *Social Forskning, særnummer*, Socialforskningsinstituttet, København, 1996, pp. 8–19.

24 SONAR and Jyllands-Posten; the investigation was implemented on 15 January 2001 based on a representative sample of 1,255 persons.

25 J.H. Petersen, 'Den danske alderdomsforsørgelses udvikling, Oprindelsen', Odense: Odense Universitetsforlag, 1985; J.H. Petersen, 'Three Precursors of Modern Theories of Old Age Pensions: A Contribution to the History of Social Policy Doctrines, *History of Political Economy*', Duke University Press, vol. 18, 1986, pp. 405–17; J.H. Petersen, 'Altersversicherung und Altersversorgung, Ein dänischer Kommentar anlässlich des hundertjährigen Jubiläums des deutschen Invaliditäts- und Altersversicherung, *Deutsche Rentenversicherung* (10–11), Verband deutschen Rentenversicherungsträger, 1989, pp. 649–63; and J.H. Petersen, 'The Danish 1891 Act on Old Age Relief: A Response to Agrarian Demand and Pressure', *Journal of Social Policy*, Cambridge University Press, vol. 19, 1990, pp. 69–91.

26 T. Fridberg, 'Hvem løser opgaverne i fremtidens velfærdssamfund?', København, Socialforskningsinstituttet, 1997.

27 The idea of a 'demostrategy' was coined by Cyril Falls in 1941: 'By this he meant in military terms, that the war could not be won unless millions of ordinary people, in Britain and overseas, were convinced that we had something better to offer than had our enemies – not only during but after the war . . . It was a call for social justice; for the abolition of privilege, for a more equitable distribution of income and wealth; for drastic changes in the economic and sociale life of the country', see R.M. Titmuss, *Essays on the Welfare State*, London: Unwin University Books, 1958, p. 82.

28 Democracy was not only understood as a formal concept of constitutional law, but included a common responsibility for economic and social solidarity; see J.H. Petersen, 'Socialøkonomi og -politik', Odense: Odense Universitetsforlag, 2000, p. 85.

29 To a growing extent the social sciences thought themselves able to uncover causal relations in a manner similar to the sciences, for example to uncover the causes of deviant behaviour, and they thought themselves able to manipulate reality as they wished.

30 Cf. N. Luhmann, *Politische Theorie im Wohlfahrtsstaat*, München: Günter Olzog Verlag, 1981.

31 OECD, *Historical Statistics: 1969–1995*, Paris: OECD, 1997.

32 Finansministeriet, *Danmark som foregangsland. Indkomstoverførsler – færre på passiv forsørgelse. Dokumentation*, København: Finansministeriet, 1997; and Danmarks Statistik, *Statistisk Tiårsoversigt 2000*, København, 2000.

33 See J.H. Petersen, n. 28, pp. 88–92.

34 See, for example, N. Smith, 'Danmark som indvandringsland – udfordringer for velfærdssamfundet', *Social Forskning, særnummer*, København: Socialforskningsinstituttet, 2000; G.V. Mogensen and P.C. Matthiessen, *Mislykket integration*, København: Spektrum, 2000; and E. Wadensjö, 'Omfördeling via offentlig sektor: en fördjupad analys', in G.V. Mogensen and P.C. Matthiessen (eds), *Integration i Danmark omkring årtusindskiftet*, Århus: Århus Universitetsforlag, 2000, pp. 279–335.

35 OECD, *Trends in International Migration*, Paris: OECD, 1999.
36 See G.V. Mogensen and P.C. Matthiessen, n. 34.
37 See A. Lindbeck, 'Welfare State Disincentives with Endogenous Habits and Norms', *Scandinavian Journal of Economics*, Oxford, vol. 97, 1995, pp. 477–93.
38 B.R. Andersen, 'Rationality and Irrationality of the Nordic Welfare State', *Dædalus*, Chicago, 1984, pp. 109–39, quote from p. 126.
39 H. Zetterberg, 'The Rational Humanitarians', *Dædalus*, 1984, pp. 75–92, quote from pp. 90–91.

13
Modernization of the European Model of Social Protection

Joakim Palme

Introduction

European countries have developed advanced systems of social protection. By establishing a universal model of social protection, where benefits and services based on residence are combined with earnings-related social insurance programmes, the Nordic countries have followed a distinctive development path. It has been a successful strategy for combating poverty and social inequalities but also for promoting employment and participation, particularly among women. However, the emergence of mass unemployment has not only threatened public finances, it has also triggered a crisis for the welfare state. Even though several aspects of the crisis are now behind us, it has highlighted a number of dilemmas for reform work, and we need a strategy for resolving these dilemmas without diluting the socio-political and moral content of the welfare state model. This chapter tries to identify important elements of such a strategy in the perspective of the 'modernization' project of European social protection.

The crisis of the welfare state has caused great uncertainty about the future of social protection in the twenty-first century. The prospects of the future appear to be heavily influenced by the recent experiences of mass-unemployment and increasing social inequalities, and large groups in society are threatened by social exclusion at the same time as the state is reducing benefit entitlements and social services, sometimes as a consequence of reduced public social expenditures, more often just as a result of increased needs. The similarities of developments in Europe and other parts of the world are striking, and it evokes several fundamental questions about the future of welfare states: are they affordable? are they desirable?

In this chapter I place the focus on the Nordic countries. One reason to consider the Nordic model is that it has a good track record in terms of socio-political performance; poverty and inequality are low while participation, not least on the labour market, is high. Another reason is that the Nordic countries are struggling with unsolved dilemmas, and if there is scope for political learning, it appears reasonable to expect that an exchange of ideas on these issues would be fruitful. European integration is creating a momentum for all European countries to take a serious grip on their national problems. Globalization of the economy should also widen our horizons on social issues; why should the diffusion of ideas and 'learning from others' be restricted to the economic sphere?

European social policy

We should perhaps start by trying to define what European social policy is about, albeit that the variation in how the various European countries have designed their systems of social protection is huge. It is therefore difficult to talk about one single European model, yet there are aspects which make Europe different from, far example, the United States. One such aspect is the degree of inclusion of different groups, also the middle classes, into the programmes of social protection. The 'modernization project' is part of the economic and political integration of the European Union.

The 'modernization project'

The basic feature of the modernization process is to adapt the system of social protection to change. Three key areas have been identified by the European Commission; the changing nature of work, the ageing of populations and the new gender balance. Why, then, is modernization necessary? One reason is that the systems of social protection, designed decades ago, are no longer effective means to, for example, fight poverty. Another reason is that the system is overburdened financially, and cannot be fully financed; read – taxes cannot be raised without jeopardizing competitiveness on the global market. It is argued in the Communication from the European Commission on modernization of social protection that policies have to be seen as a productive factor, they have to be made employment-friendly, and they have to be financially stable when needs grow stronger as populations age.[1] The proposals for reforms concern both the benefits and how to finance them. They deal with simplification of the coordination of rights, for migrant workers, individualization of rights, and with the transitions both from work to retirement and from unemployment to employment.

The Nordic model

The Nordic model has become an established concept worldwide, but views on its merits and drawbacks differ widely among different observers. Surprisingly often the extreme views are based on myths rather than reality, and it is hence a challenge to provide a more solid empirical base for discussing the model. Despite the variation in how the Nordic model is defined and understood, some labels come up again and again; universalism, generous benefits, social citizenship rights, dual-earner model, active labour market policies, and extensive social service.

Labour market policy has been developed as a form of preventive social policy. Education and training, as well as public relief work, have been expanded when unemployment has increased. The idea has been to maintain and/or improve people's skills so that they are employable when employment opportunities improve. The emphasis on and scope of the various policy instruments have been different in the Nordic countries and have changed over time, yet the costs of the transfer systems in the Nordic countries do not differ from the West European pattern. Several factors have contributed to this. The high formal pension age and the, until recently, low unemployment rate in the Nordic countries are two examples, while the high labour force participation rates among women is another important factor. However, if we include the costs of social services, the costs in the Nordic countries are also high by comparison. This has partly to do with generous provisions, partly to the high proportion of the elderly in the populations.

The Nordic countries are probably the best examples of how the 'male-breadwinner' model has been transformed into a 'dual-earner' model. It is evident that this has required policy changes in a number of respects. The fact that women, over the postwar period, have taken part in education at different levels, to a higher and higher degree, is one important factor behind their massive entrance into the labour market. Women simply developed the necessary human skills and resources. The expansion of child and elderly care are important, both as resources for women with caring responsibilities and as employment opportunities. As I shall explain below, the changes were also facilitated by changes in the tax system which provided better incentives for married women to enter paid employment.

The Nordic countries have developed universal healthcare systems. Total spending on medical care is relatively low by international standards and appears to be well under control, considering how costs have stagnated in the past 10 or 15 years. However, cost control must of course not be thought of as an end in itself; other criteria of good medical care are productivity and quality in the production of medical services, and freedom of choice for the general public. The aim of universal health insurance has been fair access to care and attention, and also, ultimately, to assure quality of health. Gustav Möller, Minister of Social Affairs during the formative decades of Swedish social policy reform, summed up the aims of universal health insurance by saying that 'only the best is good enough for the people'. One possible indicator of the efficiency of public care is the size of privately funded medical care and the extent of private supplementary insurance. In this sense, confidence in universal insurance appears to be good, because private medical insurance is of modest proportions. *But will it increase?* It seems reasonable to expect that this will primarily depend on how the public health sector performs. In all the Nordic countries there appears to be widespread popular concern about resources in the public healthcare systems being too small.

Lastly, a few words of caution are warranted: The Nordic model neither offers a coherent strategy ready to be implemented in other parts of the world, nor a ready-made solution to all the current and future social policy challenges. It is also necessary to note that the 'Nordic model' is not even something which has been equally implemented in the Nordic countries themselves.

Challenges to social protection in Europe

The challenges to the systems of social protection are many and of different kinds. Without exhausting the number of relevant factors, I would like to discuss the following changes which are affecting other European countries; the globalization of the economy, the 'crisis of the population question', exit/entry problems on labour markets, full employment, social integration/exclusion, and problems of participation along with the Europeanization of politics. These changes, in turn, create new challenges regarding the design and implementation of reforms. When it comes to what I would like to call the 'desirability' factor, I will distinguish between three kinds of arguments that, in short, go like this: (i) the welfare state does not deliver the intended social policy outcomes; (ii) the unintended efficiency losses are too large; and (iii) the state should not interfere with the family and the market, at least not as much as it does.

Globalization

The globalization of the world economy is most often perceived as a threat to national systems of social protection. It is not all that clear, however, why the welfare state project as such would not be possible for nation states with open economies. Quite the contrary, the conventional wisdom used to be that the most open economies among the advanced industrial societies had developed the most generous social security systems, in fact as an alternative to the kind of social protection that high tariffs and other import restrictions offered domestic employment.[2] The globalization process is still often used as an argument, or excuse, for welfare state retrenchments. It has been used to create 'a climate of no choice'.[3] It is thus an important challenge to seek reform-strategies that can make welfare state commitments compatible with an exposure to a globalized economy.[4] What appears clear is that the liberalization of capital implies that the profitability of investments in any country would roughly have to follow what applies in the rest of the world, otherwise investors will move the capital. This puts very clear constraints on the financing of social protection. The mobility of labour also puts restrictions on how far wages can be compressed, and how high levels of taxes can be raised in relation to the kinds of benefits and services that are provided.

The social support system may be seen as an instrument for helping individuals to deal with the projects in life that are common to all of us: the chance to get a proper education in order to find a job. Then to actually find a job. To form a family. To have children. To combine family life with participation, on the labour market, and in society at large. To be economically secure in case of exposure to unemployment and ill-health. To get a pension in old-age. To receive the necessary social services and care when physical abilities are decreasing. In modern society, these problems cannot be solved by the family and the market alone.

Unemployment

The continued very high levels of unemployment are associated with a host of social problems. The risk is very high that older workers are pushed out of the labour market and, because of the severe budget constraints, that social security provisions will not be adequate and the consequences will be more serious than when similar processes occurred a couple of decades ago. The problems are even more acute on the 'entry' side of the labour market. Newcomers are facing long queues for all vacancies, leading to very high levels of youth unemployment and very high levels of unemployment among immigrants and refugees. This creates severe problems of social integration of large segments of society with long-lasting effects, part of which are captured by concepts such as 'social exclusion' and 'social marginalization'. The younger the persons are, the longer the problems may last.

The problems of cost-control are not restricted to the high levels of unemployment. In the longer term the cost control of the public pension systems is, of course, a big challenge. The problems of high public social expenditures are aggravated by increasing problems of controlling the tax bases in a global economy, although these problems are serious enough on a European level. It is therefore a challenge to use the political mechanism to deal with the problems on the European level. If all EU countries are serious about defending the systems of social protection, then they have to leave rhetoric behind and take action. All the instruments that the Union has for economic and social policy-making should be made employment-oriented, including the European Central Bank (ECB), the central bank of Europe.

Ethical arguments

The critique of the welfare state *as such* is part of its crisis and, moreover, it is a fundamental challenge for those who believe there are rational grounds for defending the systems of social protection. The critique is not new. In reality, each step in the emergence and development of its various programmes has been followed by critical voices.[5] But it is evident that the critique has been particularly strong over recent decades. One kind of critique of the welfare state is entirely based on, what I would label, *ethical* grounds. The basic argument is that a big state is bad as such and that state interference as such should be minimized. Such arguments have to be dealt with in terms of what they are based on, that is, value judgements. The other criticisms, concerning the intended or unintended consequences, will have to be judged in terms of systematic empirical observations. Even if the theoretical claims about the negative effects are strong, the empirical evidence is scarce.[6]

Ideological issues

Efforts to secure the social protection of entire populations is also undermined by poor cost control of public expenditures. Poor management of welfare state programmes has not only wasted resources, but also contributed to problems of legitimacy. The view that, for example, abuse is common has been fairly widespread, also among the Nordic populations. It is important, though, to distinguish between reasons for eroded legitimacy which have been based on observations of mismanagement, and the critique of the welfare state that has been launched on purely ideological grounds. That 'a good state' was equal to 'a minimal state' came to dominate much of the debate in the 1980s.[7] Such a critique was fuelled by severe problems of underfinancing of welfare state programmes in some countries, contributing to increasing public debts and financial instability of the entire welfare state. In this situation privatization and marketization have been launched as solutions to an overburdened state. If and how these techniques can be used for securing the welfare of all citizens remains an open question, however.

If the incentive problem is a big issue of the critique, then it should be an important part of the modernization project to deal with these problems. First of all it is important to identify where the behavioural effect can be substantiated, and this should of course have an impact on reform priorities. In addition, it is important to take the incentive structure seriously, as a preventive strategy and as a way of accommodating equality and efficiency goals. This is important since female labour force participation is such a critical factor and women have been shown to be more sensitive to economic incentive in their labour supply.

People do not share all values, not even in the Nordic countries, but some values are related to the democratic fundamentals of our societies which is a good reason to argue that they should be part of what we have in common. I would argue that the active participation of all citizens in the political process is such a value. This means that citizenship and democracy are intrinsically intertwined with the issue of participation. The question then becomes: how do we design institutions that promote participation?

Basic security and income security

An important challenge is to accommodate the goals of basic security and income security, or, to put it differently, to both fight poverty and provide social insurance, or, to put it differently again, to find a balance between and coordinate non-contributory and contributory benefits. In this report it will be argued that this is both a desirable and a possible task, and that it can be accompanied with a sound incentive structure. Here the actual *policy design* becomes of crucial importance for how successful various systems are in pursuing the various goals. I am sceptical towards the notion that there is a *trade-off* between contributory and non-contributory programmes. This is not to claim that such a trade-off might not occur, it is rather to deny that it is a necessary element of every system of social protection that include both kinds of benefits. On the contrary, I would argue that there is evidence to suggest that the opposite dynamic is at work. If both kinds of benefits are included in the statutory system of social protection, each of them might actually work better, not least in terms of providing for the social policy goals.[8] The underlying assumption here is that the social protection budget is not fixed but dependent on the content of the entire system, the better the social protection offered by the system the stronger the willingness to pay, and the larger the proportion of the population that gets protection the broader the support for the system.

It is evident that the support of the systems of social protections are very widespread in the Nordic populations, despite the fairly widespread critique of how the systems are managed. This could be interpreted as a message to the reformers to use the same social policy approach. In any case, the political challenge is to design sustainable systems that meet the demands of the citizens without eroding their willingness to pay the economic price for them.

If we want to make the welfare state popular in the twenty-first century, it appears fruitful to rely on a double strategy of, firstly, tying the self-interest of broad majorities in the population to the health, education and social insurance programmes, and, secondly, making the systems work in the way they are intended, that is making them legitimate.

Social protection, inequality and participation

The goal of the welfare state is often defined in terms of poverty reduction, but the Nordic countries appear to have gone further and they have also included the ambition of reducing overall inequalities.[9] Modern welfare states have additional goals like providing social insurance and services of different kinds. However, all social policy boils down to redistribution. Some of that redistribution is vertical – that is, from rich to poor through the system of taxation and benefits. A great deal of redistribution is horizontal, over the lifecycle. This is the case with pensions, child allowances and parent's allowance. Another type of redistribution accompanies the distribution of risk involved by health and work injury insurance and by unemployment insurance. These risks are unevenly distributed throughout the population. Their redistribution also implies a certain degree of vertical redistribution, because the risks of illness, work injury and unemployment are greatest among people in the lowest income brackets. Consequently, most parts of the social insurance system also have an important bearing on the fight against poverty.

Even if the systems of social protections have other goals than just fighting poverty, I still would argue that the situation of the worst-off in society is a powerful indicator of how successful the entire system of social protection is. This is really following the philosopher John Rawls' principles, that we should judge societies on the basis of how we treat those who are worst-off.[10] If then, in the end, the welfare state programmes should be most important for those who lack resources derived from the family or the market, the situation of children provides a special rationale for the welfare state. Children do not choose to be born and brought up by poor parents. It can therefore be argued that governments have a responsibility to ensure that the children in their countries have the same rights to participate in education, healthcare and so on, and that they should be entitled to the necessary resources in terms of nutrition and housing so that they can take full advantage of these rights. If the children cannot be blamed for being poor, the reason why they are to be found in poverty is irrelevant. Whether it is unemployment, sickness, divorce or simply indolence and/or negligence on the part of their parents, it follows that in no case should the children be deprived of the opportunity of becoming full citizens.

In addition to the classical social policy goals discussed above, there are of course a number of other criteria for evaluating how efficient a system of social protections is. These are important because they are related to the underlying issue of combining efficiency and equality. Good examples are: administrative cost-efficiency, low transaction costs at the labour market, portability of insurance entitlements, sound incentive structures, institutional stability and predictability. The last factor is related to the fact that stable institutions, such as property rights, contribute to economic growth by maintaining stable conditions for different kinds of investments.

In the following, I will use results from a number of analyses of income distribution data from the Luxembourg Income Study (LIS) to illustrate how the Nordic countries are doing compared to countries that have applied other social policy strategies. I will start with the classical notion of lifecycle poverty and then discuss what we have called 'the paradox of redistribution'.

Lifecycle poverty

In his classical studies of poverty in York at the turn and beginning of the twentieth century, Seebohm Rowntree identified phases in the lifecycle that appeared to be particularly poverty stricken among the inhabitants of York.[11] The problematic phases occurred when there was an unfavourable balance between work-capacity and consumption-needs in the household. Thus, families with small children were facing high poverty risks. When the children grew up and started to contribute to the household income, and when they subsequently moved away from home, poverty decreased. But poverty was also high among the elderly, not primarily as a result of high consumption-needs but rather as a consequence of decreasing work-capacity. How efficient have then the expansion of social protection been in terms of reducing this kind of lifecycle poverty?

The results from a study by Kangas and Palme, based on the Luxembourg Income Study, give some indications.[12] The analysis was based on data from different time points, the first around 1970 and the second around 1990, and different countries representing different social policy traditions. Big differences were found both over time and among countries. A central tendency was that poverty rates showed a more cyclical pattern at the first time point. The cyclical pattern followed the same trajectory Rowntree had observed, that is poverty was higher among families with children and among the elderly. In the 1990s, this pattern had vanished in the Nordic countries that were included in the study (Finland and Sweden). In Canada, where old-age poverty has become very low, families with children still face clearly higher poverty risks. The cyclical component is still strong in the United States; even if old-age poverty had gone down a little compared to the situation in the 1970s, poverty had gone up among families with children.

What is interesting is that the observed cross-national variation can be linked to the design of social policy programmes. In Finland and Sweden the combination of more generous child benefits and wide coverage of subsidized childcare – enabling second earners to contribute to the household income – appears to have paid off in low poverty among families with children. Similarly, the generosity of the public pension programmes correlates with the poverty rates among the elderly. Here, of course, the universal basic pensions in the Nordic countries and Canada is the most important factor. The results show how the potential of horizontal redistribution may be explored in a successful way. However, a warning sign here is that poverty rates are high among young persons without children – even though there are severe measurement problems that prevent us from drawing very firm conclusions.

In some countries, for example the United States, poverty among families with children has even increased. The feminization of poverty is a fact, even if in Europe it is primarily connected to single parenthood. In addition, the common trends of falling birthrates, increasing divorce rates and single parenthood pose a tremendous challenge for family policy.

The paradox of redistribution

The various social policy models follow different redistributive strategies.[13] The *targeted* model follows the same principles as Robin Hood applied by following the means-testing principle and only give to the poor, and taking from the rich by financing the benefit payments from general taxation. The *basic security* model follows a simple egalitarian strategy by paying flat-rate benefits, that is providing the same benefit levels to both rich and poor. The *corporatist* model, in its classical form, redistributes resources primarily within the different corporations. The *encompassing* model, by relying on universal earnings-related social insurance benefits in fact gives more to those who already have (following the preaching of Matthew rather than that of Robin Hood). However, in reality, most countries apply combinations of different kinds of programmes and the relevance of different principles varies between different sectors. Even if the earnings-related principle might be central in social insurance, it is less applicable in, for example, the provision of social services.

The core issue is whether there are trade-offs between the provision of different kinds of benefits. With Gordon Tullock (1983) we could hypothesize that the more the welfare state programmes are directed towards the non-poor, the more the worst-off in society will lose out.[14] In reality, and contrary to Tullock's expectations, it seems to be that the more the middle class is involved in the welfare state, the better the situation will be for vulnerable groups and the more that social inequalities will actually be reduced by the tax/transfer programmes. The reason might be found in how interests are organized in different kinds of social policy models. Here a vital distinction has to be made between the distributive profile of benefits (and taxes) and the size of the sums that become subject to redistribution. Moreover, there appears to be a correlation between the distributive profile and size of sums for redistribution, the more benefits are targeted the smaller the sums will become. This gives rise to a strongly positive correlation between the size of sums and the size of inequality reduction. But, paradoxically, the more the benefits are targeted to the poor in a country the smaller is the reduction in inequality achieved by the welfare state. Instead, protection should be organized within a common framework so that the poor would not have to stand alone.[15] This inclusive strategy could perhaps be seen as the essence of the European strategy.

Equality and efficiency: sometimes an illusive trade-off

Criticism of big welfare states of the Nordic kind has focused on the incentive problems associated with the high levels of taxation involved, and the lack of control of the growth of public expenditures. Where actual labour market behaviour is concerned, however, it is hard to find any pronounced negative deviations in the Nordic patterns of economic activity as compared with the patterns prevailing in other kinds of welfare state in the Western world. On the contrary, the Nordic countries have one of the world's highest employment participation rates despite the high level of unemployment. This is largely due to the high participation among women.

The relationship between the welfare state and efficiency is under-theorized and under-studied both theoretically and empirically. Several factors contribute to that. One factor is that the intentions are confused with the actual outcomes; another is that the architects behind the systems might have feared a critical examination of the outcomes. There is also an unfortunate combination of perspectives in economics. The neoclassical starting point is that all forms of taxation mean efficiency losses. This starting point leads to a bias towards focusing on the negative aspects of all state intervention. I would argue that it is misleading to compare state intervention in the form of benefits and taxation with no intervention at all. In our kinds of society, in fact in all advanced industrial countries, the state intervenes in many but various ways, and all countries have fairly high taxes. This suggests that it is more fruitful to compare different kinds of interventions, that is how the size and design of transfers/services and taxation affect equality and efficiency, than to make references to the imagined world of no taxation.

On the other hand, Keynes is only of limited assistance for those who would like to argue in defence of the welfare state project. Notwithstanding that his countercyclical approach provided a good argument for state intervention, it could be argued that this perspective is socially 'empty' in two respects. One is that the content of the spending is not given significance. The other is that he did not develop his interest in the distributional aspects. What, hence, is needed is a theoretically motivated analysis of how the incentive structure is affected by the different kinds of policies. What is also warranted is an analysis of how public spending can be used to improve the conditions for economic growth. What is the role of education, training, health, housing, environment, social networks and so on, for promoting growth?

There are, of course, interesting attempts in this direction. Barr (1992) gives excellent examples in terms of both equality and efficiency,[16] pointing out that the potential advantages of public programmes are often neglected. With regard to administration they are much cheaper to run, because of scale effects but also because of the uniform conditions, and transaction costs are much lower. Portability is also usually much better in the public programmes. The possibility of controlling both the incentive structure and costs should be recognized. This boils down to something very similar to the approach advocated by Anthony Atkinson; we should worry less about aggregate social spending and level of taxation, and more about the actual design of both programmes and methods of financing if we are interested in improving the efficiency of welfare state programmes.[17] This is at least what the empirical research on the behavioural impact of welfare state programmes suggests.

Cost-efficiency of universal programmes

With regard to the economic criteria mentioned above, the following can be noted concerning universal and earnings-related programmes of a Nordic type. The administrative cost-efficiency of universal programmes is of course one clear advantage. Another strength of universal systems which are fully earnings-related is that they reduce the so-called transaction costs on the labour market. Individuals, firms and unions do not have to spend time negotiating about the provision of basic insurance and services like health-care. It furthermore promotes mobility and flexibility on the labour market because the universal character of the system means that workers do not lose their earned rights when they move from one job to another – the porta-bility of social insurance is high. One neglected aspect and advantage with public systems is that it is in principle possible to control the incentive struc-ture. Another important role of institutions is that they should promote stability and predictability in society. Douglass North (1990) has found that stable economic institutions – like property rights – are important for growth.[18] The fact that among the most advanced industrial nations, growth was higher in the postwar years in countries with the most stable institu-tions for mediating different and even conflicting interests. Social protec-tion has a potential to contribute here.

There are hence two critical indicators when it comes to the economics of welfare state intervention; (i) actual labour force participation, and (ii) cost control. When it comes to cost control, I would like to make two remarks. Firstly, even during the 1980s public finances appeared to be in better shape in the Nordic countries than in most of the other advanced industrial nations, even those with so-called small welfare states. This devel-opment stands in sharp contrast to the problematic developments in Finland and Sweden during the first half of the 1990s. However, as is evident from the study carried for the Nordic Council of Ministers, the situation has improved a lot recently and public finances are now in, or very or close to, balance in all Nordic countries.[19] The situation in the Nordic sphere is simply better than in EU and OECD areas on average. Consolidated public finances is not the ultimate goal of economic policies, and it is not the only instru-ment for pursuing successful economic policies. However, it is most likely a necessary preconditions for making public commitments – of securing the welfare of all citizens – viable in the longer run.

Public expenditures can of course promote growth and equality simulta-neously by affecting the distribution of at least two aspects of human resources, education and health, in a favourable direction. With regard to health it can be noted that, internationally speaking, the overall goal performance in terms of general health objectives appear to be good among the Nordic countries. Low infant mortality and long life expectancy are clear examples. Class differences with regard to health and use of caring services are smaller in the Nordic countries than in other Western countries. There are, however, disturbing tendencies where health developments are concerned. Women's health is not improving as rapidly as men's, and health inequalities are on the increase not only between men and women but also between different socioeconomic groups.

A framework for reform: universalism, incentives, resources, opportunities, rights and responsibilities

The underlying ambition with the modernization of the European model of social protection should, in my view, be to maintain and, when necessary, restore the universal approach to social protection. By this is meant not only that the entire populations should be covered within the same framework, but also that the benefits and services should be adequate enough to really provide protection for people in different situations and with different income levels. In order to make the system of protection work in practise, it is vital that we find techniques that, in essence, contribute to increase the number of taxpayers and, whenever that is possible, to decrease the number of benefit recipients.

The following questions are central when it comes to the incentive structure. How can poverty traps be avoided? How can marginal effects be reduced? How can welfare state programmes be designed so that it pays more to work while entitlements are protected? To put it differently, the question is how we can design the economic rewards so that they induce the desired behaviours.

Incentives

A rule of thumb is to use universal benefits and services rather than means-tested ones. The reason is that as soon as we start means-testing it will have consequences for how profitable it is for, particularly, low-income persons – often women – to engage in paid employment. Another strategy is to make social insurance provisions earnings-related which makes it profitable for people to work and pay social security contributions. The more they earn and pay, the better the benefit entitlements will be. A technique that has become popular in North America and the United Kingdom is to have earnings-disregards for recipients of means-tested benefits so that benefits will not be fully reduced if the recipient start to earn an income. Notwithstanding that this is very different from the Nordic tradition, where the approach to the problem has been to apply strict activity/work-tests and no one in principle should be able to say no to a job offer, it still appears worthwhile to evaluate the earnings disregard approach seriously.

Resources: skills and services

Once the incentive structure is reformed, the big issue is about resources. It is not enough to make people willing to work, they must also possess the resources to be able to work. This is partly a matter of skills, partly of adequate social services making it possible for adults in families with small children, or frail elderly relatives, to participate in the labour market. The classical strategy is education and training, as well as other forms of active labour market policy, such as public relief work and forms of subsidized employment. The aim with these measures was to improve. or at least maintain, the employability of unemployed persons. This approach has probably contributed to the overall high employment rate. However, when the Nordic countries were hit by mass unemployment, the problem was that the resources were so restricted that governments often found it necessary to give priority to cheap and 'passive' measures. The Nordic approach to resources in respect of social service has been to give heavy subsidies to public services, such as day-care facilities, which has most likely contributed to the overall high employment rate among women.

Opportunities

Even if the labour force is highly skilled, and poverty traps as well as high marginal taxes have been avoided as much as possible, this is of little comfort as long as people do not get the opportunity to exercise their skills. If there are no, or too few, jobs to apply for, good skills might not be enough to become employed. Social policies cannot make up for economic policy failures. This means that a successful strategy has to be based on successful macro-economic policy-making, and the fundamental problem of mass unemployment is that there are too few jobs. But then, on the other hand, successful macro-economic policies are not likely to be enough either if the skills of the unemployed persons do not match what the new vacant jobs demand. It is necessary to improve social policy and labour market institutions in several respects: incentives, resources (skills and services), responsibilities, and opportunities for selected groups. In sum, reforms of the social security systems have to be coupled with macro-economic policy-making promoting employment and growth.

How successful we are in finding a balance between *rights* and *responsibilities* will ultimately depend on the success in providing the proper incentives, resources and opportunities for people to enter the labour market. Hence, every strategy will have to deal with the kinds of obstacles – in terms of incentives, resources and opportunities – that face those who could seek employment. In this context the position of ethnic minorities, and other groups that are discriminated on the labour market, is of critical importance.

Pensions

In the reform work of pension systems over the past decades, it is apparent that European governments have struggled to achieve both goals of income and basic security, while trying to control costs in the longer run. I think that it is possible, within the different frameworks elaborated in the various countries, to improve the balance between the two types of benefits. For employment and gender reasons, it is an advantage to include both kinds of provisions within the framework of a statutory system. The Finnish solution is worth considering since it addresses the incentive problem of basic benefits by always giving something extra for those who have contributed to the earnings-related part of the pension system.[20] The Finnish strategy of coordination of basic and earnings-related benefits has also been followed in the Swedish 1994 pension reform.

The Swedish pension reform deserves a few additional comments since it is relevant for several of the issues raised in this report. By shifting to a defined benefit, cost-control is dealt with in an interesting way. The basic idea is that the defined contribution of 18.5 per cent of the wage sum will be fixed and pensions will be related to that, rather than a predetermined benefit level determining the contribution level. The benefit formula also provides a sound incentive structure; additional contribution will, in principle, always pay off in a higher entitlement to a future pension.

Family support

The coordination of different instruments is also important in family support. A rule of thumb, to make the system equitable, is to design the support in the form of direct payments so that all families are included and not only taxpayers. If the tax system is neutral in terms of household composition (and it is not in all Nordic countries), it will also be an excellent strategy for promoting gender equality and emphasizing the individualization of social protection. Benefits should not be subject to taxation since that has negative effects on women's incentives to work. In designing family support programmes, means-testing should be avoided as much as possible because it can create poverty traps as well as costly administration. In designing universal benefits, consideration should be given to the number and the age of children in order to avoid divisions of welfare and poverty traps. Universal benefits, with a bonus for a large number of children, is an excellent tool for supporting this vulnerable group without creating poverty traps. Designing the support to single-parent households and households with many children provides an interesting challenge but should follow the same guidelines.

Social services and the dual-earner model

However, family support cannot be isolated from issues concerning social insurance, social services and the labour market. Since cost-control appears to be reasonably good in the short-term perspective but more problematic in the longer term, a broad, dynamic and long-term strategy is warranted – and also necessary for restoring the intergenerational contract which is of crucial importance for making the welfare state sustainable.

There is a universal tendency of increased female employment and an outspoken political ambition to equalize the participation of men and women, both on the Nordic and European levels. If governments fail to respond to the needs of social services, this is likely to reinforce old and create new divisions of welfare. Low-income parents are especially dependent on subsidized social services for being able to seek and uphold employment, not to mention lone parents. I would argue that social services in this context is probably the most efficient way for lone parents to simultaneously break potential 'benefit dependency' and to improve the economic standards of their families. This should be seen as a double strategy of both improving the resources for the lone parents, and for *empowering* the children.

At the heart of the modernization project, family support should be designed to make family and worklife possible for two-earner families. Policies aimed at equal opportunities for men and women in the labour market and equal participation and responsibility in family life should be encouraged. 'Family-friendly jobs' are a necessary ingredient, which has been recognized by the Danish government in a good example of the ambition to promote both equality and efficiency by improving social cohesion – the dialogue between different actors on the labour market – and this is part of a Danish offensive to promote an international discussion on these issues.

The lack of adequate resources in terms of social services such as childcare and care for frail elderly relatives are effective barriers for primarily women to participate in the labour market but also in society in general. Social services may be seen as investments that in a dynamic way provide people with the opportunity to become taxpayers and hence to contribute to balancing state finances. Social services are also needed to ensure the full participation of all citizens in society in general, and not only on the labour market. The access to services is therefore a democratic problem.

The public–private mix

The debate about the 'proper' public–private mix of welfare is often fought with more or less ethical arguments. On one side, it is claimed that the state should leave much more room for private alternatives and that a big state involvement in the financing and provision of insurance and services is bad as such. On the other side, it is claimed that a smaller state involvement necessarily means less welfare. These approaches both appear ahistorical and lacking in empirical content. It seems more fruitful not only to identify trade-offs and zero-sum games but also to look for positive-sum games. It is moreover important to identify different dimensions of private and public, and to recognize that the ideal mix may differ not only from an ideological point of view but also depending on what policy area we are talking about.

It is not always clear what the problem with privatization is about and what can be done about it. Privatization can take place along several dimensions; it is not always a question of reducing social rights. We can also find examples of public benefits being a very important condition for making private care possible. The care allowance paid to relatives of disabled persons is one way of making it possible for family members to take care of disabled persons at home. This is often a much less expensive solution for the public purse if the alternative is institutional care. Despite the massive expansion of public care, most caring work is still provided by family members.

A puzzle with privatization is that the ideas about what it is and what it can achieve are so vague. This naïve approach is problematic in several respects. One important aspect of the coordination is how private pensions are treated. If the public and private systems are disconnected this might actually be good for household savings, because when private pensions reduce public benefits, it does not make much sense to save. An important aspect of other providers of publicly financed services is that it might enable choice, but this is not always the case. Some forms of privatization just replace public providers in specific geographical areas. It is also evident that the reasons for privatization differ. Some of it is motivated on purely ideological grounds, while sometimes it is used for introducing competition. Another problem of privatization is that there are poor instruments of quality control. This is not an argument against private providers as such, rather it points to the necessity of keeping a public responsibility also for private social services. This argument is of course especially strong when it comes to publicly financed services.

The Nordic model is rightly associated with a big public involvement in both the social insurance and social service sectors. However, it would be misleading to conclude that this necessarily implies a mechanical 'crowding-out' of private alternatives. Historically, the voluntary state-subsidized insurance for sickness and unemployment are good examples of how private and public programmes can interact. We can also find examples in the pension area. The existence of a trustworthy public pension system might in fact stimulate people to engage in private pension savings by decreasing what is usually labelled 'myopia', that uncertainty is so big that people give up on taking rational actions to decrease uncertainties.

In a study on social services in Norwegian municipalities, Kuhnle and Selle (1990) found that the private and public services have developed in tandem.[21] Rather than crowding out each other, their expansion was conditional on the existence of the other type of provision. In Denmark, public funding of private social work has been used to stimulate innovative work, of various forms, in the fields of social work and social services. Another example, of the interdependence of public and private, is provided by the care-work done by family members for frail relatives. In Sweden, public care benefits not only make private care possible, they also save public funding by relying on family members for, sometimes, 'round the clock' care.

The privatization of publicly provided services can be seen as at least having a potential for improving people's welfare by introducing choice and competition in the production of social services. However, private production of publicly financed services should not be confused with private funding of the same services. In this connection we can observe that the family is far too small a unit for risk distribution. Nor can the market provide insurance for everybody, because certain people imply much too great a risk to be insurable in a private market. On the other hand, private insurance can supplement public universal insurance, even though, here again, various kinds of state regulation and guarantees are necessary in order for the insurance to work well.

The policy towards the disabled in Sweden may serve as an example of how the public–private mix has developed and how different kinds of policies are interdependent. It is part of the universal system but has deep roots in voluntary organizations. The first of these associations were formed at the end of the nineteenth century, simultaneously with the emergence of other popular movements. One important aim was to create job opportunities and with them opportunities of self-sufficiency. Initially, the associations for the disabled frequently took things into their own hands to solve their members' problems, but caring and other services for the functionally impaired have, in various ways, now become part of the general welfare model. Persons with functional impairments are also entitled to medical care, education and childcare services, and they are also expected to work and pay tax. As part of the universal system, great improvements have thus been made to the situation for persons with functional impairments in the past few decades. This illustrates the possibility of establishing a positive link between services and employment, but also the problems of maintaining that link when unemployment is high.

Conclusion: we need 'a strategy of equality'

In the middle of the global economic crisis of the 1930s, R.H. Tawney (1931) identified the welfare state as a 'strategy of equality'. [22] Among the then existing social services, Tawney's attention was directed at healthcare, education and policies aimed at providing economic security in the case of work incapacity resulting from old age, sickness and unemployment. Already by 1951, Tawney himself appeared to be fairly optimistic about the achievements of public policies in reducing, for example, income inequality. Comparative research indicates that there is an important potential in the welfare state as a strategy of equality, a potential which, however, has remained fairly unexplored in many countries.

With the British sociologist T.H. Marshall (1950), we can also see the welfare state as a set of social rights and we can interpret the innovation of social insurance as a new stage in the development of citizenship, following the institution of equal civil and political rights.[23] Contrary to the old Poor Law systems, which denied the recipients of public support their political citizenship rights, the new programmes can be seen as an extension of these rights. However, the entitlements in social security programmes are based not only on citizenship, but on additional criteria like need and work-merit. Social rights are also accompanied by obligations and responsibilities, which can be very basically summed up by saying that every citizen must, according to capacity, earn his or her livelihood and pay tax on his or her income. Insistence on work, on active participation in the labour market, is relatively well-developed in the Nordic welfare institutions and has gained widespread political legitimacy under the device of the *work strategy*, and is ultimately about participation.

I have highlighted some of the advantages of a universal approach incorporating earnings-related social insurance benefits in comparison with other approaches to social security, such as the targeted and the corporatist models. If we are serious about defending the achievements of their systems of social protection, I would argue that it is necessary to do three different things. The first is that governments need to declare their firm *commitment* to the goal of protecting social rights. This is important because there is a lost confidence in the welfare state institutions after years of cutbacks (however necessary these might have been). The second is to critically *evaluate* the design of the existing programmes against the goal of promoting the welfare of all citizens. Good intentions are not enough to defend a programme; not only do we have to study whether the goals are actually achieved, we also have to consider unintended consequences of the programmes. The third is that it is not enough to secure the programmes on a national level. The Nordic countries were successful in using the Nordic arena for strengthening the systems of social protection during their expansionary period, both in terms of policy learning and diffusion and in terms of protecting migrants. We now need to use the *global arena* to discuss the global problems of social protection.

In comparative welfare state research, where I have my academic background, diffusion is a largely neglected aspect of the emergence and expansion of the various programmes. Despite this fact, it seems safe to conclude that the diffusion of ideas and programme design is an important factor. This goes for the emergence, the expansion and the more recent 'retrenchments' as well. It is still an open question whether it will work in a constructive way in terms of modernization as well.

The role of international organization is one part of the neglected diffusion process. Before the Second World War the International Labour Office (ILO) undoubtedly played an important role as a forum for discussion and dissemination of ideas. The ILO also actively and very systematically collected data on the systems of social protection (they do not anymore). After the war, the International Social Security Association took over the tasks to an important degree. The question is also if the different international organizations can join forces in the modernization process. From organizations like the IMF and the World Bank, both the ideological and substantive critique of the various parts of the welfare state has been very strong, but they rarely distinguish between the two kinds of arguments. In this perspective, the European Commission and the Nordic Councils of Ministers play a more constructive but far from uncritical role. And there are undoubtedly signs that, for example, the World Bank has the potential of playing a constructive role.[24] People I talked to recently claim that even the IMF is emerging as a solid partner on social issues!?

This is not to argue that the globalization of the world economy puts clear constraints on nation-states. To my mind, there are two areas where the limits are clear. The first is that profitability has to be on a competitive level. Otherwise, foreign as well as domestic capital will leave the country. The level of income taxation and the size of social security contributions is not of primary importance, yet employees and their trade unions must recognize the cost of social security. 'There is no such thing as a free lunch.' If the cost of social policy, the social wage, is not taken into consideration in wage-negotiations the result might be inflation and eroded competitiveness. This is a lesson which the Swedish and other Nordic labour movements hopefully have learnt from the past decades. Competitiveness is not threatened as long as the cost of the 'social wage' is taken into consideration in wage negotiations. Even if profit levels cannot be reduced in single countries, the division between what is paid as a direct wage and what is paid as a social wage ought to be flexible.

If we agree that the welfare state is about securing the welfare of all its citizens, it should also be evaluated in these terms, that is how it succeeds in promoting welfare in broad terms. In this context the Nordic countries developed a concept of welfare and methods to study it that has the potential of informing the general debate on the systems of social protection.[25] This multidimensional and action-oriented perspective on welfare is based on a resource perspective close to what Amartya Sen (1985) has developed.[26] This approach carries the potential to study social exclusion. Following Sen, we may define factors such as low income, ill-health and poor education as risk factors for social exclusion.[27] This perspective is also policy-oriented insofar as the risk factors to important extents can be affected by social policies broadly defined. If it can be agreed upon that social policy programmes should be judged not from what they intend to achieve but from what they actually achieve, then we have to agree on methods of evaluation. What will be argued here is that we should not rely on pure thought experiments, we need empirical data to test our ideas. Moreover, to get accurate assessments we need to assemble data that can actually answer our questions. These data are often costly and time consuming to gather, but the costs are small compared to the very large sums that are spent on the system of social protection.

Social security is ultimately about creating social identities. By sharing the costs of universal risks, the ground appears to be more fertile for building coalitions between different groups in society, groups that would otherwise have a narrower basis for forming social identities. National identities, or even nationalism, organized around social support systems for the whole population, is a more attractive scenario than nationalism based on real, or believed, ethnic, religious or other divisions.

In the end, the modernization of social protection should be put into the context of democracy and security. Failing to reform the systems of social insurance, service and assistance, when there are problems and deficiencies, not only threatens to leave many people in poverty and despair, and disable many children from exploring their full potentials in the future, it also threatens democracy insofar as it hampers the full participation of all persons as citizens and full members in society. And if democracy is threatened, this means that political security is on shaky ground. I think this holds true both in Europe and elsewhere. If European governments are serious about the European Union as a peace project, then they have to be serious about the social security systems of their own and other countries. This calls for a serious discussion of the future of social protection on a European level. I also believe that the same approach can fruitfully be applied in other parts of the world.

I would like to argue that the welfare state can be seen as – and should be – a project of civilization.[28] This means that the states should redistribute resources so that the poorest can also enjoy the degree of civilization which would otherwise be reserved only to the rich. In this civilization project, the design of systems of social protection can play a very important role. Let us not be overwhelmed by the time horizon as we enter the twenty-first century, a new millennium, and let us not be paralysed by our 'big ideas' about what *should be* in a distant future, it is urgent that we start to engage in practical policy-making to promote the fundamental values in democratic society.

Notes

1 European Commission, *Modernising and Improving Social Protection in the European Union*, Com (97) 102, 1997.

2 David Cameron, 'The Expansion of the Public Economy', *American Political Science Review*, Washington, DC, vol. 72, 1978, pp. 1243–61.

3 Colin Hay, 'Globalization, Welfare Retrenchment and the "Logic of No Alternative"', *Journal of Social Policy*, Cambridge, vol. 27, 1998, pp. 525–32.

4 Gösta Esping-Andersen (ed.), *Welfare States in Transition*, London: Sage, 1997.

5 Jens Alber, 'Is there a crisis of the welfare state? Cross-National Evidence from Europe, North America, and Japan', *European Sociological Review*, Oxford, vol. 4, no. 3, 1988, pp. 181–206.

6 Anthony Atkinson, 'Does Social Protection Jeopardise European Competitiveness?', *Bulletin Luxembourgeois des Questions Sociales*, vol. 4, 1998.

7 World Bank, *World Development Report: The State in a Changing World*, New York: Oxford University Press, 1997.

8 Walter Korpi and Joakim Palme, 'The Paradox of Redistribution and Strategies of Equality: Welfare State Institutions, Inequality and Poverty in the Western Countries', *American Sociological Review*, Washington, DC, vol. 63, 1998, pp. 661–87.

9 Robert Erikson, 'Descriptions of Inequality: The Swedish Approach to Welfare research', in Martha Nussbaum and Amartya Sen (eds), *The Quality of Life*, Oxford: Clarendon Press, 1993, pp. 67–83.

10 John Rawls, *A Theory of Justice*, Cambridge, Mass.: Harvard University Press, 1971.

11 Seebohm Rowntree, *Poverty. The Study of Town Life*, London: Macmillan, 1901.

12 Olli Kangas and Joakim Palme, 'Does Social Policy Matter? Poverty Cycles in the OECD Countries', *International Journal of Health Services*, New York, vol. 30, 2000, pp. 335–52.

13 Walter Korpi and Joakim Palme, n. 8, pp. 661–87.

14 Gordon Tullock, *Economics of Income Redistribution*, Boston: Kluwer-Nijhoff, 1983.

15 Walter Korpi, 'Social Policy and Distributional Conflict in the Capitalist Democracies: A Preliminary Comparative Framework', *West European Politics*, London, vol. 3, no. 3, 1980, pp. 296–316.

16 Nicholas Barr, 'Economic Theory and the Welfare State: A Survey and Interpretation', *Journal of Economic Literature*, Nashville, vol. 30, 1992, pp. 741–803.

17 Atkinson, n. 6.

18 Douglass C. North, *Institutions, Institutional Change and Economic Performance*, Cambridge: Cambridge University Press, 1990.

19 Nordic Council of Ministers, *Fiscal Consolidation in the Nordic Countries: Fiscal Policy for Sustainable Growth and Welfare*, Copenhagen: Tema Nord, 1997 [Joakim Palme], no. 595.

20 Olli Kangas and Joakim Palme, 'The Development of Occupational Pensions in Finland and Sweden: Class Politics and Institutional Feedbacks', in Michael Shalev (ed.), *The Privatization of Social Policy*, London: Macmillan, 1996, pp. 211–40.

21 Stein Kuhnle and Per Selle, 'Meeting Needs in a Welfare State: Relations between Government and Voluntary Organizations in Norway', in Aland Ware and Robert Goodin (eds), *Needs and Welfare*, London: Sage, 1990, pp. 165–84.

22 R.H. Tawney, *Equality*, London: George Allen & Unwin, 1931.

23 T.H. Marshall, *Citizenship and Social Class*, Cambridge: Cambridge University Press, 1950.

24 World Bank, n. 7.

25 Sten Johansson, *Om levnadsnivåundersökningen* (About the Level of Living Survey), Stockholm, Swedish Institute for Social Research, 1970. Erik Allardt, *Att ha, att älska, att vara: Om välfärd i Norden* (Having, Loving Being: Welfare in the Nordic Countries), Lund: Argos, 1975.

26 Amartya Sen, *Commodities and Capabilities*, Amsterdam: North Holland, 1985.

27 Amartya Sen, 'Social Exclusion', Paper presented at the Ministry for Foreign Affairs in Stockholm, Sweden, 1998.
28 Zsusa Ferge, 'And What If The State Fades Away? The Civilising Process and the State', Paper prepared for the European Sociological Association, Third Conference, Essex University, UK, 27–30 August 1997.

14
Recent Welfare Reforms in the United States

Asha Gupta

Introduction

The United States of America provides a unique example where the existence of the prevailing models of a welfare state or state of welfarism can neither be denied nor accepted. In fact, we find an amalgam of the behaviourist, residual, social insurance and populist forms of welfare coexisting.

The behaviourist vision is concerned with the task of inducing the poor to behave in a more socially acceptable manner. It is based on the logic that the able-bodied should work at any job available. Families should take care of the young and disabled, and social welfare should be restricted to those in dire need. This view is shared by Charles Murray (1984) in his famous book, *Losing Ground.*

The residualist view intends to rescue the victims of capitalism by giving subsistence-level relief to those who are unable to meet their basic needs. Followers of this school think that the aim of welfare should be restricted to temporary assistance and its administration should be fully decentralized. This view is shared not only by the elite in the United States but also by the middle and lower-middle classes as well.

The social insurance model of a welfare state differs from the residual model, aiming to provide social security by preventing people from falling into destitution rather than rescuing them when they have already fallen. Threats to economic security can come from involuntary employment, widowhood, sickness, injury or retirement. The social security network can be based on contribution towards social insurance in the form of general taxes, or flat payment in the form of a payroll tax. Recent schemes of social security such as PAYG (Pay as You Go) and MIRA (Mandatory Insurance Related Act) aim at linking social insurance with one's paying capacity.

Social insurance provides a measure of economic security to the entire population on a universal basis. It does not try to transform power relations through redistribution, whereas the more populist and egalitarian model of the welfare state aims at an egalitarian society through social engineering.

Though part of the anti-poverty strategy launched in the 1960s can be related with this vision, it has been least influential in designing the welfare state in the United States.

In a country like the United States, 'welfare' is generally used in derogatory terms. To be on welfare implies those who are dependent on social assistance. Americans, in general, hate those 'able-bodied' individuals who are work-shy and, therefore, on dole. This is reflected in the bill signed by Bill Clinton putting an 'end to welfare' as we know it. By 1994, the number of those on welfare had risen to a historic high of 5.1 million families, representing approximately 15 per cent of American families with children.

In 1996, President Bill Clinton ended the 63-year-old programme for the Aid to Families with Dependent Children (AFDC). Although AFDC amounted to just 1.2 per cent of federal spending in 1994, the myth prevailed that welfare in the USA was a big financial burden on the state. The economists and political analysts in the conservative think-tank played a very important role in castigating the American welfare state as 'undesirable', 'unaffordable' and 'ungovernable', and the general perception was to look down upon those who were on welfare. Very few realized that welfare constituted a very small portion of the overall social security endeavours. Nor could the general public realize that their country was actually spending more on social security, despite recent reforms in welfare through various programmes such as EITC (Earned Income Tax Credit), food stamps, Medicaid, housing assistance, subsidized school meals and SSI (Supplemental Security Income).

With the passage of the welfare reforms bill in 1996, the federal welfare policy towards AFDC was abruptly reversed, and replaced with the TANF (Temporary Assistance for Needy Families). This aimed at reducing welfare dependency, ending welfare entitlement and emphasizing mandatory work. Without creating a social catastrophe, the pro-work welfare reforms based on limited and short-term assistance succeeded in pushing many off welfare. During 1994–2001, there was a decline of 60 per cent in welfare caseloads, greatest among white families (63 per cent) and lowest among Hispanic families (44 per cent).

Around July 2001, however, the number started rising again, and as such it is difficult to say that the decline in welfare caseloads was primarily due to welfare reforms. Perhaps the boom in the economy during the 1980s and the recession during the 1990s may be the reason behind the steep decline and then the rise in welfare caseloads. During the economic boom, there was a rise of 17 per cent in hourly wages and the market was receptive to low-skilled labour and women as well. During 1996–99, expenditure on means-tested benefit under TANF rose by approximately $5.9 million, a rise of 25 per cent.[1]

Though Bill Clinton's promise to end welfare worked initially, it has led to a new form of dependency in terms of 'working families' dependent upon public support through various schemes providing aid. The expansion of social welfare spending has enhanced the number of welfare recipients, on the one hand, and led to disincentives in terms of work and marriage, on the other. For instance, if a single mother with an income of $10,000 per annum decides to marry a boy with a minimum income of $10,000, she is likely to lose approximately 75 per cent of income in terms of welfare benefits and increased taxes.

Therefore, the process of welfare reforms in the United States is not yet complete. Either TANF benefits have to be provided for a limited period of time or they have to be extended to middle-class and higher-income groups. Such efforts require either reducing benefits or raising the eligibility conditions. But, unfortunately, such increases in benefits and eligibility are likely to lead to expansion in welfare, creating problems pertaining to distribution, inequities, overuse, misuse or inegalitarian use of welfare benefits.

From the 'welfare' 'workfare'

In order to overcome some of the problems under the AFDC programme, we find a definite shift from 'welfare' to 'workfare' under recent welfare reforms. The idea is that the needy should be given aid only in return for some contribution to society and not as a legal right in the form of welfare entitlement. In 1996, the Personal Responsibility and Work Opportunity Reconciliation Act was passed to help state governments move at least 50 per cent of adults on welfare to work by the year 2002. It provided for federal funding to various state governments through block grants. Earlier, states received federal grants for AFDC cases on the basis of numerical strength, which served as a disincentive to remove those on AFDC from the welfare list. Now states could keep the grant and use it for reducing dependence of welfare recipients on state government.

The politics of recent welfare reforms in the United States represents a return to the citizenship rationale, but this time the emphasis is on obligations rather than rights. The goal is not only to complement welfare rights with work obligations, but also to codify them legally. Although the Republican Party has always considered welfare as one of the biggest problems faced by the United States, the Democratic Party tried to ward off the challenge by emphasizing 'workfare', 'wedfare' and 'learnfare' in lieu of 'welfare'.

Instead of subsidizing ever-escalating levels of social pathology, the recent welfare reforms aim at inculcating virtues, commitment and a sense of discipline among American citizens. Policy-makers rely on the traditional wisdom which recognizes that 'one-way handouts' very often hurt those very people whom they intend to help.[2] In the wake of the new welfare reforms, several states including Wisconsin, Idaho and West Virginia have made remarkable progress in reducing welfare dependency and promoting self-sufficiency under the Temporary Assistance to Needy Families (TANF).

Caseloads under former AFDC (now TANF) was cut by 90 per cent and the child poverty rate was cut by 50 per cent in those states.

In some states, welfare agencies developed special programmes for providing short-term education, vocational skills and training to those on welfare. Some states made it mandatory to search for jobs, the message to recipients of welfare benefits being clear: 'be prepared to work or be prepared to leave'. Though during the 1980s the burgeoning economy propelled reforms towards welfare, the economic decline during the 1990s made mandatory work a farce. No government could take strict measures against a single mother with two children if she expressed her inability to get a job despite her best efforts. States were forced to exempt all those on welfare beyond their time limit or provide alternate means of assistance on the ground of weak economy. It made the public look on mandatory work and welfare reforms as a 'grand bluff'.

This explains why the TANF Scheme could not be reauthorized in September 2002. Owing to disagreements among the liberals and the democrats alike, Congress had to adjourn without reauthorizing the law. There is no consensus on the issue whether to expand work requirements or increase aid to low-income families not on welfare in the form of 'benefits in kind'. These two issues have been most contentious in the debate over welfare reforms in the United States, and in order to understand the current welfare reforms under discussion, it is essential to look into the past.

The new deal and after

The traditional welfare state was based on liberal wisdom on welfare. Since the New Deal, the emphasis of welfare programmes in the USA has been on cash transfer and services in kind to supplement the market instead of supplanting the market altogether. Unlike the command economies, the welfare state in the USA preferred a *post-fisc* distribution of goods and services to a *pre-fisc* one. The Great Depression of the 1930s taught Americans an important lesson – individuals could be poor and unemployed through no fault of their own. The New Deal Programme launched by President Franklin D. Roosevelt and the War on Poverty Programme launched by President Lyndon B. Johnson taught Americans the lesson to help such individuals, so that the Great Society of America could survive as a whole.

The New Deal merely introduced certain socio-economic reforms abandoning *laissez-faire* capitalism to enter into the progressive era. This programme was not so new, but the speed with which it was carried out was really remarkable. Sincere efforts were made to cushion the administrative bodies from the likely obstacles and criticisms from vested interests. For instance, in 1933 the government passed the Agriculture Adjustment Act (AAA) to provide economic relief to farmers. Its policy was to raise crop prices by paying farmers a subsidy to compensate for cutbacks in production (only 8 per cent were engaged in agriculture at that time). The government extended loans to them through the Commodity Credit Corporation (CCC).

In its early years, the New Deal sponsored a series of legislative initiatives and achieved remarkable success in increasing production and prices, but it could not bring to an end the economic depression. The Second New Deal was an attempt to provide work and a social security net, rather than welfare. Under the Work Progress Administration (WPA), bridges, roads, railways, airports and so on were constructed to provide work to millions of Americans. Approximately 9 million people were hired up to 1943, also including people from theatre and the fine arts. In 1935, the Social Security Act was passed, that provided for social insurance for the aged, unemployed and disabled based on employer and employee contributions. This was funded in large part by taxes. The progressive era continued from Franklin D. Roosevelt to Harry S. Truman and John F. Kennedy to Richard M. Nixon. During 1961–73, legislation extended and concluded the initiations of previous years. Medicaid and Medicare (1965) provided for the health insurance that Truman had called for, the indexation of Social Security benefits (1972) insured the stability of Roosevelt's retirement benefits, whereas the supplemental security income (1972) rounded out such benefits for the indigent, aged, blind and disabled.[3]

Each of these programmes provided for 'cash transfers' and 'services in kind' – healthcare, for example, which otherwise would have been purchased or foregone. In 1964, the Economic Opportunity Act was passed on the basis of the report provided by the President's Task Force on Manpower Conservation. It found one-third of young men unqualified for military service either on physical or mental grounds. Such young persons lacked good health, education and skills owing to circumstances beyond their control, and lacked the opportunities to be effective citizens and self-supporting individuals.

Shedding myths about welfarism in the United States

Generally perceived as a 'welfare laggard', the United States has invested approximately $7.9 trillion on programmes that provide cash, food, housing, medical and social services to the poor and low-income Americans ever since President Lyndon B. Johnson launched the 'war on poverty'. Unfortunately, in this war, poverty won.[4] Despite tremendous expenses incurred on welfare, social problems grew worse in terms of rising illegitimacy, crime, drug abuse and welfare dependency.

We should not forget that in a country like America, instead of material poverty, we find behavioural poverty more alarming. The typical American defined as 'poor' by the government is not malnourished, poorly clothed and living in filthy housing, but owns a refrigerator, a stove, a washing machine, a colour TV, an airconditioner and a car. This phenomenon cannot be explained merely in terms of 'overload' or 'fiscal crisis'. It has to be explained in terms of methodological individualism, which has proved to be 'anti-structural', 'anti-functional', 'anti-normative' and 'anti-sociological'.[5]

In its formative years, the government played a very small role in providing welfare,[6] charity or welfare was generally provided by religious organizations. Before the onset of the Great Depression, the total expenditure on welfare by local states and federal government was only $90 million which grew to approximately $861 million in 1999 out of which approximately 73 per cent came from federal funding.

In 1980 when Ronald Reagan became president, welfare spending was more than five times that of 1965. During the Reagan era, welfare spending declined from 4 per cent in 1980 to 3.6 per cent in 1988. However, despite publicity to the contrary, welfare spending actually grew dramatically during the last decade in the wake of the shift from 'welfare' to 'workfare'. The welfare reforms, in fact, have affected only a few states and a few programmes launched by the federal government, the rest including public housing, food stamps and Medicaid remain primarily unchanged.

Present problems

Welfare provisions in the United States proved to be 'one-way handouts'. Benefits were bestowed as unconditional entitlements without making the recipients change their behaviour. Where benefits are unconditional, welfare caseloads are bound to be high. Welfare is reported to result not only in a high level of dependence, but also promotes the disintegration of families. For instance, when the war on poverty began, 7.7 per cent of American children were born out of wedlock. In 1999, the figure stood at 33 per cent. Amongst the black, it took precarious turn; in 1975, the rate of black illegitimate birth was reported to be 49 per cent, rising to 70 per cent in 1999.[7]

We find a lot of resentment among policy-makers and the public alike for the fact that welfare rewards illegitimacy. It established strong financial disincentives for keeping two-parent families intact. The income-tested welfare programmes proved to be anti-marriage and have had a splitting effect on most American households. Welfare benefits could be maximized only if the husband did not work or the biological parents lived apart. Some even questioned the huge expenses involved in providing counselling on marriage and individual matters by the state government under the Bush administration.

Moreover, the rise of illegitimacy has caused many behavioural and emotional problems, in general, and among children in particular. 'Out-of-wedlock children' often indulge in anti-social, hyperactive or headstrong behaviour. They have been found to be disobedient in school and have difficulties getting along with others outside school. The situation has also led to increased sexual activity at puberty, resulting in teenage pregnancies. The TANF aimed at eliminating perverse incentives to various state governments for keeping more people on welfare in order to receive more funds from the federal government; the new law allows the state governments to keep surplus federal funds in case they are able to reduce welfare dependents in terms of numbers.

Despite the profound success of workfare in reducing dependents in some states, most states have failed to achieve the desired results. At present, more than 50 per cent of adults on TANF remain idle. Most of them have a 'no work' culture. Some are involved in drug and alcohol abuse and pervasive crime, while others found the various welfare programmes meaningless and uninteresting. Instead of isolated policy changes, welfare reforms need to be carried out in terms of a series of interrelated policies in the wake of post-industrialization, post-modernization and post-democratization.

In any modern state, citizens are related to the state authority in three prominent ways – as creators of state authority, as subjects against whom the collective political will is enforced, and as dependents upon services and provisions provided by the state. In these three components we find the ideological roots of liberalism, democracy and the welfare state. Earlier, we found harmony, compatibility and mutual reinforcement among these three, but today we notice symptoms of stress, strain and contradictions. The present symptoms indicate that democratic mass politics may not work in the direction of maintenance or expansion of the welfare state.[8]

A vital debate has begun, or perhaps the old debate has been renewed, about the proper role of government and the attitudes on which it rests. We find a decline in the confidence of most Americans in their government's ability to perform social functions well or efficiently. In a mature society, in which various interests call upon the government to meet diverse needs, the cumulative costs of welfare have risen in an unanticipated way. The public perception of rising costs is complicated by their division between direct taxes – 'visible to all' and indirect tax exemptions – 'not so visible'. Whereas the people in the upper-income strata consider their fiscal benefits as 'earned', they attribute the tax burden to the 'poor' who are seen as not having earned their entitlement.[9]

Challenges and constraints

In recent decades, welfare provisions in the United States have become both a challenge and constraint on two accounts: (1) democratic governments are finding it difficult to maintain welfare programmes and policies within the existing framework of fiscal constraints; and (2) the institutional arrangements are also found to be inadequate to accommodate the new demands made by the larger number of social groups. Owing to the potential adverse reaction to the postmodern and postindustrial capitalist economy, welfare programmes and policies in the United States tend to be more 'reactive' than 'active'.

Surprisingly, the salaried and upper-middle class – the main beneficiaries of the welfare state – have declined to provide political support to it. The higher the income and privileges, the less is the need to have one's privileges tied to collective arrangements. As such, the welfare state has to face the dilemma of alienating the better-off, whose income could be used to subsidize the less-fortunate. There also seems to be an 'asymmetry' among the socio-political processes that result in the expansion of welfare programmes and benefits, on the one hand, and economic and fiscal crises that lead to various cutbacks, on the other. As such, the very legitimacy and effectiveness of welfarism and the welfare state has become a matter of public scrutiny.

The questions arise:

- What are the causes and consequences of recent shifts in public attitudes towards welfare provisions in the United States?
- What images and arguments are being used concerning welfare and poverty by the neo-liberal political ideology?
- Should the debate on welfare reforms be seen in terms of an economic device or political strategy?
- What is the role of the media in setting and reinforcing the agenda of welfare reforms?
- How can the politics and welfare cutbacks gain public support within the democratic framework?
- What is the role of electoral economism in contemporary American politics?
- How far is the American culture responsible for the politics of recent welfare reforms?
- Can the notions of 'self-help', 'self-reliance' and 'thrift' be sustained in the era of a weakening social fabric?
- Can MIRA (Mandatory Individual Retirement Account) be more effective than PAYG (Pay As You Go)?

We find sharp differences among the intellectuals, policy-makers and social actors over the nature and scope of welfare reforms in the United States. Although there has been a tremendous rise in welfare research owing to skepticism about the economic growth and public expenditure on social welfare, not much attention has been paid to shedding the myths about welfare in the United States. America, unfortunately, remains the most misunderstood welfare state to this date.[10]

It is interesting to recall that approximately 4 to 5 per cent of GDP is involved in welfare, though the media has created an image of huge national resources being squandered in the United States. There is a big gap between the perception of the elite and the general public, and there are misconceptions about welfare which have insinuated themselves into the national consciousness in the form of conventional wisdom. It is ironic that capitalism can neither coexist with a welfare state nor can it exist without the welfare state.[11] Of late, the welfare state has been constantly portrayed as a child of crisis.

The American political legacy

The American political identity is founded around distrust and opposition to authority, rather than support for it. Even civil servants see themselves as separate from the government. It is a political legacy of the distrust and revolution of the American people against the British Crown, and most Americans like to be free of government rather than rely on it for their economic security. In contrast to European nations, individualistic attitudes in the United States have led to the curtailment of the welfare state. Since the stagflation in the 1970s, we find definite shifts in public policies towards social welfare programmes in the United States, and these policies have been blamed as the main cause of prevailing socio-economic and political problems. They were no longer viewed as corrective of market failures. The welfare state has been projected as undesirable, unaffordable and ungovernable, leading to a highly pessimistic vision.

Most radical critics have expressed dismay at the rigidity of the welfare state. During the 1970s and 1980s, the dominant political tendency was conservative; the media and the think tanks played an important role in disseminating certain myths, misunderstanding and misinformation about the welfare state in the United States.[12] In the wake of a trade-off between efficiency and equity, most political and economic analysts stood for 'less government' and 'welfare capitalism'.

The economists seemed to outsmart the policy analysts in America; instead of viewing government as an authority over society, they tried to project it as one of the actors among many within it. They tried to put forward the idea that most of the problems in federal policy and administration could be solved through 'adroit use of incentives'. A purist kind of economic thinking that tends to downplay the less tangible, attitudinal and political dimensions of socio-cultural problems. Most of the analysts tried to highlight the material dimension to the neglect of behavioural problems.

Such federal analysts operated in a 'protective cocoon of computers, models and statistical regression', out of touch with reality. Their analyses proved to be academic and unreal to those who were actually responsible for administering welfare provisions. In the economic analysis, people suffering from poverty or dependency were understood in dependent terms and its causes in independent terms. In political analysis, it could be the other way round. People under political analysis cannot be treated as mere passive or reactive actors, but as active participants.

Welfare spending and economic growth

There is a clear lack of correlation between social welfare expenditure and economic growth. Social welfare spending was commonly measured in terms of GNP or GDP, which made the general public think of it as a drain on the economic output. It missed the point that such spending consisted mostly of transfer payments rather than direct purchases. It did not, therefore, affect the freedom of the public to consume or invest as much of GNP after the transfer as before.

Similarly, it was a myth to equate the growth of welfare spending with the growth of poverty or the failure of eradicating poverty from America. It is commonly held that the American welfare state grew dramatically during the 1970s and 1980s, but it is a mistake to equate 'welfare' with the 'welfare state'. Indeed, social welfare and welfare spending followed radically different paths in America. For instance, if we look at the spending on AFDC, commonly equated with welfare, we notice that it was lower in 1987 than in 1971. In fact, welfare forms a 'minuscule fraction' of the American welfare state.[13] Attempts are now being made to relate welfare benefits with personal contributions and to make individual insurance mandatory. It is again a myth to project that welfare promotes dependency. In his famous book *Losing Ground*, Charles Murray (1984) propagated the thesis that the welfare state aggravates the problem it is ostensibly designed to solve.[14]

Murray holds the welfare state responsible for the increase in the number of latent poor, but his arguments are based on misunderstanding and misdiagnosis about the effects of welfare or the welfare state on the poor.[15] Murray often indulges in overgeneralizations in his work, when in fact most of the problems that related to post-industrialization and postmodernization couldn't be blamed on welfare or the welfare state.

As such, welfare cannot and should not be held responsible for causing poverty, illegitimacy and flight from work. Nor should the meaning of welfare be confined to mere AFDC or means-tested programmes. There are approximately 75 programmes run by the federal government in the United States; what is needed is a new vision of welfare rather than the scrapping of welfare. It is a mistake to regard the welfare state as part of a problem rather than part of a solution, and it is necessary to shed persistent myths about welfare in the wake of enduring realities. The welfare state in America is not a disaster or a failure as is often projected by its critics. In fact, welfare constitutes a very small proportion of social security in America in contrast to what prevails in advanced European and Scandinavian welfare states.

Moreover, the public psyche in America has always been in favour of the 'deserving poor', though not in support of 'healthy adults' on welfare. Therefore, it is wrong to be carried away by the current debate on welfare reforms as we cannot really carry over the current trends into the future. The economic incentives cannot lead to desirable public behaviour, nor are the purposes unitary as far as welfare programmes prevail in America. As such, failure in one direction cannot amount to failures in all directions.

State–federal dynamics

The current politics of welfare reforms in the United States has to be visualized in the context of state–federal dynamics. The rhetoric of hyperinflation of reforms has, in fact, never aimed at fundamental change in welfare provisions as a political agenda. Washington has never been able to set uniform standards ever since the American constitution came into operation. The federal government lacks the power to impose 'work' or 'wedding' on its citizens in the wake of welfare reforms.

The federal government can make no direct provisions for welfare, health, education, housing and social security, it can only provide grants to the various state governments and local agencies. It cannot control or enforce various welfare provisions and reforms directly. Details of the philosophy, management and administration of provisions have to be worked out by the states. Washington, therefore, is made the servant and not the master of its people. Expressing this sentiment, George Will asserted:

> [M]odern liberalism . . . has given us government that . . . is big but not strong; fat but flabby; capable of giving but not leading. It is invertebrate government, a servile state. . . . But a government obsessed with responsiveness is incapable of leadership. Leadership is, among other things, the ability to inflict pain and get away with it – short-term pain for long-term gain. . . . The one thing we do not have is strong government.[16]

This explains why most of the welfare reforms pertaining to workfare could not be implemented in practice. This welfare non-work cannot be seen in terms of a mere technical problem, but it has to be seen in terms of behavioural dilemmas in social policy. One of the HEW (Department of Health, Education and Welfare) spokesmen, Russell Long, dismissed the low number of welfare clients in WIN (Work Incentives) as a statistical anomaly.

There are many constraints to the implementation of various welfare reforms in America. The federal government lacks the mandate to impose work or other conditions on the welfare recipients at the state and local level, and the states are capable of bending welfare reforms, like the earlier provisions, to serve their own ends. The various state governments control the administrative apparatus and they do not consider themselves as subordinate to the federal government. Federal authority is often used not to impose requirements like work on the dependent, but to keep the state or local governments from doing so. It demands rights for its recipients more than it imposes obligations on them. For instance, under the AFDC law, the federal government saw to it that the aid to welfare mothers was not denied for illegitimacy, or compensation denied to those who refused to accept work for a variety of reasons. The federal policies have been generally client-oriented in contrast to morality imposed by some of the state agencies.

The question arises: why can't the responsibility of providing welfare to the needy and deserving be provided at the local and state level to make it more effective? Most Americans look at the federal government as a provider of benefits and grants but resist its power and authority in the wake of general distrust of government. The problem is an old one in American politics, but it is acute in social policy matters.

American political leaders spend more time on controlling authority rather than using it. The conservatives are found to counter dependency by resorting to cutbacks rather than enforcing welfare reforms, which has made the work requirement more symbolic than real. The liberals also aim at expanding opportunities for the individual instead of creating a fundamentally different kind of society. They encourage individuals to stand on their own and consider dependency on welfare as a social stigma.

The future ahead

For both liberals and conservatives, welfare stands as a force for disorder rather than discipline. They blame individuals for their woes and believe that there are ample opportunities in a country like America for every individual to grow provided he or she is willing to work extra hard. They have no sympathy and concern for those who are apparently lazy, indifferent and unwilling to fulfil their responsibilities as Americans.

Both the liberals and the conservatives desire the welfare state to be less disciplined than private society, and hope to put the welfare 'genie back into the bottle'. They believe in confining welfare only to the aged, blind or disabled, and not to those who are employable. The general perception is to put a stop to the expansion of welfare through federal grants and make the state governments responsible for providing basic services such as health, housing, education and transportation. For John Rarick:

> The constitution contains no authority that provides that the Government shall force the tax payers to pay for health services, food, clothing, transportation, housing, legal services, jobs, birth control devices, or even education to citizens. . . . The only guarantee owed by the Federal Government to the States is a republican form of government.[17]

As a legacy of the political culture prevailing in the United States, the recent welfare reforms aim at 'more individual responsibility and less government' and 'not individual liberty through government'. The combination of Lockean philosophy and distrust of authority have led Americans away from government rather than towards it. Americans believe in a government that is big but not strong; fat but not flabby; capable of giving but not leading. For Americans, their rule in American political culture can be best defined as 'participatory subjects'. Though they distrust authority and power, they also obey laws and discharge their obligations coming from the government. This cultural imbalance is the result of the historical legacy.

The opposition between freedom and authority remains an age-old problem in the United States. The expansion of federal government is allowed in the name of freedom, but its authority disallowed in the wake of sharing responsibilities. This problem is traceable to the New Deal that allowed federal government to dispense certain benefits at the national level without truly regulating them. Whereas, the democrats remain more democratic in responding to 'group claims on government, the republicans remain more statist in their willingness to govern'. The republicans have never reconciled themselves to the expansion of welfare programmes since the New Deal, just as the Democrats have never accepted the need to limit the claims. The Republicans want to exert 'authority without programmes', while the Democrats want 'programmes without authority'.[18]

Despite the shift from 'welfare' to 'workfare', 'wedfare' and 'learnfare', the need for a welfare state and a welfare society remain. The old welfare is gone but the new welfare is bigger and more popular with working families. Earlier, the idea of welfare or well-being was confined to the satisfaction of physiological needs of individuals, to the neglect of their psychological and emotional needs. But without fulfilling both the physical and psychological needs of the individual, no state or society can function properly.

With 'welfare' as an end and the 'welfare state' as the means to achieve that end, the horizons of the 'welfare society' broaden to include both the individual and the state. Unless and until citizens are prepared to share the burden with government, the welfare objectives can no longer be achieved. Those who are unable to share the rising costs of social welfare should be prepared to work extra hard or be prepared to tolerate lower living standards during fiscal crises and economic decline.

At the dawn of the twenty-first century, we need to differentiate between 'good life' and 'goodness of life', between 'holistic well-being' and 'rising consumerism', between 'immediacy' and 'importance', between 'identity' and 'independence', and so on. This requires a new vision and fundamental rethinking on the very presence of human beings on this planet earth not as 'predators, polluters and consumers' but as 'protectors, producers and caretakers'. This is possible if the 'being model' is promoted in lieu of the 'having model' of development. What really matters is 'what you are' rather than 'what you have'.

Notes

1   Douglas J. Besharov, 'The Past and Future of Welfare Reform', *The Public Interest*, Washington DC, no. 150, Winter 2003, pp. 4–21.
2   Robert Rector, 'Welfare: Broadening the Reform', in Stuart M. Butler and Kim R. Holmes (eds), *Issues 2000: The Candidate's Briefing Book*, Washington, DC: The Heritage Foundation, 2000.
3   Daniel Patrick Moynihan, *Miles to Go: A Personal History of Social Policy*, Harvard: Harvard University Press, 1996.
4   *Ibid.*, p. 213.
5   Asha Gupta, *The Changing Perspectives of the Welfare State: The Issue of Privatization*, New Delhi: Pragati Publications, 1994, p. xii.
6   Robert F. Rector and William F. Lauber, *America's Failed $5.4 Trillion War on Poverty*, Washington DC: The Heritage Foundation, 1995, Appendix ii.
7   *Ibid.*, p. 8.
8   Asha Gupta, n. 5, p. ix.
9   Lawrence M. Mead, *Beyond Entitlement: The Social Obligations of Citizenship*, New York: The Free Press, 1985, p. 196.
10   Theodore R. Marmor, Jerry L. Mashaw and Philip L. Harvey, *America's Misunderstood Welfare State: Persistent Myths, Enduring Realities*, New York: Basic Books, 1990.
11   Claus Offe, *Contradictions of Welfare State*, Cambridge, Mass.: MIT Press, 1984, p. 153.
12   Theodore R. Marmor *et al.*, n. 10, pp. 53–81.
13   *Ibid.*, p. 86.
14   Charles Murray, *Losing Ground: American Social Policy, 1950–1980*, New York: Basic Books, 1984.
15   Franz Yaver Kaufmann, 'Major Problems and Dimensions of the Welfare State', in S.N. McLanahan *et al.* (eds), *Losing Ground: A Critique*, IRP Special Report no. 38, *New York Review of Books*, 1985, pp. 1–12.
16   George Will, quoted by Mead, n. 9, p. 176.
17   John Rarick, quoted by Mead, n. 9, p. 199.
18   *Ibid.*, p. 217.

15
Canada's Changing Welfare State

*B. Vivekanandan**

Introduction

In the construction of a modern welfare state system in Canada, the *Report on Social Security for Canada* prepared by Leonard C. Marsh in 1943 was a landmark.[1] But, historically, Canada's social policy began to evolve following the British North American Act of 1867 which gave provinces authority over social affairs. The two world wars gave the needed impetus to the federal government to pay attention to the problems of those who were injured during the wars, while between the wars, in 1927, Canada enacted the Federal Old Age Pension Act.

The Great Depression of the 1930s and the Second World War had created a favourable climate for the introduction of a sharing welfare state system in Canada. The initiative in this regard came from the social democrats; in the wake of the Depression, a number of social democrat leaders met in Regina in 1933 and published a manifesto demanding major changes in social policy. The Cooperative Commonwealth Federation (CCF) Party of Saskatchewan Province adopted this manifesto, and the party was elected to power in the province in 1944, enabling it to introduce reforms in healthcare.[2]

In the wake of the social disruption caused by the Depression, which made about 20 per cent of the population dependent on municipal social assistance, in 1935 the Federal government proposed the introduction of an Employment and Social Insurance Act in order to help the unemployed and their families. But, that measure was declared unconstitutional in view of the 1867 British North American Act. Following this, in 1940, the constitution was amended to enable the federal government to fund social

* A shorter version of this chapter was published in the January–March 2000 issue of *International Studies*, New Delhi, published by Sage Publications. The author is grateful to the Shastri Indo-Canadian Institute in New Delhi and Calgary for the support extended to undertake this study.

programmes. Till then, needy people had to depend upon charity organizations or muncipalities, after passing through a humiliating means test.

Notable influences in shaping Canada's social policy came from Britain,
Scandinavia and the United States. It may be noted that the US President
Franklin Delano Roosevelt's 'Four Freedoms' included 'freedom from want'.
Similarly, among the stated aims of the Atlantic Charter of 1941 were 'social
security' and 'fair labour standards'. The other influence came from Britain
through the Beveridge Report. Following the lead given by Britain in terms
of postwar reconstruction through the appointment of the Beveridge
Committee, Canada followed suit by appointing the Marsh Committee for
a similar exercise in Canada. In addition, Leonard C. Marsh, the Chairman
of the Committee, was considerably influenced by the construction of
welfare state system in Scandinavia in the 1930s which he visited in 1937.

The Marsh Report

The Marsh Report examined the nature of social insurance and social
minimum standards for Canada. One section was fully devoted to employment, but it also dealt with social insurance other than unemployment
insurance. It underlined the need to review the existing provisions like
workmen's compensation, old-age pension and mothers' allowances and to
get them integrated into an insurance programme. The Report examined the
issues of finances and social security legislation and focused on the reasons
why unemployment should dominate most other considerations, noting
that 'If earning power stops all else is threatened'.[3] This was also the lesson
Canada learned during the Depression of the 1930s, causing policy-makers
to realize that provision for unemployment was essential, both economically and socially, in a security programme of a modern industrial economy.

The Marsh Report gave convincing arguments in favour of institutionalization of social insurance in Canada which was perceived as 'a direct and
complete remedy' for the humiliating need test under Poor Law. The Report
noted that:

> Social Insurance brings in the resources of the state, i.e., the resources of
> the community as a whole, or in a particular case that part of the
> resources which may be garnered together through taxes and contribu-
> tions. . . . The contributors who do not draw from the fund help to aid
> the unlucky ones who suffer unemployment or some social casualty.
> Some social insurance provision may have to be frankly viewed as no
> more than the gathering together of a fund for a contingency whose total
> dimensions are uncertain, but whose appearance in some form or mag-
> nitude is certain. In any circumstances, it is better than having no col-
> lective reserves at all, or leaving the burdens to be met by individuals in
> whatever way they can.[4]

The Report underlined: 'there has been increasing recognition of the advantage of this pooling of individual risks by collective means along with state controls [social insurance] and participation'. The Report also examined the possibility of combining both contributory and tax revenue methods. 'In effect, it is this combination which the Beveridge recommendations propose to develop extensively'. It said: 'The genius of social insurance is that it enlists the direct support of the classes most likely to benefit, and enlists equally the participation and controlling influences of the state, at the same time as it avoids the evil of pauperization, and the undemocratic influence of excessive state philanthropy'. In an emphatic argument, the Report said that social security has become

> one of the concrete expressions of 'better world' which is particularly real to those who knew unemployment, destitution, inadequate medical care and the like in the depression periods before the war. To others . . . it is an intelligible recognition that it is one way of realizing nationally a higher standard of living, and of securing more freedom and opportunity through the use of such income as is available once social insurance has taken care of the minimum.[5]

Another argument put forth by the Report in favour of the institutionalization of social insurance was the necessity of 'the maintenance of the flow of purchasing power' for economic stability:

> From the standpoint of the economic system as a whole, social insurance can aid in maintaining consumer purchasing power if national income exhibits a tendency to shrink and thus can assist maintaining unemployment in higher levels. The general sense of security which would result from the continuity of income provided by those various types of protection would provide a better life for the great mass of people.

Therefore, the main concern of the Marsh Report was how to devise methods to cover, 'through family income maintenance in particular, some of the most widespread contingencies'.[6]

The Report stressed on the need to make collective provisions for certain categories of needs such as unemployment, sickness and medical care, disability, old age and retirement, family needs, and so on. It underlined the effect of unemployment on family income, and the problems of need which may arise from it 'that the whole phenomenon is a major risk which has to be met in any modern society by collective as distinct from individual provision, is beyond question'. On sickness and medical care, the Report said that:

Sickness as a risk in the life of the individual as breadwinner or as a member of the family may be simply a problem of securing proper medical care. But it is a problem which has to be met by collective provision because individual incomes are not sufficient to provide for the contingencies, or to pay for the desirable amount and quality of services. ... A serious and prolonged illness means not only medical or hospital bills but destitution if there are no sources to fill the gap created by the cessation of wages.[7]

The measures recommended by the Marsh Report to deal with these contingencies included instituting social insurance, unemployment insurance, disability pensions, mothers' allowances, old-age pensions, provisions for children, and so on. Social insurance was to be instituted by organizing provision collectively by securing contributions from various groups for needs that could not be left safely to individuals' or family's resources. The measures were concerned basically with raising and broadening the national minimum and its extension to cover the whole population.[8] But the provision of unemployment insurance was confined only to employees. In many respects it was superior to the earlier workmen's compensation because the unemployment insurance would now be a 'national and unified structure'.[9]

Part II of the Marsh Report dealt with the issue of 'A National Employment Programme', noting that: 'The only basic answer to unemployment is employment ... employment carrying a reasonable level of remuneration and reasonably satisfactory working conditions.'[10]

Part III of the Report dealt with 'Universal Risks' like sickness, invalidity and old age. The remedies it recommended were health insurance, insurance against industrial accidents and diseases, workmen's compensation, disability and invalidity pensions, old-age pensions and retirement provisions, retirement insurance, and so on.[11] Health insurance and unemployment insurance were recommended as 'two basic administrative systems for Canadian social security'.[12]

The Heagerty Report

Another important report which made a great impact on the construction of the welfare state in Canada was the Report of the Special Advisory Committee on Health Insurance, appointed in 1942 under the Chairmanship of J.J. Heagerty, then Director of the Public Health Service in the Department of Pensions and National Health. The Committee submitted its report to the Parliamentary Committee in 1943, simultaneously with the Marsh Report.[13] The recommendations of the Heagerty Report formed the basis of Canada's National Health Insurance Act. The Heagerty Report, like the Marsh Report, recommended that national health insurance, with unemployment insurance, should be nationally coordinated but provincially administered, and jointly financed by flat-rate personal contributions and government subsidies. The Report recognized healthcare as a basic social service, spanning from public health and disease control to baby clinics and preventive aspects of healthcare, and meeting a wide range of pertinent requirements like access to doctors and other medical personnel. In all these respects, people have experienced tremendous inequality in terms of availability of services. Since the responsibility in the matter lay with the provinces, Canada had a variety of arrangements in this regard, and in the absence of nationwide coordination of the healthcare system, many outstanding issues like national extension of community health centres and other modes of group practice remained unattended. The system that had prevailed till then was composed of government-coordinated insurance plans for hospital costs, free or subsidized medical care for indigent persons, and prepayment schemes, like monthly contributions, run by private medical associations.

The Draft Bill on Health Insurance was based on the recommendations of the Heagerty Report and the measures included in it were compulsory and contributory insurance, encompassing everyone in Canada, by agreement with the provinces. When the Draft Bill was presented by Ian Mackenzie, Minister of Pensions and National Health, in 1943, it was made clear that in order to provide health insurance, it would be necessary to create a Health Insurance Fund comprising money contributed by insured persons, employees, the provincial government and the Dominion government. It was argued that by so distributing costs, the financial burden would be considerably lessened. Under the Bill, all residents would have the right to choose a doctor from the list provided. The method of payment to doctors and other medical personnel was left to the decision of the Provincial Health Insurance Commission. The services of physicians could be utilized for both prevention as well as treatment. The objective of the National Health Insurance Act was the integration of public health and medical care for the purpose of raising and maintaining the standard of health of the people of Canada.[14]

Royal Commission Report

A significant report which needs to be taken into account in this context is the Royal Commission Report – The Rowell–Sirois Commission Report – of 1940, which largely dealt with Dominion–Province financial relations.[15] The Report dealt with Canada's unity in diversity, but from the point of view of our present analysis of the welfare state system of Canada, it also made a few recommendations pertaining to unemployment, old-age pensions and public health, medical and hospital services. On the question of unemployment, the Commission recommended that the Dominion government

> should take over full responsibility for the unemployed employables. The Dominion Government alone is capable of carrying the burden of unemployment relief and grappling with the problem of unemployment.... With the responsibility for the unemployed employables must go the

right to administer unemployment relief and to enact and administer any scheme of compulsory unemployment insurance.[16]

The Commission made a distinction between the unemployment of employables and the unemployment of the unemployables. It recommended that while the responsibility for unemployed employables should be transferred to the Dominion government, 'the responsibility for unemployables should remain with the Province, or, through the Province, with the municipality'.[17]

On old-age pensions, the Commission recommended the continuation of the system already in operation whereby the Dominion government paid 75 per cent of the cost of the pension, and the Provincial government paid 25 per cent and the cost of administration. It said that,

> should it be decided to establish a contributory old age pension scheme, it should be administered by the Dominion, and the Dominion should also have the power to include provisions for widows and orphans . . . and provision for pensions on retirement from industry due to invalidity or permanent disability.

On public health, medical and hospital services, the Commission said that due to differences from Province to Province in Canada, medical and hospital services should remain a provincial responsibility. At the same time, it held the view that 'the Dominion might be in a better position to collect the fees for health insurance, especially if there should be a Dominion scheme of compulsory unemployment insurance or contributory old-age pensions'.[18]

In 1944, the federal government had brought about the Family Allowances Act which gave all mothers entitlement to receive an allowance on behalf of their children below 16 years, and in 1948 it offered a National Health Grant Programme which provided grant-in-aid for health services planning and hospital construction, and demonstration grants for public and mental health. In 1951, the government introduced a universally applicable old-age pension system, which gave entitlement to all Canadians, above 70, to a pension.

In 1957, the federal government and provinces reached an agreement on the terms of hospital insurance grants, and in 1968 on medical care insurance. Under the agreement, the amount of grant-in-aid for both these programmes varied according to the wealth condition of each province. But, on average, each province could claim around 50 per cent of its expenditure. To qualify to receive this grant-in-aid, provinces had to agree to accept four basic medical-care principles: (1) universality; (2) comprehensiveness; (3) portability; and (4) public administration. The principle of equity of access was added to them in 1984 under the Canada Health Act.

Welfare reforms in the 1960s

A new chapter in the construction of the welfare state system in Canada was opened after the Liberal leader, Lester Pearson, became Canada's Prime Minister in 1963, with the support of the New Democratic Party of social democrats which had always supported the establishment of a welfare state system in Canada. Indeed, much of the social reform measures in Canada were introduced during the period between 1963 and 1968 as a result of the joint efforts of the Liberals, under Lester Pearson, and the New Democratic Party of social democrats of Canada. The period witnessed the introduction of social security, health insurance and public housing.

In 1964, a Royal Commission on Health Services made certain recommendations to ensure the best possible healthcare for all Canadians. It gave more emphasis to children's healthcare programmes; it recommended that the nation's resources should be mustered to establish universal, comprehensive health services programmes in the 10 provinces and two territories;[19] and it said that the coverage of health services should be continuous with portability of benefits assured to individuals moving from province to province, and wherever the services are rendered.[20] It said that: 'The provision of an adequate standard of health services for all Canadians . . . will require the participation of the Federal Government in the planning of health care programmes and the establishment of national standards. There remains the question of the division of revenue and expenditure.'[21] The Royal Commission recommended that the federal government should meet '50 per cent of the cost of publicly financed programmes'.[22] Following this, in 1966, the federal government passed the Medical Care Insurance Act which affirmed the government's commitment to finance healthcare programmes.

Lester Pearson's government piloted three major social legislations – Medicare, the Canada Pensions Plan and the Canada Assistance Plan. The Canada Pensions Plan was passed in 1965. It ensured social-insurance protection for retirement, disability and benefits for survivors. The Medicare Act was passed in 1966, providing for the federal government's contribution to the provincial governments' medical care insurance plans. These were followed by the introduction of the Guaranteed Income Supplement, medicare grants, education grants, and so on. The programme was further strengthened by public housing, unemployment insurance provision and other measures. In 1975, the federal government introduced the Spouses' Allowance under which old-age pensioners' spouses, aged 60 and above, would receive an allowance to help to maintain a certain standard of living.

However, by the 1960s there was a substantial growth of private and voluntary pre-payment health schemes everywhere in Canada, and according to a Royal Commission Report, by 1961 about 60 per cent of the population were members of one or other such scheme.[23] By 1970, this had grown to about 70 per cent of the population. Yet a significant proportion of the poor – the most needy, or what are sometimes called 'medically indigent' – were left out of these schemes. In the absence of comprehensive health insurance cover, these medically indigent people had to depend upon hospitals, local agencies and the medical care which was available as part of social assistance – in other words, a stigmatized state medicine for the underprivileged. Comprehensive health insurance would have meant providing a national fund, contributed by everybody through tax revenues equitably collected, with benefits equitably available to everyone, and such a comprehensive national health insurance scheme was finally put in place in 1968.

Taken together, these measures transformed Canada into one of the most highly advanced welfare states in the world. Pertinently, it may be noted that the social security programme in Canada is the responsibility of the government in the sense that it gives direct financial assistance to individuals and families. Family allowances, old-age pensions, provincial and municipal social assistance programmes and so on fall under this category.

The Canada's welfare state

Canada has 10 provinces and two territorial administrations. In the division of responsibilities under the Constitution, the provinces are responsible for social assistance, education, healthcare and social services, whereas insurance programmes, including employment insurance (EI), are a federal responsibility. The provinces are responsible for social affairs and regulate the provision of provincial social assistance to the needy who do not enjoy contributory entitlements. The social assistance policy provides for cash support to those who otherwise are not able to provide for themselves, but would facilitate their return to a position where they can support themselves. Since provinces and territories plan social assistance programmes and decide on benefit rates, the benefit rate varies from province to province and territory to territory. But, everywhere, the level of social assistance payment is limited to barely meeting the immediate necessities like food, clothing and other recurring household expenditures. In any case, it is not intended to exceed the income level of low-income households. For the Canada Pension Plan, the federal government shared responsibilities with provinces, and in a few provinces municipal governments are involved in the administration of social services and social assistance.

The welfare state system in Canada provides considerable benefits to people in the form of social services (or income in kind) and social transfer payments. Social services are funded and delivered by three sources – the governments (or public sector), the private sector for profit, and the private non-profit sector (voluntary sector). Certain social services are free and fully funded by the government, but others are based on full or partial payment, depending upon the income of the recipient. Social services cover a wide spectrum of areas, ranging from healthcare and education to promotional activities. The social transfer payments have been attuned to replace or supplement income from employment and other sources. If a person's income stops due to eventualities like unemployment, illness or retirement, social programmes like unemployment insurance, social assistance and old-age security pay a portion of that income. The income-tax system has also been used to extend social benefits through tax credits, exemptions and deductions, like the retirement savings plan.[24]

Decisions as to who qualifies and for what assistance are based on certain criteria. For instance, universal programmes like old-age security (OAS), or family allowances (which was discontinued in 1992), entitle everyone to receive benefits, irrespective of their income. After the introduction of the 'clawback' by the federal government, the OAS has been robbed of its truly universal character as the 'clawback' system takes back benefits from pensioners and families belonging to higher income brackets. Social insurance programme cover workers in the paid labour force who retire or become unemployed, or who have suffered a work-related disability. This category of beneficiaries is covered by programmes like the Canada and Quebec Pension Plans and the Federal Unemployment Insurance, which are funded by contributions from employers and employees. The benefits received from them depend upon the size of employees' earnings. In addition, there are two other programmes of social assistance – one income-tested, the other need-tested. The income-tested programme assists individuals and families whose income has fallen below a stipulated level, while needs-tested programmes give assistance to families and individuals who are in 'need' irrespective of the cause of their need. Indeed, most of the provincial social assistance programmes are needs-tested.

Canada's social security system

Canada's social security system is built on a series of insurance programmes involving both the governments as well as private agencies. The basic approach followed in this regard is that in order to meet the contingencies of life, like temporary unemployment, sickness, injury, disability and so on, and to provide for retirement, everyone should set apart a portion of his/her income and contribute the savings to an insurance plan administered by the federal government. Insurances above these basic levels are provided through private insurance, but in order to meet large and unforeseen expenditures like medical and hospital bills, the government has established special or universal hospital and medical insurance plans.

The social security system in Canada has been structured on several federal, provincial and joint federal–provincial schemes. Most important among them are: unemployment insurance (now renamed as employment insurance); child benefits; old-age pensions; and the Canada Assistance Plan (CAP).

Unemployment insurance

Unemployment insurance (UI), an income-support programme, was introduced in Canada way back in the 1940s and was expanded in the 1970s in order to provide for sickness and maternity benefits. The Unemployment Insurance Act 1940 was the first federal welfare state programme introduced in Canada. The Act stipulated that unemployment insurance should be funded by the premiums paid by the employer and employees, backed by the Consolidated Revenue Fund. The Act established the following basic principles which would guide all future unemployment insurance legislations: (1) benefits would be related to earnings, as opposed to being flat-rated; (2) the normal standard of the wage-earner should be protected; and (3) it should cover at least 75 per cent of wage-earners' income (implying that it would largely exclude rural occupations and personal service activities from its ambit). The Unemployment Insurance Act 1971 expanded the programme's ambit by reducing eligibility conditions and expanding compulsory coverage to include all kinds of employees. It also enhanced the benefit level to an extent that the insured employee would receive about two-thirds of his wages. Through this legislation, insured employees were made eligible to receive unemployment benefits for reasons like temporary sickness, disability or pregnancy. In 1985, the federal government decided to separate the UI from the Consolidated Revenue Fund.

Until the 1990s, the UI scheme covered about 90 per cent of the unemployed in Canada. But subsequently, for example in 1995, the figure reduced to 58 per cent following the tightening of the eligibility criteria in the 1990s. The UI (now EI) benefits include maternity, parental and sickness benefits. Pertinently, the Government of Canada, in a White Paper published in 1945, is committed to the maintenance of a high level of employment and income. The UI has been designed as a corollary to it, specifically to provide income to workers during temporary periods of unemployment. Therefore, the extent of UI utilization has depended very much on the extent of unemployment in the country. The programme provides income support for workers who temporarily lose their jobs, and provides sickness benefits and maternity, parental and adoption benefits for parents. Sickness benefits may be claimed up to a period of 15 weeks; parental benefit up to 10 weeks by both natural and foster parents while they are caring for a newborn or adopted child. This benefit can be claimed by the mother or father, or it can be split between the parents if both are eligible. Self-employed people, other than self-employed fishermen, are not eligible for UI benefits.

In order to qualify for regular unemployment insurance benefit, workers have needed between 10 and 20 weeks of insurable employment. In areas where the unemployment rate has been over 15 per cent, workers have needed 10 weeks of paid employment to qualify, but in areas where the unemployment rate has reached only 6 per cent they have needed 20 weeks of work. The normal UI benefit in 1992, for example, was 60 per cent of the average weekly insurable earnings, up to a maximum of $426 a week, and the payment of benefits would start after a two weeks waiting period and last for 17 to 50 weeks, depending upon the employee's insurable earnings and the regional unemployment rate. But, workers who quit their jobs without a proper reason, or who are dismissed for misconduct, or unemployed workers who refuse to accept suitable jobs, get UI benefits of 50 per cent of insurable earnings rather than 60 per cent, and their benefit period is delayed by 7 to 12 weeks in addition to the normal waiting period. Since 1993, however, the first two categories of workers have been denied UI benefits altogether. Since then, the maximum UI benefit has also been cut from 60 per cent to 57 per cent of insurable earnings.

It is important to bear in mind that UI stands apart from other social programmes because it is not funded by the government. The federal government only administers the programme, and the funds come from employers' and employees' contributions. The UI is a self-sustaining programme, and the federal government covers only temporary shortfalls in the fund which are reimbursed from future UI premium revenues.[25] The National Council of Welfare, through its research findings, has pointed out the correlationship between the length of UI beneficiary rolls and the total number of people who are unemployed. The UI beneficiary rolls invariably lengthened as and when unemployment rose in Canada, as happened in 1991.[26]

The UI Act was once again revised in 1990. As a result of this revision, while the benefit structure was simplified, waiting periods were increased and the maximum benefit period was curtailed. A penalty clause was introduced for quitting a job 'without just cause' or for being dismissed for misconduct. In 1993, UI benefits were reduced from 60 per cent to 57 per cent and tough measures were introduced against quitters to prevent misuse of the system. UI regulations were further tightened in 1994 and 1995 when $2 billion was cut from the total annual cost of $10 billion of the programme.

Reform of unemployment insurance (now EI) in the 1990s has been publicly resented because, as a result of the reforms, the federal costs of EI were reduced while the provincial costs increased. The changes that took effect on 18 November 1990 under the Mulroney government also reduced unemployment insurance coverage. In some parts of the country the minimum period of work in order to qualify for UI benefits was increased from 14 to 20 weeks, and benefits were now paid for periods of 35 to 50 weeks instead of the previous 46 to 50 weeks. The net result of these changes has been the shifting of some employable people who are temporarily out of work from the UI rolls to the welfare rolls.

However, there has been a perceptible decline in the number of those who are entitled to the UI (EI) benefits after the recent reforms. Statistics show that while the ratio of regular EI beneficiaries among the unemployed in

1989 was 83 per cent, in 1999 the figure reduced to 42 per cent.[27] This was partly due to shrinkage of the EI coverage of unemployment, and partly due to EI reform which restricted access to and the duration of EI benefits. As a result of the reform, the federal government is responsible for a smaller portion of the employed. Owing to stringent needs testing, only a small proportion of EI claimants enter the Social Assistance Programme, a provincial responsibility, after the expiry of EI.

Child benefits

Canada's welfare state system provides for child benefits. Provision for children was one of the recommendations of the Marsh Report which said that children should have an unequivocal place in social security policy, and favoured the recognition of a children's cash allowance as a specific social security measure.[28] Therefore, children's allowances were already in place long before Parliament passed its resolution on child benefits in 1989. However, when the House of Commons passed a unanimous resolution on 24 November 1989 to 'seek to achieve the goal of eliminating poverty among Canadian children by the year 2000', a national approach on child benefits was crystallized. However, despite this resolution, serious efforts to improve the system of child benefits were not made until 1996 following the release of the *Report to Premiers of the Ministerial Council on Social Policy Reforms and Renewal*. As a result of provincial initiative, the Report proposed income support for poor families with children. The federal government responded favourably, and opened discussions on improving benefits for children. At the First Ministers' meeting held in June 1996, the federal prime minister and the provincial premiers decided to make eradication of child poverty their priority. A national approach was informally developed, and the speech from the throne in October 1999 made explicit the federal government's intention to prepare a national plan to provide support to families. Meanwhile, the government introduced a Child Tax Benefit (CTB) system in July 1998 and successive federal governments have targeted their financial support to low-income families. This was significant because it was the first new major federal social spending scheme in many years intended to improve the conditions of families on welfare. But, in actual practice, most provinces and territories except Newfoundland and New Brunswick decided that the new money should be clawed back from families on welfare. Under the CTB, the federal government has provided all families with income up to $20,921 with a Supplement to the Canadian child tax benefit. For families with one child, the annual supplement is $605. Families with two children would receive an annual supplement of $1,010. Yet, according to the National Council of Welfare (NCW), only those families on welfare living in Newfoundland and New Brunswick saw an increase in their incomes through this supplement, in other provinces and territories these benefits have been 'clawed back' in different ways.[29]

Old-age pensions

Old-age pension, introduced in 1952, provides a basic non-contributory income for people above 65 under the federal old-age-security (OAS) programme. In 1965, the federal government of Canada introduced contributory pension schemes in the form of Canada/Quebec Pension Plans. Prior to that, in 1927 the federal government had enacted the Old-Age Pensions Act, which was replaced in 1951 by the Old-Age Assistance Act. The 1951 legislation provided for means-tested support for those above 70, but the age limit was reduced from 70 to 65 subsequently. In order to help low-income pensioners, the government introduced a guaranteed income supplement in 1967. Therefore, since 1951, Canada's old-age security programme had operated as a universal social programme for senior citizens above 65. Spouses of OAS pensioners aged 60–64, whose income is below a certain level, receive a spouses allowance (SPA). However, in 1989 the government decided to claw back the OAS benefits of high-income seniors, undercutting the universality of the programme.

In addition to OAS, there are also earnings-related pensions based on compulsory contributions to cover retirement, disability and death. Two plans operate the earnings-related pension scheme, the Canada Pension Plan (CPP) and the Quebec Pension Plan (QPP), both introduced simultaneously in 1966. The Canada Pension Plan – the retirement pension – is not funded through general tax revenues, it is contributory – contributions are paid by employees, their employers and self-employed people and from the interest earned on the investment of that money. Employer and employee pay 50:50 for the CPP. Similar to this is the operational aspect of the Quebec Pension Plan, the sister plan of the CPP, which operates in Quebec Province. Together, these two contributory plans cover practically every member of the paid labour force, providing pension benefits to retired workers, survivor's benefits for spouses of deceased CPP/QPP subscribers and a lump-sum death benefit in order to meet funeral expenses. And those expenses are insulated against inflation. In fact, these two plans are the major source of income of seniors, in addition to the federal government's old-age security pension and the guaranteed income supplement.[30] The Canada Pension Plan and the Quebec Pension Plan are administered by the governments, but are not financed with government money. The government is the custodian of the money contributed by workers and employers.

In 1995 Canada proposed a new set of seniors' benefits, to be brought into force from 2001. Under this programme, in 2001 the old-age security Pension and the guaranteed income supplement for seniors would be combined into a new Seniors' Benefit. Simultaneously, the special tax credit for seniors and the credit for the first $1,000 income from an occupational pension plan would also disappear from the income tax system. The centrepiece of the new proposal is that a new seniors' benefit would replace the old-age security pensions and guaranteed income supplement. Under the new scheme, the maximum benefit for low-income seniors would be $120 a year, per household, higher than old-age security and the GIS combined. Low-income single seniors would get an extra $120 a year, and low-income senior couples would share the extra $120. Under the new scheme, family income, rather than individual income, would be used for calculating all benefits. The new scheme would not disturb the existing spouse's allowance programme for low-income people aged 60–64. Widows and widowers would also get an additional $120 a year under the spouse's allowance. Under the new seniors' benefit, the most economically disadvantaged senior citizens would receive the largest benefits and the benefit structure is tied to the amount of income seniors receive from other sources. According to one calculation, a single pensioner with no other income would receive $11,420 a year in 2001, $120 a year more than the estimated value of the old-age security pension and GIS at the maximum rate for single people.[31] The new Seniors' benefit would be non-taxable.

Canada' retirement income system has two major objectives: (1) to ensure that elderly people have incomes high enough to enable them to live in dignity, irrespective of the circumstances during their working years; and (2) to maintain a reasonable relationship between incomes before and after retirement so that old age does not bring a drastic reduction in a person's quality of life. According to National Council of Welfare, neither of these objectives have been achieved as more than half a million senior citizens live in poverty, and as many workers with average incomes have experienced notable fall in their living standards after retirement.[32]

In Canada, the CPP and QPP are the major source of income of seniors. The Canada Pensions Plan operates on a 'pay-as-you-go' financing basis, and the funds needed to pay today's CPP pensioners come from contributions of today's workers and employers. The original rate of CPP contributors was 3.6 per cent of contributing earnings – that is, 1.8 per cent from workers and 1.8 per cent from employers. Although the CPP and QPP are totally separate, the benefits they provide are identical. These two plans were designed to provide retirement income equal to 25 per cent of career earnings up to the average industrial wage. According to 1996 figures, these two plans provided more than $14 billion a year as retirement benefits to 3 million seniors.[33]

The Canada Assistance Plan (CAP)

The Canada Assistance Plan (CAP) constitutes a key element of Canada's welfare state system. Prior to its creation in 1966, welfare was a collection of loose programmes that varied widely from province to province, targeted only towards people who fell into specific categories of need. In 1966 the federal, provincial and territorial governments reached agreement to set up the CAP as a framework for financing social security of last resort. The Plan led to the development of a series of social services for low-income and middle-income families. The federal legislation which established the CAP stipulated that the provinces and territories would have to base their welfare programmes on a 'needs test' and no residence restriction should be allowed. The legislation required that welfare assistance be provided to cover the cost of food, shelter, clothing, fuel, utilities, household supplies, personal care, religious obligations and recreation.

The CAP finances programmes which provide income to Canadians in need, and also subsidizes the cost of social services for people below the poverty line and for people who are in danger of falling into poverty without some outside help. Prior to the introduction of the CAP in 1966, the federal government shared the cost of assistance, but not of welfare services. But under the CAP, welfare services and community development were included as measures of developing greater emphasis on preventive and rehabilitative measures in provincial programmes. Under the CAP, the federal government contributed half of the cost of assistance payments and of improving and extending preventive and rehabilitative and administrative services. In the case of Quebec, special fiscal arrangements replaced cost-sharing. Under federal–provincial agreements, all provinces agreed to use needs tests as a method of determining the amount of assistance and services, to provide for appeal procedures against the decisions of the welfare officials, and to refrain from erecting and maintaining residence barriers.

Under the CAP, agreements concluded between the federal government and the provincial and territorial governments, provinces and territories would provide financial help to all Canadians judged to be 'in need'. Under the federal law, 'people in need' are those who are unable to provide adequately for themselves and their dependents due to their inability to get jobs, loss of a principal family provider, illness, disability, age or other reasons. 'Need' is determined through a needs test, a detailed examination of the means of support available to a family or individual compared to the cost of the bare necessities of life. If a family's basic expenditure is higher than its income, the family is 'in need' and qualifies for support under CAP. However the amounts provided by the provinces or territories for basic assistance usually remained far below the poverty line.

In addition to these welfare supports, the CAP provided social services to persons in need and to 'persons who are likely to become persons in need unless such services are provided'. The CAP Act refers to such services as 'welfare services', but they are also available to those who are not on welfare. Welfare services are aimed to lessen, remove or prevent poverty, child neglect or dependence on public assistance. For those who are not welfare recipients, the services are available under different conditions, with eligibility determined through an 'income test' rather than a 'needs test', and the services would be provided by public or non-profit agencies. For the income test, the provinces and territories set limits on the amount of income a family or individual can have in order to qualify for subsidized welfare services under the CAP. However, most of the health-related services do not come under the CAP, and are financed through another federal-provincial arrangements entitled 'Established Programmes Financing' (EPF).[34]

In Canada, the CAP was viewed as the social safety net of last resort because it gave protection to people – men, women and children – who are not protected by other social safety nets. A key feature of the CAP was that it not only replaced the patchwork of a series of programmes operated and funded by different tiers of administration, but the welfare support was made available to everyone in Canada who could not provide for their own needs. There was no longer any residence requirements for welfare support. Besides welfare and social services, the CAP also provided money for more than 7,000 homes for special care, for certain healthcare costs not covered by medicare or supplementary programmes, and for child welfare services. The provision for special care included care homes for the aged, shelters for battered women and their children, residences for the handicapped, rehabilitation centres for drug or alcohol addicts, and so on.

At the operational side of the CAP, the provinces and territories provided income support and other assistance to the needy in the first instance and submitted the details of the expenditure incurred to the federal government for verification and reimbursement of 50 per cent of the costs of all eligible expenditures.

The original deal on CAP lasted until 1990 when the Progressive Conservative government, headed by Brian Mulroney, in the federal budget speech, announced a 'cap on CAP' in three rich provinces – Ontario, Alberta and British Columbia. The federal government unilaterally declared that it would not increase its share of the cost of CAP in these three provinces by more than 5 per cent a year; any increases above 5 per cent would have to be borne by the provinces themselves. The cap on CAP was approved by parliament against opposition from the Liberal Party and the New Democratic Party. The measure was later extended up to 1995. But, by 1992–93, the federal share of the CAP fund was down by 28 per cent for Ontario and by 36 per cent for British Columbia. Alberta was not much affected yet since the provincial government in Edmonton decided to cut down its welfare programmes.

Canada health and social transfer

A radical shift from CAP was proposed by the new Liberal government of Jean Chretien in the federal budget speech of 27 February 1995. It proposed the repeal of the CAP, and suggested a sea-change in the way the federal government contributed to the cost of welfare and social services. Instead of sharing the social costs incurred by the provinces and territories, the federal government would provide money to the provinces and territories under a new system of block funding. The two reasons cited for bringing this change were: (1) to cut federal government spending; and (2) to give provincial and territorial governments flexibility by reducing restrictions on the use of federal money. The Budget Implementation Bill 1995, had three pertinent features: (1) repeal of the Canada Assistance Plan; (2) creation of a Canada Health and Social Transfer to help provinces to pay for welfare and social services as well as for medicare and post-secondary education; and (3) cuts in federal financial support to all of these programmes. The Bill said that there would be no more cost-sharing of welfare and social services after 1 April 1996, and that the provinces and territories would be given four years to settle their outstanding accounts with the federal government for the amounts paid in the previous years and that the CAP would be repealed formally by 31 March 2000.[35] Pertinently, the original proposal in the budget speech on 27 February 1995 was for the creation of the Canada Social Transfer. But, three weeks later, it was renamed as the Canada Health and Social Transfer (CHST). It expanded the scope of the programme of federal block-funding arrangements to encompass medicare and post-secondary education, besides welfare and social services.

CHST is not a cost-sharing system. Under the CHST, provinces and territories would receive block-funding for welfare, social services, medicare and post-secondary education. But, unlike in the CAP, none of the money would be legally earmarked for any of the four areas. Though obviously it gives flexibility to the federal and territorial governments in terms of its administration, there is a potential danger of this money now spent on welfare and social services getting channelled to medicare or post-secondary education, making the poor people depending upon welfare and social services losers. Similarly, social programmes of a preventive nature – for example better-nutrition programmes and prenatal care for pregnant women which could improve the health of newborns – could also suffer neglect or low priority. However, it has been observed that the amount which actually got transferred to the provinces under the CHST was much lower than that transferred under the CAP. Moreover, it has also been observed that there has been a decline in the total federal transfers to the provinces (annually on average a per capita reduction of 3.4 per cent of transfer spending) since 1995. However, the federal transfers account for between 14 and 42 per cent of revenues of the provinces.[36] In addition, the funds are reallocated through 'equalization' grants, based on the province's relative revenue-raising capacity, to provide provinces with approximately the same level of public services. The provinces which do not generally get any benefit from the equalization fund are the rich provinces – Alberta, Ontario and British Columbia. The highest beneficiaries of the equalization fund are the maritime provinces or the 'have-not' provinces.

In Canada, post-secondary education is a provincial responsibility and has been funded by and large by the government.[37] Earnings from tuition fees have amounted to only about 5 per cent of the total expenditure. But, this pattern was sought to be changed in the 1990s. In a Discussion Paper presented to parliament on 5 October 1994 by Lloyd Axworthy, federal Minister for Human Resource Development, the government indicated the choice of phasing out cash transfers for post-secondary education and developing a system of 'income-contingent repayment loans'. Instead of providing support for institutions of higher learning, the government would provide loans to students and stipulate repayments on students' ability to pay after graduation and getting a job.[38] This policy has been criticised as Ottawa's attempt to balance its budget by offloading its own financial responsibilities onto the provinces/territories, or onto university students by offering them education loans to finance their own studies.

Housing assistance

Canada has a federal housing assistance programme operated through the Canada Mortgage and Housing Corporation, which has been dovetailed to help low- and moderate-income families. It has its counterparts at the provincial level as well, with several housing assistance programmes for the general public which include non-profit housing, rent supplements, residential rehabilitation assistance, emergency repair assistance, and so on. While in certain programmes the cost is shared between the federal government and provinces, other programmes are funded and administered either by the federal governments or by the provincial government. As a result, there are a number of social housing units for low-income families. In fact, subsidized housing constitutes about 5 per cent of Canadian households. As the social assistance scheme covers the actual cost of housing at a level decided by the provincial governments, those who live in social housing units do not receive supplementary shelter benefits in addition to their normal social assistance entitlement.[39] However, the rents of social assistance recipients in social housing are settled through negotiations between social welfare and housing authorities. The rent paid by low-paid employees comes to about 25 to 30 per cent of their income.

Attacks on the welfare state

If the 1960s witnessed the flowering of Canada as an advanced welfare state, the 1980s witnessed mounting attacks on the role of the state as provider. This was partially stimulated by the growing demands on public expenditure due to increasing unemployment and due to demographic changes caused by the growing size of the ageing population in the country. The main focus of these attacks was on the universalistic element ingrained in the welfare state programmes. This was also the time when massive and sustained attacks on the welfare state system were launched by the Thatcher and Reagan administrations in Britain and the United States, breaking the bipartisan consensus that had prevailed in Britain and the United States on the publicly funded welfare state systems. The Thatcher–Reagan attack was directed against the role of the state in the public welfare sector, and their plea was to leave public welfare to free-market forces and private enterprises. Under the influence of this ideological offensive, and by using public debt and deficit financing as excuses, the federal government in Ottawa initiated a cost-cutting exercise with a view to bring down public expenditure. Social security programmes like healthcare, family allowances, unemployment benefits, old-age pensions and so on came under special scrutiny in this context, with the objective of redesigning them. As a result, the eligibility criteria for social security benefits, including unemployment benefits, were modified, and social services were sought to be privatized or contracted out.

The Wealthy Banker's Wife and Shooting the Hippo

Canada also launched a move to take the public welfare system into the US pattern. The arguments and the moves which the neo-Conservatives in Canada had put forth to prepare the Canadian psyche to accept the otherwise unacceptable solutions were brilliantly dissected by Linda McQaig, famous Canadian journalist, in her two well-known books, *The Wealthy Banker's Wife: The Assault on Equality in Canada* (1993) and *Shooting the Hippo: Death by Deficit and Other Canadian Myths* (1995).[40] In these two celebrated works, McQaig encapsuled the carefully crafted strategy of the then Canadian administration led by the Progressive Conservatives.

McQaig tells the story of how the advanced welfare state system of Canada has been systematically undermined by the Conservative-led Canadian administration since 1985 by effecting drastic spending cuts in sectors like healthcare, education, pensions, family benefits and social assistance. She also focuses on how Canadians have been repeatedly told by the government that they had no choice but to cut back spending in order to compete in the global market, to inveigle them to accept an otherwise unacceptable solution. The role model presented to them at that time was the US-model welfare system where social programmes are minimal and where prosperity and drudgery coexist with a large underclass living in squalor. In *The Wealthy Banker's Wife*, McQaig contested the 'no-choice' argument of the neo-Conservatives and said that Canadians had a choice in the impressive European models, particularly the Scandinavian model – a combination of a strong welfare state system and strong competitive economies. According to her:

> The Europeans manage to maintain extensive social welfare systems and strong economies while the Americans have convinced themselves that they can't afford anything more than the most minimal programmes. Canada, which has traditionally been situated somewhere between the two models, has recently been drifting in the American direction.[41]

However, the key element of McQaig's findings is that the concerted attack on social programmes in Canada was indeed an attack by those who were ideologically opposed to equality and distributive justice. She found little evidence to support the argument that a strong welfare state interfered with economic growth. On the other hand, the welfare state promoted equality and distributive justice in society. She noted that:

> there is no evidence that a strong welfare state interferes with economic growth and competitiveness. What a welfare state does do, however, is divide up a society's resources more equitably. And it is this – not the welfare state's alleged impact on economic growth – that has led to the attack on the welfare state by those unsympathetic to the egalitarian cause.[42]

Though the Mulroney government's election manifesto promised preservation of Canada's universal social programmes as a 'sacred trust', when it assumed power it breached that promise through 'complex and obscure budget changes' and through effectively cutting expenditure on health and education on a massive scale from 1986 onwards. According to McQaig, this was done insidiously without even announcing its intentions and by quietly withdrawing from funding and overseeing the vital areas of social welfare.[43] McQaig focused on the perils of handing over crucial areas of human development, like medical care and education, to the private marketplace for the poor where the quality of service would depend on the financial resources of the customer. Inevitably it would lead the poorer sections of society to end up with poorer healthcare and poorer education:

> the people calling for an end to our universal system are those who benefit least from a reduction in inequality – people like the wealthy banker and his wife. In fact, it could be said that these sorts of people are comfortable with inequality – an inequality where they are among the privileged few.

Therefore, demands for government spending cuts for welfare were in many ways constituted an attack on the very egalitarian goals of the welfare state, she contended.[44]

Of course the marketplace would produce large disparities between the rich and the poor, and McQaig criticized the Mulroney government's actions to reduce protection offered by Canada's unemployment insurance system. The government's decision to withdraw federal funding from the Unemployment Insurance Fund, leaving the system financed by contributions from employers and employees, was eventually a move to end the government's responsibility for unemployment – especially for the reduction of unemployment or for pursuing a full employment policy in the country.

In her other book, *Shooting the Hippo*, McQaig focused on how the advanced egalitarian welfare state system of New Zealand was transformed into a free-market jungle, with massive unemployment and growing inequality. She explained how Canada was systematically enticed in to following New Zealand's path – by lowering the expectations of what a society can do for its citizens, by rolling back the frontiers of government and by reducing the government to merely an enforcement agency of certain legal and political rights of people, rather than expanding its role as a provider and equalizer – to establish a market-based welfare system. Of course, in the marketplace there are no automatic rights or entitlements, except the right to sell services to those who have money to pay for them.[45]

However, the fact remains that by the end of 1981 the Canadian economy came into the grip of deep recession. As jobs began to disappear and unemployment rates reached double digits in Canada, businesses went bankrupt. This provided a good opportunity for the anti-welfare state elements to launch attacks on Canada's welfare state system. They included not only Brian Mulroney and his Progressive Conservative Party, but also the neo-Conservative think-tanks like the C.D. Howe Institute, named after the most outstanding opponent of the welfare state system.[46] Soon, the Howe Institute stepped up its demand for cuts in government spending and called for reforms to unemployment insurance, welfare, pensions, healthcare and education with a view to reducing their cost, size and scope.[47] The Mulroney government, which assumed power in 1984, prepared the ground for mounting attacks on Canada's welfare state system on two planks – the 'debt crisis' and 'anti-deficit'. They argued that the debt problems had become so acute that there was no choice but to cut social spending. The deficit screw was tightened to such an extent that opponents were forced to submit without any further resistance. However, in the wake of recession and from an earlier full employment situation, unemployment in Canada had grown to double digits, which had an adverse impact on social and business lives in the country. In November 1981, about 100,000 unemployed people staged a demonstration on Parliament Hill in Ottawa to protest against high interest rates and the damaging effects on employment and the economy. It is an established fact that high interest rates favour the affluent sections of society and squeeze employment, by and large hitting low-income earners the hardest. As McQaig said, a 'tight-money policy reinforces inequality in two ways – its high interest rates disproportionately reward the rich, and the resulting unemployment disproportionately punishes the poor'.[48]

The 1980s and 1990s witnessed drastic changes in the structure and policies of the Canadian state. On the one hand there was a shift of power from the national governments to the international investing community, with headquarters in New York, Washington, London, Frankfurt or Tokyo, with no accountability to the people, and on the other hand, the states' role in economic regulation became drastically reduced during this period.

Indeed, rightwing parties all over the world were trying to hollow out the state and thereby weaken the state's capacity to intervene effectively in the field of social welfare. According to some analysts, the Canadian state 'is dismantling itself in terms of distributive policies, while strengthening its capacity to regulate in favour of the priorities of the market':

> A steady process of trade liberalization, winding down of capital controls, and internationalizing of production has undermined the state's capacity to regulate the entire country as one economic unit. However, what has been noticed in Canada is the reduced role of the federal government in setting minimum national standards for social assistance. At the same time it has given greater role for provinces to administer labour market services. The decision to move towards free trade through the Canada–United States Free Trade Agreement (FTA) of 1989, for example, signalled that the state was willing to move its regulatory powers elsewhere – in this case, to an international treaty that set limits on state actions.[49]

A changing welfare state

Gilles Seguin, a senior official of the Ministry of Human Resource Development in Canada, has observed that Canada's welfare state system is ideologically close to Europe, but in practice it is close to the US system.[50] It is true that the welfare state system in Canada evolved greatly under the influence of European ideas and experiences, particularly the British and Scandinavian experiences. At the nascent stage, the American influence remained marginal, but today the situation is becoming reversed. Canada's welfare system is moving considerably closer towards the minimalist one that characterizes the USA. This development is taking place particularly following the United States and Canada becoming partners through their Free Trade Agreement.

Yet Canada ranks among the most advanced welfare states in the world, with several strands of welfare benefits disbursed through a string of programmes ranging from universality, to those which disburse specific welfare benefits to categories of the population through multiple kinds of insurance and social assistance programmes. Different programmes provide protection to different categories of people – some provide long-term and others short-term benefits. Some provide income in relation to previous or current income, while others provide assistance on the basis of 'need'. While each of these programmes has specific purposes and targets specific groups of people, together their protective arm reaches everyone in Canada.

Although Canada comes under the category of a liberal welfare state in terms of its social transfer payments, compared to other countries Canada has relatively low social transfer payments, despite 11 per cent unemployment. This is mainly because though the Canadian welfare state recognizes the right to protection against basic risks like unemployment, sickness and old age, its programmes are enjoined by stringent eligibility criteria, shorter duration of benefits and low levels of income replacement. Compared to many other countries, Canada relies more on low, income means-tested benefit payments. According to 1980 figures, means-tested benefits accounted for 15.6 per cent of Canada's public expenditure compared to Sweden's 1.1 per cent,[51] and the situation has remained broadly the same since then. This limited benefit coverage in Canada has encouraged the growth of private, but government regulated, savings plans and insurances in the country. This has given openings to commercial service providers in the private market, which has led to the growth of dualism in the welfare state system in Canada – a typical feature of a liberal welfare state system – one for people on the margins and the other for the affluent. The two sectors where this dualism has not yet been found are healthcare and primary education, though post-secondary education has already been put slowly onto the track of this dualism.

Constraints

Success for a welfare state needs strong political commitment, backed by organized political and other forces in society, as in the case of Scandinavia. Those kinds of conviction and backing have been lacking in Canada since the push for a welfare state in the country came from civil servants and from the prodding of a relatively small New Democratic Party (NDP) in the 1960s and 1970s during the prime ministership of Lester Pearson. The NDP government in Ontario pushed the welfare state reforms first, and in the political spectrum of Canada only the NDP (earlier CCF) has been firmly committed to the welfare state system. However, there is little hope of the NDP returning to power in Ottawa in the near future. The Progressive Conservatives are at the other end of the spectrum, opposed to the welfare state system, whilst the centrist party, the Liberal Democrats, has positioned itself in between, with no strong commitment either way; their commitment to the welfare state cannot therefore be considered strong.

Canada's welfare state system, therefore, has been built on fragile political foundations. Unlike in many European countries, Canada does not have a strong labour movement to back up the welfare state agenda. Politically, the CCF, now the NDP, which is the moderate social democratic party of Canada, remains weak and does not currently enjoy the clout it enjoyed during the prime ministership of Lester Pearson, when much of the welfare provisions were put in place in Canada. Moreover, the linkage between organized labour and the NDP remains weak, which forfeits them the necessary strength to further advance the universalistic welfare state agenda. Quebec is an exception in this regard, where the system remains more progressive. On the other hand, there exists a strong linkage between organized capital, which is opposed to the welfare agenda, and the Progressive Conservative and Liberal parties which not only apply effective brakes on further advancement of the welfare agenda, but put constant pressure on the government to withdraw from many areas of welfare. However, no government in Canada can totally reverse the welfare state system in the country. When the Progressive Conservative government sought to go whole hog on it in the 1990s, the party was practically wiped out from parliament in the 1994 elections. Its strength in the House of Commons was reduced to two representatives.

The claw-back

When Pierre Trudeau's Liberal government was defeated by the Progressive Conservatives under Brian Mulroney's leadership in 1984, the new Conservative leadership began to press to cut social spending stating that the budget deficit in Canada was caused by social spending in excess of revenues raised in taxes, an assessment which was refuted by the National Council of Welfare through its empirical studies. McQaig also questioned this assessment of the Progressive Conservatives. However, the argument over the deficit became the springboard on which the Mulroney government launched its stealthy attacks on welfare state policies. Its first budget, in May 1985, contained an attack on old-age pensions when it proposed that old-age security (OAS) payments be only partially indexed. The controversy this raised was punctuated by a televised encounter between Prime Minister Mulroney and a fragile protester, Solange Denis, who accused Mulroney of going back on his election pledge that old-age pensions were a 'sacred trust'. This forced the Mulroney government to backtrack on the issue. But, in the 1989 federal government's budget, old-age security and family allowances were converted to income-tested programmes, through a devious method known as 'social benefits repayments', or 'clawback', as it is popularly called.

The clawback undermined the universality principle applied on old-age pensions. Under the clawback system, senior citizens who have incomes above a threshold ($50,000 in 1989) have their old-age security benefits curtailed by 15 per cent of other net income, besides the income taxes they pay on their OAS benefits. This has meant that, the higher the net income, the larger will be the clawback and smaller will be the old-age pension. Under the system, when the net income of a senior exceeds a stipulated level, he/she has to refund to the federal government the entire amount of OAS received in the previous year. The clawback became fully operational in 1991, and it brought an end to the universal elderly and child benefits. In 1993, the Mulroney government completed its reform of child benefits and replaced family allowances and child tax credits with a single income-tested Child Tax Benefit. The return of the Liberals to power in 1994 did not change the course of reforms being pursued by the Mulroney government. The 1995 budget of the Chretien government formally stated the end of universal old-age pensions, family allowances now no longer exist in Canada.

What impact did the ideological pressure Thatcher and Reagan had launched on welfare state systems have on curtailing welfare benefits in Canada? One cannot say that it had any major impact. In Canada, the issue was put more in the context of federal–provincial relations and also in the context of cutting the federal deficit. Although the privatization programme was pushed forward under the argument that there was a lack of money for public spending, many well-informed analysts thought that the supposed lack of money was a phoney argument, and that the economic argument lacked substance. Perhaps Canada's Free Trade Agreement with the United States, followed by the NAFTA agreement, might have had a greater impact on the Canadian government than anything else to whittle down welfare benefits in Canada to bring it closer to the US pattern, than what Thatcher or Reagan had stated during their tenure in office in the 1980s. Although the Free Trade Agreement was hastily concluded by Mulroney's Conservative government without mature scrutiny and 'in a most unbecoming way', and 'gave away everything', the Liberals, though aware of the implications, did not have the mind to renegotiate when they returned to power in 1994.[52]

However, the curtailment of welfare benefits was carried out after building up considerable domestic pressure under the facade of the deficit argument, which became more convenient for the neo-Conservatives to argue against the public-funded welfare state system. The medical bill of senior citizens, for example, went up following the cutting down of the provision of free medical aid after 65. According to Prof. V. Subramaniam, what is happening now is that both Canada and the USA are trying to imitate the worst parts of each other's welfare systems.[53]

Stealth attacks

Though initial attacks on Canada's welfare state system began to surface in the late 1970s, the actual cuts in the welfare programmes started only in the 1980s under the Conservative administration of Brian Mulroney. Cuts were introduced in the federal public service and a cap put on the CAP. Though people hoped that the new Liberal government in Ottawa, which assumed power in 1994 after unseating the Conservatives, would reverse the policy, their hopes were belied by the new government's acquiescence to the policy pursued by the Mulroney government. The Liberal government wound up the CAP and replaced it with a new programme of National Health and Social Transfer, with further federal cuts in the social transfer. This indicates that the priorities and perception of the Liberals had also changed. Like the Conservatives, the Liberal government started listening to the business community of Canada on welfare matters. The business community had always pressed the government to cut down social transfer in Canada, and reduce the cost of labour, using the logic that a reduction of welfare would make labour cheaper in Canada. A lower labour standard in Canada would mean higher competitiveness with the United States. Similarly, for the business community welfare means more taxes and less welfare means less taxes. They argued that in order to compete with the United States, social cuts and lower labour standards in Canada were necessary,[54] since in their perception the social security system made labour in Canada expensive.

It may be found that every welfare reform introduced in Canada during the last two decades has gone against distributive justice in Canada. This is what McQaig also focused on in her two books. Unlike in the 1960s and 1970s, when people spoke about egalitarianism and distributive justice, no major political party in Canada today pursues its policies on those lines.

According to Professor Wallace Clement, the ideological attack on Canada's welfare state system was not direct, but stealthy, and through Free Trade Agreements, first with the USA, and subsequently through NAFTA, which had the effect of undercutting the welfare state in Canada. It came through a process of Canada's endeavour of levelling the playing field with the United States, and through undercutting the state funding for the welfare state.[55] Though the primary responsibility for the welfare state remains with the provinces and territories, federal transfers play a critical role. Any reduction in those transfers would weaken the system.

Apart from the challenges from free trade arrangements, Canada's welfare state system is also faced with challenges from inside. In terms of commanding power and resources, Canada is a shrinking state. All suggestions advanced by Conservative forces have been aimed at harnessing the hollowing-out of the state of Canada, and weakening its resource base and capacity to effectively intervene. This is another way of attacking the welfare state system by stealth. If the resource base of the state is undermined, it will inevitably result in spending less and less on sectors like public health, education, housing, welfare and so on, through a process of pulling out funding from underneath. It will also lead to a retreat from the universalist approach towards a limited and targeted approach, covering less and less people. Universal, cross-country welfare state programmes will increasingly give way to provincial welfare state systems on a much smaller scale.

Despite these stealthy attacks on the welfare state system in Canada, two important programmes – healthcare and the education system – remain basically fully public-funded. Healthcare in Canada still remains basically universal through health insurance programmes, whereas in the United States it is much more privately based. Therefore, compared to the United States, Canada's welfare state system remains much more substantial and vast, but it is increasingly under attack, mainly due to the exigencies of its deepening partnership with the USA through the free trade arrangement. The objective seems to be to take the Canadian system closer to that established in the United States, and in this regard there is little difference between the Progressive Conservatives and the Liberals.

Privatization

Privatization has been a factor in the reform of the welfare state system in Canada. The process was again introduced subtly and, to a considerable extent, by stealth, mainly pursued through a method of contracting-out services. Even in healthcare, though done through a public insurance system and public hospitals, services have been given mostly through private doctors and clinics. Indeed, in Canada only about 20 per cent of doctors are attached to the government. The rest are private doctors who give normal services to patients on a fee fixed and paid by the government. Canada today has two types of health insurance – public health insurance, and private health insurance – which cover all extra needs of healthcare, such as better rooms in hospitals, dental care, eye care, drugs, and so on. And payments for these are made to the private doctors separately by the insurance companies, although the doctor's fee is set through a public system. Thus healthcare in Canada has a mixture of private and public, but there are no private hospitals, only public hospitals and private doctors.

Though education remains a public-funded system, in post-secondary education the government is trying to partially shift the financial burden onto the shoulders of students by raising tuition fees and by providing student loans. These changes represent a stealth attack on public education. Students provide more revenue to the universities which were hitherto primarily reliant on the state. Earlier, the ratio was 95 per cent government funding and 5 per cent from tuition fees, now the proposal is 25 per cent from tuition fees, 5 per cent from private funds and 70 per cent from government funds. Therefore, the move is to reduce the government share and increase the student share in funding the universities through an increase of tuition fees from $3,000 to $15,000, a kind of privatization within the system by stealth, while higher education still remains a public-funded system. It is estimated that, today, an arts graduate comes out of university with a debt of on average $25,000. For students from poor families, this poses a new barrier for higher education. The prospect of thousands of dollars debt burden at the age of 21 or 22 will deter many students from the lower income strata from seeking higher education in universities, and increasingly transform universities to preserves of the rich, or reduce them to training centres for high-priced jobs so that its students may earn incomes large enough to repay their personal debts. The social purpose and the notion of universities as centres of creativity and creative thinking is likely to be lost in the process.

The changing pension system

The pension system in Canada is shifting from being rights-based to needs-based. Pensions in Canada operate in a mixed manner – employment-based, private-based or universal state-based, but the mix between private and public pension plans is changing. A privatization plan is being strengthened within the mix; a free-market system is slowly being introduced and individual private pensions are very much part of the mix. The healthcare sector has already opened up; while doctors' fees are highly regulated, drugs, dental care, eye care and so on have become market-driven. There are market-driven private clinics supported by public funds through services given to people, and there is now a programme – the Registered Retirement Savings Plan (RRSP) of Canada – which is private and free market-driven. Big US international companies are involved in this plan.

Though the free-trade agreement with the United States is slowly sucking Canada towards Americanization, in many sectors Canada still remains strong *vis-à-vis* the United States. In the financial sector, Canadian capital still remains quite strong, and so strong is Canada's position in the insurance sector that Canadian companies can effectively compete with US companies. Therefore, these sectors are not yet in the track of Americanization.

Demographic change

In addition to the challenges noted above, the Canadian welfare state system is faced with certain other domestic challenges. A notable development in this context is the demographic change now sweeping Canada. The ageing process is already making an impact on the welfare state system in the country, and as the baby boom generation of the postwar period grows old, the cost of maintaining the existing social support system looms large in the minds of Canada's policy-makers. It is estimated that by 2030, Canada will have two-and-a-half times more old people than the country has now, and the aged population will constitute about one-fourth of the total population.[56] This is expected to place considerable strain on the social support system due to the high cost it will face. In recent decades, Canada has experienced a declining number of live births, which, along with enhanced life expectancy, is effecting serious demographic change in Canada.[57] This will have serious repercussions on Canada's pension policy. Keeping that prospect in view, the debate on pensions policy has already shifted from how to strengthen its anti-poverty element, to how to sustain the public part of the pension system in future. The ageing of the population and slow economic growth will jeopardize pay-as-you-go public pensions programmes.

Another factor which has enhanced social expenditure in Canada is the growth of single-parent families in the country, to about 14 per cent in 1999. This, together with the demographic changes, has led to an increasing proportion of social expenditure moving from younger people and families to the ageing population and single-parent families. As a result, there is a marked decline in non-health-related public social spending on the non-aged population.[58]

Poverty levels

The welfare state system in Canada also aimed to eradicate poverty in the country, but before that objective could be achieved, the system has been brought under dilution and mutilation during the last two decades. According to the latest figures available (1997), Canada still has 5.1 million (17.2 per cent) poor people who live with incomes much below the poverty line. In fact, the number of people living at less than 50 per cent of the poverty line has grown significantly during the last decade – from 143,000 families and 287,000 unattached individuals in 1989, to 277,000 families and 456,000 unattached individuals in 1997.[59] Despite the House of Commons resolution to eliminate child poverty in Canada by 2000, the child poverty rate in the country still remains high. The poverty rates are particularly high among families headed by single-parent mothers under 65 with children under 18 (57.1 per cent), and by single-parent mothers under 25 (93.3 per cent). Similarly, there was a rise in the poverty rate for families with heads under 25 (from 28 per cent in 1989 to 43.6 per cent in 1997), and for unattached individuals under 25 (from 47.8 per cent in 1989 to 58.2 per cent in 1997). At the same time, the figures showed that the poverty rate among senior citizens declined to a level of 17 per cent in 1997.[60]

Cuts in social spending

The 'debt crisis' and 'anti-deficit' slogans have been kept as frills throughout the 1980s and 1990s to whittle down the welfare state system in Canada. Though the change of government in 1994, to the Liberals under Chretien, raised hopes that the new government would reverse the trend set by the previous Conservative administration under Mulroney, the new government also continued with the same policies. Despite the fact that the new Liberal government had appointed a known progressive leftwinger of the party, Lloyd Axworthy, as Minister of Social Welfare, in whom the social welfare advocates entertained high hopes of reversing the anti-welfare policies of the Mulroney government, Axworthy was found pursuing the same policy pursued by the previous government and followed approximately what the Howe Institute had suggested for overhauling the social safety net. When Axworthy made his proposals for reviewing the social spending policy as soon as he became minister, the proposals contained were very much in tune with the suggestions of the Howe Institute – for example deep cutbacks in social spending. His proposals included measures to cut back on unemployment insurance, a stipulation that the unemployed should work for their cheques, shifting the cost of higher education progressively to individual students, and so on.[61] The objective was to effect a cut of $7.5 billion in social spending, but the Howe Institute mocked the government and, in a publication entitled *The Courage to Act*, suggested that the government should effect a deeper cut of $17 billion and drastically reduce spending in every area of the social arena, including unemployment insurance, welfare, health, higher education, pensions, and so on.[62]

Following the US model

After the conclusion of the free trade agreement with the USA, the US influence in Canada has grown in leaps and bounds. That influence has transcended trade matters and has had a tremendous impact on the gamut of economic and social policies of Canada. A tendency has grown in Canada to look towards US examples in dealing with new situations, as a result of which a dilemma has persisted in Canada as to how to reconcile the traditional welfare policy, which was by and large patterned after the European models, with the US model, which is based on the market system and known for its minimal social welfare. Indeed, in the USA, unlike in Europe where social welfare is universal with all-embracing programmes designed to ensure the well-being of everyone, social welfare is stigmatized and is little more than a system of government handouts, like receiving food stamps, to the poor. However, Canada has followed the US example in cost-cutting on welfare expenditure.

Canada's welfare state system, as has been established today, is a 'liberal' welfare state system – a model characterized by a minimalist approach designed to induce workers to accept jobs unmindful of the working conditions. The system has a large private welfare sector where the government encourages families and the market to meet the beneficiary's welfare needs outside government programmes. As a result, the 'liberal' welfare state system, as characterized in Canada, has erected 'an order of stratification that is a blend of a relative equality of poverty among welfare state recipients, market-differentiated welfare among the majorities, and a class-political dualism between the two'.[63]

The current debate

A major current debate in Canada on the welfare state system pertains to whether the system should be universal, or selective and targeted to those in need. There is strong support for retaining the principle of universality in providing welfare benefits, and the arguments based on budget deficits have lost their élan as Canada's budgets are no longer in deficit. Another key debate in the country pertains to the question of moving employable social assistance recipients into the workforce as the federal and some provincial governments have begun to follow a carrot-and-stick policy in this regard. The federal government capped the CAP in 1994–95 to heighten the pressure on unemployed employables to join the workforce, irrespective of working conditions, and introduced the system of 'workfare', which was opposed by welfare think-tanks like the National Council of Welfare (NCW).[64] The NCW demanded that 'workfare' should be discontinued;

encouraging welfare recipients to work is reasonable, but assigning them to specific menial or dead-end jobs as a condition for welfare is tantamount to servitude. In addition, forcing parents on welfare into demeaning jobs creates serious stresses which may undermine their ability to take care of their children.[65]

Findings of the National Council of Welfare

According to the National Council of Welfare, the welfare state system in Canada has been attacked through certain misperceptions, that: (1) people on welfare are young people who should be out working; (2) the welfare rolls have fallen significantly since Canada started coming out of recession in 1991; (3) unmarried teenagers make up most of the single-parent mothers; (4) long-term dependence on welfare is rare in Canada; (5) almost all people on welfare are adults; (6) disability is not a major reason for people relying on welfare; (7) many single parent mothers have lots of kids in order to boost their welfare cheques; (8) most people on welfare do not really have it so bad because they get a break on their housing costs by living in subsidized housing; (9) most people on welfare also have income from part-time work or employment insurance or government pensions; and (10) people who are well-educated almost never wind up on welfare.[66] In a highly researched report, conducted in 1997 when about 10 per cent of the population – men, women and children – were on welfare, the NCW refuted, with empirical evidence, all these misperceptions. Indeed, the NCW study found that only 4 per cent of the heads of welfare cases (in March 1997) were below 20 years, and another 12 per cent were between 20 and 25. Similarly, it was found that only 3 per cent of single parents on welfare were below 20 years. According to the report, 54 per cent of welfare cases (in March 1997) had been on welfare continuously for 25 months or more; dependent children under 18 years accounted for nearly 1.1 million of the people on welfare; and it was found that 27 per cent of heads of families recieving welfare had a disability as a reason for being on welfare. Contrary to the popular impression, the report found that nearly half of all single-parent families on welfare had only one child and another 31 per cent had only two children. It was similarly found that only 7 per cent of the welfare cases were in subsidized housing, only 29 per cent of cases had outside income from work, government pensions, support payments, employment insurance, and so on. It was also found that education did not offer absolute protection from welfare; 11 per cent of the heads of families receiving welfare had attended some form of post-secondary education.[67]

Together, the findings in the report exposed many misperceptions and showed that millions of Canadians have turned to welfare only after exhausting all other sources of income, and that welfare provides a vital support for children as well as adults and has become a long-term source of income for a large number of Canadians. The report noted that 'the welfare rolls are made up of older people as well as people who are able-bodied, and people who are well-educated as well as people who are poorly educated'.[68] More than one million people on welfare in March 1997 were found to be children under 18 years, and they were on welfare because their parents were on welfare. In conclusion, the NCW report noted that: 'It is sad to think that governments have been unable to come up with better ways of managing the economy and creating more job opportunities for the people who are willing and able to take advantage of them.'[69] Regarding better ways to deal with the problem of long-term dependency on welfare, the study pointed to the provision of more and better jobs for people, and 'improving financial support for single parents, and promoting government income support for people with severe disabilities that are more appropriate than welfare'. It concluded: 'Better welfare policies are in the interest of all Canadians, because everyone is at risk of falling on welfare at some point of their lives.'[70]

Popular support for universalism

The vicissitudes of the welfare state system in Canada during the last two decades have been punctuated by several moves to hollow out the Canadian state from the welfare sector. Without making any frontal attack on the welfare state system itself or its universal character, the undercutting of the system was carried out by stealth, through a cost-cutting process launched on the bases of debt competitiveness and budget deficit. While some mutilation of the system has taken place that has made it less universal, the core elements of the system still remain more or less intact. Key sectors like healthcare and education still remain universal and state-funded. The attacks waged on the system in the 1980s and 1990s for reasons based on debt and budget deficits have turned out to be phoney since the pre-1980 levels of welfare benefits have not yet been restored to the people, now that Canada is no longer under a budget deficit.

Despite right-wing attacks on the universalist system, public support in Canada seems to favour universal programmes in the welfare sector. This is mainly because a universal welfare system has a certain degree of dynamism of its own because everyone is a partner in it as both benefactors and beneficiaries – in the sense that everyone pays and receives benefits, and thus feels part of the system. But if the system moves away from universalism and become increasingly targeted to the poor only, it would stigmatize beneficiaries on the one hand, and at the same time would lead to resentment among those taxpayers who would not receive any benefit. However, it must be recognized that though universality is preserved in healthcare and education, massive federal cutbacks have weakened the egalitarian character embedded in these two key sectors of the Canadian welfare state system. At the same time, it must be recognized that attempts to undermine the welfare state system through privatization, liberalization and deregulation have not been fully successful. Pertinently, in an attempt to introduce privatization of the healthcare system, Alberta is currently engaged in an exercise of testing the waters through its recent Bill-11 (2000): Alberta's Health Care Protection, which contains a proposal for 'approved surgical facility'.

Conclusion

In the construction of modern Canada as a compassionate and responsive society based on civility, equality and distributive justice, the welfare state idea and the pertinent moves towards its realization have played an outstanding role during the last half-century. Stealthy attacks on it based partly on ideological grounds and partly on economic grounds have not convinced the Canadian people to discard the system. As Liora Salter and Prick Salter (1977) have said:

> Whatever the failings and contradictions of the welfare state, it reflected a commitment . . . to some measure of redistribution and equity. What now threatens to supplant it – the decentralized, politically-oriented, process-oriented mix of public and private functions – is unlikely to effect significant redistribution precisely because it is highly decentralized and involves much more than the state and capital as traditionally understood. Nor is there much indication that those who now take up the tasks previously assigned to the welfare state have any strong commitment to equity.[71]

Notes

1 Leonard C. Marsh, *Report on Social Security for Canada: With a New Introduction by the Author and a Preface by Michael Bliss*, Toronto, University of Toronto Press, 1975.

2 For details, see Malcolm G. Taylor, *Health Insurance and Canadian Public Policy: The Seven Decisions that Created the Canadian Health Insurance System*, Montreal: McGill-Queen's University Press, 1978, pp. 69–104.

3 Leonard C. Marsh, n. 1, p. 7.

4 *Ibid.*, p. 11.

5 *Ibid.*, pp. 12–15.

6 *Ibid.*, pp. 16–19.

7 *Ibid.*, p. 21.

8 *Ibid.*, p. 24.

9 *Ibid.*, p. 93.

10 *Ibid.*, p. 76.

11 *Ibid.*, p. 117.

12 *Ibid.*, p. 186.

13 Canada, House of Commons, Special Committee on Social Security, *Health Insurance: Report of the Advisory Committee on Health Insurance appointed by Order in Council, PC 836 dated February 5, 1942*, Ottawa, 1943.

14 *Ibid.*, pp. 3–5.

15 See S.A. Saunders and Eleanor Back, *The Rowell–Sirois Commission*, Part I, *A Summary of the Report*, Toronto, Ryerson Press, 1940.

16 *Ibid.*, p. 28.

17 *Ibid.*, p. 39.

18 *Ibid.*, pp. 40–1.

19 Canada, *Royal Commission on Health Services*, Vol. I, Ottawa, Queen's Printer, 1964, p. 18.

20 *Ibid.*, p. 20.

21 *Ibid.*, p. 872.

22 *Ibid.*, p. 875.

23 Canada, *Royal Commission on Health Services*, Hall Commission, Ottawa, Queen's Printer, 1964.

24 Isabella Bakker and Cathrine Scott, 'From the Post-war to Post-Liberal Keynesian Welfare State', in Wallace Clement (ed.), *Understanding Canada: Building on the New Canadian Political Economy*, Montreal: McGill-Queen's University Press, 1977, pp. 290–1.

25 Canada, National Council of Welfare, *A Blueprint for Social Security Reform*, Ottawa: NCW, 1994, pp. 11–12.

26 *Ibid.*, pp. 26–7.

27 OECD, *The Battle Against Exclusion: Vol. 3, Social Assistance in Canada and Switzerland*, Paris, 1999, p. 137.

28 Marsh Report, n. 1, pp. 197 and 200.

29 Canada, National Council of Welfare, *Welfare Incomes 1997 and 1998*, Ottawa: NCW, 1999–2000, pp. 12–13, 68.

30 Canada, NCW, *Improving the Canada Pension Plan*, Ottawa: NCW, 1996, p. 1.

31 Canada, NCW, *A Guide to the Proposed Seniors Benefit*, Ottawa: NCW, 1996, pp. 1–3.

32 Canada, NCW, *A Pension Primer*, Ottawa: NCW, 1996, p. 1.

33 Canada, NCW, *Improving the Canada Pension Plan*, Ottawa: NCW, 1996, p. 17.

34 For details of the shift in funding arrangements for extended healthcare from CAP to EPF, see Canada, Parliamentary Task Force on Federal–Provincial Fiscal Arrangements, *Report*, Ottawa, 1981.

35 Canada, National Council of Welfare, *The 1995 Budget and Block Funding*, Ottawa: NCW, 1995.

36 See *Finance Canada*, 1999.

37 Canada, Ministry of Foreign Affairs and International Trade, *Facts Canada: Education*, Ottawa, 1994, p. 1.

38 Canada, National Council of Welfare, *A Blueprint for Social Security Reforms*, Ottawa: NCW, 1994, p. 44.

39 OECD, *Social Assistance in OECD Countries, Vol II, Country Reports*, London: HMSO, 1996, p. 98.

40 Linda McQaig, *The Wealthy Banker's Wife: The Assault on Equality in Canada*, Toronto: Penguin, 1993; *Shooting the Hippo: Death by Deficit and Other Canadian Myths*, Toronto: Viking, 1995.

41 Linda McQaig, *The Wealthy Banker's Wife*, ibid., p. 8.

42 *Ibid.*, p. 3.

43 *Ibid.*, p. 4.

44 *Ibid.*, p. 43.

45 Linda McQaig, *Shooting the Hippo*, n. 40, p. 7.

46 C.D. Howe was a powerful political figure in Canada from the 1930s to the late 1950s. He put up a strong opposition in 1944 when the government introduced Family Allowances – a monthly allowance paid to each child – which had significantly enhanced family income in Canada. He was a champion of free enterprise and free-market solutions, and wanted the market to be left alone.

47 Linda McQaig, *Shooting the Hippo*, n. 40, p. 253.

48 *Ibid.*, p. 273.

49 Gregory Albo and Jane Jenson (1977), 'Remapping Canada: The State in the Era of Globalisation', in Wallace Clement (ed.), *Understanding Canada*, n. 24, pp. 216–17.

50 Gilles Seguin, in an interview with the author on 1 June 2000 in Ottawa.

51 Isabella Bakker and Catherine Scott (1977), 'From the Post-War to the Post-Liberal Keynesian Welfare State', in Wallace Clement (ed.), *Understanding Canada*, n. 24, p. 291.

52 Prof. V. Subramaniam, Distinguished Professor, Carleton University, Ottawa, in an interview with the author on 12 June 2000 in Ottawa.

53 *Ibid.*

54 Joanne Roulston, Senior Researcher and Policy Adviser, National Council for Welfare, Ottawa, in an interview with the author on 6 June 2000, in Ottawa.

55 Professor Wallace Clement, Director, Institute of Political Economy, Carleton University, Ottawa, in an interview with the author on 2 June 2000 in Ottawa.

56 Frank T. Denton and Byron G. Spencer, 'Population Aging and the Maintenance of Social Support Systems', *Canadian Journal on Aging*, Guelph, Ontario, vol. 16, no. 3, 1997, p. 425.

57 Robert L. Brown, 'Security for Social Security – Is Privatisation the Answer?', *Canadian Journal on Aging*, ibid., p. 503.

58 OECD, *The Battle Against Exclusion*, n. 27, vol. 3, p. 26.

59 Canada, National Council of Welfare, *Poverty Profile 1997*, Ottawa: NCW, 1999.

60 *Ibid.*, p. 2.

61 Linda McQaig, *Shooting the Hippo*, n. 40, p. 254.

62 *Ibid.*, p. 256.

63 Gösta Esping-Anderson, *Politics Against Markets*, Princeton, NJ: Princeton University Press, 1985.

64 Canada, National Council of Welfare, *Welfare Incomes 1997 and 1998*, Ottawa: NCW, 1999–2000, p. 70.

65 *Ibid.*

66 *Ibid., Profiles of Welfare: Myths and Realities*, Ottawa: NCW, 1998, p. 1.

67 *Ibid.*, pp. 2–3.

68 *Ibid.*, p. 60.

69 *Ibid.*, p. 61.

70 *Ibid.*, pp. 61–2.

71 Liora Salter and Prick Salter (1977), 'Displacing the Welfare State', in Wallace Clement (ed.), *Understanding Canada*, n. 24, p. 334.

16
Welfare Designs and Peripheral Realities: The Brazilian Dilemma

Dilip Loundo

Introduction

This chapter analyses the welfare policies in Brazil since the 1930s, when efforts towards state-led industrialization took place. It argues that welfare rhetoric and policies ended up serving a model of economic development where capital accumulation resulted, to a great extent and paradoxically, from incremental inequality and poverty among large contingents of the urban and rural populations. Even if social sacrifices were expected in a process of late/peripheral industrialization, there was hope that the state would have functioned as balancing broker. But far from that, the state established a bureaucratic network of social control ranging from populist/corporatist to repressive/clientelist approaches, which propelled patrimonialism, corruption and external dependency.

In the beginning of the 1990s, there were imminent signs of implosion: recession, hyperinflation, external debt and, above all, continued poverty. Externally, globalization and the end of socialist regimes took centre-stage. The combination of those factors demanded a purging action, and it came with President Cardoso's substantive reform of the state's functions. Against this backdrop, this chapter analyses Cardoso's two-term mandate (1995–2002), his institutional reforms and the social policies pursued. It draws attention to Cardoso's theoretical evolution, particularly his move from dependency to the third way.

Exclusion, dependency and the world system

One of the biggest challenges facing social scientists in developing countries is the imperative need to derive from specific historical structures, the theoretical frames required to understand the complexity and abundance of their ground realities. There is a recurrent risk of falling into a *conceptual trap*, that is into the temptation of utilizing, more or less acritically, theoretical paradigms evolved and associated with developmental processes in central

272

economies. This is dramatically true in the case of Latin American cultures and histories on account of a general perception of their belonging to the so-called 'Western civilization'. Terms like 'modernity', 'liberalism', 'democracy', 'fascism', 'populism' and others have been freely used to describe phases, periods and situations which reflect more often dissimilarities than otherwise to the original models of reference.

It is a fact that in many cases the models are not absolutely devoid of empirical consequences since they were adopted by the region's political and economic elites as prospective designs subsuming the formulation of state or corporate policies. However, the specific interests at stake and the complex process of interaction between the elites and the masses within multicultural formations, were two of the major factors responsible for the historical surgeries at the political and social levels that lent those concepts a new organicity and semantics. The full realization of their meaning and scope calls for a deliberate effort to understand local processes and acknowledge alternative variants to conventional meanings. The temptation to look at reality as a mere negative qualification to external paradigms makes the former prey to an absolute 'morality' of an alien history. Latin America becomes the locus, *par excellence*, of incomplete, residual or deviant conceptual realizations of European or North-American designs: a realm of 'pre-modernity', 'limited democracy', 'oligarchic liberalism', 'semi-fascism', and so on.

It goes to the credit of the centre–periphery model and, particularly, the subsequent *dependency studies* undertaken by major Latin American social scientists in the 1960s and 1970s, the postulation of a credible framework to positively situate the alleged deviations.[1] The dialectical analysis of the world international order was able to show that 'pre-modernity' was just another name for the specific forms of modernity developed in peripheral nations which were the counterpart and condition of existence of the 'full-fledged modernity' of the central industrialized nations. The basic role of post-independent Latin American economies as suppliers of raw-materials and the social regimes of slavery or serfdom which prevailed therein, were not part of a pre-industrial stage, but elements of a definite marginal role in the capitalist system and a reversal expression of the possibility of industrialization in Europe and North America. The attempts at industrialization of the 1950s and 1960s onwards were not the result of late arrivals in the capitalist system, as the concept of 'newcomers' or new industrialized nations may suggest, they were impelled by the state's ability to sponsor it against international pressures but for which they terribly needed foreign capital. Dependency theoreticians varied in their perception of the role of transnational corporations and foreign loans in this process of peripheral development. While some presented a gloomy picture, looking at the internal reproduction of dependency as leaving no margin for social upliftment within the capitalist system, others favoured a more optimist approach looking at the progressive incorporation of the labour force as a definitive conquest which would enable a nation to move from pure dependency to *asymmetrical interdependency*.[2] The success story of Southeast Asia was seen as a concrete expression of that possibility.

The dependency theory has now lost much of its appeal, but it has left an important legacy: it looked at the world system of modernization/colonialization and neo-colonialization as a paradigm to understand local histories of development. Some of its critics endeavoured to take it beyond the notion of development understood as a materialistic socio-economic process. In their view, most of the social impasses in the region were related to a fundamental process of cultural exclusion.[3] They called for the inclusion of the cultural paradigm as a means to understand the overall implications of a situation of dependency. Cultural dependency was the other side of modernity in the periphery as neocoloniality of power. For them, the developmentalist model pursued by most of the Latin American states in their projects of industrialization was based on an erroneous postulation of the nation-state as a cultural uniformity or synthesis. Thus, developmentalism as a dominant – yet non-hegemonic – nationalist ideology had an intrinsic ethnocidal or culturecidal character, similar to the eurocentric civilizing mission of the nineteenth century. Challenging the alleged affiliation of Latin America to Western civilization, they drew the critics' attention to the multicultural formation of the region wherein a diversity of ethnicities, races and subcultures had come together to constitute a heterogeneous whole.

Understood in an extended manner to include both developmental dependency, now upgraded to *asymmetrical interdependency*, and the multiplicity of cultural dependencies, the peripheral factor seems to be an appropriate criterion to analyse, on the one hand, the historical nuances of welfare systems in the region and, on the other, social exclusion as its historical counterpart with a plurality of manifestation – the exclusions from inside, viz. class exploitation, and the exclusions from outside, viz. ethnic segregation, racial discrimination, subcultural inequalities and others. Thus, the evaluation of any peripheral project of development should match the quantum of welfare, justice, citizenship and human rights against a more comprehensive understanding of the ground reality of social exclusion.

The interventionist state and world crisis

When in 1991 Collor de Mello, the first elected President after military rule (1964–85) announced his plans to disengage the state from its main regulatory and productive functions, a historical process was about to begin in Brazil of radical revision of over 60 years of state intervention as a basic dimension of the project of social and economic development. Internally, the announcement followed the major economic crises of the 1980s (the *lost decade* characterized by inflation, recession and huge external debt) whose immediate cause was a crude form of state interventionism represented by the military dictatorship. The rhetoric of state disengagement tended to associate authoritarianism with interventionism in general, and the latter with the model of development pursued, viz. the *import substitution* policies. In other Latin American industrialized nations, the scenario was not different. The newly democratic leaderships that succeeded the wave of military dictatorships in the region moved quickly in the direction of deregulation, privatization and liberalization.[4] The ultimate source of inspiration and perhaps emulation were the neo-liberal policies implemented by the Thatcher and Reagan administrations in Western Europe and the USA, respectively. Meanwhile, in Eastern Europe, the socialist form of state intervention was equally on the brink of a collapse following the end of the Soviet experiment and the unification of Germany. All this against the growing processes of economic, trade and financial globalization which pressed for a free flow of commodities and factors of production among nation-states. Thus, more than the victory of capitalism as some authors have put it, the international scenario at the beginning of the 1990s seemed to conspire against the major established forms of state intervention.

The concurrence in time in different regions of the globe of the crises of the interventionist state certainly wasn't a matter of coincidence. The globalization of capitalism as a peculiar phase of its development as a world system acted, to a great extent, as the most determinant common external input. And yet it would be incorrect to assume that the *neo-liberal* model would emerge as a consensus therapy to be employed. First of all, globalization with its network of information and technology pointed to the establishment of transnational centres of economic control to ensure a free market. This demanded an active participation of states in negotiating various modalities of insertion and in ensuring the continuity of their cultures and sovereignties in renewed socio-political terms. Accordingly, the neo-liberal wave of the 1980s in Europe was followed in the mid-1990s by the resumption of revised versions of social democracy and a protectionist regional integration. Besides, the attempts to raise the banner of the free-market to dismantle the socialist-bureaucratic structures formed over decades in Eastern Europe and Russia, failed to establish healthy capitalist economies, and have been responsible for the exponential increases increment in social costs.

Thus, the sheer identification of globalization with the adoption of neo-liberal policies could perhaps be better understood as part of a bargaining strategy of some nations *vis-à-vis* others. The exalted rhetoric and hasty policies of President Collor de Mello favouring the idea of a minimum state in Brazil, could be a credit to the recurrent practice among some of the region's elites to adopt acritically the dominant discourse of central economies without properly scrutinizing its deep ground reality or ascertaining the adjustments required to take it beyond the short-term interests of particular groups.[5] The social mobilization that followed not only exposed the naïve proposals as a cover-up for a major scheme of state corruption which ultimately caused the impeachment of Collor de Mello, but also demanded a greater participation of civil society in determining the future of the nation and the role of the state.

A comparative analysis of the three models of state interventionism in the perspective of the welfare policies adopted can easily reveal the enormity of differences among them. The Western European model, of which social democracy is perhaps the most accomplished form, envisages welfare policies, compensatory or preventive, as a state-led initiative to curb the excesses of free-market and private capitalist entrepreneurship. As a direct response to unionist demands, it seeks an intervention within a given situation of industrialization with the basic goal of reversing the functional distortion of an increasing commodification of workers without abandoning the basic fundamentals of a capitalist system, viz. private ownership. Thus, the role of social democracies and other welfare states was not that of a substitute to private agency, but one aiming at regulating the latter's actions in order to ensure citizenship and social justice to all members of a consolidated nation-state. In the socialist state, on the other hand, welfare policies were not compensatory or preventive to functional distortions of the capitalist system, but part of a radical project of abolishing the latter. A welfare society rather than a welfare state was ultimately what they were looking at, as the only means to achieve the goal of decommodification of human beings. Apart from the reasons for their crises or failures, in both cases welfare policies represent a genuine concern and an intrinsic design of state intervention.

The interventionist state in the tropics: labourist 'welfare'

Lets us now turn our attention to Brazil where state interventionism and its welfare designs/rhetoric has a rather unique history, which stretches roughly from 1930 to 1990. As in any social democratic state, the formulation of welfare policies was part of a sustained faith in the capitalist system. But the similarities stop there. As a successor to oligarchic liberalism, based on agricultural production for the international market, state intervention was basically committed to industrializing the country. Different from the social democratic model, the state assumed a double and contradictory role: (1) to promote industrialization as a countercurrent project to external and internal 'vocations' by filling, to a large extent, the gap represented by the absence of a spontaneous bourgeoisie; and (2) to promote social welfare through policies aiming to protect the marginalized elements of society. For a country having to jump over conventional capitalist stages after inheriting a huge social debt, it is clear that the task ahead could hardly be able to reconcile the need to generate massive capital accumulation with income distribution. The 'import-substitution model' based on commercial protectionism and export-led growth gave the tone for the methodology to be followed. An all-powerful state with no definite compromise with any organized sector or movement but very much grounded on charismatic leaderships – mostly dissidents from rural oligarchies – or a military establishment, was responsible for organizing and controlling the incipient economic agents – labour and capital – by nourishing their class-awareness within a corporatist model which promised harmony and concerted efforts in the process of industrialization.

The politics/rhetoric of welfare in Brazil prevailing during that period – more specifically, from 1930 to 1964 – became known as *labourism*, but the similarities with the British model stop there. The closest source of inspiration was Mussolini's corporatist/fascist system. But far from being the outcome of any social struggle, labour legislation in Brazil was a concession of the state.[6] It included separate social security provisions for public servants and other urban employees, a minimum wage, regulation of the work of minors and women, concessions of holidays, a limit of eight hours for daily work, a pension system and formal access to health and educational services. To be entitled to those benefits, workers had to be affiliated to the corporatist unions which were kept under total control of the state in terms of funding, management and strategies. Even the right to strike was prohibited or made dependent on a declaration of legality by the government. Calls for alternative forms of unionism by leftist forces met with all sorts of repression including bans and exile. On the other hand, workers of rural areas were totally excluded from the labour legislation. The timid reforms introduced in 1964 did not fundamentally change the situation. Thus was formed the three-layer pyramid of the Brazilian salaried classes: on the top the privileged public servants, in the middle urban private workers and at the bottom the wretched of the rural areas.

The congenital weakness in self-organization together with the corrosive power of inflation was responsible for nullifying the self-styled benefits of the labour force. The historical correlation between inflation and the minimum wage shows that most of the benefits of the workers were transferred to the capital sector through public deficits originated either from the policies to compensate the rural oligarchies for the fluctuation of commodities prices, the payment of interest and royalties due to massive international loans and investments, and the costs of the clientelist and corrupt forms of co-optation of labour and middle-class leaderships within the state bureaucracy or within the state corporations.[7] The fiscal burden, one of the highest among industrialized nations, favoured concentration instead of redistribution. In sum, welfare policies and particularly the minimum wage provision proved to be one of the most important internal sources of capital accumulation. Instead of transferring resources from capitalist agents to the labour force, the welfare policies were turned upside down and made to function as a complement to the internal circulation of resources within sections of the capital. Whereas the resources transferred from the rural oligarchies and international capital to state and private capital would make their way back in different ways and proportions to the donors, the resources transferred from the salaries had no return in sight.

A retrospective analysis of the scope and efficacy of those policies shows their major subservience to the process of capital accumulation. As the manager of both accumulation and distribution, the interventionist state was able to put the former at the service of the latter. A sort of *excluding inclusion* – or, perhaps, the other way round – was underway in urban industrial centres: on the one hand, industrialization created jobs for the unemployed but, on the other, the state imperative of capital accumulation and social control rendered welfare policies an additional and rather paradoxical factor towards wealth concentration. A more explicit form of social exclusion resulted from the absence of any welfare scheme for other historically backward groups. Among these one should mention the peasantry which formed, since the slavery system in colonial and post-colonial times, the bulk of the labour force of the peripheral economy. The rationale of the 'import-substitution' model demanded the preservation of the oligarchic system in rural areas, closing the doors for any attempt to reform the half-slavery forms of labour relations prevailing therein. One could also mention the large masses of urban unemployed, which included large numbers of the black and *mestizo* populations, internal migration from rural areas, and recent immigration from Europe and Asia. Still further away from any type of welfare consideration were the marginalized cultural and subcultural groups including the original Amerindian population. The elites' perception of their being, instead, an obstacle to any project of development and industrialization, became clear in the policies pursued during the 1970s in the Amazon region.

The interventionist state in the tropics: populism and the military

The dynamics of state interventionism in Brazil passed through different political phases, ranging from formal democracy to authoritarianism. The initial turning point was the civil dictatorship of Getúlio Vargas (1937–45), and the climax the military-bureaucratic dictatorship (1964–85). The first launched the bases of a corporatist state anchored on a nationalist ideology which called for the mutual cooperation of urban agents – workers, private and state capital – in a process of industrialization based on national resources. The populist rhetoric wooed the urban poor with a discourse centred on industrialization as the only means to achieving social inclusion and eliminating all social evils of the past. Vargas' authoritarian regime was succeeded in 1945 by a populist democracy that lasted till 1964, leaving intact the mechanisms of control (corporatism) and the ideology of legitimation (nationalism). The prevailing political party system found itself contaminated by the corporatist spirit, being as it was a direct inspiration of Getúlio Vargas. He himself sponsored the creation of the two major political parties of the period, viz. the Brazilian Labour Party (PTB), the official spokesman of the corporatist workers, and the Social Democratic Party (PSD) which gave shelter to diffuse interests of private and state capital. With a deficient form of political representation and increasing levels of industrialization being matched by equal levels of social inequity, Brazil experienced in the beginning of the 1960s a radicalization of the labour political praxis with calls for socialism and base reforms.

The elite's reaction came in 1964 with a political turnover which brought the military to the forefront of the national destiny, with a mission to establish a more accomplished form of interventionist-developmentalist model based on political repression. The new leadership launched a severe attack on the politics of populism/nationalism after diagnosing it as counterproductive as far as the goal of capital accumulation was concerned. The *populist consensus* was substituted by the *technocratic truth* supported by a politics of repression where the major channels of popular participation were blocked. External investments and loans were given a major role as co-partners in the technocratic project to upgrade the technological park of the country. With state participation in the economic process reaching unthinkable levels, the period experienced high rates of growth and the development of strategic industries. However, the foundations were weak. Mega-projects of dubious relevance coupled with maladministration and corruption in state bureaucracy, led to an absolute incapacity of the government to provide sustainable ways of repaying the external debt. The Amazon region was the theatre of environmental and human crimes. Huge agricultural and mineral projects and a self-styled 'agrarian reform' functioned as a license for indiscriminate deforestation and destruction of indigenous Indian populations. A huge and inefficient bureaucracy unable to provide basic services, economic recession, public deficits and high inflation not only defied economic theories but also undermined the nominal benefits of workers and the middle classes, being directly responsible for the enormous growth of poverty rates and disparities in income. As a result of social and political pressures, the military handed over the power to civil leadership in 1985.

Thus, the transition from a populist democracy to a military-technocratic dictatorship did not imply any significant change of route, but a disagreement over conjunctural patterns of capital accumulation and strategies of social/political control: the former pursued an endogenous, nationalist-developmentalist and corporatist approach; whereas the latter, an exogenous, pragmatic-developmentalist and repressive one. Their common axis was clear: (1) a rejection of any non-capitalist path of industrialization, and (2) an imperious need to evolve strategies to check the growing influence of the working classes.

In sum, the history of state intervention in Brazil from 1930 to 1990 was characterized by a conservative modernization, which made welfare policies subservient to broader control policies meant to ensure social discipline of the labour force in the project of industrialization. As an instrument of the state for private and bureaucratic interests, labourism favours little decommodification, if not instead recommodification. Different from the social democratic experiments, welfare policies do not exist *per se*, but as a tool in the process of capital accumulation. In other words, they become prey to their own symbolic dimension, viz. the ideology of developmentalism: industrialism *is* welfare. The real politics at stake was neatly exposed by a statement attributed to Delfim Neto, a former finance minister of the military regime: 'First one has to bake the cake [industrialization] and only then one will be able to eat it [distribution]'. (Neto denied it, but it became emblematic of the policies pursued by the military regime.) This being so, whether democratic or otherwise, the *interventionist model has proved to be intrinsically authoritarian*. Its toll was painfully felt not only in the failures of the developmental model pursued, but also in the compromises it made with the cultural plurality of the country. Here lie the genuine local sources of later aspirations to radically modify that model.

The state at the crossroads

If we set aside, for a moment, the guiding principle of welfare, we have to acknowledge that in the beginning of the 1990s Brazil was an industrialized nation with concrete advances in leading sectors such as nuclear energy and space exploration. The ratio between the rural and urban population had almost inverted, making Brazil a predominantly urban nation.[8] Industrialization itself, bereft of any meaningful welfare policy, had been responsible for giving jobs to thousands of unemployed people. And yet a huge economic and social debt, high levels of poverty, land and income concentration, and a deficient system of primary education and health formed the background for the economic crises of the 1980s which signalled the exhaustion of the import-substitution model.

Authors may disagree whether this state of affairs and the authoritarian character of state intervention were the necessary cost for the country's industrialization within the periphery of the capitalist system. But whatever one's posture may be, the fact remains that the internal logic for reforming the state (intervention) in Brazil varies radically from that of traditional welfare states in Europe. In the latter, we have a welfare system that has effectively provided social benefits in the past but is now facing internal and external signs of weariness. In the former, we have a model of industrialization which is showing signs of exhaustion exactly, among other reasons, because it did not evolve an effective welfare system. If so, the impact and influence of globalization on the process of state reform in Brazil has to be measured with different parameters of analysis. It makes little or no sense to speak about the challenges posed by globalization to a (practically) nonexisting welfare system.

The redemocratization in Brazil from the middle of the 1980s onwards reflected, directly, the desire to do away with a military repressive regime and, indirectly, with the need to eliminate the outstanding defects of previous democratic and authoritarian periods of state developmentalist intervention. The sharp increase of social movements was indicative of the growing level of awareness of civil society and its struggle to institutionalize more participant mechanisms of political control and eliminate both the paternalistic and the repressive state. Among these forces, the new unionist movement is of paramount importance. As a spontaneous and autonomous development in a sector dominated by international capital (the car industry), the creation of the Unified Labour Union (CUT) and, subsequently, the Workers Party (PT) under the leadership of Luiz Inácio Lula da Silva was a major blow to the already weakened corporatist scheme. The social action of the church through the Basic Ecclesial Communities played equally an important role in organizing communities at the regional level, particularly the peasantry. From these grassroots organizations emerged the most articulate social protest in rural areas, the Movement of Landless People (MST). Their voice echoed among the urban middle classes as a reminder of the systematic exclusion of the rural labour force. On the other hand, the well-known sociologist and social worker Herbert José de Souza, better known as 'Betinho', launched several initiatives with the support of local communities, in the fields of environment, defence of Amerindian groups, agrarian reform and poverty. The programme Citizenship Action against Misery and for Life earned massive popular support and exerted enormous pressure on the government.

Equally worth mentioning are the social provisions of the new Constitution promulgated in 1988. It expanded and strengthened individual rights and mechanisms of political participation much beyond the traditional forms.[9] It ensured a major participation of non-governmental organizations and movements in the decision-making process and adopted a unique provision granting them a direct role in legislative procedures through popular amendments. It incorporated important conquests in the area of education and healthcare, a full chapter dedicated to environmental protection and another ensuring the native Indian population eternal rights to their traditional lands and to the pursuance of ancient habits and customs. On the other hand, the new political party system presented no signs of continuity with the previous corporatist/populist democratic period (1945–64). Born afresh as a natural development of the hyper-controlled two-party system that had prevailed during the military regime, the new arrangement gave greater intelligibility to the electoral process and confined the traditional nationalist/populist/clientelist/corporatist parties to very limited electorates. However, the excessive proliferation of new political forces and the traditional political culture of often ideological loyalties continued to underscore the difficulty of evolving clear national projects.

Reforming the state: alternatives and imperatives

At the beginning of the 1990s, some analysts argued that Brazil had reached a similar stage to that of Western European countries prior to the adoption of social democratic models: industrialization, an independent organized labour force, social debt and unemployment, and the facts seemed to reinforce this perception. The Constitution had been quite innovative and progressive as far as the social order was concerned and, at the same time, it had been quite conservative in retaining the mechanisms of state intervention in the economic system. The basic assumption among leftist parties was that the reform of the social and political order would generate sufficient moral ground for a more effective and socially oriented state intervention. This seemed to favour both the Workers Party (PT) which represented the new unionism and a proposal of native socialism, and the Party of Brazilian Social Democracy (PSDB) a centre-left outfit created in 1988 – an outcome of the natural fragmentation of the major opposition front to the military regime – which opted for a formal social democratic profile of European style. And, in fact, in the presidential elections of 1991, PT's candidate Luiz Inácio Lula da Silva lost by a very narrow margin to Fernando Collor de Mello. The dispute reflected, as never before, a clear demarcation of the political spectrum between the left and the right. The subsequent failure of a rather primitive and naïve neo-liberal discourse of president Collor de Mello added fuel to the leftist presumption that its time had arrived.

But the impressions proved wrong. Indications to the contrary were equally available in abundance to make one suspicious about the long-term approach likely to emerge to tackle the crises of the interventionist state. First, peripheral histories do not repeat phases and stages of central capitalism, as the positivist model would suggest. Second, the collapse of the socialist regimes in Eastern Europe and the acceleration of the process of globalization, especially in information networks and financial markets, had shaken the foundations under which traditional economies and social democrats in Europe were used to operating in. Third, the fantastic growth in world trade had put enormous competitive pressures on Brazil, compelling economists to explore different strategies. The first domestic reactions were felt in the heterodox plans of economic structural adjustment at the end of the 1980s and the beginning of the 1990s.[10] Though most of them failed, they reflected the amount of international coercion put up by international agencies such as the IMF and the World Bank. On the other hand, efforts to achieve economic integration with Argentina and other countries of South America led to the formation in 1991 of the regional common market known as Mercosur. And finally the success of the programme of economic stabilization known as the Real Plan, conceived by Fernando Henrique Cardoso as Finance Minister in 1993, was explicitly conditioned to the transformation of economic order through trade liberalization, privatization, revision of the fiscal system and social security, and flexibility of the labour market.[11]

The transformations taking place at the same time among social movements around the world and the expansion of the left's electorate much beyond the social democrats' and socialists' traditional reliance on the industrial working class is equally worth mentioning. In Brazil, there was a curious convergence between transnational postmodern discourses on gender, environment, ethnicity and human rights, and a local urgency to address old problems of cultural and regional exclusion. This favoured close linkages between international NGOs and local organizations dealing with fundamental internal issues such as the subcultural marginalization of rural communities; racial discrimination inherited from the slavery past and the absence of compensatory policies; and ethnic cleansing related to denial of existence, outside the developmental model, to the remaining indigenous populations. These groups tended to be historically suspicious of the state's authority and to advocate grassroots participation and self-management of their lives.

On the eve of Fernando Henrique Cardoso's resounding victory in the presidential elections of 1993 under the banner of the social-democrat PSDB, there were clear indications, in the social and economic spheres, both internally and externally, that a major transformation of the interventionist state was about to take place in Brazil. The tremendous success of the Real Plan and the immediate social benefits it produced by bringing down dramatically the rates of inflation gave Cardoso the necessary popularity and legitimacy to initiate his mandate with the announcement of dramatic changes in the socio-economic order. He embarked in a largely orthodox and market-oriented programme which not only shattered the inflated character of the state in Brazil, but also some of his own party's traditional social-democratic tenets. What again surprised the political establishment was the political alliance of Cardoso's PSDB with a right-wing party – the Party of the Liberal Front (PFL) – meant to ensure a broad parliamentary support for the constitutional amendments required to implement the economic reforms. The justification for that marriage of convenience was their mutual agreement on the need to reform the state and, particularly, the economic order, notwithstanding the differences in overall policies and ideology.

Fernando Henrique Cardoso's theoretical evolution

Although most analysts have used the word 'neo-liberal' to designate his policies and programmes, Cardoso strongly resists that adjective. Instead he describes them as part of a broader process of rationalization of state functions, within which the liberal measures should be contextualized. In other words, Cardoso maintains that the reform of the state is not informed by any ready-made neo-liberal doctrine but prompted by the need to improve its efficiency in a globalized world by making it free from the clientelist, patrimonialist and populist web of the past. Only then will the state be able to finally discharge its socio-economic duty. The four major pillars of Cardoso's reforms are: (1) reformulation of state institutions and mechanisms of representation; (2) regulation, stabilization and liberalization of the economy; (3) formulation of social programmes to eradicate poverty and social exclusion and; (4) negotiation of global integration. The specific points related to the so-called 'neo-liberal' package include (a) flexibilization, or even elimination, of state monopolies; (b) concession of public services to private initiative; (c) intensification of the process of privatization of state corporations; and (d) liberalization of trade by lowering import barriers.[12]

It is still early to assess the overall implications of the state reforms put in process by Cardoso during his two-term mandate (1994–2002), and the long-term implications in terms of incremental welfare of his social policies. The benefit of the doubt should refrain one from giving definitive labels. Meanwhile, in some intellectual circles, there is a deep-rooted impression that Cardoso's reforms amount to a rejection of his former theoretical theses, particularly the dependency theory propounded during the 1970s. Others are inclined to justify the apparent contradiction of past and present postures as a strategy of adjustment to present times: just like in the past Vargas was a man of the right with a discourse of the left, Cardoso represents exactly the opposite – a man of the left with a discourse of the right.

What is Cardoso's assessment of his own ideological leanings? In several interviews given in different periods of his presidency, he reiterates his commitment to social causes and defines himself as a social democrat.[13] Thus, a preliminary assessment of state reforms implemented by a man who completed in 2002 an unprecedented second term in office in Brazilian democratic history, should turn its attention to three fundamental aspects: (1) Cardoso's theoretical reflections on his programmes and policies; (2) the PSDB's doctrinal evolution; and (3) the preliminary outcome of the policies themselves as reflected in social welfare trends and indicators. Is the new state weaker or is it smaller and yet better, that is more effective and just? Is social disinvestment the necessary consequence of economic disinvestment, or is the latter opening new and effective alternatives to traditional social democratic policies within a continued spirit of social welfare?

Although disagreeing with Cardoso's present policies, Theotônio dos Santos – another major proponent of the dependency theory – acknowledges that they are not in contradiction with but represent a *possible evolution* of his former postures.[14] Cardoso had since long – more precisely, in 1976 – admitted the possibility of a positive way out for a dependent capitalist country like Brazil in the following words:

> At least in some peripheral countries, the penetration of industrial-financial capital accelerates the production of incremental surplus, strengthens the productive forces and, if it causes unemployment in phases of economic recession, it absorbs the labour force in expansive cycles, producing, in this particular, similar effects to those seen in central economies, where absorption and unemployment, health and misery co-exist.[15]

In other words, the association between national and international capital did not proscribe – as the dominant Marxist currents within the dependency school sustained – the possibility of a substantive economic development in the periphery. Here lies the element of continuity and coherence: for a long time Cardoso had placed himself within the capitalist paradigm. In that scenario, however, social disparities would persist and, therefore, what role would one expect from the state? Here lies the element of evolution in Cardoso's thought. The programme of the PSDB could give us a clue. The initial orientation in 1988 shows a commitment towards a European style of welfare state with a flexible role and relative freedom from past populism and nationalism.[16] To a certain extent, this resulted from the experiences of exile of many of the PSDB's leaders during the political struggle against military rule, which led to the establishment of close linkages with European social-democratic and socialist parties. And yet the policies pursued by Cardoso from 1994 onwards departed from those basic social-democratic commitments. For Dos Santos and others, the evolution was nothing but a tilt towards neo-liberalism.[17] But things are far more complex. Cardoso's evolution is not an isolated case; it includes his own party and, above all, it moves along the lines of some stalwarts of European social democracy. Thus, Cardoso's contention should be evaluated in the context of the evolution of the social-democratic paradigm.

The tropical *third way*

To understand this line of argument, we should consider the reformist trends in European social democracy at the beginning of the 1990s with the advent of New Labour in the United Kingdom. Anthony Giddens gave it a theoretical basis by advocating the *third way*.[18] He argued that the world had changed substantially and the classical instruments of social democracy in practice – nationalization, a broad welfare state, and statist solutions to all problems – were exhausted and had been severely challenged by neo-liberals. However, the core of third-way politics would remain social-democratic in view of the permanence of a set of lasting values. In other words, he meant that policies and instruments would have to change, whereas intrinsic values such as equality, citizenship, community, transparency and democracy would be preserved as principles to guide the state's political actions.

The reformist trend did not take long to hit the PSDB on the eve of its assumption to power in 1994. Not without dissident voices, the party embarked on a programmatic reform along the theoretical lines of the third-way's new left. Ironically, what perhaps favoured the move and the compromises it implied was the PSDB's historical lack of a strong basis within the unionist movement. Different from the PT and other European social-democrats, PSDB's electoral basis has never been the organized labour force but the progressive and moderate middle classes and also a good number of intellectuals responsible for bringing into the social discourse the aspirations of the other spheres of exclusion such as ethnicity, race, gender and environment. The traditional left (populists and communists), the PT and its strong affiliated unions – whom Cardoso labelled the 'backward left' – denounced the PSDB's departure from its original platform as a rightward tilt which further justified the party's alliance with traditional rightwing liberal forces. At the same time, the proliferation of autonomous unions affiliated to the different shades of the political spectrum – including the newly created Social-Democratic Union – gave the PSDB a sufficient margin of maneuvering to go ahead with the reforms.

Meanwhile, Cardoso and other intellectuals of repute and leftist background, such as Bresser Pereira, began to address the fundamental questions posed by the adoption of the third way.[19] Would it be feasible to modernize social democracy in a country with no major social democratic tradition? What type of adjustments were required to implement the third way of social democracy in a country which had not experienced its traditional or classical variant? Prompted by the desire to contribute to the intellectual exercise and share mutual experiences, Cardoso sought a close association with the movement. And, in 1999, he had the unique distinction of being the sole leader from the developing world to be invited to a brainstorming discussion held in Italy on 'Progressive Governance' where he joined Tony Blair, Lionel Jospin, Gerhard Schroeder and Bill Clinton.

The evolution of Cardoso's social thought is presented in an essay written in 1990. While reflecting on the processes of globalization, he distinguishes the new ideas from the neo-liberal thought:

> Those facts [process of globalization] generated, contradictorily, the impression (ideological) that the contemporary world is moving towards

the reinforcement of the maket and liberalism. But, in fact, negotiations are being conducted politically by the governments, economic alliances bind the interests of great oligopolies of production and distribution at a world scale, and a new system of 'spontaneous and prospective planning' has been created . . . . The state should no longer be a substitute to civil society but should create conditions for a better articulation of the latter. By a 'better articulation', I mean two things: local businessmen should find conditions and stimuli for investment and the government should support fiscal policies which may be able to revert the present situation of income hyperconcentration. And I repeat: nothing of sorts will happen unless there is an 'educational revolution' and policies of welfare that may lead to rising levels of equality – the practical support of freedom – as well as to higher levels of technical competency and social organization.[20]

With a language of compromise between the present and the past, Cardoso sounds pretty close to Gidden's emphasis on both rights and duties of citizens. The stress on duties underscores the idea of *devolution of powers* to civil society – the public realm *par excellence* that transcends and encompasses the sphere of the state.[21] In federal structures like Brazil, devolution may take place within the state itself, through decentralization and strengthening state units and municipalities. The call to civil society to shoulder responsibilities in defining policies, supervising their execution and curbing their subversion, through mechanisms other than traditional political representation, amounts to the rejection of a state that delivers the goods (or ought to deliver) and a passive citizenship who accepts them as a client, that is as a mere reactive factor.[22]

Designs, programmes and results: the economic sphere

Cardoso's eight years in power profoundly changed Brazil, and it is widely undisputed that the period saw the consolidation of democratic institutions and had its climax with an exemplary political transition to the newly elected president Luis Inácio Lula da Silva of the Workers Party in 2003. Yet, 'many years will pass before one can make a dispassionate judgement of Cardoso's weaknesses and strengths'.[23] This is particularly true in the case of his social policies and the effectiveness of a renewed concept of welfare as defined by the third way. Nevertheless, available trends and indicators give us a basis to initiate the debate.

The reform of the state has already produced a major transformation of character. Brazil, says Rubens Cysne, 'has made a clear transition – perhaps a little linear (given the country's relatively lack of experience in this sphere) – *from an entrepreneurial to a regulatory state*' (my emphasis).[24] The programme of privatization of state corporations in production, infrastructure and public service areas – perhaps the largest in developing world – has been driven by the desire to eliminate redundancy, inefficiency, bureaucratism, clientelism and ensure universality. It was followed by the creation of government agencies meant to regulate the various economic sectors such as electricity, telecommunications and the oil industry. As an expression of the state's new role, they substitute ministerial bureaucracies and seek partnerships with civil society by involving representatives of the public and consumers in the decision-making process.

Despite serious losses during the last year of his second and last term, mostly caused by the crises in neighbouring Argentina in 2002, economic stability was one of the major achievements of Cardoso's years. Since the implementation of the Real Plan in 1994, inflation has been kept under control with an average below 10 per cent – a complete reversion of the hyperinflation and hyperindexation of the previous years.[25] From 1994 to 2002, the average annual growth rate of GDP was a modest yet stable 2.7 per cent whereas the average annual per capita income stood at 1.7 per cent.[26] Meanwhile, foreign direct investments increased steadily. The annual average from 1994 to 2001 was 13 times higher than in the beginning of the decade, making Brazil one of their main destinations among developing nations.[27] On the negative side, endangering the benefits of stabilization, were the huge external and internal deficits. The former was stimulated by a policy of overvalued exchange rates, which forced a major devaluation in 1999, and the subsequent adoption of floating rates. The latter was stimulated by high interest rates needed precisely to attract the financing for the external deficit. This perverse cycle demanded a structural corrective measure and that was the much-needed reform of the tax system and its regressive character. But Cardoso failed to carry out this important reform, partially because of political constraints. Nevertheless, an important piece of legislation was passed – viz. the Law of Fiscal Responsibility – forcing states and municipalities to adjust their accounting procedures.

Trade liberalization and privatization did not affect, as initially expected, the level of unemployment. Major reasons were its phased implementation, the positive response of private industry to cope with international competition and uplift its levels of productivity, and the positive results of Mercosur as part of a strategy of gradual insertion in a global world. After a high of 7.6 per cent in 1998, unemployment ended 2002 at an acceptable level of 7.3 per cent despite the present negative conjuncture.[28] A scheme of unemployment insurance introduced in the mid-1980s as part of the social security system has grown steadily during Cardoso's administration, and partially softened the negative impact of state economic disinvestment.

For a country plagued by hyperinflation, eight years of relative economic stability produced in itself a redistributive impact among the most backward sections of society. However, conjunctural economic benefits without long-term social policies can only remain marginal in a country where poverty and social inequality constitute a structural/historical predicament.

Designs, programmes and results: the social sphere

After a timid first term, Cardoso's social agenda gained pace from 1999 onwards. Here there is a wide consensus among critics that his best legacy lies in the sphere of primary education, which holds the key – perhaps more than traditional redistributive policies – for the long-term solution of structural social inequality. In fact, more than contrasts between a few rich and millions of poor, inequality in Brazil reflects the existence of an enlarged upper/middle class in urban areas benefitting from prevailing differential wages between the more and the less educated. Official statistics show that primary education is now practically a universal good – 97 per cent among children between 7 to 14 years of age in 2000 – whereas middle education recorded an expansion of 71 per cent during the period 1994–2001.[29] Concomitantly, rates of repetition and dropout, which were traditionally high in the past, have fallen significantly. Decentralization and the devolution of power seem also to have gained ground with the establishment of associations of teachers and parents to function as co-partners of the government in the management of funds in public schools. An indication of the positive impact of these and other more specific initiatives is the decline of the rate of illiteracy – that fell from 13.9 per cent in 1996 to around 11.4 per cent in 2001.[30]

Another structural area of social emphasis was land reform, and here a good deal of credit goes to the pressures of civil society, particularly the Movement of Landless People (MST). Since the mid-1980s, the MST has drawn the attention of Brazilian public opinion to the continued plight of the peasantry, as a result of the model of industrialization pursued. As a major force of opposition, the MST opted for tactics of occupation of unproductive lands, which often led to violent encounters with security forces at state and municipal levels. Despite a tense relationship, the legitimacy of the cause ended up by persuading the government of the urgency of the case. The results were significant, particularly if seen in the context of the country's long history of land concentration. During the period 1995–2001, 588,173 families were settled in unproductive lands – a 170 per cent increase over the total number of previous 30 years.[31] With a view to ensuring economic viability for the settlements, state agencies were asked to ensure credit and maximize the scale of production. However, defective implementation of those schemes and influential agro-industry lobbies threaten their sustainability and tend only to render the landless poor into poor small farmers.

When Cardoso assumed office, the social security system was in financial collapse, but the reasons had little in common with similar problems faced in Europe. In Brazil, the system envisaged two very distinct categories, viz. civil servants, and the general public. The comparative benefits of the former – and particularly small pockets of it – served the corporatist/clientelist nature of the state and turned upside down the distributive goal. It favoured income concentration, corruption and financial mismanagement. Saturation was reached with most of the population far from benefitting from the system, ageing groups on the rise, and productivity still low. After much controversy and political debate, part of Cardoso's reform package was passed in 1998. For civil servants, early retirement was restricted, and a combination of age limits and time-of-service requirements was imposed. This was coupled with an administrative reform that brought employees of state corporations under general legislation and discouraged inefficiency among those of direct administration by abolishing the provision of 'stability'. For the general public, the new security measures included minimum age and length-of-contribution requirements, abolishing special pensions and the right to retire on a pension proportional to length of service. The half-measures were clearly insufficient to balance public accounts and kept intact the inequities between social classes. Perhaps the greatest failure was Cardoso's inability to set a clear line of demarcation, and sell it to the general public, between a patrimonialist bureaucracy – 'privileged groups that surround it [state] from the outside and colonize it from within'[32] – and legitimate security conquests of public servants. When Cardoso stepped down in 2002, social security expenditure amounted to a high 5.2 per cent of GNP.[33]

The constitution of 1988 had established the Unified Health System (SUS) as an important dimension of the social security system as a whole. Targeting universalization, quality and decentralized management, the implementation of the SUS was slow but recorded institutional and topical achievements such as the public health agents programme targeting over 50 million Brazilians, the family doctor programme, the women's health programme and programmes combating infant mortality. The positive results can be seen in the 17 per cent decline in the infant mortality rate during 1995–2001: around 30 children in every 1000;[34] and in the continuing improvement in life expectancy: from 67.26 years in 1995 to 68.82 in 2001.[35] Besides, an initiative aimed at promoting generic drugs to make them available to the population at prices considerably cheaper than the branded ones was successfully implemented. Finally, Brazil's response to the global AIDS epidemic not only produced effective results – HIV cases fell around 27 per cent during the period 1995 to 2000[36] – but also became a model for the developing world for its incisive social orientation. Free healthcare is now provided for the poor, and generic AIDS medication is made available to all concerned at reduced prices, much against the pressures of multinational drug companies.

Besides social initiatives of general reach, Cardoso initiated or pushed forward antipoverty and redistributive programmes specifically targeting urban and rural backward groups. The bulk of those initiatives came during the second term and, in many cases, as a response to specific pressures by social movements, antigovernmental organizations and political parties, including Cardoso's PSDB. By and large, they were considerably affected by recurrent budget surgeries meant to savage public deficits.

In order to rationalize and bring efficiency to different initiatives, Cardoso created the Social Protection Network under whose umbrella more than a dozen programmes were run serving potentially 32 million people. They targeted the reduction of infant mortality, eradication of child labour, compensation to poor families for ensuring children's education, supply of basic food stuffs, the generation of jobs, incentives for handicrafts, empowerment of adolescents and women, improvement of housing and sanitation conditions, unemployment insurance, small-scale farming, among others. To precisely identify beneficiaries, the government created a Unified Database of the poor based on which Unified Cards were issued – a personalized magnetic card meant to facilitate and debureaucratize the access to benefits. In 2001, the government launched the Alvorada Project to boost social action in specific backward areas with a view to targeting regional inequality. States and municipalities with Human Development Index (HDI) below the national average were given priority in the implementation of healthcare, educational and infrastructural programmes. Other initiatives include the Solidary Community, an attempt to involve civil society in a partnership with different NGOs in defining and implementing social actions.

Two spheres of great symbolic relevance for a multicultural nation like Brazil were the object of government action. The first relates to the black population and their old demands for affirmative action. A past of slavery and its abolition without compensation had voted Afro-descendents to social backwardness and racial discrimination. More than 100 years after abolition, the Brazilian state finally acknowledged past exploitation and present prejudices. Acting upon presidential recommendation, several organs of direct administration, ministries and others, and several public educational institutions passed specific legislation reserving quotas for the black population. The second relates to the remaining indigenous populations, totalling around 350,000 people and mostly located in the Amazon region. Acting on the constitutional provisions, Cardoso's administration demarcated 41 million hectares of land during 1995–2001, representing 40 per cent of all indigenous land demarcated since independence. Brazil's indigenous groups are now growing at a rate of 3.5 per cent a year and are legally entitled to around 12 per cent of national territory.[37]

Judging by the facts and the figures given above, Cardoso's reform of the state has achieved modest yet definitive social gains. This is confirmed by an improvement of the UN's Human Development Index: from 0.734 in 1995 to 0.750 in 2000.[38] Similarly, official social indicators show a decline of poverty and indigence: the former from 42 per cent in 1994 to 32 per cent in 2000; and the latter from 20 per cent in 1994 to 13 per cent in 2000.[39] Some of these gains resulted from spontaneous transferences due to economic stabilization and low inflation; others from specific intervention in structural areas such as primary education, healthcare, human rights, land reform and administrative reform; and still other from antipoverty programmes. As compared to economic stabilization, the role of antipoverty policies and intervention in structural areas is small, reflecting the limited effectiveness of the former and the long-term character of the latter. Accordingly, inequality remained almost unchanged.

Conclusion

Sociologist Gilberto Freyre once stated that 'Brazil has never been a country of extremes'.[40] What he did not say is that undermining such a cultural disposition was a structure of perverse *social extremes*. For decades, Brazil has held the dubious record of being one of the most unequal nations in the world. The promise of industrialization initiated in the 1930s to redeem its colonial and post-colonial causes has not been fulfilled. Instead, the emergence of a rhetoric of welfare and the policies pursued in its name ended up serving a model of economic development where capital accumulation resulted, to a great extent and paradoxically, from incremental inequality and poverty among large contingents of the urban and rural populations. Even if social sacrifices were expected in a process of late/peripheral industrialization, there was equally hope that the state – the propelling agent and guarantor of such a process – would have functioned as a moderating and balancing broker. Far from that, the state established a bureaucratic network of social control ranging from populist/corporatist to repressive/clientelist approaches, which propelled patrimonialism, corruption and external dependency.

In the beginning of the 1990s, the expressions of an imminent implosion were clear: recession, hyperinflation, external debt and, above all, continued poverty. Externally, the winds of globalization and the end of socialist regimes had taken centre-stage. If internal predicaments made it imperative to purge the state, external factors favoured a purging process in the form of a substantive reform of its past functions. Cardoso's eight years of mandate went consciously down that road. As a social democrat, he lost no time in seizing the theoretical tenets of the Third Way to justify the move and distinguish it from neo-liberalism. But Brazil is not Europe. To reform an accomplished welfare state is something quite different from reforming 'an ill-fare state that takes from the poor to give to the rich and well-to-do'.[41] It demands (1) institutional/structural alternatives, and (2) effective/lasting social results. As regards the first point, a good number of Cardoso's reforms seem irreversible. Some ensured economic stability and administrative transparency; some ensured base transformations with potential long-term social benefits; and others ensured power devolution befitting a multicultural society like Brazil.[42] As regards the second point, the accomplishments were modest, despite improvements in some specific social indicators and institutional initiatives.

To conclude, it's possible that Cardoso's policies of deconstructing/reconstructing state structures and pursuing economic stabilization amidst successive global financial crises may prove to be a positive platform to ensure future sustainability and efficacy of substantive welfare designs. The initial policy postures of the newly inaugurated administration of the Worker Party's candidate Luiz Inácio Lula da Silva lend credit to that perception.[43] President Lula's democratic socialism and his past as an independent labour leader lend credibility to his welfare proposals and ensure a level of political support among the working class that Cardoso never enjoyed. The announcement of a large-scale programme to eradicate poverty, which strengthens and integrates actions of different areas and ministries, came hand in hand with a call to consolidate the institutional parameters of economic stability and push forward social security and tax reforms. Time will tell if today's moves are tomorrow's achievements in social justice.

Notes

1 For an insider's critical account of the development of dependency studies in Latin America and in the USA see Fernando Henrique Cardoso, *As idéias e seu Lugar*, Petrópolis: Vozes, 1993, pp. 125–50.

2 The two main currents are: (1) the neomarxists such as Theotônio dos Santos and André Gunder Frank; and (2) the neo*Cepalians* such as Oswaldo Sunkel and Fernando Henrique Cardoso. *Asymmetrical interdependency* is an expression used by Fernando Henrique Cardoso. *Ibid.*, pp. 21–2.

3 That is the case of Anibal Quijano and Enrique Dussel 'who are indebted to the impact of dependency theory in its critique to "development" as the new format taken by global designs once the "civilizing mission" was winding down with the increasing process of decolonization'. Walter Mignolo, *Local Histories/Global Designs. Coloniality, Subaltern Knowledges, and Border Thinking*, Princeton: Princeton University Press, 2000, p. 54.

4 The political transitions to democracy took place mostly during the 1980s (e.g., Argentina 1983; Brazil, 1985; Uruguay, 1985; Chile, 1988). For a critical account of those processes see Guillermo O'Donnel *et al.* (eds), *Transitions from Authoritarian Rule*, Baltimore: Johns Hopkins University Press, 1986, and also Guillermo O'Donnel *et al.* (eds), *Issues in Democratic Consolidation: The New South American Democracies in Comparative Perspective*, Notre Dame: University of Notre Dame Press, 1992.

5 This is perhaps better understood in the framework of 'internal colonialism' or 'colonial difference'. See Mignolo, n. 3, p. 281.

6 The labour legislation based on the Carta del Lavoro of fascist Italy was enacted from top to down, i.e., from the state to the 'poor masses'. The weakness of an emerging working class diluted, at the time, the possibility of a distinct 'class awareness'.

7 See Fernando Henrique Cardoso, *Dependência e Desenvolvimento na América latina*, Rio de Janeiro: Guanabara, 1970, pp. 91–113.

8   Population in 2000: urban – 81.25 per cent; rural – 18.75 per cent. *Source*: IBGE www1.ibge.gov.br/brasil_em_sintese/populacao.htm

9   Political scientist Bolívar Lamounier stresses: 'From a doctrinal point of view, the Brazilian Constitution of 1988 raised substantially the importance of "direct" democracy *vis-à-vis* "representative" democracy'. *A Democracia Brasileira no Limiar do Século 21*, São Paulo: Fundação Konrad-Adenauer-Stiftung, 1996, p. 33. 'Do ponto de vista doutrinário, a Constituição brasileira de 1988 aumentou substancialmente a importância da democracia 'direta' em relação à democracia "representativa"'.

10 These were the plans: the Cruzado Plan in 1987, the Bresser Plan in 1988, the Summer Plan in 1989, and the Collor Plans in 1991 and 1992.

11 The Real Plan consisted of a number of economic measures aimed at curbing hyperinflation and eliminating financial indexation. It was named after the new currency adopted, the *real*.

12 Fernando Henrique Cardoso, 'Notas sobre a Reforma do Estado', *Novos Estudos/CEBRAP*, no. 50, março 1998, p. 9.

13 For example, see Fernando Henrique Cardoso, 'Ser Social-democrata', *Veja*, 1997 veja.abril.com.br/100997/p_022e.html

14 Theotônio dos Santos, *A Teoria da Dependência: Balanço e Perspectivas*, Rio de Janeiro: Civilização Brasileira, 2000, p. 121.

15 Cardoso, n. 1, p. 143, '. . . pelo menos em alguns países da periferia, a penetração do capital industrial-financeiro acelera a produção da mais-valia relativa, intensifica as forças produtivas e, se gera desemprego nas fases de contração econômica, absorve mão-de-obra nos ciclos expansivos, produzindo, neste aspeto, um efeito similar ao do capitalismo nas economias avançadas, onde coexistem desemprego e absorção, riqueza e miséria'.

16 Different from Mexico and Argentina, Brazil's state reform and liberalization were led by a non-populist party, the PSDB. On this subject read Edward L.Gibson, 'The Populist Road to Market Reform: Policy and Electoral Coalitions in Mexico and Argentina', *World Politics*, Princeton, 1997, pp. 339–70.

17 Santos, n. 14, pp. 151–8.

18 Anthony Giddens, *Beyond Left and Right: The Future of Radical Politics*, Cambridge: Polity Press, 1994. It was followed by two other publications in 1998 and 2000. For a discussion on the *third way* in the context of recent Brazilian political life see Timothy Power, *The Third Way in the Third World: Theoretical Considerations and a Case Study of Cardoso's PSDB in Brazil* (crab.rutgers.edu/ ~goertzel/power.doc)

19 See Luiz Carlos Bresser Pereira, 'Um Novo Estado Para a América Latina', *Novos Estudos/CEBRAP*, no. 50, março 1998, pp. 91–8.

20 Cardoso, n. 1, pp. 234, 243, 'Estes fatos deram origem, contraditoriamente, à noção (ideológica) de que o mundo contemporâneo marcha para uma revalorização do mercado e do liberalismo, quando, na verdade, as negociações são conduzidas politicamente pelos governos, as alianças econômicas soldaram interesses entre grandes oligopólios de produção e distribuição, ramificados à escala mundial e criou-se um novo sistema de "plenejamento espontâneo e prospectivo". . . . Não mais, entretanto, para que o estado *substitua* a sociedade civil, e sim para que ele permita melhor articulação desta última. Por "melhor articulação" entendo duas coisas: que o empresariado local encontre condições e estímulos para investir e que os governos sustentem políticas de rendas que comecem a reverter a atual situação de hiperconcentração de riqueza. Nada disso será feito, repito, sem uma "revolução educacional" e sem políticas de bem-estar que levem

tanto a mais igualdade, que é o suporte prático da liberdade, como a níveis mais elevados de competência técnica e de organização social.'

21 Cardoso, n. 12, pp. 7–8.
22 *Ibid.*, p. 8.
23 Ted Goertzel, 'Eight Years of Pragmatic Leadership in Brazil', 2003 (crab.rutgers.edu/~goertzel/fhc.htm)
24 Rubens Penha Cysne, 'Macro and Microeconomic Aspects of the Reforms', in Renato Baumann (ed.), *Brazil in the 1990s: An Economy in Transition*, New York: Palgrave Macmillan, 2002, pp. 39–40.
25 IBGE (Brazilian Institute of Geography and Statistics), in *Brasil, 1994 a 2002: Realizações do Governo*, 2002 (www.brasil.gov.br/relatorio/relatorio01.pdf)
26 IBGE (www1.ibge.gov.br/brasil_em_sintese/contas.htm)
27 BC (Central Bank), in Report no. 24.
28 IBGE (www1.ibge.gov.br/brasil_em_sintese/trabalho.htm)
29 MEC (Ministry of Education), in *Brasil, 1994 a 2002: Realizações do Governo*, 2002 (www.brasil.gov.br/relatorio/relatorio10.pdf)
30 IBGE (www1.ibge.gov.br/brasil_em_sintese/educacao.htm)
31 MDA (Ministry of Agrarian Development), in *Brasil, 1994 a 2002: Realizações do Governo*, 2002 (www.brasil.gov.br/relatorio/relatorio21.pdf)
32 Fernando Henrique Cardoso, *Mensagem ao Congresso Nacional: Oito Anos de Estabilidade, Desenvolvimento e Conquistas Sociais*, Brasília: Presidência da República, 2002 <www.planalto.gov.br/publi_04/mens2002.htm>, '... grupos favourecidos que o envolvem por fora e o colonizam por dentro'.
33 In Fernando Dantas, 'After Eight Years Lula Inherites a Better Country', *Estado de São Paulo*, 1 January 2003.
34 IBGE, in *Brasil, 1994 a 2002: Realizações do Governo*, 2002 (www.brasil.gov.br/relatorio/relatorio09.pdf)
35 IBGE (www1.ibge.gov.br/brasil_em_sintese/trabalho.htm)
36 Cardoso, n. 32.
37 FUNAI (National Foundation for the Indian Peoples), in *Brasil, 1994 a 2002: Realizações do Governo*, 2002 (www.brasil.gov.br/relatorio/relatorio06.pdf)
38 UN's *Human Development Report*, 2002 (www.undp.org/hdr2002)
39 IPEA (Institute of Applied Economic Research)/IBGE, Report 1.
40 Gilberto Freyre. 'Slaves in Newspaper Ads', in Ilan Stavans (ed.), *Latin American Essays*, New York: Oxford University Press, 1997, p. 345.
41 Cardoso, n. 32. 'O Brasil ... era um exemplo acabado de Estado do mal-estar social, que tirava dos pobres para dar aos ricos e remediados.'
42 Political scientist Cândido Mendes, a vocal critic from his own party, was ready to acknowledge those advances: 'However, the essential point to be said is the much, in a wider perspective – one that lasts and impels history forward – the present administration has achieved as far as institutional advances, civic awareness and human rights are concerned.' Cândido Mendes, *A Presidência Afortunada*, Rio de Janeiro: Record, 1999, p. 108. 'O essencial, entretanto, a indicar-se é o quanto, no ritmo maior – o que fica e impulsiona a História – o tucanato apresenta um enorme saldo no que respeita ao nosso avanço institucional, representado pelo ganho da consciência cívica e dos direitos humanos.'
43 That is also the opinion of sociologist Bernardo Sorj, expressed in his work *A Construção Intellectual do Brasil Contemporâneo: Da Resistência à Ditadura ao Governo FHC* (Rio de Janeiro: Jorge Zahar Editor, 2001). He says: 'Fernando Henrique Cardoso's government created, paradoxically, the conditions of governability for

a future opposition government from the left, to the degree that he applied stabilization policies and carried out reforms that would have been hotly contested by the labour union base of the Workers Party. . . . A government of the left in Brazil should be guided by the experience of the Chilean government in the sense of a coalition of the Christian Democrats and Socialists, learning to live with liberal reforms, building a dialog with civil society and strengthening social policies, respecting the limits of fiscal discipline, and welcoming productive foreign investment', cited in Goertzel, n. 23.

17
South Africa: Reflections on Establishing a Welfare State

Albert J. Venter

Introduction

The purpose of this chapter is to reflect on the advances made towards, and the possibility of, establishing a welfare state in South Africa. The emphasis is on reflection, contemplation and debate. It is not merely an empirical checklist – that is that there is a list of indicators of a welfare state and whether South Africa meets or does not meet the criteria for a 'welfare state'. It is time that South African intellectuals engage with this debate, instead of merely swallowing hook, line and sinker the liberal orthodoxy that the welfare state is on its way out and that the minimal state is 'in'. This essay is an effort to stimulate debate on this matter and is therefore in the final analysis not specifically prescriptive on the question whether the South African economy should be managed towards a welfare state of some kind. Rather it reflects on the question whether social forces and structural circumstances will usher in a welfare state in South Africa in the course of the development of its political economy.

In contemplating this problem, let me first summarize what is meant by the term 'welfare state'. The underlying normative commitment in the welfare state is aimed at improving the quality of life of the population by promoting economic (or material) equality through the redistributive power of the democratic state. Unregulated, free-wheeling economic competition is condemned as unacceptable, since it encourages greed, avarice and social conflict. This type of free and unfettered competition is seen as inefficient and unproductive. However, the modern welfare state does not dispense with the advantages of the free market altogether. Indeed it tries to establish a symbiotic relationship with the free market: the free market is utilized to produce the economic surpluses needed to fund the welfare state. Exactly how this is accomplished differs from state to state and from epoch to epoch within the ideology of state welfarism. In Britain, for instance, immediately after the Second World War the state tried to manage wealth-creating enterprises by a policy of nationalization of private industry. This failed, and

Thatcher's Conservative Party privatized much of these state enterprises. In France, the state is still much involved in managing and owning production capacity. The general tendency in the twenty-first century welfare state is, however, to leave business to business and let the state redistribute resources by the use of its political power to intervene in the economy.[1]

The virtue of the welfare state, in this defence, is that it takes the distribution of wealth away from the vagaries of the market to ensure that all citizens have a stake in society and that each individual has an incentive to contribute to the common weal. This conception of the welfare state subscribes to the principles of formal equality before the law and equality of opportunity for every citizen or member of society. Moreover, in the welfare state some measure of equality of outcome is encouraged, which means that the state intervenes in the economy through its monopoly on political power to ensure, and if necessary enforce, an equitable distribution of income, wealth and other social goods. The apologists of the welfare state defend the redistribution of wealth on the grounds that it promotes justice and social community (solidarity).[2]

The social consensus that underpins a welfare state

The modern welfare state as it exists in much of Western Europe rests on a social consensus that has developed over the last century or so. In my view the social consensus on the idea of the welfare state comprises the following elements. In the first place social welfare transfer payments (often hailed 'welfare entitlements') are seen as a social right of citizenship, a form of civil contract between the various social classes in society. Second, the welfare state's mode of being requires that the present contributors of resources show generosity towards their less fortunate fellow citizens. By the same token, the less fortunate should show modesty and constraint in collecting benefits, since both groups acknowledge the reversibility of roles over time.[3]

Furthermore the individual is conceptualized as a victim of external circumstance beyond his/her control: war, famine, redundancy, disease, inflation, economic recession, foreign economic competition and similar incidents and circumstances that lead to human insecurity. The welfare state tries to compensate for most of the disadvantages and inconveniences inflicted on the individual by life itself. In other words, the welfare state acts as insurance against the insecurities and neuroses of life. The European welfare state ideal typically assumes that people live their entire lives in the country of their birth and that their mutual solidarity is nationally delimited.[4] People managing well will be willing to finance welfare benefits, since they may themselves one day find themselves in similar social stress: old age, unemployment, disease, disability.[5]

Some welfare states such as the German (Bismarckian model) and the British (Beveridgean model)[6] rely on the principle that social insurance and benefits are related to previous employment and contributions. In essence they are reciprocity systems and presuppose a *quid pro quo* relation. The Scandinavian model relies heavily on tax-transfer mechanisms and is in essence a model of role reversibility. Role reversibility means that one imagines what help one would have appreciated if one were in the other's place. Almost Biblically, it relies on the idea that one is one's fellow's keeper.[7]

The social consensus on which the (West) European welfare state has been constructed claims the following successes: (a) reduction and alleviation of poverty; (b) weakening of social exclusion and polarization; (c) developing an equitable income distribution; (d) smoothing the income stream in an individual's life; (e) providing individual security; (f) weakening social tensions; and (g) increasing the supply of social services not provided by either the market or charity.[8]

These are significant benefits and many societies in the Third World are striving for just such a society. The emigration of people from the so-called Third World into the European welfare states is partly explained by the generous benefits that these welfare states supply.

South Africa on its way to a welfare state?

In order to reflect on the question whether South Africa's political economy is being managed towards becoming a welfare state, I shall do the following. First, a brief comment on its political economy is offered. Second, some key theories and actors that could influence the South African political economy moving towards a welfare state will be identified. Third, I shall reflect on the question whether such a movement is taking place as well as the likelihood of a welfare state developing in South Africa over time.

South Africa's political economy

South Africa's current economic problems – mainly deep inequalities in income, poverty and lack of international competitiveness – go back to the mid-nineteenth century. The discovery of gold and diamonds in the nineteenth century on the highveld of South Africa spearheaded its transformation from a backward agrarian economy to a mining and industrial economy in the middle of the twentieth century. The country's industrial development was initially focused on mining with little job-creation elsewhere,[9] and the manpower needs of the mines caused economic development in rural areas to stagnate. The mining-industrial economy came to be dominated by a few huge mining-financial conglomerates, with an in-built oligopolism. With the absence of real competition as well as the elimination of African peasants, little other economic development took place in African rural areas.

The political economy of apartheid led to a huge racially based wage gap. The industrial base was built behind tariff walls and import substitution.

Due to its international political and economic isolation, South Africa was forced to maintain a macro-economic policy of import substitution during the 1970s and 1980s when Latin America and Southeast Asia started on the road to export-based industrialization. Moreover, the ideological costs of apartheid, such as resettling workers far away from the industrial cities and a policy of state-aided industrial decentralization, which made no economic sense, led to an inefficient economy.[10]

The political economy has created deep inequalities in terms of the distribution of wealth. Moreover, these inequalities were perpetuated into participation in the economy: whites had open access to economic opportunities, blacks were restricted. Numerous laws, rules, regulations and practices benefited the white population. Businesses and industries were established in mainly 'white' areas; job reservation was legislated by statute by the various National Party governments, starting with the Hertzog government in 1924 and ending, in reality, with the De Klerk government in 1994.[11]

These practices, linked to its international economic position, resulted in a duality in the South African economy. On the one hand the country developed a political economy in which the distribution of wealth was (and mainly still is) skewed in favour of the white minority. This means that the economy is divided along racial lines with its wealth primarily benefiting the white population. The richest 10 per cent of the country's population earns 50 per cent of the national income, the poorest 20 per cent only 1.5 per cent; and 85 per cent of the poor are black. The country's Gini coefficient is calculated at 0.68, which reflects this inequality.[12] The second duality within the economy is one typical of a developing country – the rural/urban divide. Economic activities are largely restricted to urban areas, with areas or 'islands' of economic development concentrated in the Gauteng province, the Durban-Pietermaritzburg area of KwaZulu Natal, the Port Elizabeth-Uitenhage area of the Eastern Cape and the Cape Town-Bellville complex in the Western Cape. This means that rural poverty and deprivation is rife and that urbanization, as in many other parts of Africa, grows at a rate which makes it difficult to plan urban development properly.[13]

South Africa struggles with a problem of high unemployment. Formal unemployment/underemployment at present, September 2001, ranges between 26 per cent and 35 per cent.[14] Of the formally unemployed, approximately 50 per cent are engaged in the informal sector; these are quite often marginal economic activities, like hawking, which do not necessarily eliminate material poverty. Some commentators claim that South Africa's unemployment ratio is the highest recorded for a middle-income economy.[15]

Moreover, the dependency ratio – the proportion of youths (under age 15) to economically active adults (ages 15 to 64) – places a heavy burden on the economy. Half the population is under 24, and under-four-year-olds are the biggest age group. High unemployment together with a big youth dependency ratio leads to a low revenue base for government. Consequently, government has smaller material resources at its disposal to create or encourage the creation of employment and to provide social security nets for the poor. Taxation levels are disproportionally high in South Africa, creating an onerous tithe for the wealthier but relatively small for the middle class in the country. High taxation, low labour productivity and government dissaving through deficit financing of its budget result in low domestic savings and investment and therefore low capital accumulation. This makes South Africa highly dependent on foreign investment and loans for economic development, and increases the country's vulnerability to international capital flows and financial crises.[16]

The major failure of economic policy since the establishment of the Union of South Africa in 1910 was that the fairly rapid economic growth of the first 70 years of the Union's history was never transformed into economic development that embraced the majority of the population. Economic *development* means that the whole or majority of the population experiences sustained improvement in their standard of living. Economic *growth* merely points to an increase in average wealth but does not mean that its distribution benefits the population as a whole. South Africa experienced economic growth, but not economic development – the majority of its population remained poor, while the distribution of new wealth was limited to the white population. Furthermore, and as was the case with most African economies in this era, growth was highly dependent on the earnings from the export of minerals and other commodities.[17]

These developments – and, of course, in a different sense, a *lack* of development – has left the South African political economy in the year 2001 with, amongst others, the following features:

1 ownership of land is still largely in the hands of a white minority (for example 1.0 per cent of the white community, mainly farmers, who comprise 0.125 per cent of the total population, own 85 per cent of agricultural land);
2 an oligopolistic corporate business sector dominated by 10 large corporations;
3 whites in general still enjoy levels of health, education, social services and general living standards far superior to those of the majority of the black population;
4 the growth of a black middle class during the last five years, largely facilitated by the change in the political power base in South Africa; employment creation has occurred within the public sector rather than within the private sector. Class differences within the black community now emulate those between black and white in South Africa, and political transformation has led to the rapid economic empowerment of a new

black elite by the state. Some of the instant riches of black interests have been breathtaking in the last seven years;

5   the country is increasingly subject to problems related to regionwide endemic poverty and deprivation, such as illegal immigration, crime, drug and small-arms smuggling;

6   neglect of human development, particularly in the field of formal education, makes for a shortage of skilled labour and managerial skills necessary to develop the economy's productivity and competitiveness, while unemployment is growing; and

7   despite high levels of unemployment, the cost of labour in South Africa is high and, together with low productivity of all factors of production (not only labour), international competitiveness is curtailed.[18]

The following key economic indicators are pertinent to the above analysis:[19] (1) in the last decade, GDP per annum increased by an average of 2 per cent per annum, while public expenditure increased by 3.5 per cent per annum in real terms. Even the 'good years' of 1999 and 2000 produced growth rates of only 2 per cent in 1999, 3 per cent in 2000 and 2.5 per cent in 2001; (2) over the past five years gross domestic savings as a percentage of GDP has declined from 19 per cent per year to 16 per cent of GDP; (3) the deficit in the current account of the balance of payments has been an average of $1.3 billion per year (3–4 per cent of GDP, but declining) for the last five years. The low savings rate as well as the deficit on the current account clearly makes South Africa reliant on uncertain foreign capital flows; (4) employment has been declining at 1.6 per cent per annum for the last decade; (5) inflation has declined from a rate of 13.6 per cent in 1989–93 to 7.5 per cent in 1994–2001, but this is still almost three times higher than that of the country's major trading partners, leading to a steady depreciation in the rand; (6) the average budget deficit of the state increased from 4.3 per cent in 1989–93 to 5.7 per cent the next five years. However, this has now been brought down to less than 2.5 per cent in the current 2000/01 fiscal year; (7) high domestic consumption, high increases in salaries and wages and a continuing state budget deficit have led to restrictive monetary policies by the SA Reserve Bank. The prime overdraft rate for the last decade was on average 19 per cent, but declining steeply in the period September 1999 to September 2001, when the prime overdraft rate was 13 per cent; (8) however, much of the strict monetarist policy of the ANC government in the last five years has strengthened the state's financial position and South Africa's macro-economy is in much better shape than seven years ago when the ANC came to power.[20]

The ANC government's macro economic policy

When the present ANC-led government took power in 1994, the South African economy had become stagnant and uncompetitive. It needed to be completely overhauled and made more equitable and inclusive from a racial point of view, but also internationally competitive. Basic social services had to be extended to African people, human capital development fostered, subsidies to commercial farmers, mines and industry had to be scrapped, and state expenditure at the same time had to be reduced in real terms. Inflation had to be brought down. For political reasons, the ANC government did not choose the route of a Southeast Asian low-wage, full employment economy. Investment in human capital and strengthening the skills of the workforce to make it more competitive globally is the basis of the ANC government's economic policy.[21]

The government's current macroeconomic policy is known by the acronym Gear (Growth, Employment and Redistribution). Gear is a strategy to rebuild and restructure the economy; it creates a context to 'successfully confront the related challenges of meeting basic needs, developing human resources, increasing participation in the democratic institutions of civil society and implementing the RDP (reconstruction and development programme) in all its facets'.[22]

Gear's aim is to 'catapult' South Africa into a 'new burst of economic activity' with higher levels of growth, development and employment and a 'significantly improved distribution of income and opportunities'. The higher growth path depends on attracting foreign direct investment, higher domestic savings and a strong export performance. The strategy also includes greater industrial competitiveness, a tighter fiscal stance, moderation of wage increases, accelerated public investment, efficient service delivery and a major expansion of private investment.[23]

The state's macroeconomic policy can thus be described as neo-liberal, but includes some socialist components such as the redistribution of income and building homes for the poor – as set out below. The policy is guided by the following key elements: (a) to create a competitive fast-growing economy; (b) redistribution of income to the poor and disadvantaged of society; (c) achieving sustainable economic growth and job-creation; (d) improve police and streamline the criminal justice system; (e) build homes for the poor, improve municipal infrastructure and living conditions; and (f) target poverty relief.[24]

The national budget prioritizes spending on education, health and welfare. Policies have been put in place to fund productivity skills training, but this is funded off-budget by a training levy on enterprises. A glance at the 2001–02 national estimates of expenditure reveals one major weakness in the state's budget: servicing of public debt. In 2001/02 it consumed R48 billion, that is 18.6 per cent of the total budget, or 5.5 per cent of the GDP.[25] Compare this figure with the expenditure for education in the same budget, which was R58 billion, and one can understand what type of restriction the servicing of the public debt places on social spending. The public debt ratio, as a proportion of GDP, is not inordinately high at 55 per cent of GDP, and, moreover, the state is dissaving at present and has been doing so for the last decade. The 2001–02 budget deficit is 2.5 per cent of GDP, down from 9 per cent in 1994, while the consolidated national expenditure (the state budget), consumes 27.1 per cent of GDP. Therefore the public debt has been declining as a percentage of GDP during the last five years and is a considerable improvement to its predecessor.[26]

Likewise, the state's dissaving has been improving steadily. The state dissaving for 2001 was 0.25 per cent of GDP, compared to 4.4 per cent in 1994. The target is to eliminate state dissaving in the medium term. However, the cumulative effect of state dissaving in the last decade has led to continued high interest rates in the country. In 2001 the prime overdraft rate was 13 per cent, inflation was 6.5 per cent, yielding a high real interest rate of 7.5 per cent.[27]

Spending on social welfare

The state's budget is quite strongly restricted in what can be done in terms of improving the conditions of life of poorer members of South African society. Moreover, 58 per cent of the 2001 national budget was spent on social services – education, health and welfare. The largest single redistributive programme of the government is the system of social grants to the elderly, disability and child support grants, providing support to three million South Africans every month. This amounts to 7.5 per cent of the population. However, the income tax burden in South Africa is shared by a relatively small section of the population. Only about 12 per cent of South Africa's economically active population pay income tax; the wealthiest members of society are taxed at a marginal rate of 42 per cent on an income of R200,000.00 per annum, which is high by industrialized world standards.[28]

However, within the restrictions pointed out above, the ANC government has clearly embarked on a redistributive social spending policy. It is redistributing resources from rich to poor and from white to black. Tables 17.1, 17.2 and 17.3 indicate how the ANC government changed its social spending priorities between 1993 and 1997: the social spending gap between rich and poor, as well as the gap between whites and blacks.[29]

The four-year trend of Table 17.1 shows that social expenditure has been redistributed from the wealthiest 20 per cent to the poorest 40 per cent of the population, and the same trend is demonstrated in the percentage share of the expenditure of the five quintiles. The redistributive tendency is clear: the wealthiest 40 per cent saw their share in social expenditure decline from 30.3 per cent of the total to 23.4 per cent, while the poorest 40 per cent saw an increase in their share of social expenditure from 49.3 per cent to 56.5 per cent.

Table 17.2 shows that the expenditure per capita on blacks increased substantially in the six-year period, that is by 39.9 per cent. The trend shows

Table 17.1 Increases in social expenditure per capita 1993 compared to 1997. The figures are per quintile, 1 = poorest 20 per cent of population, 5 = richest 20 per cent of population

	Social expenditure per capita				
	1	2	3	4	5
1993	R1730	1280	1464	1790	1673
1997	R2320	1977	1743	1334	1924
% increase 1993–97	34.1	54.4	28.0	–2.6	–20.2

	Percentage share of expenditure				
	1	2	3	4	5
1993	27.4	21.9	20.5	17.6	12.7
1997	30.7	25.8	20.1	14.7	8.7

Source: South Africa, Department of Finance, *Budget Review 2000*, www:SARS.gov.za/budget_2000/review, p. 6.

Table 17.2 Social spending per racial group per capita, 1993 compared to 1997

	Social spending per capita				
	Black	Brown	Indian	White	Total
1993	R1439	2014	2529	1732	R1555
1997	R2012	1812	2000	1435	R1924

	Percentage share of spending				
	Black	Brown	Indian	White	Total
1993	70.1	11.2	4.2	14.5	100
1997	80.2	8.2	2.6	9.07	100

Source: South Africa, Department of Finance, *Budget Review 2000*, www: SARS.gov.za/budget_2000/review, p. 6.

lucidly that white, brown and Indian people saw their share in social expenditure decrease in the four-year period, while blacks received a significant increase.

Table 17.3 shows a clear upward trend in the relative share of the budget being spent on social services, which is in line with the above quoted Gear policy that the ANC-led government intends redistributing wealth to the poor and to target poverty relief as one of its priorities.

Table 17.3   Total government expenditure on welfare services: social services, health and education, fiscal years 1997/98–2001/02

	Welfare expenditure				
	1997/98	1998/99	1999/00	2000/01	2001/02
Amount (R billions)	88.6	98	103	129	155
% of budget	46.6	47.7	47.2	50	58
% of GDP	14.6	15.1	14.6	15.3	16.0

Sources: South Africa Yearbook 1999, p. 308, and South Africa, Budget Review 2001, p. 22.

Social policy in South Africa

Since the demise of apartheid and the instigation of a new political order, a radical new paradigm has been introduced in the country's social policy. The intellectual framework of democratic socialism drives the social policy of the ANC-led government, with an emphasis on equality and equity in human relations. The government has enacted a number of new laws since 1994 to put into practice its ideological views. Amongst the most important are: the abolition of the death penalty; laws on gender equality; affirmative action employment laws; legalization of abortion on demand in the first 15 weeks of pregnancy; laws which protect the right of collective bargaining in the workplace; laws which prohibit unfair dismissal in the workplace; land reform, including restoration of land rights or payment of reparation to people of colour who were unfairly deprived of their land since 1913; use of the national budget as a redistributive mechanism to benefit the poorer (and mostly black) people of society; laws to improve the lot of women in traditional African communities as far as property and inheritance rights are concerned; and laws protecting the right of individuals to choose their own sexual orientation and to protect such persons against discrimination based on their sexual orientation.[30]

The government's social welfare policy makes provision for: (a) promotion of self-reliance to empower people to play a meaningful role in society; (b) use of auxiliary workers, volunteers and family and community-based models of care, rather than institutionalized care; (c) state grants to the elderly, poor children and the disabled; (d) restorative justice in dealing with children and families in trouble with the law; (e) a law against domestic violence, to strengthen families and to make domestic violence a statutory rather than common law offence; (f) biological fathers are given the right to participate in deciding whether children born out of wedlock can be given up for adoption; (g) family advocates (lawyers) and councillors are appointed at state expense to submit recommendations to the court regarding the well-being of children in divorce cases; and (h) a project to aid children and youths who run foul of the law. The principle is that children are best cared for by their families.[31]

Taking the above sketch of the ANC government's economic and social policies into consideration, one can address the question of the trends towards a welfare state in South Africa. In particular, what builds a welfare state? Is South Africa on its way to a welfare state?

A number of theories have been advanced to explain the development of the welfare state, and three well-known ones are briefly summarized below and applied to present-day South Africa.

The industrialism thesis[32]

This theory builds on the fact that the industrialization of a political economy leads to a migration of workers towards cities, where they are exposed to the vagaries of free-market competition The main socio-economic problem is that market-based industrial economies are not able to solve the phenomenon of economic cycles. Consequently, the working class is subject to retrenchment and is ill-equipped to face the risks of the marketplace. Therefore, in industrializing societies that are also democratizing, pressure builds up for state intervention in the economy to supply some security for the industrial working class through social insurance, socialized health and welfare services and free or nearly free education. Moreover, the welfare state becomes possible in an industrialized economy because sufficient wealth is created that can be redistributed to the working class to ensure its material security.

In present-day South Africa, much of this theory applies. The country has been industrializing since the late nineteenth century, and since the middle of the 1970s African-led labour unions have been lobbying governments vehemently for job security, minimum wages, pensions, social security payments and the right to strike. Retrenchments since 1994 in the restructuring of the economy led to the shedding of 500,000 jobs, which increased pressure by organized labour on the democratic ANC government for more regulated job security as well as state intervention to ensure economic benefits for workers.[33]

The contradictions of capitalism thesis[34]

According to neo-Marxist theories, welfare states originate in the contradictions of capitalism. Capitalist political economies need to ensure conditions favourable to capital accumulation; capital needs the state to ensure social peace and labour needs the state to limit the predations of capital. The state presides over a social contract: it accedes to the demands of labour by establishing social welfare policies funded by economic surpluses generated by the capitalist economy. It keeps the loyalty of capital and ensures a favourable investment climate by keeping the demands of labour in check and ensuring reasonable tax limits on capitalist enterprises.

To placate 'capital',[35] the present South African government subscribes to the so-called Washington consensus on economic policy,[36] derived from the theories and practices of neo-liberal economics and the general policy prescriptions of the Bretton Woods Institutions, which are situated in Washington DC and the USA. This doctrine holds that the private sector is the primary engine of economic growth; governments should keep inflation low through strict monetarist policies, maintain price stability and shrink the size of the state bureaucracy. The state should maintain a balanced or close to balanced budget, keep taxes low, maintain low tariffs on imported goods and promote exports. Moreover, states should remove restrictions on foreign investment, privatize state-owned enterprises and utilities, deregulate capital markets, promote a convertible currency and allow free repatriation of capital, interest and dividends to foreign investors. Industries, stock and bond markets should be opened to foreign competition. Lastly, states should strive towards 'good governance', eliminate government subsidies and kickbacks to the private sector, and manage state services through public–private partnerships.[37]

As pointed out above, the South African government is quite strongly sympathetic to labour demands for security against the vagaries of the (global) marketplace. For instance the Basic Conditions of Employment Act grants workers maternity and paternity leave, regulates hours of work to 45 hours per week, gives preference to regulation of workplace agreements via collective bargaining at industry level and prohibits child labour. It also protects workers against arbitrary hiring and dismissal, and in a wide-ranging number of industries minimum wage levels are prescribed. The Employment Equity Act forces employers to implement affirmative action plans which are monitored by the Department of Labour. Entrepreneurs regularly complain that the labour system in South Africa is unnecessarily rigid and makes businesses uncompetitive against low-wage Asian Economies, while labour complains that they are still insufficiently protected against the vagaries of Asian and other low-wage economic competition.[38]

Since 1994, the government has succeeded in managing the contradictions of capitalism reasonably successfully, but not without a price. Ministers have been heckled at Labour Union Annual Congresses and many investors are wary of investing in an economy which has 'inflexible labour laws'.[39] These contradictions regularly have the government defending capitalism to labour unions and labour rights to capitalists.[40]

Nation-state building

This theory supposes that welfare states arise through the strategies of capitalist elites to integrate workers into the capitalist political economy of the national state. In order to do this, the state offers social protection as a rational-legal and impersonal form of state action. Social protection now becomes a matter of rights of the citizen against the state. These rights are acquired through democratic processes and are justiciable. The elites legitimate the political power of the state by incorporating the working classes through the mechanisms of social security.[41]

The South African government is committed to a programme of 'nation-building', although this is primarily a political ideology against ethnic and racial fragmentation. The government does not have the economic resources to implement a typical West-European welfare state, but its state spending priorities in successive budgets have been redistributive in nature, favouring poorer sections of the population and taxing wealthier sections (cf. Tables 17.1–17.3 above). To operationalize the transfer of resources, taxes on the wealthy are often imposed by direct-user fees such as toll roads, school fees,[42] stamp duties, transfer duty on fixed property, inheritance tax, tax on pension funds and the like. The poor and working classes benefit from this redistribution in rational and legal ways, such as the right to an old-age grant, a children's grant, free medical treatment for pregnant women and children under six years of age at state hospitals, free and compulsory education, housing subsidies for the working class and a limited supply of free water and electricity to the poor. In this way the legitimacy of the ruling party, the state and its ruling power elite is accomplished. In other words, a nation-state is being consolidated by the use of economic redistribution and limited welfarist policies.[43]

The resources of power thesis

This thesis holds that the growth of reformist (or 'progressive') trade unions and the ascendancy of labour-based political parties to executive power are the main forces in devising and developing public policies designed to bring about greater equality between classes in a bourgeois capitalist state. The social and political transformation of a capitalist society rests on the balance of power achieved between the classes (capitalists and working classes). Where a strong labourist political party is in power for a significant period of time, supported by a well-organized and disciplined trade-union movement, the state is likely to embark upon social policies that are redistributive and welfarist in orientation. The ideology of the ruling party in power is important for determining the type of options and actions that will be followed to shape a welfare state in such a society. Such parties will try to reduce inequalities in society – which will affect the poor and labour classes. These in turn form the basis of such a labour party and will tend to help it in remaining in power. Transforming a capitalist state to a welfare state is in essence a political process that intervenes in the political economy of such a state to redress economic and social inequities if not inequalities.[44]

This is probably the strongest theory supporting the ultimate development of a welfare state in South Africa. The ANC is a centrist to left-of-centre African nationalist-labour coalition and is supported by a strong labour union movement. Indeed the ANC, the South African Communist Party and the Congress of South African Trade Unions are in a formal governing alliance, the so-called *Tripartite Alliance*. In its own words the ANC is

> A broad multi-class, mass organization, uniting the motive forces on the basis of a programme for transformation. It must strive to remain a broad democratic movement by accepting into its ranks all those who accept and abide by its policies and objectives.

> Among these forces are the organizations of the working class – the South African Communist Party and the progressive trade union movement, represented by COSATU, in particular. . . . This Tri-partite Alliance is therefore not a matter of sentiment, but an organizational expression of the common purpose and unity in action that these forces share.[45]

However, at present a black capitalist elite is developing in the ranks of the ANC that has strong ideological bonds with the governing party; members often leave active politics to start out in very lucrative private capitalist ventures. Therefore, the governing party faces in itself the 'contradictions of capitalism' thesis mentioned in the first theory above to explain the welfare state. As shown above, in the brief exposition of the ANC government's social policies, these are quietly redistributive. The policies do, however, not only favour the poor working classes of South Africa, but also the previously disadvantaged members of the black elite through explicit affirmative action programmes. Inasmuch as class differences develop within the ANC, the contradictions of capitalism will also make itself felt in the ranks of the ruling party. If the resources of power thesis is correct, and the economy becomes sufficiently industrialized and produces significant surpluses, the ANC Alliance may well make welfare state-like compromises between (black) capitalists and black labour unions.

Comment and conclusion

From the above highly condensed analysis it is clear that the ANC government is determined to redress imbalances of the past through state intervention policies in the political economy. However, as much as some of its rhetoric is socialist, it is hampered by the fact that the ANC does not only represent the workers of South Africa. An African nationalist elite controls the ANC, and unsurprisingly its policies also favour this constituency. A strong movement towards the embourgeoisement of Africans in South Africa is underway and undermines the idea of working-class solidarity. The ANC has to manage a precarious balance of power between the aspirations of the poor and working classes of South Africa and the economic desires of the aspiring African/black elite as well as the capitalist business enterprises and their class supporters. In fact, the black elite have done very well out of the state transformation of South Africa since 1994, while the poorest sector of black society have been left behind.[46]

In the light of the evidence presented above, South Africa is clearly not a typical welfare state – the economic resources to support a fully-fledged welfare state are not available, and the global economic power structures do not favour such an economy. A glance at the level of welfare expenditure as a percentage of GDP confirms the minimalist welfare state in South Africa. During the last five years, the state spent around 15 per cent of GDP on its welfare budget: education, health and social security.[47] The typical Scandinavian welfare budget is around 30 per cent of GDP. Even fastidious, Thatcherite Britain spent around 27 per cent of GDP on these welfare items. Moreover, strong class divisions, reinforced by racial divisions in South Africa, at present impede a national feeling or even conception of social solidarity, so necessary in promoting the welfare state. The middle classes, mostly white, have very little welfare protection. Middle-class persons in South Africa have limited access to state-aided healthcare, unemployment insurance and old-age pensions. The quality of state-provided healthcare is low,[48] and unemployment insurance and old-age social grants are strictly means-tested.[49] Consequently, many middle-class persons do not qualify for unemployment insurance or old-age grants. Social grants for the aged are non-contributory grants from the public purse. The state-managed unemployment fund is a Bismarckian contributory type of fund, and is not universally available to all employed people. Only lower-middle-income earners qualify for membership and the benefits are meagre. After six months, most of the benefits are cut off. Yet at the same time, the middle classes are taxed fairly heavily to provide for the minimalist social grants made to poorer sections of society. This class-based welfare discrimination does not enhance class-based social solidarity and is divisive.

The Scandinavian welfare state promotes social solidarity by the idea that both contributions to welfare as well as the drawing of benefits are universal. Therefore every working or (income-generating) individual must contribute by way of the social security tax in order for everyone to share in the benefits of the welfare state. The type of social benefits paid out by the South African state, as well as its distinct redistributive policies[50] do not comply with the principle of social solidarity of a welfare state. Taking from the rich and giving to the poor does not enhance the idea of reciprocity of the Beveridgean or Bismarckian welfare state, nor of the idea of role-reversal inherent in the Scandinavian conception of the welfare state. At best, state social welfare in South Africa is aimed at poverty relief and a minimalist social protection.

However, one should also consider the substantial influence of the limited social redistribution that is taking place within the constraints of current economic capacity. The Minister of Finance referred to this in his budget speech, and I reiterate that the largest single redistributive programme of the government is the system of social grants (R31.6 billion) to the elderly, disability and child-support grants, providing support to 3 million South Africans every month. This amounts to 7.5 per cent of the population. Moreover, the size of the education budget (R58.5 billion) and health budget (R29.6 billion) point to considerable 'social welfare spending' in South Africa.

Despite its redistributive policies, the ruling ANC has made provision for the role of free markets in the restructuring of South Africa's political economy. In constructing and reconstructing South Africa's political economy, the South African government has chosen to let a free-market economy take its place alongside the cautious welfarist policies it has embarked upon. Wealth has to be created before it can be redistributed. Private and NGO welfare, private insurance and extended family care – leaving part of the welfare function to private individuals and respecting their autonomy – augment state welfare in South Africa.[51]

In my view a welfare state will most likely develop in democratic South Africa over the longer term – depending on the success of economic growth and development. The thrust of the government's Gear programme is to create wealth in order to redistribute it; as more wealth is created in the modern sector of the economy, a further increase in urbanization can be expected as in other industrialized states. A crucial coalition of workers and the ruling ANC, as a social democratic movement, will find ways and means to redistribute resources to the working classes through the typical political mechanisms of the welfare state. The bourgeoisie – the majority of whom will be 'black' – will progressively be brought into the welfare net. As more resources become available, welfare services will improve and a larger proportion of the state's budget will be allocated to fund welfare. The 'resources of power' path towards the welfare state will conceivably be followed. The successes of the redistributive measures of the ANC government so far should enhance the power of the ruling party and help it to stay in power. The ANC has been successful in selling the idea to its electoral constituency that only the ANC can improve their economic conditions once in power.[52] Thus, while South Africa is not a welfare state, in my judgement the indications are that increased economic prosperity will lead to a more comprehensive welfare state.

All three theses discussed above on the development of the welfare state support the conclusion. The 'contradictions of capitalism thesis' holds that the state uses social welfare to pacify workers to ensure favourable conditions for capital accumulation. The ANC government is doing this, indeed it is criticized by key members of the Tripartite Alliance of coddling up to capitalists.[53] The 'nation-state thesis' argues that the welfare state is a rational aid to the ruling elite to incorporate the working class into the capitalist economy by way of social security measures. The foregoing analysis in the section on the macro-economic policy of the ANC government and

Tables 17.1–17.3 illustrate how the ANC government has been doing this. The 'resources of power thesis' reasons that labour-based coalitions which hold executive power tend to devise public policies that are designed to bring about greater equality between the classes, and the redistributive policies of the ANC government have been working towards such an outcome in the last seven years. It has been more successful in racial terms than in class terms, but the (black) poor have benefited, as argued above.

Inasmuch as the present social transfers in South Africa do not promote social solidarity – since it takes from the rich and gives to the poor, without the middle classes benefiting – progressively improving social benefits over time would enhance social solidarity and the feeling of reciprocity. Once the middle classes are brought into the social security net, they will have a vested material interest in the expansion of the welfare state and its consequent benefits. The point is this: the modern capitalist economy has not solved the problem of the vagaries of the free market and its cyclical nature. As such, the more society is exposed to a modern industrial and service-based economy, the more vulnerable its members become towards its inevitable business cycles. Politics under such circumstances tend to become the politics of welfarism, where the electorate looks towards the state and its political power to intervene on their behalf to ensure them against economic vulnerability. The welfare state in Europe has been tenacious and resilient, despite two decades of relentless pressure against its benefits by what is popularly known as the neo-liberals.[54] My contention is that in South Africa, the strong labour lobby by their partial capture of state power through the ANC is laying the groundwork for a welfare state. With increased economic capacity the clamour for social benefits will remain, and South Africa will steadily progress on the route towards the typical welfare state, so well-travelled in the industrialized world, unless economics as a discipline finds an answer to the business cycle. Try as it might, after the last two hundred years of capitalist progress and Marxist socialist failure, that answer does not seem to be forthcoming. The welfare state is the consequence as political forces drive elected politicians towards using state power to protect society against the failures of the market and the vagaries of life. There is little reason to believe that under the aforesaid circumstances, South Africa will be an exception.

Notes

1 This description has been gleaned from the vast literature of the welfare state. For a good overview see R. Erikson, 'Descriptions of Inequality: The Swedish Approach to Welfare Research', in M. Nussbaum, and A. Sen, *The Quality of Life*, Oxford: Clarendon Press, 1993; and A. De Jasay, *The State*, Oxford: Basil Blackwell, 1985, chapter 4; as well as G. Esping-Andersen, 'After the Golden Age? Welfare State Dilemmas in a Global Economy', in G. Esping Andersen (ed.), *Welfare States in Transition: National Adaptations in Global Economies*, London:

Sage, 1996; E. Scarbrough, 'West European Welfare States: The Old Politics of Retrenchment', *European Journal of Political Research*, Oxford, vol. 38, 2000, pp. 225–59; D. Marsland, *Welfare or Welfare State?* London: Macmillan, 1996; and Joakim Palme in Chapter 13 of this book.

2   A reviewer requested some evidence regarding what is termed the 'roll back' of the welfare state in Europe. This is a popular stereotype of neo-liberal-oriented financial journalists. A proper analysis of the welfare state in Europe demonstrates that it is alive and well, while of course going through adjustments. But the salient and underlying assumptions of the welfare state in Europe are intact. In fact it would be political suicide for any party in Western Europe to 'significantly roll back' the welfare state. See for instance Scarborough, *ibid.*, Petersen in Chapter 12 of this book as well as Marsland, *ibid.*, for persuasive arguments and statistics regarding this question. Marsland is a vehement critic of the welfare state and finds much evidence, indeed, to his distaste, that the welfare state is alive and well in Western Europe and Britain.

3   J.H. Petersen in Chapter 12 of this volume.

4   In real-life situations in Europe, this assumption can no longer be defended, since immigration into the European economies is needed to augment an ageing workforce. *Ibid.*

5   *Ibid.*

6   See Marsland, n. 1, for a discussion of the Bismarckian and Beveridgean models of social security.

7   J.H. Petersen, n. 2.

8   *Ibid.*, c.f. also S. Kuhnle, 'European Welfare lessons of the 1990s', in S. Kuhnle (ed.), *Survival of the European Welfare State*, London: Routledge, 2000, p. 234.

9   For an analysis of South Africa's early history of industrialization, see M. Lipton, *Capitalism and Apartheid. South Africa 1910–1986*, Cape Town: David Phillip, 1987.

10   Cf. Alec Erwin in *F & T Weekly*, Sandton, South Africa, 21 August 1999, p. 21; Lipton, *ibid.*, pp. 227–30.

11   C. McCarthy, 'Apartheid Ideology and Economic Development Theory', in N. Nattrass and E. Ardington, *The Political Economy of South Africa*, Cape Town: Oxford University Press, 1990, p. 53. M. Schoeman, 'The Political Economy of South Africa in a Global Context', in A.J. Venter (ed.), *Government and Politics in the New South Africa*, 2nd edn, Pretoria: J.L. van Schaik, 2001, p. 324.

12   Schoeman, *ibid.*, p. 326.

13   *Ibid.*, p. 325.

14   The figures differ according to which method of calculation is used. The *Labour Force Survey* calculates unemployment at 35.9 per cent in September 2001, while the *Survey of Employment and Earning* calculates it to be 25.8 per cent. Cf. South Africa Reserve Bank, *2001 Annual Economic Report*, Pretoria, Reserve Bank, 2001, p. 12.

15   N. Nattrass, in Centre for Development and Enterprise (CDE), *Report 1998*, Johannesburg, CDE, 1998, p. 4; SA Reserve Bank, *2001 Annual Economic Report*, *ibid.*

16   Schoeman, n. 11, pp. 325–6.

17   *Ibid.*, p. 327.

18   *Ibid.*, pp. 325–6.

19   This information has been gleaned from the CDE Report of 1999 as well as checked against the latest, September 2002, *Annual Report* of the SA Reserve Bank. Where necessary, specific page numbers and/or references have been indicated. The full report is available from www.resbank.co.za/economics/annua2002/domes.html

20 *CDE Report* 1999, pp. 97, 98, 100, as well as SA Reserve Bank, *2001 Annual Economic Report*, n. 14, p. 1.
21 Alec Erwin, n. 10.
22 South Africa, *Department of Finance*, Pretoria, Department of Finance, 1996, p. 20.
23 *Ibid.*, p. 3, *South Africa Yearbook 1999*, Pretoria, Government Communication and Information System, 1999, p. 288.
24 *South Africa Yearbook 1999, ibid*, p. 307.
25 Progress has been made in bringing down the relative size of the public debt; however, it still consumes significant resources which could have been used elsewhere.
26 T.A. Manuel, *Budget Speech of the Minister of Finance*, Pretoria, South African National Assembly, 21 January 2001, pp. 7–8.
27 South Africa reserve Bank, n. 15; T.A. Manuel, *ibid.*, p. 8.
28 However, the South African Revenue Service (SARS) has been quite effective in bringing more taxpayers into the tax net. In 1999 for instance it brought 50,000 citizens into the tax net (CDE Report 1999, p. 90). See also the Budget speech of the Minister of Finance, February 2001, p. 21, in which he indicated that the SARS has been improving its tax collection capacity considerably (CDE Report 1999, p. 90, budget speech of the Minister of Finance 2001, n. 26, p. 19); R.P. Gouws, *Tax and Savings in South Africa*, unpublished paper delivered at the South African Savings Institute, Sandton, 2001, p. 3.
29 T.A. Manuel, n. 26, p. 3.
30 *South Africa Year Book 1999, ibid.*, pp. 405–6.
31 *Ibid.*, p. 406.
32 Scarborough n. 1, pp. 228–9.
33 CDE Report 1999, pp. 57, 85; SARB September 2001, n. 14, pp. 12–16.
34 Claus Offe, *Contradictions of Welfare State*, London: Hutchinson, 1984.
35 This term is used here within the context of the contradictions of capitalism thesis as summarized.
36 See the 'Gear Policy' of 1996.
37 T. Friedman, *The Lexus and the Olive Tree*, New York: Farrar, Strauss & Giroux, 1999, pp. 121–8.
38 CDE Report 1999, n. 35, pp. 84–5; *South Africa Year Book 1999*, n. 24, pp. 295–6.
39 The acrimonious exchanges between Minister Fraser-Moleketi and the Public Service Unions in early October 2001 are illustrative of this tension. *F & T Weekly*, 4 October 2001, p. 4.
40 CDE Report 1999, n. 33, pp. 85–97.
41 Friedman, 'After the Golden Age? Welfare State Dilemmas in a Global Economy', in G. Esping Andersen (ed.), *Welfare States in Transition: National Adaptations in Global Economies*, London: Sage, 1996. J. Alber, 'Continuities and Change in the Idea of the Welfare State', *Politics and Society*, London, vol. 16, 1988, pp. 451–68.
42 School fees and toll roads, it goes without saying, is a regressive tax on poorer sections of the community. A government school in South Africa, may not exclude a child on the grounds of its parent's ability to pay the school fees. This is in keeping with section 29(1) of the South African constitution which gives everyone the right to a basic education. It can also be argued that the recently implemented tax on pension funds is regressive at least to the poorer members of such a fund.
43 Also see CDE Report, 1999, n. 33.
44 M. Shalev, 'The Social Democratic Model and Beyond: Two Generations of Comparative Research on the Welfare State', *Comparative Social Research*, Oslo, vol. 6,

1983, p. 317. G. Esping-Andersen, *Politics against Markets*, Princeton: Princeton University Press, 1985

45   ANC Policy Statement, 1996.

46   The income of black people in the high-income group in South Africa has increased from a share of 13 per cent in 1996 to 23.7 per cent of GDP in 2001. A very significant increase in five years, *Beeld*, 20 February 2001, p. 6.

47   See Table 17.3.

48   The private sector spends around R35 billion per year on health services, much of this financed by medical aid schemes (*F&T Weekly*, May 2001, p. 23). The funding of these medical aid schemes in terms of a welfare state, is nothing else but a private tax to provide adequate healthcare to the wealthier sections of society. This type of private tax in my judgement mitigates against the feeling of social solidarity needed to maintain a welfare state.

49   Unemployment insurance is only available to persons earning less than R93,000 per annum. Old-age social grants are low – R650.00 per month – and means-tested. Persons owning property and receiving an income are tested by a social welfare officer in terms of Act 59 of 1992. From 1 December 2001 the property clause will be scrapped. However, in terms of the Law, 'grants are not meant for people who have enough money to care for themselves. Grants are meant for those who are in most need.' See www.welfare.gov.za/socialgrants

50   A further complication in South Africa is that the state's redistributive policies are not only class-based; due to its apartheid history, the distribution of wealth in South Africa is visibly racial or colour-based. Thus wealthy whites perceive redistribution in class as well as in racial terms. Often, ANC government rhetoric creates the impression in white capitalist circles that they are the undeserving rich who have to fork out their wealth to the undeserving (black) masses.

51   A reviewer of this article poses the question whether this is not almost similar to Western Europe. It is not. A person in the European welfare state, whether Bismarckean, Beveridgean or Scandinavian, can draw life-supporting social benefits without resorting to private charity. The complaint of critics of the European welfare state is that it has destroyed the sense of charity of ordinary Europeans. For an incisive critique see Marsland, 1996, n. 1, pp. 201–2.

52   The ANC Alliance has won two national elections as well as two local government elections with overwhelming majorities since 1994. T. Lodge, *The South African General Election of 1999*, Johannesburg, EISA, 1999, chapter 1.

53   The statement of the SA Communist Party Executive after its meeting of 15 and 16 September 2001 is illustrative of this type of criticism, *Beeld*, Johannesburg, 17 September 2001, p. 2.

54   For a discussion of the resilience of the welfare state in Europe, see Scarbrough, 2000, n. 1, pp. 230–3.

18
The Welfare State in Japan and China: Development and Challenges

Christian Aspalter

Introduction

In this chapter I examine the different stages of welfare state development in Japan and mainland China, and discuss current challenges forcing the welfare state systems in these two countries. It may serve as a source for comparison of social policy practices in both countries, since it reveals striking similarities in the attitudes of the governments of Japan and China (after 1978) towards dependency-generating and potentially laziness-producing social assistance programmes. As White, Goodman and Kwon[1] have noticed, the Chinese welfare state system is becoming more and more similar to that of its neighbouring countries. The study here may also serve for a closer look at the similarities between the 'iron rice bowl system' (*tie fan wan*) of Communist China and the occupational welfare system in Japan which both create exceptionally strong company–labour relationships and which both lack risk-pooling and disrespect the needs of the labour market and a healthy economy because there is no firing of those workers and employees profiting from these systems. Moreover, both welfare systems cover only a very limited segment of the workforce, and represent special variants of a wage-earners' welfare state. In analysing the subject matter, I apply a historical case study approach; after giving a historical review of welfare state development in Japan and China, the essay encapsulates the major changes of the welfare state systems and goes on to focus on the present and potential challenges to them.

The development of the welfare state in Japan

Prewar developments

By the end of the Second World War, Japan had already established a residual welfare state system, with generally meagre welfare benefits. Only a limited range of welfare services and benefits were offered on a statutory basis. The first welfare programme of the modern Japanese welfare state system was established in 1874, when the government set national criteria for local poor relief, stipulating up to 50 days of support for people too old, young, poor, sick or disabled to work, provided they had no relatives to care for them. An annual average of 20,713 people received assistance from 1891 to 1900, 17,200 people from 1921 to 1930. In 1899, tuberculosis caused 7.1 per cent of all deaths, but the state did not build urban clinics for tuberculosis patients until 1914. The subsequent development of the Japanese welfare state system up to 1945 may be characterized by a very conservative stance on social welfare policy, where a short democratic period in the 1920s, which was shaken by political and social crises, did not succeed to implement more peacetime welfare programmes. In the absence of sustainable democratic politics, social and economic crises, natural disasters and wars came to carve the history of the first half of modern welfare state history. Important events that pushed for welfare state initiatives were the 1918 Rice Riots, the Great Kanto Earthquake, the Great Depression, the Second Sino-Japanese War and the Second World War. In 1918, the governing elite of the Japanese Empire had been severely threatened by a countrywide rebellion, that is the Rice Riots, which lasted for two months. A second major event that shook the Japanese nation was the Great Kanto Earthquake in 1923. Though the government had seen the consequences of major social problems caused by poverty and natural disasters, it did not launch any new social welfare programmes that could have helped the poor and stabilized the country. The only important piece of legislation in the first 10 years following the First World War was the Health Insurance Law of 1922 that provided social security for employees. But, this new law was not implemented until 1927 due to the consequences of the Great Kanto Earthquake. The Health Insurance Law of 1927 applied to workers employed for over 60 days in enterprises subject to the Factory Law. It provided benefits for sickness, injury, death and childbirth and managed to cover 38 per cent of the workforce, but excluded managers, temporary workers and workers in small enterprises. Employers and employees contributed equally, while the state paid 10 per cent of the cost. In the 1920s Japan possessed a fairly democratic regime, known as the Taisho Democracy, but this parliamentary government was not rooted deeply enough to withstand the economic and political pressures of the early 1930s, when military leaders became increasingly influential and eventually took over power.[2]

In 1929, the Japanese parliament, the Diet, passed the Relief and Protection Law, intended to solve the most stringent needs of the very poor. This law was the outcome of political forces in Parliament and in district-level administration that demanded new governmental social assistance schemes. The national government itself did not wish to upgrade the meagre benefits of the social assistance system, and as the government refused to grant the necessary financial means, the new social assistance programme could not be implemented before 1932. Public assistance under the new scheme again covered only those who were unemployable, that is the handicapped, the very sick, the chronically sick and the very old. In 1935 the Japanese government introduced, partly in response to the new politics of the New Deal in America, a minimal unemployment assistance programme. Thereafter, from 1937 to 1945, war outweighed all other factors in causing Japan's welfare transformation. Just before the outbreak of the Second Sino-Japanese War in 1937, the government decided to set up a new Ministry of Health and Social Affairs, as a response to the military's concern about health conditions of new draftees in light of the approaching war. A year later, in 1938, the government also enabled Japan's vast rural population to join the national health insurance scheme. The Social Work Law of 1938 authorized government officials to license and to regulate private relief activities, and also systematized official support for private efforts, and state aid to private relief services increased five times from 200,000 yen in 1937 to 1,000,000 yen in 1939.[3]

The Second World War led to increased government efforts to extend the welfare system. The Seamen Insurance Scheme of 1939 was a very comprehensive social security system covering the risks of sickness, unemployment, old age and accidents. In 1941, the new Workers' Pension Insurance Law had been enacted and, three years later in 1944, the Parliament also passed the Welfare Pension Insurance Law. The newly created pension system for workers included benefits for old-age retirement, invalidity and death.

Postwar developments

Before the Second World War, the Japanese welfare state system was patterned after the German model of social security, since Germany represented a politically and economically powerful industrialized country, while after the defeat of the Japanese and Germans in 1945, America served as the prime model for governmental policies. However, with regard to the Japanese welfare state, other determinants than foreign influences determined the path of welfare state development in the postwar period. Under the leadership of the Supreme Commander of Allied Powers after the War, the Japanese government implemented a series of new social legislation, for example the National Assistance Law of 1946 that widened the scope of social assistance; and the Accident Compensation Law and the Unemployment Insurance Law of 1947 which significantly enlarged the social security of workers. In the early 1950s, the government continued to extend the social welfare system. First, it upgraded the level of social assistance with the Livelihood Protection Law of 1950. Then, in 1953, the government introduced a new health insurance scheme for day labourers. In 1954, the employee pension system was extended to companies with five and more employees. The next giant step towards a more developed welfare state system was brought by the New Health Insurance Act of 1958, which established a mandatory universal health insurance system, finally implemented in April 1961. Only three years later, virtually all of the population was benefiting from the protection of national medical insurance, with the new health insurance system administered at municipal level. In 1959, the National Pension Law set up a new pension insurance scheme for all those who could not participate in the employee pension scheme – farmers, workers in small companies and self-employed persons. Furthermore, the new pension law also provided non-contributionary pensions for those who could not benefit from the existing pension system – people who had reached 70 and above, the handicapped and those who had lost their breadwinner like widows with children.[4] These far-reaching extensions of Japan's health and pension insurance systems in the late 1950s were motivated by the Socialists' appeal for new pensions, increased labour conflicts and the ruling Liberal Democratic Party's need to ensure the support of workers in small firms and farmers.

Though the Japanese social security system had been constructed to a large extent in the 1940s and 1950s, the level of state expenditures remained very low throughout the first three decades after the war. The reason for this was that, first, the Japanese economy started to boom in the 1960s, and thus the postwar emergency period had come to an end; and, second, after the Allied Powers occupation was over, Japan's conservative government resorted to the politics of avoiding and cutting down welfare expenditures. Japanese welfare capitalism at that time focused increasingly on the provision of employment as a functional equivalent for welfare services and benefits. Thus, labour market policies became an intrinsic element of the Japanese welfare state after the Second World War. Trade protectionism, industrial policies and minimum wage policies all focused on the pursuit of the full-employment principle. The extent of state-financed social assistance benefits was kept at very low levels, and the vast majority of welfare state expenditures, hence, were concentrated in the field of healthcare and pensions.[5] The developmental strategy of postwar conservative Japan was to concentrate resources for generation of economic growth and to avoid redistributive programmes.[6]

As a consequence, large enterprises created their own type of occupational welfare that has become so famous throughout the world. These large corporations promoted a core workforce within their companies (often counting for only 30 per cent of total employees) that profited from relative guarantees of employment until the age of 55, systematic promotions and wage increases, a series of bonuses and subsidies related to family size, need and company profitability, as well as free healthcare and recreational services.[7]

In the early 1970s, the Liberal Democratic Party lost more and more of its electoral support in the working and middle classes. Therefore, it was compelled to seek support from minority parties in securing a sound parliamentary majority. The Liberal Democratic Party had to cut the ground from under the left-wing parties' feet by launching popular social policies that had formerly been promoted by socialists and communists. Socialist and Communist local governments had already implemented free healthcare services for the elderly.[8]

The government lured members of the middle classes with universal social welfare benefits, for example child allowances. The Child Allowance Law was enacted in 1971 and the scheme went into operation in January the next year. In 1973, the government also introduced free healthcare services for those aged 70 and over. However, the new plans of Prime Minister Tanaka Kakuei of extending the Japanese welfare state system in 1973 were buried in the same year as they came into being. The government's intention to raise overall social welfare provision of the state had to been taken back owing to the economic crisis of 1973 caused by the sudden upsurge of world-wide oil prices. Since the Liberal Democratic Party regained control of the majority of seats in the Diet, the welfare state ambitions of the purely conservative Japanese government in the 1970s and for the most part of the 1980s came to a stop. In 1984, the government conducted a reform of the earlier-introduced nationwide free medical care system for the elderly, that is those aged 70 and over – 65 and over in Tokyo – so that from then on the elderly had to pay, in the beginning, 10 per cent of the costs of medical services. Whereas in the 1970s the share of social security expenditure of GDP doubled, this share remained unchanged in the 1980s, at around 14 per cent.[9]

Rising concerns about the needs of the fast-ageing society and the increasingly competitive political system caused the implementation of improvements in the welfare services sector for the elderly. In the early 1980s, the Liberal Democratic Party started to believe that the existing social insurance and social welfare provision was highly inadequate for the elderly and that there was an urgent need for government action. In 1985, the government started to pay particular attention to the problem of the ageing of society and the lack of social welfare provision for the elderly. The newly created basic pension scheme included provisions for the disabled, the elderly and surviving dependants. Both major national pension schemes, the Employment Pension Insurance and the National Pension Scheme, incorporated this new basic pension programme. This new reform, in essence, could be regarded as a partial unification of the pension insurance system. In the meantime, that is since the beginning of the 1980s, the social security system had been gradually transformed from a cash-based to a care-based system. After the introduction of the Gold Plan in 1989, new care services for the elderly were set up and the level of the existing ones upgraded. Six years later, the New Gold Plan raised the level of benefits anew.[10]

In addition, facing the worsening social conditions of the fast-growing elderly population, the government introduced a new Chronic Care Insurance in December 1997, covering all residents aged 40 and over. Social administrators had studied the possibility of introducing such a programme as early as the mid-1980s, but the final scheme, however, was fully installed only in April 2000, after a two-year preparation period.[11]

The ruling Liberal Democratic Party lost its parliamentary majority for the first time in 1993, and within a year three prime ministers had fallen from power. In summer 1994, the long-term ruling Liberal Democratic Party regained power. Together with its new junior partners in succeeding government coalitions, the LDP was forced to make concessions to the growing constituency of senior citizens of the Japanese electorate since party competition in national elections had become closer than ever before. The government estimates that by the year 2025, nearly 60 per cent of all communities in Japan will have more than a third of their total population over the age of 65. In the year 2030, it is estimated that 29 per cent of the population will be elderly people. At this time Japan has entered a new era, that of a *super-aged* society, and has to prepare itself for '*the century of the elderly*'.[12]

In the 1990s, the welfare rights of women had become the second major concern of the government. In the past, the responsibility of caring for the elderly, the sick and children had been considered as women's problems. As a result, the conservative government did not accept any responsibility for providing social welfare in those fields. Up to the mid-1970s, Japan's women's movement supported women being housewives, as family wages of male breadwinners had been rising in a fast-expanding economy since the 1950s and 1960s. But, from then on, the women's movement switched to support an economically active role of women on the formal labour market, which considerably increased the need for government welfare over time, on top of Japan's worrisome population development. Ito Peng notes that the political and demographic imperatives faced by the Japanese welfare state in the 1990s should serve as a good illustration of what happens when the family becomes overburdened by 'traditional' care and welfare responsibilities.[13]

Though the Left could not manage to come to power at the national level, the Liberal Democratic Party had to react to reform proposals of the Left and to compete with them by proposing new social policies. Other pressures stemming from officials of local and national social welfare authorities as well as non-governmental pressure groups, such as the women's movement, also contributed to the pressure the government faced in the field of social welfare. The Liberal Democratic Party, then, had to alter its basically anti-welfare stand and to extend the long-term existing social welfare and social security schemes.[14]

However, until the 1980s, the government was successful in passing the responsibility of providing social security and welfare on to the companies. Today, the Japanese welfare state system is still characterized by its dualism between the separately administered social security schemes of employees and that of the rest of the population. With regard to traditional social policy or the welfare state in a 'narrow' sense, Japan still largely resembles Western welfare models, with long-term care insurance becoming a sort of model perhaps even for the West, as it develops in an expansive direction. Looking at the Japanese welfare state in a 'wider' sense, welfare objectives of the Japanese 'welfare society' indeed predominate in the sense that a priority has been giving to policies that have enhanced people's living standards through the tax system and employment-support policies (such as trade protection, competition-inhibiting regulations, price subsidies, and so on), rather than policies that characterize traditional welfare state programmes. Thus, there is a strong resemblance to Australia situation, with regard to its regime characteristic of a *wage-earner's welfare state*.[15]

A new development on the horizon for Japanese welfare politics is the growing strength and independence of NGOs in welfare provision, which is very much needed in the light of the growing gap between the welfare needs of a fast-ageing society and the provisions made available by the state.[16]

Development of the welfare state in China

Establishing the iron rice bowl system

The Iron Rice Bowl was a central theme in the establishment of the socialist economy and society under Mao Ze-dong. The 'iron rice bowl' meant that once a person was employed by the government, he or she had stability and security; this was a great benefit to the urban population. The Communist Party of China (CPC) began, as early as the late 1940s, still during the Civil War with the Nationalists, to implement a comprehensive social security system in Manchuria. The CPC managed to set up an extensive system within only a short period of time, and then in 1948 established the first labour insurance programme in Manchuria, which at that time was under the control of the Communist forces. After the retreat of the Kuomintang to Taiwan, the Communist government announced the Labour Insurance Regulations in October 1950 that implemented the labour insurance programme nation-wide. The labour insurance provided benefits, for example to the sick, the disabled and pensioners, as well as expecting and nursing mothers. The labour insurance scheme covered those employees who worked in state-operated, joint state-private, cooperative and private factories and mines, with more than 100 workers and staff. The coverage of the labour insurance was extended significantly after only two years of operation, when it brought units of factories, mines and transport enterprises, communication services and state-run construction enterprises also under its ambit.[17]

Labour insurance in state-owned enterprises was administered by the All China Federation of Labour Unions and its local branches. All the contributions to the labour insurance came from employers, who had to pay 3 per cent of wages to the labour insurance fund. This fund was operated jointly by both companies and labour unions, and 30 per cent of the fund was given to companies that got into serious financial difficulties. Amendments of the Labour Insurance Regulations in 1956 and 1957 extended the coverage, so that by 1958 participants in the programme had risen to 45 million.[18]

From then on, the development of social insurance in China experienced a slight setback in terms of coverage. As a consequence of the political turmoil of the Great Leap Forward and the Cultural Revolution, the government, party and the labour organizations were significantly weakened. In 1969, the administration of the pension system, therefore, was given into the hands of enterprises on an *ad hoc* basis. Hence, understanding the development of the Chinese welfare state is intertwined with understanding state institutions and their structures.[19] Only in the early 1980s did the state begin to relocate the management of the pension system and other social security systems to higher administrative levels. Nonetheless, the Chinese welfare state system continued to develop during the 1960s and 1970s, during which time the government focused its attention on the provision of public housing, medical care services and special homes for the elderly, the disabled and orphans.

The outstanding feature of the Chinese welfare state system was and still is the great dualism of welfare rights between people living in the cities and people living in the countryside. Although about 81 per cent of the population were residing in the countryside in the 1970s, the welfare state system was particularly designed for workers and employees in the cities who might have represented an acute danger for the Communist regime in times of social discontent. The state intervention that was aimed at improving the welfare of city dwellers helped to sustain the legitimacy of the state and the power of enterprises over the workforce,[20] thus considerably decreasing the likelihood of social uprisings and increasing support for the long-term ruling Communist government of China. By the late 1970s, the Chinese welfare state catered to about four-fifths of the urban population, while only 19 per cent of the population were living in the cities at that time. This means that the Chinese welfare state was only existent in the cities, not in the countryside.

The communist welfare state from the early 1950s to the late 1970s came to be known as the iron rice bowl system; a Chinese version of 'the cradle-to-the-grave' welfare system in Sweden. The Chinese system was attuned to benefit urban workers who were employed by the government, state-run companies and collective enterprises – the vast majority of the urban workforce. As already noted, this was for the reason of the government's need, in the past, to ensure social peace in the cities. Nonetheless, the argument that people living in the countryside, most of whom were farmers, were not in such a need of social insurance benefits because they were living in an archaic society, is also valid.[21] The dualism between urban and rural China in terms of social development is highly linked to the different stages of economic development of the respective areas. Since China was, at that time, still a Third World country, it would have been impossible to set up a social insurance scheme financed by the national budget that would have incorporated the vast majority of the population living in non-developed parts of China.

The Chinese government first had to tackle other, much more urgent tasks; for example safeguarding the minimal standards of living in the cities, where people could not rely on vegetables planted by themselves or livestock raised by themselves, and where people could not rely on the support of family members, relatives and neighbours as much as people in the countryside. As a result, the Chinese government focused on the development of social care service institutions and other welfare sectors, such as public housing. Another important task the government began to concentrate on was the demographic development of the population, since it wanted to make an end to the miserable conditions of its people and to enhance economic and social development at the same time. For these reasons, the government heavily promoted a new birth control policy aimed at reducing the number of children a couple had to only one. The one-child policy included a great number of incentives and disincentives in order to ensure its compliance. The new birth-control measures were much more effective in the cities than in the countryside.[22]

After the introduction of reform and open policy

The year 1978 marked a watershed not only in Chinese politics as a whole, but also in social politics. Prior to 1978, the state ran a sort of cradle-to-the-grave welfare system for most of the city dwellers tied to the workplace providing pension and sick-leave benefits, healthcare benefits, public housing, various social assistance programmes and a great number of community and cultural facilities. Thereafter, the government began to introduce major reforms of the healthcare system, especially a new responsibility for medical and healthcare institutions, diversifications to allow medical professionals to run private practices, and the introduction of medical cooperatives to reduce inefficiencies by allowing the joint usage of technical equipment and human resources of formerly strictly separated medical institutions.[23]

The state also upgraded the pension system from the company level to the provincial government level. In 1985, the Chinese government acknowledged the need for setting up new social insurance programmes for workers and employees of government institutions as well as state-owned, collective-owned and other enterprises in the Seventh Five Year Plan for National Economic and Social Development. The new social security system of China, to be sure, continued to focus on the protection of the strong, while neglecting the needs of the weak and the poor. Since only permanent workers in cities were covered, the Chinese welfare state system cannot be properly called a 'socialist social security system with Chinese characteristics' which has been put forward as the new vision for Chinese social policy-makers since the 1990s.[24]

The government emphasized the limits it had set for its responsibilities for social security and pointed out the need to focus on the welfare functions provided for families and communities. The principle *'each according to his work'* guided the implementation of new social policies, and the government intended to wipe out the phenomenon of *'eating from the same rice pot'*. They increasingly promoted the idea that welfare dependency is 'potentially parasitic and feckless'.[25] After 1994, the government speeded up the pooling of pension funds, considerably extended healthcare services and also started to unify maternity benefit schemes. The new reforms also led to the sharing of the financial burden of social security provision. Now, the premiums of employers and employees would help the government to reduce the heavy load of financing the social security system. As a response to new mass unemployment caused by economic restructuring in the state-owned enterprises, the government created a new unemployment insurance system in 1986. In the 1980s and 1990s, over 100 million farmers left their home villages and poured into the cities, especially those situated in the East. This new development aggravated the social conditions in China's coastal cities and larger inland cities, and it was for those reasons that the Chinese government was very keen on the extension of the existing pension and unemployment systems.

With the economic reforms in 1978, the state Council began to issue new pension regulations that aimed at reaffirming certain pension rights. The government granted new and higher benefits, with replacement rates of 60, 70 and 75 per cent (for 10, 15 and 20 or more years of service respectively), and introduced major incentives for early retirement, making early retirement an option, in some cases from as early as 35 years of age (which mainly served as a means to reduce the number of the unemployed after restructuring the state-owned enterprises). In only a decade, the number of pensioners jumped from 3.14 to 22 million, and expenditures grew rapidly, multiplying almost 19 times. Over the same period, contribution rates also rose from 2.8 to 10.6 per cent of wages. From the 1980s onwards, the government set in motion a series of experiments that aimed at finding new solutions to the pension problem. These experimental/pilot programmes focused primarily on: (1) introducing a social pooling system, effectively changing the enterprise-based system into a social-insurance-based system; (2) introducing individual contributions and raising overall contribution rates to counteract the explosive development in pension costs; and (3) establishing individual savings plans to supplement pensions. In 1995, the state Council proposed two models providing pension security; one involving individual accounts, and the other social pooling. Localities could opt for one of the two, or a combination thereof. Plan I emphasized individual accounts, while Plan II emphasized the social component. The state Council Document 26 of July 1997 specified the social pooling and individual account arrangements. Provinces were to pool funds from enterprises (no more than 20 per cent of payroll) and individual workers (4 per cent of wages, gradually increasing to 8 per cent). The pay-as-you-go pillar is financed entirely by 13 per cent of the enterprise contribution and intends to offer a 20 per cent replacement rate. The individual accounts are funded by the remaining 7 per cent of the enterprise contribution plus the employee contribution.[26]

Besides its efforts in reforming the pension system, the government also set up a new plan of extending the coverage of health insurance to 70 per cent of the urban population. The Ninth Five Year Plan, covering the period from 1996 to 2000, set out to incorporate 50 million new members into the health insurance system.[27] But, as of today, the Chinese healthcare system is established only marginally in the countryside, since 80 per cent of all hospitals and doctors are concentrated in urban areas. The reform of the Chinese economic system has also brought along an enormous change of the education system. From 1998 to 2000, the enrolment of universities and colleges – though still lagging behind other developing countries – doubled to reach two million.[28]

The traditional economic and societal system of the backward areas is going to change in the years ahead. This inevitable trend will necessitate implementing a welfare system in the countryside. The Communist Party of China is aware of this and has, therefore, been undertaking great efforts to fulfil this strenuous task. This is especially the case since the overheating of the economy started to become a top priority of the Chinese government in early 2004, while rural development and the increase of farmers' incomes became a new priority among the governing circles.[29] The growing middle class in the countryside, especially in developing small and medium-sized towns, is beginning to demand a modern lifestyle – for example cars and modern housing facilities, and also raises the demand for government welfare and social security provision.

In the last two decades, the Chinese welfare state system has developed into a more universal social security system; that is, the social insurance system in China is no longer divided occupationally. However, there are differences among provinces and especially between the cities and the countryside. Up to now, the function of the Chinese welfare state system has been to address the social welfare needs of the urban resident population. With the ongoing industrialization of the Chinese hinterland, the Chinese system will certainly be extended to include more and more of China's vast rural population.[30] In the meanwhile the Chinese welfare system has continued to grow at an accelerated speed. Coverage of the old-age insurance programme increased from 86.71 million in late 1997 to 108.02 million by the end of 2001. The number of those currently enjoying basic old-age pensions also increased from 25.33 to 33.81 million over the same period, with the average monthly basic pension per person growing from 430 to 556 yuan.[31]

Conclusion

A comparison of the history of social policy in Japan and China (see Table 18.1) reveals the dramatic changes of development of these welfare state systems as well as their major determinants. Prior to 1945, the development of the Japanese welfare system hinged on the occurrence of economic and natural disasters, as well as the involvement in wars. After the Second World War, the new Constitution stipulated that 'the State shall use its endeavours for the promotion and extension of social welfare and security, and of public health' (Art. 25/2).[32] However, it was not the Constitution which determined postwar social politics, but certain political circumstances that directly led to welfare state extensions. Only in the late 1940s and early 1950s can the new social policy legislation be directly ascribed to the impact of the Constitution and the political circumstances of the years under foreign occupation.

In the decades following the War, both working-class and middle-class members were highly attracted to political parties of the Left. Since the left-wing parties heavily promoted new social policies, the Liberal Democrats had to climb on the bandwagon in order to secure its single-party rule.[33] The economic crises of the 1970s, however, led to a major reevaluation of the government's role in providing social welfare. Beginning in the mid-1980s, the Japanese government introduced a new social policy designed for the aged, especially in social care services. In the early 1990s, the long-term ruling Liberal Democratic Party not only lost its majority of seats, but was also excluded from government formation twice. The New Gold Plan of 1995 and the Chronic Care Insurance of 1997 were the first major steps of the government in addressing the problems of the fast-ageing society in a more competitive political environment.

The Chinese welfare state system (Table 18.1), on the contrary, started to develop only after 1945. The Communist Party introduced a nationwide labour-insurance programme from the very beginning of its rule, and by the late 1950s China had already developed a welfare state system at a comparatively high level when compared to other countries at the same developmental stage. Although the late 1960s represented a major setback for the development of the Chinese welfare state, the Communist Party began to introduce new social policies in the 1970s, especially with regard to pensions, healthcare and housing.

Between 1978 and 1984, the government prepared for a major reform of the social insurance system and, thus, launched a series of studies, discussions and dialogues. Major reforms, however, took place only after 1984.

Table 18.1   Summary of major historical changes

Japan	Mainland China
1 Late 1930s and early 1940s: massive involvement in wars made governmental social welfare (especially social insurance systems) necessary	Late 1940s to the late 1950s: victory of communism and establishment of a labour insurance system following the Russian model of social insurance at factory level (thus covering only workers and employees in industry and government institutions, known as the 'iron rice bowl system')
2 Late 1940s and early 1950s: impact of foreign occupation and the Japanese Constitution	Late 1950s until late 1960s: weakening of state institutions hindered the development of the labour insurance system
3 Late 1950s: new social policies promoted or strengthened left-wing parties at the local level and forced the LDP to implement major changes in the fields of pension and health insurance	In the 1970s and early 1980s: a stronger focus on public housing and social care services
4 In the early 1970s: electoral losses compelled the LDP to make short-term commitments to social welfare policies; and subsequent economic recessions of the 1970s caused the abolishment of those plans	From the mid-1980s to the late 1990s: reform of social insurance programmes, especially the pension system, solving the problem of absent risk-pooling by establishing pension funds at Provincial levels; and introduction of unemployment insurance
5 From the mid-1980s to the present: a rising concern about the fast ageing of society; the vast gap between future needs and existing social insurance provisions has become visible, and politicians start addressing the problem	From the late 1990s onwards: reform of the health insurance programme and extension of membership of social insurance
6 From the early 1990s to the present: increasing electoral competition, use of election promises in order to win elections becomes more popular	

The efficiency of the healthcare system has been largely improved by structural reforms and opening of the health sector. The pension insurance scheme was upgraded from enterprise to local and provincial government levels, solving the problem of absent risk-pooling of former pension funds

Table 18.2 Summary of major challenges for the future

Japan	Mainland China
1 The ageing of society and the diminishing capacity of the family to take care of the elderly	Economic development and the resulting transformation of society (i.e. farmers become city dwellers who cannot rely on traditional forms of social security, such as the family, friends, neighbours and the village)
2 The rising share of women participating in the labour market and increased demand for social welfare services	The ageing of society, the diminishing capacity of the family to take care of the elderly, and the effect of the one-child policy on age-structures, especially in the large cities

that were implemented at the factory level only. Furthermore, employee contributions were introduced and extended, and individual accounts created to shore up old-age pension security. In July 1986, the government installed unemployment insurance for state-owned enterprises in response to the massive layoffs in the state sector. From the late 1990s onwards, the government began to focus on the reform of the health insurance system and extension of membership into the countryside.[34]

The government's policies towards migrant workers are not accommodative. The social exclusion of migrant workers is strengthened by the practice of household registration and, generally, social security, social assistance and social provision (for example kindergartens, schools) for migrant workers are not available. Today, only 3.4 per cent of migrant workers are covered by old-age insurance, while only 2.7 per cent of them can enjoy medical insurance.[35] Migrant workers are left to organize their own kindergartens and schools, and they are discriminated against (by the public authorities) in all major aspects of life, for example with regard to housing and labour welfare. Thus, the biggest threat to the construction of a more universal welfare system in China is the obvious neglect of the issue of welfare and equal treatment of the migrant versus the resident population in the fast-growing cities.

In 1989, the Japanese government took up more responsibility for the elderly population. In 2000, Hiromu Nonaka, the Secretary General of the Liberal Democratic Party, expressed the government's deep concern about the rapidly ageing society by stating that in the twenty-first century Japan's population will be the 'oldest of any' in the world.[36]

The imbalance between the proportions of the working young and the elderly will cause a great strain on the Japanese social security system (Table 18.2). By 2020, approximately every two workers will be supporting one pensioner, while in 1992 the ratio of workers to pensioners was five to one. The Japanese government also acknowledges the increased need for social workers and care specialists and has started to promote these two professions, while the Gold Plan and the New Gold Plan are mainly to focus on long-term projects for the future, in which the current working generations have their interest at stake. The living standards of the current elderly population, however, has only attracted marginal attention of top policymakers and the government still places emphasis on Confucian ethics, even though more and more elderly are living in poverty. Huck-ju Kwon notes, that 'what should now urgently be called for is not Confucian ethics but state action for the elderly'. He continues that 'Confucian ethics are still working, but it alone cannot work, while the rapid ageing process in East Asia has put increasing strain on the family'. This needs to be taken into account while reforming the Japanese welfare model at the transition into a super-aged society.[37]

Another major challenge of the future is the decreasing capacity of the family to take care of the elderly in combination with high female labour-force participation rates. The existing social security system discourages women from participating in the workforce since the government has presumed that women would continue to exercise welfare functions according to traditional care-role models of the patriarchal Japanese society. However, in recent years a lager proportion of women have chosen to work instead of staying at home to be housewifes or nurses for the young, the sick and the old. This new development creates a major challenge for the Japanese welfare state system.[38]

China today also faces two major problems (Table 18.2): first, changing social institutions along with rapid economic development (especially in the rural areas) and, second, the ageing of society in combination with the outcomes of the one-child policy (especially in the cities). Widespread dire poverty in the countryside calls for a massive extension of the social security system. The government poverty alleviation strategy is exclusively focused on a limited number of very poor rural counties, and social security provision by collectives is no longer significant. Nonetheless, dire poverty can be found across all regions and in almost all counties, and economic development of the Chinese hinterland will inevitably cause social instability. Modern lifestyles demand the implementation of modern social security institutions.[39]

When the traditional extended families are replaced by nuclear families, and when the young migrate to the cities, the elderly are left behind without subsistence support. It is estimated that 100 to 200 million peasants have left their farms – serving as a cheap workforce for the booming economy – adding to the pressure for developing a more inclusive welfare state system. Moreover, the fast-ageing society, especially in the cities where the implementation of the one-child policy has been much more successful, not only increases the need to upgrade social insurance provisions, but also social care services for the elderly. This leaves the government no choice but to rethink its current welfare policies and extend the existing welfare state institutions as early as possible. However, the emphasis in the reform of the social security system will be on social insurance, leaving the task of providing social assistance and social care services to the informal and private sector.[40]

Notes

1   Gordon White, Roger Goodman and Huck-ju Kwon, 'The Politics of Welfare in East Asia', in R. Maidment, D. Goldblatt and J. Mitchell (eds), *Governance in the Asia-Pacific*, London; Routledge, 1998.

2   See Chitoshi Yanaga, *Japanese People and Politics*, New York: John Wiley & Sons, 1956; Takeshi Takahashi and Yoshiko Someya, 'Japan', in J. Dixon and H.S. Kim, (eds), *Social Welfare in Asia*, Kent: Croom Helm, 1985; Stephen J. Anderson, *Welfare Policy and Politics in Japan: Beyond the Developmental State*, New York: Paragon House, 1993; Arthur Gould, *Capitalist Welfare Systems; A Comparison of Japan, Britain and Sweden*, Harlow, UK: Longman, 1993; Bernard S. Silberman *et al.*, *Japan in Crisis: Essays on Taisho Democracy*, Ann Arbor, MI: University of Michigan Press, 1999; and Gregory J. Kasza, 'War and Welfare Policy in Japan', *Journal of Asian Studies*, vol. 61, no. 2, pp. 417–35, 2002.

3   See Sheldon Garon, *Molding Japanese Minds: The State in Everyday Life*, Princeton: Princeton University Press, 1997; Naomi Maruo, 'The Development of the Welfare Mix in Japan', in R. Rose and R. Shiratori (eds), *The Welfare State, East and West*, New York: Oxford University Press, 1999; Anderson, n. 2; Takahashi and Someya, n. 2; and Kasza, n. 2.

4   See Gould, n. 2; Anderson, n. 2; JMHW, Ministry of Health and Welfare, Japan, 'Development of Japan's Social Security Policies, 2000, www.mhw.go.jp/ssp_in_j/services; Takahashi and Someya, n. 2; and Mitsuya Ichien, 'Japanese Social Security: Its Past, Present and Future', in J. Dixon and R. Scheurell (eds), *Social Security Programs: A Cross-Cultural Comparative Perspective*, Westport, CT: Greenwood Press, 1995.

5   See Joji Watanuki, 'Is there a Japanese-Type Welfare Society?', *International Sociology*, vol. 1, no. 3, pp. 259–69; Roger Goodman and Ito Peng, 'The East Asian Welfare States: Peripatetic Learning, Adaptive Change, and Nation Building', in G. Esping-Andersen (ed.), *Welfare States in Transition*, London: Sage, 1996; and compare John Ceighton Campbell, 'Japanese Social Policy in Comparative Perspective', WBI working papers, Washington, DC, World Bank, 2002.

6   Bai Gao, 'Japan's Economic Dilemma: The Institutional Origins of Prosperity and Stagnation', Cambridge, UK: Cambridge University Press, 2001.

7   See Christian Aspalter, *Conservative Welfare State Systems in East Asia*, Westport, CT: Praeger, 2001; Ezra Vogel, *Japan as Number One*, Harvard: Harvard University Press, 1979; and T.J. Pempel, 'Japan's Creative Conservatism, Continuity under Change', in F. Castles (ed.), *The Comparative History of Public Policy*, Cambridge, UK: Polity Press, 1989.

8   See Gould, n. 2; and Aspalter, n. 7.

9   See Nelson W.S. Chow, 'Social Security in Japan – A Historical and Structural Analysis', *The Hong Kong Journal of Social Work*, vol. 18, no. 1, pp. 23–8, 1984;

Anderson, n. 2; Maruo, n. 3; and Akiko Hashimoto, 'Ageing in Japan', in D. Phillips (ed.), *Ageing in East and Southeast Asia*, London: Edward Arnold, 1992.

10 See Gould, n. 2; Ito Peng, 'Japanese Welfare State: Perspective and Patterns of Change', paper presented at the Conference on New Prospects for Social Welfare System in East Asia, National Chi Nan University, Puli, Taiwan, 1998; and Ito Peng, 'Gender and Welfare State Restructuring in Japan', in C. Aspalter (ed.), *Discovering the Welfare State in East Asia*, Westport, CT: Praeger, 2002.

11 See Ito Peng, 'Gender, Demography, and Welfare State Restructuring in Japan', in K. Marshall and O. Butzbach (eds), *New Social Policy Agendas for Europe and Asia: Challenges, Experiences, and Lessons*, Washington, DC: World Bank, 2003; Nobuhiko Yamazaki, 'The National Experience of Japan', in ISSA (ed.), *Social Security Challenge in Asia and the Pacific*, Social Security Documentation no. 25, Manila, ISSA, 2000; On-kwok Lai, 'Long-Term Care Policy Reform in Japan', *Journal of Aging and Social Policy*, vol. 13, no. 2., 2002; and Christian Aspalter and On-kwok Lai, 'Welfare Capitalism in Japan: Past, Recent and Future Developments', in C. Aspalter (ed.), *Welfare Capitalism Around the World*, Hong Kong: Casa Verde Publishing, 2003.

12 See Ito Peng, n. 11; and Scott A. Bass, Robert Morris, and Masato Oka (eds), *Public Policy and the Old Age Revolution in Japan*, Binghamton, NY: Haworth, 1996; and Janet Primono, 'Nursing Around the World: Japan – Preparing for the Century of the Elderly', *Online Journal of Issues in Nursing*, 31 May 2000.

13 See Ito Peng, n. 11.

14 See the *driving forces thesis* of the author, which holds that party competition in democratic elections and pressure arising from the formation and protests of social movements are the key explanatory variables in determining welfare state construction and extension, especially over longer periods of time; Christian Aspalter, *The Driving Forces Behind the Welfare State: Party Competition and Social Movements*, dissertation, University of Linz, Austria, 1999; Christian Aspalter, *Importance of Christian and Social Democratic Movements in Welfare Politics: With Special Reference to Germany, Austria, and Sweden*, New York: Nova Science, 2001; and Christian Aspalter, 'Exploring Old and New Shores in Welfare State Theory', in C. Aspalter (ed.), *Discovering the Welfare State in East Asia*, Westport, CT: Praeger, 2002.

15 See John Ceighton Campbell, n. 5; and Christian Aspalter, 'Welfare Capitalism in Australia', in C. Aspalter (ed.), *Neoliberalism and the Australian Welfare State*, Hong Kong: Casa Verde, 2003.

16 See Gerald Hursh-Cesar and Jeremy Silverman (eds), *Social Welfare in Japan: At the Crossroads of Top Down and Bottom Up*, Washington, DC, Forum for Intercultural Communication, 2004, www.globalwoman.org/news/japan.pdf

17 See Nelson W.S. Chow, *Socialist Welfare with Chinese Characteristics: The Reform of the Social Security System in China*, Hong Kong: Centre of Asian Studies, The University of Hong Kong, 2000; and Nelson W.S. Chow and Christian Aspalter, 'The Welfare State in Mainland China: From Enterprise-based to Insurance-based Social Security', in C. Aspalter (ed.), *The Welfare State in Emerging-Market Economies: With Case Studies from Latin America, Eastern Europe, and Asia*, Hong Kong: Casa Verde Publishing, 2003.

18 See Peter Nan-shong Lee, 'Reforming the Social Security System in China', in S. Nagel and M. Mills (eds), *Public Policy in China*, Westport, CT: Greenwood Press, 1993.

19   See Christian Aspalter, 'Politics and its Impact on Social Policy in Taiwan, Hong Kong and Mainland China', *Social Policy Review*, vol. 13, 2001; and Sheying Chen, *Social Policy of the Economic State and Community Care in Chinese Culture, Aging, Family, Urban Change, and the Socialist Welfare Pluralism*, Aldershot, UK: Avebury, 1996.

20   See Linda Wong and Ka-ho Mok, 'The Reform and the Changing Social Context', in L. Wong and S. MacPherson (eds), *Social Change and Social Policy in Contemporary China*, Aldershot, UK: Avebury, 1995.

21   See Christian Aspalter, 'The Chinese Welfare State in International Comparison: A Comparison of Sweden, the United Kingdom, the United States, Australia, Italy, Japan, Singapore and China', paper presented at a lecture at the Medical College of Shantou University, Guangdong, China, 25 October 2000.

22   See John E. Dixon, *The Chinese Welfare System, 1949–1979*, New York: Praeger, 1981; Mark Selden and Lai-yin You, 'The Reform of Social Welfare in China', *World Development*, vol. 25, no. 10, 1997, pp. 1657–68; Lee, n. 18; Guihua Ma, 'Silver Tide in China', *China Daily*, 19 April 1999; Nelson W.S. Chow, 'Aging in China', *Journal of Sociology and Social Welfare*, vol. 26, no. 1, 1999, pp. 25–49; and Gabe Wang, *China's Population: Problems, Thoughts and Policies*, Aldershot, UK: Ashgate, 1999.

23   See Aidi Hu, 'Reforming China's Social Security System: Facts and Perspectives', *International Social Security Review*, no. 3, 1997, pp. 45–65; and Guangde Sun, 'Health Care Administration in China', in S. Nagel and M. Mills (eds), *Public Policy in China*, Westport, CT: Greenwood Press, 1993.

24   Nelson W.S. Chow and Christian Aspalter, n. 17.

25   See Nelson W.S. Chow, 'Social Security Reforms in China', in J. Dixon and R. Scheurell (eds), *Social Security Programs: A Cross-Cultural Comparative Perspective*, Westport, CT: Greenwood Press, 1995; Gordon White *et al.*, n. 1.

26   See Ivonne Sin, 'Pension Systems in East Asia and the Pacific', World Bank report, www.worldbank.org, 2004; and World Bank, 'Old Age Security Pension Reform in China', Washington DC: World Bank, 1997.

27   See Nelson W.S. Chow, 'Social Security Reforms in China – An Attempt to Construct a Socialist Security System with Chinese Characteristics', in L. Wong and S. MacPherson (eds), *Social Change and Social Policy in Contemporary China*, Aldershot: Avebury, 1995; and Nelson W.S. Chow, 2000, n. 17.

28   See Yongdong Niu, 'Welfare of the Elderly in China', *Research Paper*, Medical College, Shantou University, Guangdong, China, 2000; Hu Zhao, 'Social Security Reform in China, *Research Paper*, Medical College, Shantou University, Guangdong, China, 2000; Baoxia Zhu, '*Health for All* Remains Country's Prime Target, Medical Care Reform Pools Funds from State, Employees, Employers', *China Daily*, 3 October 2000, p. 5; and Nei Guo, 'Education Moves Forward: New Strategy Pushes Reform of Schools', *China Daily*, 4 October 2000.

29   See Patricia M. Howard, *Breaking the Iron Rice Bowl: Prospects for Socialism in the Chinese Countryside*, New York: M.E. Sharpe, 1988; and see e.g. Hong Kong Trade Development Council, 'China's Recent Tightening Measures', www.tdctrade.com/econforum/tdc/tdc040502.htm, 2004.

30   See Christian Aspalter, 'Late Industrialization and Welfare State System in China', paper presented at The 2004 International Conference on the Origin and Structure of Asian Welfare States, Korean Political Science Association, Daejon, Korea, 25 June 2004.

31   White Paper on Labour and Social Security in China, Office of the State Council of the People's Republic of China, Beijing, 29 April 2002.

32 See the Constitution of Japan, www.uni-wuerzburg.de/law
33 See the findings of Christian Aspalter, *Democratization and Welfare State Development in Taiwan*, Aldershot, UK: Ashgate, 2002.
34 See Aimin Chen, Gordon G. Liu and Kevin H. Zhang (eds), 'Urbanization and Social Welfare in China', Aldershot, UK: Ashgate, 2004.
35 See *China Daily*, 'Social Security Plan Has Long Way to Go', 20 May 2004.
36 See Liberal Democratic Party, 'Concerning the Implementation of the Nursing Care Insurance Programme, Statement from the Secretary General, 2000, www.jimin.or.jp/jimin/english/e-index.html
37 See Mikiso Hane, *Eastern Phoenix: Japan since 1945*, Boulder, CO: Westview Press, 1996; and Harry Kaneharu Nishio, 'Japan's Welfare Vision: Dealing with a Rapidly Increasing Elderly Population', in L. Katz Olson (ed.), *The Graying of the World: Who will Care for the Frail Elderly?*, Binghampton, NY: Haworth Press, 1994; and John W. Traphagan and John Knight (eds), *Demographic Change and the Family in Japan's Aging Society*, Albany, NY: State University of New York Press, 2003; Huck-ju Kwon, 'Income Transfers to the Elderly in East Asia: Testing Asian Values', CASE paper, no. 27, London School of Economics, June, 1999.
38 See Machiko Osawa, 'The Changing Women's Employment and the Role of Social Policies in Japan', in B. Koskaiho (ed.), *Women, the Elderly and Social Policy in Finland and Japan: The Muse or the Worker Bee?*, Aldershot: Avebury, 1995; and Ito Peng, n. 10.
39 See Carl Riskin, 'Social Development and China's Changing Development Strategy', in D. Ghai (ed.), *Social Development and Public Policy: A Study of Some Successful Experiences*, Basingstoke, UK: Palgrave Macmillan, 2000; and Xiangqun Chang, 'Fat Pigs and Women's Gift: Agnatic and Non-Agnatic Social Support in Kaixiangong Village', in J. West, M. Zhao and Y. Cheng (eds), *Women of China: Economic and Social Transformation*, Basingstoke, UK: Palgrave Macmillan, 2000.
40 See Nelson W.S. Chow, 1995, n. 25; Zhenglin Guo and Daming Zhou, 'Rural Development and Social Security', in G. Guldin (ed.), *Farewell to Peasant China: Rural Urbanization and Social Change in the Late Twentieth Century*, Armonk, NY: East Gate, 1997; and Shangquan Gao, *Two Decades of Reform in China*, Singapore: World Scientific Publishing, 1999; and Nancy H.H Chen, interview with, at International Symposium on Comparative Social Policy: Taiwan in the Global World, Graduate School of Social Policy and Social Work, National Chi Nan University, Puli, Taiwan, 31 May 2004.

19
The Welfare State System in India

Anand Kumar

Introduction

The evolution of welfare states has been a major factor in promoting and protecting democratic citizenship in nation-states of the modern world system. This is often perceived as a synthesis of the idea of 'rights' and the quest for 'equality', because the welfare states are guided by three institutional principles: economic management, provision of services for all citizens and social insurance.

According to T.H. Marshall, the welfare state is a critical stage in the long struggle for equal citizenship.[1] What then is equal citizenship? It is constructed on the basis of togetherness of three sets of rights – civil and legal rights, political rights, and social rights through various stages over the last several centuries. These rights are anchored in the recognition of 'equal social worth' of all members of society. They promote the ideal of enabling the process of achieving full membership in the community, and to participate in 'valued and worthwhile ways of living'. This also include a concern with social integration, or social solidarity, with promoting enough commonality in the social experiences and ways of life of different sections of the society so that genuine equality of respect will be possible. Equal social worth is closely tied to the idea of self-respect, and equality of respect is a necessary condition for self-respect in a democracy.[2] In other words, the democratic welfare state is an attempt to solve a serious challenge to social integration that necessarily results from the central role of markets in the organization of modern society where some people are deprived of the very means of survival and the possibility of maintaining their well-being and dignity due to poverty which causes undeserved exile from society.[3]

The Indian trajectory in making a democratic welfare state represents a good conjunction of the imperatives of political freedom, economic justice and social reforms. The ideas of eradication of poverty and discrimination and the goal of establishing a free 'Republic of India' through removal of foreign rule were considered as two sides of the same coin. This essay about the welfare state in India is organized in such a way to give a historical view of the process of its conceptualization in the Indian setting, the rediscovery of 'poverty' since independence, the impact of liberalization, an overview of its functioning and impact during the five decades of freedom, and the new challenges in the context of liberalization and globalization since the 1990s.

An attempt to comprehend the Indian experience of construction of its welfare state in the last five decades needs to recognize that India is a post-colonial society where the colonial heritage in the state-craft, and the legacy of an anti-imperialist national movement in the political community and political culture, play critical roles in a contradictory manner. This relationship between the 'colonial past' and 'democratic present' is very significant for understanding the changing nature and orientation of the state in India since independence in 1947. It is also necessary to remember the differences between the rise of democratic polity in Europe and the emergence of a welfare state in India. To quote Jawaharlal Nehru:

> In Western countries, full blooded democracy with adult suffrage came to the people very late, in the Twentieth Century. They had in the meantime profited by the Industrial Revolution. They got the resources before they gained democracy so that when the demands came for better living conditions they had the resources to fulfill them. In India we have full blooded democracy but not the resources. . . . I think that India will advance along the particular path of democracy with a large measure of socialism – not doctrinaire socialism but practical, pragmatic socialism – which will fit in with the thinking of India and with the demands of India.[4]

These specific and comparative aspects of India help us in contextualizing the project of nation-building through planning for a welfare state. To be precise, the Indian political processes are being shaped by continuous interaction between the imperatives of: (a) interest groups dynamics; (b) democratization; (c) decolonization; and (d) nation-building. These four factors provide the basis for legitimacy of the post-colonial state. They also give content to the concepts of 'public welfare' and 'national interest'. As a consequence, there are several changes in state and society relationship in India in this period which have caused: (i) a decline of politics and rise of economics; (ii) a rise of dominant caste coalitions and decline of upper caste hegemony; (iii) erosion of a national constitutional consensus and rise of centrifugal movements; (iv) stress on decentralization along with weakening of the process of centre-formation including planning; (v) the rise of movements of erstwhile marginalized categories of people like women, depressed classes, minorities, ethnic groups, and so on; (vi) a rolling back of the state under the pressure of global forces of liberalization; and (ix) attempting a new configuration between community, state and market to address the problems of poverty, citizenship and nation-building.

Conceptualization of the welfare state in India

What are the landmarks in the conceptualization of the welfare state in India? It has been accomplished in two phases: (i) the period of a national movement for freedom from foreign rule; and (ii) the making of the Indian Constitution.

The Indian national movement was led by a leadership conscious of the importance of freedom and planning for social and economic development. It was able to focus the attention of the masses upon growing poverty and the recurrence of famine which was due to defective policies of the colonial government. It was the considered view of leading public men like Dadabhai Naoroji (1825–1917), M.G. Ranade (1842–1901) and R.C. Dutt (1848–1909) that no solution could be found for the social and economic backwardness of India by the British government pledged to a policy of *laissez-faire*, but that only a national government which actively promoted development by direct government action could bring about improvement in living standards.

The resolutions of the Indian National Congress from 1929 onwards emphasized the need 'to make revolutionary changes in the present economic structure of the society and to remove grave inequalities in order to remove poverty and ameliorate the condition of the masses'. The resolution of 1931 underlined that 'political freedom must include real economic freedom of the starving millions' and elaborated the fundamental rights which should be included in the Constitution of free India to provide a basis for it. It was followed by the formation of a National Planning Committee on the initiative of Subhas Chandra Bose who was President of the Indian National Congress. It consisted of 15 members including industrialists, economists, financiers, professors and scientists in addition to representatives of provincial governments. The Committee created wide interest in the country about the need of a welfare state for coordinated planning as the only means of bringing about a rapid increase in the standards of living through fundamental changes in the social and economic structure.[5]

A complementary process of conceptualization was contributed by the constant debate about the nature and priorities of the state in post-colonial India among the Gandhians, socialists, communists, radical humanists and other ideological groups in the national movement. The charters of demands adopted by various class organizations of industrialists, merchants, peasants and industrial workers also had a significant impact.

The concept of the welfare state became the lodestar of the Constituent Assembly of India. It made its impact upon the orientation of the leading lights of the Assembly who wanted to secure 'justice – social, economic and political' for all citizens of the Republic. They were very clear in their minds that without social and economic democracy, political democracy had no meaning in a poor country like India. The Preamble, Fundamental Rights (Articles 12 to 35), Directive Principles of State Policy (Articles 36 to 51), and the special provisions for scheduled castes and tribes and backward classes (Articles 330 to 342) are significant dimensions of the Indian Constitution from this perspective. They created the thrust for progress from political democracy to social and economic democracy which means 'working for a certain measure of well-being for all'. In fact, for founding fathers like Dr B.R. Ambedkar, social and economic democracy was the real aim and ultimate goal.

The Preamble of the Constitution commits the state to the development of a free society based on the dignity of the individual in which there would be equality of status and opportunity and justice – social, economic and political. The state has to endeavour towards harmonization of interests between individuals, between groups and between individuals and groups on the one hand, and interests of the community on the other. It is most significant that the Preamble places justice higher than the other principles of liberty, equality and fraternity.[6]

The values embedded in the Preamble are elaborated in the Fundamental Rights and the Directive Principles. The Fundamental Rights covered all the traditional civil and political rights included in the Universal Declaration of Human Rights. There are five broad categories of fundamental rights: (1) The right to equality including equality before law and the equal protection of laws (Article 1), prohibition of discrimination on grounds of religion, race, caste, sex, or place of birth (Article 15), equality of opportunity in matters of public employment (Article 16); and abolition of untouchability and the system of titles (Articles 17 and 18): (2) the right to freedom including the right to protection of life and personal liberty (Article 21), and the right to freedom of speech and expression, assembly, association or union, movement and to reside and settle in any part of India, and the right to practice any profession or occupation (Article 19); (3) the right against exploitation, prohibiting all from of forced labour, child labour and traffic in human beings (Articles 23 to 28); (4) the right of minorities to conserve their culture, language and script and to establish and administer educational institutions of their choice (Articles 29 and 30); and (5) the right to constitutional remedies for the enforcement of all these Fundamental Rights (Article 32).

The Directive Principles of State Policy, constituting Part IV of the Constitution, are basically inspired from the concept of a welfare state.[7] Article 37 declares that the Directive Principles are 'fundamental in the governance of the country' and that 'it shall be the duty of the State to apply these principles in making laws'. Article 38 defined the aim as follows: 'The State shall strive to promote the welfare of the people by securing and protecting as effectively as it may a social order in which justice, social, economic and political shall inform all the institutions of the national life.' In Article 39, stress was laid on the right to adequate means of livelihood equally for men and women; equal pay for equal work for both men and women; conditions of work ensuring health and strength and protection of children and youth against exploitation and against moral and material abandonment. It is also laid down that the state should ensure that 'the ownership and control of the material resources of the community are so distributed as best to sub-serve the common good'; and that the 'operation of the economic system does not result in the concentration of wealth and means of production to the common detriment'.

Furthermore, the duty is enjoined on the state that 'it should, within the limits of its economic capacity and development, make effective provision for securing the right to work, to education and to public assistance in case of unemployment, old age, sickness and disablement, and in other cases of undeserved want' (Article 41). The state should also provide for 'securing just and humane conditions of work and for maternity relief', and 'secure to all workers – agricultural, industrial and otherwise – work, a living wage, con-ditions of work ensuring a decent standard of life and full enjoyment of leisure and social and cultural opportunities' (Articles 42 and 43). Particular stress is laid on special assistance to the weaker sections of the people, including the Scheduled Castes and the Scheduled Tribes, with a view to promoting their educational and economic interests and to protecting them from social injustice and all forms of exploitation. In regard to rural economy, Articles 40 and 48 enjoin the application of modern scientific methods to agriculture and animal husbandry and the implementation of programmes and improvements through self-governing Panchayats. Article 43 requires the promotion of cottage industries on an individual and coop-erative basis. Article 45 fixed a definite time limit under which 'the State shall endeavour to' provide within a period of ten years from the commencement of this Constitution, for free and compulsory education for all children until they complete the age of 14 years. These general principles were given a more precise direction when Parliament accepted in December 1954 the socialist pattern of society as the objective of social and economic policy.

In 1976, the Forty-Second Amendment Act added certain new directives in the Constitution of India: (a) that children are given opportunities and facilities to develop in a healthy manner and in conditions of freedom and dignity; (b) that the operation of the legal system promotes justice, on a basis of equal opportunity, and in particular the state provides free legal aid in cases of economic and other disability; (c) that the participation of workers in management of industries is secured; and (d) that the environ-ment is protected and improved and the forests and wild life are safeguarded.

It may be relevant to add that the Directive Principles are non-justifiable. But they have acted as the guiding principles for the Union and state legis-latures in initiating social reform legislations. They have been cited by the courts in interpreting the constitutional provisions, and are accepted by the Planning Commission as basic guidelines for evolving their approach to nation-building on a democratic bases.[8]

Rediscovery of poverty in 1960

The foundation of the welfare state in post-colonial India was laid down during the three Five-Year Plans between 1951 and 1965. Self-reliance was the basic goal, but the strategy of 'incremental democratic modernization' encountered a series of problems from 1962 onwards which made the Nehruvian approach obsolete in many spheres of state policies. A new set of national issues regarding food scarcity, price rises, national defence, foreign dependence, economic stagnation and regional inequalities generated a cumulative stress between 1963 and 1967. As a consequence, a new agenda called the Ten-Point Programme came into being. The dilemma of dependent accumulation and declining dominance of the Congress Party created a shift in India's development direction. The slogan of 'Jai Jawan – Jai Kisan' (Victory to soldier – victory to peasant) symbolized the new thrust of the state. According to Rajni Kothari:

The issue was brought up dramatically when the country was faced by accumulation of events: two successive years of drought, a fall in export earnings and foreign aid (following the war with Pakistan), consequently a shortage of crucial raw materials and spare parts, a peculiar combination of industrial recession and rising prices, and conditions of acute scarcity and political uncertainty all around. The disequilibrium between agriculture and industry, under such conditions, virtually halted the economy and created a situation of grave crisis. These conditions set in motion a decisional process that ultimately led to a comprehensive review of economic strategy, an overhaul of programme priorities and administrative routines, and a rethinking in ideological attitudes and coalitional style.[9]

The 1960s saw a wave of disenchantment with the entire planning process, and was a period of rediscovery of poverty in political discourse. The condition was succinctly put by Hanson in the following words:

Despite the formidable amount of intelligence and experience of which the [Planning] Commission disposes, Indian planning seems to have gotten into a rut. Approaches and methods are persisted with, even when their results are disappointing, and there is some reluctance to admit, even privately, that anything can be fundamentally wrong. It is time, therefore, for the planners to ask themselves whether the things they are trying to do are really the right things. Every aspect of planning, from

the distribution of industrial investment to the organization of community projects, bears looking at again with fresh, unprejudiced eyes.[10]

The occasion was utilized by the socialists of India under the leadership of
Dr Ram Manohar Lohia to take the initiative in presenting an alternative
approach for promoting peoples' welfare through democratic planning. This
became the rallying point for all non-Congress political formations in the
national election of 1967. It also created pressure for a reorientation of the
Congress Party, which resulted in a new agenda for the state in the form of
the Ten-Point Programme (see Table 19.1).

The programme of non-Congressism conceptualized by the socialists
emphasized the need to not only change national priorities from industrialization and sectorwide modernization to providing irrigation to all agri-

Table 19.1 Comparison of the Socialist and Congress Party programmes, 1966–67

The Socialist programme[11]	*The Congress Party's ten-point programme*[12]
1 Uniform primary education	Social control of Banks
2 Abolition of land revenue on uneconomic holdings and introduction of the agricultural income tax	Nationalisation of general insurance
3 Five/seven-year plans for irrigation	State control over foreign trade
4 Removal of English as a medium from all sectors of public life	State trading in food grains
5 Rs1000 limit on monthly personal expenditure	Expansion of cooperatives
6 Classless trains	Regulation of monopolies
7 Ban on private car production and exclusive production of buses, tractors, and taxis for 20 years	Provision of minimum needs
8 National price policy for parity between agricultural and industrial goods	Ceilings on urban property and income
9 60 per cent opportunities for backward communities	Comprehensive development of rural areas
10 Maximum two houses per family	Abolition of the privy purse for ex-rulers
11 Effective land reforms and price control	

cultural land and economic strength to small landholding cultivators, but also of promoting a new social order through preferential opportunities to the Backward communities (including women). It sought egalitarian primary education, agricultural income tax, a national price policy, and a ban on personal expenditure above Rs1000 per month. The Lohia Programme considered the removal of English from affairs of the state, judiciary, business and education as a critical component of the new social order, as it was a colonial legacy which prevented the use of Indian languages and blocked the masses from access to institutions of governance and mobility. Thus, it called for a total challenge to the Indian elite and their three sources of privileges: (i) caste; (ii) wealth; and (iii) English language. In response, the Congress Party moved towards populist nationalism and accepted the need of taming market forces through welfare state mechanisms.

These two programmes created a countrywide debate on the challenge of poverty. The priorities of the planning process and responsibilities of the Indian state were reviewed beyond the conceptual frame of the early decades of freedom. After a period of political instability at the Centre and a wide variety of non-Congress coalition governments in major states of India, the years from 1971 to 1975 became dominated by the theme of putting distribution ahead of growth as the development strategy. It became recognized as a political imperative of democratic governance as a large number of people (more than half of the Indian population) were still trapped in economic settings which forced them to live below the levels of subsistence. It was legitimized by the slogan of *Garibi Hatao* (Eliminate Poverty) by the Congress Party under the leadership of Indira Gandhi who routed most of the anti-Congress political parties in the general elections of 1971–72. It appeared that, after a long wait, the moment had arrived for fulfilling the dreams of *Swaraj* by creating an egalitarian social order based upon economic self-reliance and democratic social transformations. It is another matter that the electoral mandate was not translated into effective socioeconomic measures due to a variety of internal and international reasons. Low savings, limited investment, sluggish industry, a steep rise in the money supply and a sharp decline in agricultural production were the prominent features of economic administration. The problems were further complicated by international 'price revolution' and a phase of 'stagflation' in the world economy. The inflation of prices in 1973–74 had turned everything topsy-turvy, and it was also coupled with the crisis of leadership within the Congress Party. The situation gave rise to multiple political pressures and student-youth movements and working-class protests which culminated into a national movement against the failures of the government in terms of checking corruption, controlling price rises, creating employment and providing relief to the poor.

In other words, the collapse of the welfare functions of the state had become the cause of national unrest. It was led by Jayaprakash Narayan, a top freedom fighter and founder of the Indian socialist movement (who later joined the *Sarvodaya* movement for reconstruction of the Indian society, economy and polity to promote welfare for all) and supported by socialists and others. After a phase of indifference and tolerance, the ruling party declared a State of Emergency due to the intensity of internal protests. At the same time, it had to adopt a 20-Point Programme of welfare measures to show that even in an emergency regime for the repression of the protest movements, the government was committed to continue the process of relief and welfare for the poor sections of society.[13]

In spite of these adversities, the change in the orientation of the political community and policy-makers in the early 1970s was remarkable. According to C.T. Kurien:

When a small group in the Planning Commission proposed in 1962 that the central concern of our planning has to be the removal of poverty as early as possible, it was a novel and consequently very suspicious idea. But within a decade it had become not only the accepted economic dogma, but also a highly articulated political programme.[14]

The new mood was reflected in the documents of the Fifth Five-Year Plan. For example, *Towards An Approach to the Fifth Plan (1974–79)* proclaimed:

There would seem to be a conspicuous element of historic inevitability in a direct approach to reducing poverty becoming the main thrust of the Fifth Five-Year Plan. The Plan is being formulated by a government that has massive mandate from the people, both in the Parliamentary election of 1971 and the state elections of 1972, on the basis of programme whose center-piece is *Garibi Hatao*. The homogeneity of the Governments in the Centre and most of the states during the formulation and early years of the Fifth Plan is guaranteed. This should enable bold and imaginative proposals being put through on the basis of an enlightened national consensus.[15]

Thus, the Fifth Five-Year Plan of post-colonial India was a landmark in the progress of forming a welfare state in India due to its special thrust, to make the maximum possible dent on low-end poverty while ensuring that the country moves one more step in the direction of economic independence. It was also remarkable due to its recognition that the Indian economy has reached a stage where a larger availability of resources made it possible to launch a direct attack on unemployment, underemployment and poverty. It clearly admitted that the twin causes of poverty are underdevelopment and inequality, and that it is inadmissible to ignore or underplay either factor. Therefore, the problem of poverty cannot be overcome within the foreseeable future by efforts in one direction only.

The era of liberalization

India entered a phase of liberalization in the 1980s under Prime Minister Rajiv Gandhi, and the process continued in spite of changes in prime ministers. The year 1991 was the beginning of an explicit phase of rolling back the state due to the pressure of liberalization. A relatively higher growth was recorded during 1980–2000, particularly during the 1990s which was a decade of structural economic reforms. The period also showed a decline in poverty and improvements in health and literacy levels of the people of India. But India continues to suffer with high levels of illiteracy, a high rate of infant mortality, a high incidence of disease, disability and malnutrition even after half a century of freedom and democracy. Our allocations for health and education have been only around 4 per cent of GDP, lower than other developing post-colonial countries like Malaysia and Sri Lanka.

The reorientation of state policies from nationalization to liberalization has been viewed with great apprehension in several quarters. To quote Bipan Chandra:

The inspiration and ideological-political structuring provided by the national liberation struggle are increasingly receding, the Congress Party is directionless and in shambles; the secular opposition parties and groups are unable to cohere; the Left is dissipated and bereft of any fresh ideas; communal parties and groups are growing and becoming respectable; the bureaucracy is demoralized and politicized i.e. it caters to whosoever is in power; the intelligentsia has defaulted and abdicated its social role, nor is it anymore trusted by the people – it is increasingly becoming irrelevant, the bourgeoisie has grown rapidly but has lost cohesion – this is signified by the absence of a dominant leadership of the class; the working class is fragmented by a multiplicity of trade union centers as also by the pattern of industrial development so that there is a small well paid section in technologically advanced industries, a medium paid section in traditional industries such as cotton textiles, jute, sugar, tea and coffee plantations, and a vast mass of under-paid, unorganized workers in the informal small scale sector, the rich peasant is fighting for hegemony over non-social development; the vast mass of agricultural labourers and poor peasants are completely disorganized and atomized; and the middle classes gripped by consumerism are losing the ideological edge and have abandoned all pretence of being guardians of social values and societal welfare, being increasingly engulfed by individual greed and social pessimism.[16]

According to economic analysts, the expenditure on social-sector schemes, as part of the welfare oriented programmes of the Indian state, has been increasing in real terms in the era of liberalization (see Table 19.2). At the

Table 19.2 Expenditure on the social sector in India as a percentage of total public expenditure

	1990–91	1996–67	1999–2000
Education, sport, youth welfare	11.20	11.41	12.28
Public health and water supply	4.23	4.39	4.48
Family welfare	0.60	0.56	0.56
Housing and urban development	0.99	1.40	1.66
Broadcasting	0.39	0.32	0.29
Social security and welfare	2.50	2.97	2.84
Labour and employment	0.47	0.42	0.42
Other social services	1.15	1.29	1.09
Food subsidies	1.58	1.86	1.77
Rural development	3.32	3.69	3.32
Basic minimum services	–	0.76	0.76
Total	24.85	27.22	27.69

Source: S. Mahendra Dev and J. Moij, 'Social Sector Expenditure in the 1990s', *Economic and Political Weekly* (Bombay), 2–8 March 2002.

same time, it has also been pointed out that this has been done mainly through increased expenditures by the central government. The state governments are easing themselves out of their constitutional commitment to sustain programmes in social sectors, which is a matter of concern. However, in the present context, social-sector expenditure is defined as the total expenditure on social services and rural development. The social services include education, health and family welfare, water supply and sanitation. Rural development expenditure relates mostly to anti-poverty programmes and is presented as 'economic services' in budget documents.

In empirical terms, the total combined Union and state expenditures, in 1993–94 prices, for (a) education, sport and arts; (b) medical [public health and family welfare]; (c) water supply and sanitation; (d) welfare of scheduled castes, scheduled tribes and other backward classes; (e) rural development; (f) urban development; (g) labour and unemployment; (h) family welfare; (i) social security; (j) scientific services and research, etc.; (k) social and community services; and (l) housing, accounted 7.4 per cent in 1999–2000. This compares to 7 per cent of GDP for the total period of 1991 to 2000.

As a percentage of aggregate expenditure, India spends 24–28 per cent on the social sector. In terms of per capita real expenditure, social sector spending has increased from Rs623 in 1990–91 to Rs959 in 2000–01, an increase of 54 per cent in 11 years. The percentage started to increase in the middle of the 1990s. Since 1995–96, the percentage has been higher than that of the 1980s. In other words, a higher percentage of government expenditure goes to the social sector now than when the reforms started, or during the last year preceding the reforms. This is partly due to the introduction of a programme for basic minimum services (BMS) in 1996–97, that consisted of seven basic services: safe drinking water, primary education, primary health, housing, midday meals for primary school children, rural roads, and a public distribution system.

In this context, it is important to keep four aspects in mind to make a better reading of Table 19.2. First, the ratio of expenditure by the states and the centre in India in the total social sector is 80:20. Secondly, the role of the centre is more important than the states because it sets the priorities and the policy direction for the country as a whole. Thirdly, the contribution of the centre to the overall social sector is increasing, particularly in the area of rural development. Finally, there has been a decline in the proportion of spending on social services in the states in the post-reform period.

This picture has to be further clarified by looking at the per capita real expenditure in various states. Because, if the states are divided into three categories of rich, middle and poor states, then it may be concluded that the rich states (Gujarat, Goa, Haryana, Maharashtra and Punjab) have done better in education and overall. The middle-income states (Andhra Pradesh, Karnataka, Kerala, Tamil Nadu and West Bengal) have put more money than the others into health and rural development. Among the poor states (Bihar, Madhya Pradesh, Orissa, Rajasthan and Uttar Pradesh), Bihar and Uttar Pradesh have been found the most negligent in the areas of health and education. Thus, the state level variations make it difficult to use the national picture for basic generalizations, as Table 19.3 shows.

The internal diversity has to be also juxtaposed with the international location of India in terms of the share of expenditure allocated to social services. India ranks 115 in the community of nations in terms of the Human Development Index, which is lower than Korea (27), Malaysia (56), Thailand (66), Sri Lanka (81) and Egypt (105). The share of expenditure for social services in India is much lower than in East Asian countries and all developing countries. Our input in education is higher than the other South Asian countries, but lower than in East Asian countries. In the case of health, it is lower than even the other South Asian countries. Thus, the need to step-up social-sector expenditure and efficient utilization of allocated funds in several states of India is self-evident in spite of increasing attention of the central government in the post-reform years.

Public expenditure on education (including higher education) has been the single largest item of expenditure by far, increasing from 3.29 per cent in 1998–99 to 3.7 per cent of GDP in 1999–2000. Despite an increased allocation during the last decade to the medical, public health and family welfare sectors, both the state and the central expenditure as percentages of GNP did not attain the same level as enjoyed during 1990–91. The relative share of central expenditure on rural development declined substantially

Table 19.3 Per capita expenditure on social services and literacy by selected states
(in Rs current prices; year 1998–99)

States	Per capita expenditure Rs, 1998–99	Ranking by literacy rate (2001) %
Andhra Pradesh	973	28 (61)
Bihar	476	35 (47)
Goa	3069	4 (82)
Gujarat	1211	15 (69)
Haryana	1111	20 (68)
Karnataka	1001	22 (67)
Kerala	1096	1 (90)
Madhya Pradesh	942	25 (64)
Maharashtra	1045	10 (77)
Orissa	782	26 (63)
Punjab	1157	16 (69)
Rajasthan	1037	29 (61)
Tamil Nadu	1205	13 (73)
Uttar Pradesh	571	31 (57)
West Bengal	740	18 (69)

Sources: Reserve Bank of India *Bulletins; Census of India 2001.*

from 42 per cent in 1998–99 to 35 per cent in 1999–2000. The performance
of several major poverty alleviation programmes that were initiated were
not satisfactory in recent years. For instance, the Employment Assurance
Scheme for rural areas had a target of generating 409 million man-days
for the rural poor living below the poverty line in the drought prone,
desert, tribal and hill areas, but only 262 million man-days of work were
generated.[17]

The realities of 'reforms' have created new challenges for India in the
context of pursuing the basic objectives set since independence. These challenges are: (a) that so far mostly the better-off sections have been able to
respond to market signals while the rural population has benefited less; (b)
India is suffering marginalization in a globalized world and has lost domestic market-share due to the unfettered entry of foreign companies under
WTO provisions; and (c) the role of the government in economic and social
matters is shrinking which has caused apprehension about the future of
protective discrimination for weaker sections. These challenges are better
recognizable through an overview of the process and consequences of developing the welfare state in India since 1947.

An overview

India had completed five decades of freedom as well as forming a democratic welfare state by the end of the millennium. This provides us scope for

Table 19.4 Estimates of the incidence of poverty in India, 1973–2007

Year	Poverty ratio (%)			Number of poor (millions)		
	Rural	Urban	Combined	Rural	Urban	Combined
1973–74	56.4	49.0	54.9	261.3	60.0	321.3
1977–78	53.1	45.2	51.3	264.3	64.6	328.9
1983	45.7	40.8	44.5	252.0	70.9	322.9
1987–88	39.1	38.2	38.9	231.9	75.2	307.1
1993–94	37.3	32.4	36.0	244.0	76.3	320.3
1999–00	27.1	23.6	26.1	193.2	67.1	260.3
2007*	21.1	15.1	19.3	170.5	49.6	220.1

*Poverty projection for 2007.
Source: India Planning Commission, *Tenth Five-Year Plan*, Vol. 1.

attempting an overview of the progress achieved in its journey towards a socio-political order around the objective of human development encompassing the quality of life, the level of well-being and access to basic social services. Poverty, labour and employment, illiteracy, poor health conditions and the marginal status of the weaker sections of society, have been five outstanding concerns of the nascent welfare state. Let us glance at the changes in these five major domains of national life between the 1950s and 2000 to gain an overall picture of the role of the welfare state in the Republic of India during these critical years.[18]

Issue of poverty

The impact of the anti-poverty strategy is reflected in the decline in the combined poverty ratio from 54.9 per cent in 1973–74 to 26.1 per cent in 1999–2000. While the proportion of the poor in rural areas declined from 56.4 per cent to 27.1 per cent, the decline in urban areas has been from 49 per cent to 23.6 per cent during this period (see Table 19.4). But the process of poverty reduction has demonstrated wide interstate disparities, and it is a matter of concern that Orissa and Bihar continue to be the two poorest states with poverty ratios of 47 and 43 per cent respectively.

It is important to underline that the Tenth Five-Year Plan (2002–07) has been aimed at reducing the poverty ratio by 5 per cent by 2007, and by 15 per cent by 2012. The anti-poverty programmes have been continued during the recent years of liberalization to create additional employment through asset formation as well as by imparting technical and entrepreneurial skills.

Labour and employment

The labour and employment scenario was marked by the findings of the 55th Round (1999–2000) Survey of the National Sample Survey Organization (NSSO), and the recommendations of the National Labour Commission

(2003).[19] It shows a distressing situation in comparison to the reported progress in poverty eradication in a variety of national studies and reports.[20] First, there has been a decline in the rate of growth of employment from 2.7 per cent per annum in 1983–94 to 1.07 per cent annum in 1994–2000 (Table 19.5), associated with a sharp decline in the rate of growth of the labour force, and a decline in the labour intensity of production. Second, the absolute number of unemployed as well as the incidence of unemployment has increased during this period. Third, the decline in the overall growth rate of employment in 1994–2000 was largely attributable to a near stagnation of employment in agriculture; as a result the share of agricultural sector in total employment dropped substantially from 60 per cent in 1993–94 to 57

Table 19.5 Past and present macro-scenario of employment and unemployment (person years)

	(Millions)			Growth per annum (%)	
	1983	*1993–94*	*1999–2000*	*1983 to 1993–94*	*1993–94 to 1999–2000*
All India					
Population	718.20	894.01	1003.97	2.00	1.95
Labour force*	261.33	335.97	363.33	2.43	1.31
Workforce**	239.57	315.84	336.75	2.70	1.07
Unemployment rate (%)	8.30	5.99	7.32		
No. of unemployed	21.76	20.13	26.58	−0.08	4.74
Rural					
Population	546.61	658.83	727.50	1.79	1.67
Labour force	204.18	266.38	270.39	2.15	0.96
Workforce	187.92	241.04	250.89	2.40	0.67
Unemployment rate (%)	7.96	5.61	7.21		
No. of unemployed	16.26	14.34	19.50	−1.19	5.26
Urban					
Population	171.59	234.98	276.47	3.04	2.74
Labour force	57.15	80.60	92.95	3.33	2.40
Workforce	51.64	74.80	85.84	3.59	2.32
Unemployment rate (%)	9.64	7.19	7.65		
No. of unemployed	5.51	5.80	7.11	0.49	3.45

*Labour force includes all employed and unemployed men and women above the age of 18 years.
**Workforce includes only those men and women, above the age of 18 years, who were in paid employment, at work, self-employed or with a job but not at work during the reference period.
Source: India Planning Commission.

per cent 1999–2000. Fourth, at the same time, employment growth in all the sub-sectors within services (except community, social and personal services having negative growth rates) exceeded 5 per cent per annum. And fifth, there is also growth of the casualization of labour, and the total volume of casual labour in total employment has been going up. The NSSO covers five major features of the employment scene – population, the labour force, the workforce, the unemployment rate, and the number of unemployed in rural and urban settings between 1983–2000 (see Table 19.5).

It is important to remember that only a small percentage (nearly 9 per cent) of the total workforce of the country is employed in the organized sector. Secondly, the public sector accounts for more than two-thirds of the total organized sector employment and the growth of employment in the public sector has been negligible due to the push for liberalization since the late 1980s (see Table 19.6).

This is a critical situation in view of the centrality of employment generation in the overall process of socio-economic welfare and development. Therefore a special group was commissioned to target 10 million employment opportunities per year over the Tenth Plan period (2002–07), to address the issue of decline in employment generation and to take India out of the 'job–less growth syndrome'. The group has recommended promotion of labour-intensive activities in the fields of agriculture and allied activities, small and medium industries, information technology, construction, tourism, the financial sector, education and health and so on.

Turning to the state-wise employment scenario, it is important to understand that there is a wide economic disparity between the states of India. A glance at the various states in Table 19.7 shows that Andhra Pradesh, Himachal Pradesh, Kerala, Rajasthan, Tamil Nadu and West Bengal have experienced very low employment growth in the era of liberalization. Similarly, Andhra, Assam, Kerala, Tamil Nadu and West Bengal have higher unemployment rate than the All India average. On the other hand, Gujarat, Haryana, Himachal, Madhya Pradesh, Punjab, Rajasthan and Uttar Pradesh have reported lower unemployment rates than the national average in 1999–2000.

National Labour Commission recommendations

In the arena of labour welfare, there has been a turn from a 'labour friendly' to a 'capital friendly' path in the last two decades of Indian polity and economy. The National Labour Commission has presented a set of new recommendations to improve the welfare of working men and women, particularly in the unorganized sector (which provides work opportunities for more than 90 per cent of the working population in India). It has urged the need for an 'adequate safety net' for the workers in the context of any changes in the labour laws. The recommendation for formulation of schemes for pension and unemployment benefits for the unorganized sector

Table 19.6 Sectoral employment growth

Sector	Employment (in millions)				Annual growth (%)			
	1983	1987–88	1993–94	1999–00	1983 to 1987–88	1987–88 to 1993–94	1983 to 1993–94	1993–94 to 1999–00
Agriculture	151.35	163.82	190.72	190.94	1.77	2.57	2.33	0.02
Industry								
Mining and quarrying	1.74	2.40	2.54	2.26	7.35	1.00	3.68	-1.91
Manufacturing	27.69	32.53	35.00	40.79	3.64	1.23	2.26	2.58
Electricity, gas and water supply	0.83	0.94	1.43	1.15	2.87	7.19	5.31	-3.55
Construction	7.17	11.98	11.02	14.95	12.08	-1.38	4.18	5.21
Services								
Trade, hotels and restaurants	18.17	22.53	26.88	37.54	4.89	2.99	3.80	5.72
Transport, storage and communications	6.99	8.05	9.88	13.65	3.21	3.46	3.35	5.53
Financial, insurance, real estate and business services	2.10	2.59	3.37	4.62	4.72	4.50	4.60	5.40
Community, social and personal services	23.52	27.55	34.98	30.84	3.57	4.06	3.85	-2.08
All sectors	239.57	272.39	315.84	336.75	2.89	2.50	2.67	1.07

Source: India, NSSO, different rounds.

Table 19.7 The employment scenario in the states

	Employment (000s) 1999–00	Employment growth, 1993–94 to 1999–00 (% p.a.)	Unemployment rate		Employment Elasticity 1993–94 to 1999–00	GDP growth (% p.a.) 1993–94 to 1999–00
			1999–00 (%)	1993–94 (%)		
Andhra Pradesh	30,614	0.35	8.03	6.69	0.067	5.2
Assam	7,647	1.99	8.30	8.03	0.737	2.7
Bihar	30,355	1.59	7.32	6.34	0.353	4.8
Gujarat	18,545	2.31	4.55	5.70	0.316	7.3
Haryana	5,982	2.43	4.77	6.51	0.420	6.8
Himachal Pradesh	2,371	0.37	2.96	1.80	0.052	7.1
Karnataka	20,333	1.43	4.57	4.94	0.188	7.6
Kerala	8,902	0.07	20.97	15.51	0.013	5.5
Madhya Pradesh	28,725	1.28	4.45	3.56	0.272	4.7
Maharashtra	34,979	1.25	7.16	5.09	0.216	5.8
Orissa	11,928	1.05	7.34	7.30	0.262	4.0
Punjab	8,013	1.96	4.03	3.10	0.426	4.6
Rajasthan	19,930	0.73	3.13	1.31	0.104	7.0
Tamil Nadu	23,143	0.37	11.78	11.41	0.052	7.1
Uttar Pradesh	49,387	1.02	4.08	3.45	0.185	5.5
West Bengal	22,656	0.41	14.99	10.06	0.056	7.3
All India	336,736	1.07	7.32	5.99	0.160	6.7

Source: India Planning Commission.

workers is a major step forward to improve their social and economic conditions. It has also recognized the need for cluster development to improve the quality of employment, and has pointed out that the health, safety and welfare of workers must be kept in view while reviewing the labour laws. At the same time, the recommendations for allowing state governments to make provincial laws and giving more powers to employers of small and medium-scale units have been criticized by the trade unions.

The gender gap in work participation and low female work participation rates are two of the critical shortcomings in the workforce in India. A majority of women workers are employed in rural areas, primarily as labourers and cultivators, and their employment in the organized sector was only 4.9 million (17.8 per cent of the organized sector employment) in 2001. The distribution of women employees across industries reveals that community, social and personnel services sectors employed 55.6 per cent of women workers, followed by manufacturing (20.7%), agriculture and allied occupations (10.9%) and finance, insurance, real estate and business (4.7%).

The existence of child labour is a major national concern, but the number of working children in the country has declined from 2 per cent of the total population and 6 per cent of the total workforce in 1981 to 1.34 per cent of the population and 3.59 per cent of the total workforce in 1991. The estimated number of working children in the country according to the latest survey (2000) was 10.4 million. These children are mostly employed in the unorganized and home-based industries. The state with the highest child-labour population in the country is Andhra Pradesh. Madhya Pradesh, Maharashtra and Uttar Pradesh also have more than a million child-labour workers. The problem of child labour has attracted global criticism. The policy of the Indian government is to ban the employment of children below the age of 14 years in factories, mines and hazardous employment, and it has launched about 100 National Child Labour Projects covering 211,000 children in 13 states where child labour is relatively high. Their activities include the establishment of special schools to provide non-formal education, vocational training and supplementary nutrition. It is claimed that, so far, about 150,000 children have been mainstreamed into a formal education system.

Illiteracy eradication and basic education

Educational opportunities are critical inputs in the welfare of citizens. The problem of illiteracy has been one of the hurdles in the process of nation-building since independence, as 72 per cent of men and 91 per cent of women were found to be trapped in illiteracy in 1951. In last fifty years the literacy rate has increased to 75 per cent among men and 54 per cent among women (see Table 19.8). The thrust towards universalizing primary education and eliminating illiteracy was given a fresh constitutional impetus through the 93rd Amendment of the Constitution by making free and

Table 19.8 Literacy rates in India, 1951–2001 (%)

Census year	Persons	Males	Females	Male–female gap in literacy rate
1951	18.33	27.16	8.86	18.30
1961	28.30	40.40	15.35	25.05
1971	34.45	45.96	21.97	23.98
1981	43.57	56.38	29.76	26.62
1991	52.21	64.13	39.29	24.84
2001	65.38	75.85	54.16	21.70

Source: Census of India.

compulsory elementary education a fundamental right for all children in the age group of 6–14 years.

There were 638,738 primary schools and 206,269 upper primary schools in India in 2000–01, with 3.2 million teachers at the elementary level. It is recorded that out of the estimated population of 193 million in the age group 6–14 years in 2000–01, nearly 81 per cent attended school. But this still left 19 per cent beyond the reach of the school system. If we combine this figure with the drop-out rate of 40.3 per cent at the primary level, especially in the case of girl students, then the situation looks very unsatisfactory from the perspective of the commitment of Education for All and the global goal of eradication of illiteracy by 2015.

In this context the government has launched the National Literacy Mission which expects to achieve full literacy, that is a sustainable threshold level of 75 per cent literacy by 2005. Out of 600 districts in the country, 587 have since been included under Adult Education Programmes. The government has also recognized the great potential of non-governmental organizations (NGOs) in furthering its programmes and schemes in this historical mission.

Healthcare

Eradication of epidemics and improvement in the health status of the population has been a thrust area under the welfare state system of India. A vast health infrastructure and manpower at the national level has been built up which has resulted in a substantial improvement in the health status of the population and a decline in mortality (see Table 19.9). However, there is still a vast variation in access to healthcare facilities between states, urban–rural, and across different sections of society.

Therefore, areas of attention in the Tenth Plan include the reorganization and restructuring of the existing healthcare infrastructure. An appropriate delegation of powers to Panchayati Raj Institutions is one of the basic features of the new strategy to promote the National Health Policy (2002) to

Table 19.9   Trends in healthcare, 1951–2000

	1951	1981	2000
SC/PHC/CHC*	725	57,363	1,63,181
Dispensaries and hospitals (all)	9,209	23,555	43,322
Beds (pvt. and public)	117,198	569,495	8,70,161
Nursing personnel	18,054	1,43,887	7,37,000
Doctors (modern system)	61,800	2,68,700	5,03,900
Malaria (cases in millions)	75	2.7	2.2
Leprosy (cases/10,000 population)	38.1	57.3	3.74
Smallpox (no. of cases)	>44,887	Eradicated	
Guinea worm (no. of cases)		>39,792	Eradicated
Polio (no. of cases)		29,709	265

*SC = Sub-Centre, PHC = Primary Health Centre, CHC = Community Health Centre.
Source: *National Health Policy 2002.*

provide Health for All in the near future. It is to be noted that (1) malaria (2.03 million cases in 2001), (2) kala-azar (an epidemic in West Bengal, Jharkhand and Bihar), (3) tuberculosis (targeted coverage of 271 million population in 102 districts), (4) leprosy (declined from 24 per 10,000 population in 1992 to 3.2 per 10,000 population in 2002), (5) blindness (7 million) and (6) HIV/AIDS (3.97 million infected in 2001, with a high prevalence of 1 per cent in Karnataka, Tamil Nadu, Andhra Pradesh, Maharashtra, Manipur and Nagaland) are being given top priority in the National Health Policy (2002) to improve the overall health status.

The Government of India has also been engaged in promoting family welfare programmes to encourage smaller family groups since the early 1970s. India has adopted a path of transition from 'high birth rate–high death rate' to 'low birth rate–low death rate'. It has been recognized by the state's policy-makers that the goal of population stabilization may be achieved only when child survival, maternal health and contraception issues are addressed in a wholistic way. Among the major states, Kerala and Tamil Nadu have already achieved a replacement level of fertility (total fertility rate of 2.1), while Andhra Pradesh, Gujarat, Karnataka, Maharashtra, Orissa, Punjab and West Bengal are in the direction of achieving it. Assam, Madhya Pradesh and Haryana are relatively slow in their progress. Only Rajasthan, Uttar Pradesh and Bihar have recorded a total fertility rate of 4.1 to 4.7, which is far above the desired national level.

In short, India has succeeded in enhancing life expectancy from 36 years (1951) to 65 years (2001), and in reducing infant mortality from 146 per 1000 (1951–61) to 68 per 1000 (2000) due to its healthcare initiatives. It has also promoted a couple protection rate from 10 per cent (1971) to 48 per cent (1998–99) and brought down the total fertility rate (per woman) from

Table 19.10 Selected health indicators

	1951	1981	1991	Current level
Crude birth rate (per 1000 population)	40.8	33.9	29.5	25.8 (2000)
Crude death rate (per 1000 population)	25.1	12.5	9.8	8.5 (2000)
Total fertility rate (per woman)	6.0	4.5	3.6	3.2 (1999)
Maternal mortality rate (per 100,000 live births)	n.a.	n.a.	437 (1992–93) NFHS	407 (1998)
Infant mortality rate (per 1000 live births)	146 (1951–61)	110	80	68 (2000)
Child (0–4 years) mortality rate per 1000 children	57.3 (1972)	41.2	26.5	20.4 (1999)
Couple protection rate (%)	10.4 (1971)	22.8	44.1	48.2 (1998–99) NFHS
Life expectancy at birth				
Male	37.2	54.1	59.7	62.3
Female	36.2	54.7	60.9 (1991–95)	65.3 (1996–2001)

NFHS: National Family Health Survey; n.a. = not available.
Source: India Office of the Registrar General.

6 (1951) to 3.2 (1999) in the last five decades which is a significant level of progress (see Table 19.10). At the same time, there is a need to promote a better strategy so that the interstate, and intercommunity disparities may be eliminated in the near future.

It is significant that addressing the issues of (a) the nutritional deficiency syndrome, and (b) the prevalence of water-born diseases, are integral aspects of the healthcare schemes of the Indian state. It is reported that one half of children under the age of five years in India are often malnourished. 30 per cent of new-born children are significantly underweight and nearly 60 per cent of women are anaemic. Therefore the Integrated Child Development Scheme (ICDS) has been promoted to improve the nutritional status of mothers and children.

Similarly, according to the Census of 1991, there were only 62 per cent of households in India with access to safe drinking water. This consisted of 81 per cent of urban households and 56 per cent of rural households. Safe drinking water and improved sanitation play a major role in the overall well-being of the people, in the control of infant mortality, the decline in the death rate, and improvements in longevity. But, in 1991, less than one-fourth of households in the country had toilet facilities within their premises. Such facilities were available for less than 10 per cent of rural and about 64 per cent of urban households. The Ministry of Rural Development was assigned the task of providing safe drinking water in all rural habitations by April 2004, and in the economic survey of 2002–03, 91 per cent of rural habitations had been fully covered and 7 per cent partially covered.

Attention to weaker sectors of the population

Given the precolonial and colonial principles of India's power structure, nearly all women and the scheduled castes and scheduled tribes were found to be on the margins of the systems of opportunities and mobility on the eve of Independence. They also constitute the weaker sections of Indian society along with the other backward classes.

The condition of women has been one of the major concerns since the colonial era. The continuity of their powerlessness in post-colonial India was highlighted by the first national committee on women in 1975–76 through the well-documented report *Towards Equality*.[21] This alerted the nation in general, and women in particular, towards mobilizing society into urgent steps to promote gender justice through women's empowerment. The achievements of the women's movements during the last two decades are remarkable as they have promoted (a) legal reforms, (b) economic opportunities and (c) political participation of women in a substantial manner. Making stricter laws to prevent as well as punish violence against women, provision of a 33 per cent reservation in the elected membership in Panchayats, Municipalities and District Boards, and the formation of a National Commission for Women for promotion of women's health, education and economic well-being are the most outstanding consequences of the new orientation of the Indian state since the emergence of the national women's movement in the 1970s.

In the last decade, the Ninth Five-Year Plan (1997–02) adopted the strategy of a Women's Component Plan under which not less than 30 per cent of funds and benefits were earmarked in all women-related sectors, for women-specific programmes. The Tenth Plan (2002–07) aims at empowering women through translating the recently adopted National Policy for Women (2001). Providing training in new technologies, managerial and marketing support for productive activities, employment-linked training in various traditional and non-traditional trades and encouragement at self-help groups and individual enterpreneurial initiatives through Rashtriya Mahila Kosh credit support have been the significant components of economic aspects of the empowerment process.

Protection of women from widely prevalent domestic violence has been brought onto the state's agenda in recent years due to mobilizations by NGO media and other bodies. The new initiatives include new legislation through the Domestic Violence Bill (2002), a network of short-stay homes, gender sensitization drives among police, judiciary and schools and colleges, and better provisions for the rehabilitation of women in difficult circumstances. Improving the conditions of female children and adolescent girls in the context of health and education are two major concerns of the state in recent years.

In the case of the scheduled castes, scheduled tribes and the other backward classes, the state through the Ministry of Social Justice and Empowerment is addressing the constitutional obligation of ensuring effective implementation of plans for protecting the interests of these groups. According to official documents, the Tenth Plan is dedicated to promoting a three-pronged strategy for social empowerment to be carried forward through removing the persisting inequalities and disparities, besides providing easy access to basic minimum services. Economic empowerment is being accelerated through promotion of employment-cum-income generation activities, and social justice is to be furthered by supporting the elimination of all types of discrimination with the backup of legislative support, affirmative action and awareness generation.

As education is the prime requirement for the empowerment of this process, efforts are being made to address the school drop-out problem and improve retention rates through a variety of educational aids and support, and similarly to abolish the practice of untouchability and check the high rate of crimes against the Scheduled Castes and Scheduled Tribes. To these ends a new law has been introduced through the Scheduled Castes and Scheduled Tribes Prevention of Atrocities Act 1989. The continuing presence of scavangers in a large number of our cities (more than 650,000 in 2001) is also a cause of serious concern in this context. A national scheme for the Liberation and Rehabilitation of Scavengers has provided support to 146,000 scavengers for training and 384,000 for rehabilitation up to 2000–01, is a special drive of the state to address the challenge of putting an end to one of the most degrading occupations and rehabilitating the persons so engaged.

There has been a continuous mobilization among the tribal communities of India (which constitute 8.6 per cent or 67 million of the total population) for the last several years for a comprehensive welfare approach. As a response, the Ministry of Tribal Affairs was set up in 1999 as the nodal ministry for the reorientation of national policies and programmes. A Commission under Article 339 of the Constitution of India has been appointed to report and review on the administration of the scheduled areas and the welfare of the scheduled tribes. Protecting the tribals from land alienation and the related problems of indebtedness and exploitation, the formulation of a national policy for rehabilitation of displaced persons, promoting tribal participation in forest-centred activities and strengthening tribal economies, protecting the Primal Tribal Groups, and ensuring tribal participation in the development process through democratizing the decision-making process at various levels are major components of the Tenth-Plan approach. Food and nutrition security, educational development, support for income-generating activities, and the creation of infrastructural support are the explicit targets of the government's initiatives.

The social welfare groups in India include the following categories: (a) persons with disabilities (estimated at 50 million or 5 per cent of the total population in 2001); (b) the social deviants who come into conflict with the law; and (c) the other disadvantaged groups, like older persons (7 per cent of the population – 70.6 million in 2001), and children in distress. The state has engaged itself in pursuing a three-dimensional strategy since the Ninth Plan: (1) *Empowering* the disabled; (2) *Reforming* the social deviants; and (3) *Caring* for the other disadvantaged. The programmes of empowering the disabled are backed by the provisions of Persons with Disabilities (equal opportunities, protection of rights and full participation) Act 1955, which has identified over 130 districts for providing comprehensive rehabilitiation services, and 83 District Disability Rehabilitation Centres have already been brought into existence. The state is also engaged in promoting an active partnership with non-govermental organizations for promoting training and rehabilitiation services.

Similarly, reform and rehabilitation of social deviants is the core idea of the 'Progamme of Juvenile Justice', where a network of mandatory homes is one of the distinguishing features of this sector. Similarly, a community-based approach has been evolved to curb the growing problems of alcoholism and drug abuse in the county. The government is also engaged in supporting a good number of counselling Centres and treatment-cum-rehabilitiation centres. But the large number of high-risk groups like street children, sex workers, truck drivers and so on, and the growing influence of drugs in rural areas and the north-east suggests that the country needs a more effective strategy for addressing this set of persons.

Caring for the 'other disadvantaged' is becoming a growing concern due to the rapid decline of family support systems. The state has to respond to the needs of the uncared aged, the orphaned or abandoned, the destitute and street children. There is an Integrated Programme for Older Persons, which is being run through state–NGO partnerships for managing old-age homes, day-care centres, and mobile medicare units. A national old-age pension scheme is also in the process of gradual growth to cover aged men and women who are slowly trapped in destitution due to growing age combined with lack of assets, family support and their declining capacity of income generating activities.

Similarly, a national scheme for Welfare of Children in need of Care and Protection has been initiated to cater to child workers and potential child workers. It is engaged in providing opportunities to facilitate their entry into mainstream education.

To sum up this descriptive overview of the expanding role of the welfare state in India, it may be underlined that there has been a gradual evolution of the state's orientation in the context of the imperatives of welfare of various needy sections. This has been catalyzed by the constitutional framework, social mobilizations and international concerns expressed through UN agencies. On the other hand, there has been a new thrust, since the 1980s, to move from state-managed welfare schemes to state-supported public–private partnerships with increasing involvement of non-governmental organizations (NGOs). The new orientation has been variously termed as a rolling-back of the state, 'government as guide and not manager', 'new spaces for civil society groups', 'imperatives of corporate social responsibilities', and 'the rise of people-centric welfare regimes'.

Conclusions

The socio-political dynamics of the making of a welfare state and the consequences of the liberalization-globalizaton drive for the state and society in India have been summarized by Yogendra Singh as a state versus market dilemma:

> The extent to which the power of market increases and expands, the significance of the state as a supreme political institution undergoes major alterations. Idealistically, some protagonists of market even anticipate the end of the notion of sovereignty. For societies such as India, where nation-building has still not reached the level of integrative maturity, such fears of the end of sovereignty or a threat to it due to unhindered play of the global market force cause not only an acute anxiety but also poses a challenge.[22]

On the other hand, it has been recognized by policy-makers that:

> freedom from ignorance, disease and fear, along with freedom from want, are the best guarantors for human development. But education, health care, water and sanitation services, which can ensure these freedoms, are not accessible to all. To ensure easy accessibility, there is need of public action in these areas if human development has to gather momentum. Together, these facilities comprise a nation's social infrastructure that is as critical as physical infrastructure for a widely shared and inclusive development. Therefore a set of new goals are adopted in the field of education, health, and safety nets.[23]

Thus, there are new tasks basing India in moving further in the direction of a welfare state. These the new challenges demand a new interface between the nation-state and the modern world system at the global level, and between the community, the state and the market in Indian polity.

So far the shift of paradigm has been carefully utilized by the neo-rich dominant caste elite, by metropolitan centres and global financial firms. It has promoted consumerism among the middle classes and scams in the power elite. It has also created a new wave of people's movements by political parties and non-party organizations to demand freedom from illiteracy, hunger, diseases, environmental degradation and unemployment. The pressure groups for social justice and political empowerment are becoming increasingly visible and assertive – the Dalit movement, the women's movement, the movement of indigenous peoples for control over land, forest and water resources. The movement for a Right to Information and pressure for electoral reforms are becoming significant. The pressures are growing to move India towards a system of participatory democracy through planning for decentralization of power and empowerment of the weaker sections like women, the scheduled castes and the scheduled tribes based upon the twin goals of rapid growth and the elimination of poverty for a just social order. It is obvious that the heritage of the Indian national movement, the basic values of the Constitution of India (including the Directive Principles) and the continuous widening of the social base of democracy in India in the last five decades may provide the required support in this project for a better welfare state in the era of liberalization and global market mediation.

Notes

1 T.H. Marshall, *Class, Citizenship and Social Development*, Chicago: University of Chicago Press, 1977.
2 G.W.F. Hegel, *The Philosophy of Right* (trans. T.M. Know), Oxford: Oxford University Press, 1952.
3 T. Donald Moon, 'The Moral Basis of the Democratic Welfare State', in Amy Guttmann (ed.), *Democracy and The Welfare State*, Princeton: Princeton University Press, 1988, pp. 27–52.
4 Jawaharlal Nehru, *Jawaharlal Nehru's Speeches*, Vol. 4, New Delhi: Publications Division, 1964, pp. 151–2.
5 V.T. Krishnamachari, 'Planning for Economic Development', in the *Gazetteer of India, Vol. III*, New Delhi: Publication Division, 1975. Also see, Bipan Chandra, Mridula Mukherjee and Aditya Mukherjee, *India After Independence (1947–2000)*, New Delhi: Penguin Books, 2000, chs 2–5.
6 Subhash C. Kashyap, *Our Constitution*, New Delhi: National Book Trust, 1994, p. 65.
7 *Keshavanand Bharati* vs. *State Of Kerala*, India, AIR 1973, Supreme Court 146.
8 Granville Austin, *The Indian Constitutions Seamless Web*, New Delhi: Rajiv Gandhi Foundation, RGICS Paper no. 15, 1994. He has contributed some of the best-known commentaries on the Indian Constitution.
9 Rajni Kothari, *Caste in Indian Politics*, New Delhi: Orient Longman, 1970, p. 346.
10 A.H. Hanson, *The Process of Planning: A Study of India's Five Year Plans 1950–61*, London: Oxford University Press, 1966, p. 231.

11 *Mankind*, Hyderabad, December, 1966, pp. 3–8.
12 Resolution of the All India Congress Committee, 23 June 1967 as quoted in A.M. Zaidi (ed.), *The Encyclopaedia of the Indian National Congress*, New Delhi: S. Chand, 1983, pp. 351–3.
13 Anand Kumar, *State and Society in India: Making of the State's Agenda*, New Delhi: Radiant, 1989, ch. 6.
14 C.T. Kurien, *Poverty, Planning and Social Transformations*, New Delhi: Allied Publishers, 1978, pp. 22–3.
15 Planning Commission, *Towards an Approach to the Fifth Plan*, New Delhi: Planning Commission, 1973.
16 Bipan Chandra, *Essays on Contemporary India*, New Delhi: Har-Anand, 1993, p. 49.
17 S. Mahendra Dev and Jos Mooij, 'Social Sector Expenditures in the 1990s', *Economic and Political Weekly*, Bombay, 2 March 2002, pp. 853–66.
18 Most of the material presented in this section is based upon the latest *Economic Survey* by the Government of India. For further details see *Economic Survey 2002–03*, New Delhi: GOI Press, 2003, pp. 207–46. Also see India, *Tenth Five Year Plan*, New Delhi: Planning Commission, 2002, Vol. I.
19 Ravindra Varma, *Report of the National Labour Commission*, New Delhi: Akalank Publications, 2002.
20 K.C. Pant, *National Human Development Report*, New Delhi: Oxford University Press, 2002, ch. 3.
21 Government of India, *Towards Equality*, New Delhi: Publication Division, 1976.
22 Yogendra Singh, *Culture Change in India*, Jaipur: Rawat Publications, 2000 p. 240.
23 Government of India, *Economic Reforms: A Mid Term Perspective (Recommendations of Prime Minister's Economic Advisory Council)*, New Delhi: Ministry of Information and Broadcasting, 2001, p. 22.

Bibliography

Åberg, R. (ed.) (1987) *Welfare State in Transition*, Oxford: Clarendon Press.

Alban, A. and Christiansen, T. (eds) (1995) *The Nordic Lights: New Initiatives in Health Care Systems*, Odense: Odense University Press.

Alcock, P. and Craig, G. (eds) (2001) *International Social Policy: Welfare Regimes in the Developed World*, Basingstoke/New York: Palgrave Macmillan.

Alestalo, M., Allardt, E., Rychard, A. and Wesolowski, W. (eds) (1994) *The Transformation of Europe: Social Conditions and Consequences*, Warsaw: IFIS Publishers.

Anderson, S.J. (1993) *Welfare Policy and Politics in Japan: Beyond the Developmental State*, New York: Paragon House.

Anker, R. (1998) *Gender and Jobs: Sex Segregation of Occupations in the World*, Geneva: International Labour Organization.

Aspalter, C. (2002) *Discovering the Welfare State in East Asia*, Westport, CT: Praeger.

Aspalter, C. (2002) *Democratization and Welfare State Development in Taiwan*, Aldershot: Ashgate.

Atkinson, A.B., Rainwater, L. and Smeeding, T.M. (1995) *Income Distribution in OECD Countries*, Paris: OECD.

Atkinson, A. and Morgensen, G. (1993) *Welfare and Work Incentives: A North European Perspective*, Oxford: Clarendon Press.

Baker, D. *et al.* (eds) (1998) *Globalization and Progressive Economic Policy*, Cambridge: Cambridge University Press.

Baldwin, P. (1999) *The Politics of Solidarity: Class Bases in the European Welfare State, 1875–1975*, Cambridge: Cambridge University Press.

Bauman, R. (ed.) (2002) *Brazil in the 1990s: An Economy in Transition*, New York: Palgrave Macmillan.

Bauman, Z. (1998) *Work, Consumerism and the New Poor*, Buckingham: Open University Press.

Beck, W., van der Maesen, L. and Walker, A. (1997) *The Social Quality of Europe*, The Hague: Kluwer Law International.

Becker, H. and Hermkens, P.L.J. (eds) (1994) *Demographic, Economic and Social Change, and its Consequences*, Amsterdam: Thesis Publisher.

Bergham, J. and Cantillon, B. (eds) (1993) *The European Face of Social Security*, Aldershot: Avebury.

Beveridge, W.H. (1942) *Social Insurance and Allied Services*, London: HMSO.

Birch Sorensen, P. (ed.) (1998) *Tax Policy in the Nordic Countries*, London: Macmillan.

Bonol, G., George, V. and Taylor-Gooby, P. (2000) *European Welfare Features*, Cambridge: Polity Press.

Bouget, D. and Palier, B. (eds) (1999) *Comparing Social Welfare Systems in Nordic Europe and France*, Paris: MIRE-DREES.

Boyer, R. and Drache, D. (eds) (1996) *States Against Markets: The Limits of Globalization*, London: Routledge.

Bradshaw, J. (1993) *Household Budgets and Living Standards*, York: Joseph Rowntree Foundation.

Brooke Ross, R. and Zacher, H. (1983) *Social Legislation in the Federal Republic of Germany*, London: Bedford Square Press.

Buchanan, J.M. and Wagner, R.E. (1977) *Democracy in Deficit: The Political Legacy of Lord Keynes*, New York: Academic Press.

Burden, T., Cooper, C. and Petrie, S. (2000) *Modernising Social Policy: Unravelling New Labour's Welfare Reforms*, Aldershot: Ashgate.

Burden, Tom. (1998) *Social Policy and Welfare*, London: Pluto.

Cardoso, F.H. (1978) *O Modelo Politico Brasileiro*, Rio de Janeiro: Guanabara.

Castles, F.G. (ed.) (1989) *The Comparative History of Public Policy*, New York: Oxford University Press.

Castles, F.G. (ed.) (1993) *Families of Nations: Patterns of Public Policy in Western Democracies*, Aldershot: Dartmouth.

Castles, F.G. (1998) *Comparative Public Policy: Patterns of Post-War Transformation*, Cheltenham: Edward Elgar.

Chow, Nelson, W.S. (2000) *Social Welfare with Chinese Characteristics: The Reform of the Social Security System in China*, Hong Kong: University of Hong Kong.

Clarke, J., Cochrane, A. and McLaughlin, E. (1994) *Managing Social Policy*, London: Sage.

Clasen, J. (1994) *Paying the Jobless: A Comparison of Unemployment Benefit Policies in Great Britain and Germany*, Aldershot: Avebury.

Clasen, J. (ed.) (1997) *Social Insurance in Europe*, Bristol: Policy Press.

Clasen, J. (ed.) (1999) *Comparative Social Policy*, Oxford: Blackwell.

Clement, W. (ed.) (1977) *Understanding Canada: Building on the New Canadian Political Economy*, Montreal: McGill-Queen's University Press.

Compston, H. (ed.) (1997) *The New Politics of Unemployment: Radical Policy Initiatives in Western Europe*, London: Routledge.

Danziger, S., Sandefur, G. and Weinberg, D. (eds) (1995) *Confronting Poverty: Prescriptions for Change*, Cambridge, MA: Harvard University Press.

Deacon, B. (1998) *Global Social Policy: International Organizations and the Future of the Welfare*, London: Sage.

De Swann, A. (1988) *In Care of the State*, Cambridge: Polity Press.

Dixon, J.E. (1981) *The Chinese Welfare System, 1949–1979*, New York: Praeger.

Dixon, J. and Kim, H.S. (eds) (1985) *Social Welfare in Asia*, Kent: Croom Helm.

Dixon, J. and Scheurell, R.P. (eds) (1995) *Social Security Programmes: A Cross-cultural Comparative Perspetive*, Westport CT: Greenwood Press.

Duncan, A.S., Gilles, C. and Webb, S.J. (1994) *Social Security and Women's Independent Incomes*, Manchester: Equal Opportunities Commission.

Eardly, T. Bradshaw, J., Ditch, J., Gough, I. and Whiteford, P. (1996) *Social Assistance in OECD countries: Synthesis Report*, London: HMSO.

Easton, B. (1980) *Social Policy and the Welfare State in New Zealand*, Wellington: Allen & Unwin.

EC Commission (1997) *Modernising and Improving Social Protection in the European Union*, Brussels: EC Commission.

EC Commission (1998) *Social Protection in Europe 1997*, Luxembourg: Office for official Publications of the European Commiunities.

Ellwood, D. (1988) *Poor Support: Poverty in the American Family*, New York: Basic Books.

Ellwood, D. and Bane, M. (1994) *Welfare Realities: From Rhetoric to Reform*, Cambridge, MA: Harvard University Press.

Elsenhans, H. (1992) *Equality and Development*, Dhaka: Centre for Social Studies.

Erikson, R., Hansen, E.J., Ringen, S. and Uusitalo, H. (eds) (1987) *The Scandinavian Model: Welfare States and Welfare Research*, Armonk: M.E. Sharpe.

Esping-Andersen, G. (1985) *Politics against Markets*, Princeton: Princeton University Press.

Esping-Andersen, G. (1990) *The Three Worlds of Welfare Capitalism*, Cambridge: Polity Press.

Esping-Andersen, G. (ed.) (1996) *Welfare States in Transition: National Adaptations in Global Economics*, London: Sage.

Esping-Andersen, G. (1999) *Social Foundations of Postindustrial Economies*, Oxford: Oxford University Press.

Evers, A. and Winterberger, E. (eds) (1988) *Shifts in the Welfare Mix*, Vienna: Eurosocial.

Ferge, Z. and Kolberg, J.E. (eds) (1992) *Social Policy in a Changing Europe*, Frankfurt: Campus/Verlag.

Finland (1996) *Social Security in Finland, 1994*, Helsinki: Ministry of Social Affairs and Health.

Finland (1999) *Financing Social Protection in Europe*, Helsinki: Ministry of Social Affairs and Health.

Flora, P. (ed.) (1986) *Growth to Limits: The Western European Welfare States Since World War II, Vol. 1: Sweden, Norway, Finland, Denmark*, Berlin: Walter de Gruyter.

Flora, P. and Heidenheimer, A.J. (eds) (1981) *The Development of Welfare States in Europe and America*, New Brunswick: Transaction Books.

Fox, A.J. (ed.) (1989) *Health Inequalities in European Countries*, Aldershot: Gower.

Friedman, M. (1962) *Capitalism and Freedom*, Chicago: University of Chicago Press.

Friedman, R., Gilbert, N and Sherer, M. (eds) (1989) *Modern Welfare States: A Comparative View of Trends and Prospects*, Brighton: Wheatsheaf.

Gallie, D. and Paugam, S. (eds) (2000) *Welfare Regimes and the Experience of Unemployment in Europe*, Oxford: Oxford University Press.

Gao, S. (1999) *Two Decades of Reform in China*, Singapore: World Scientific Publishers.

Garon, S. (1997) *Molding Japanese Minds: The State in Everyday Life*, Princeton: Princeton University Press.

George, V. (1973) *Social Security and Society*, London: Routledge & Kegan Paul.

George, V. and Miller, S. (eds) (1994) *Social Policy Towards 2000: Squaring the Welfare Circle*, London: Routledge.

George, V. and Taylor Gooby, P. (1996) *European Welfare Policy: Squaring the Welfare Circle*, London: Macmillan.

George, V. and Wilding, P. (2001) *Globalization and Human Welfare*, Basingstoke: Palgrave Macmillan.

Ghai, D. (ed.) (2000) *Social Development and Public Policy: A Study of Some Successful Experiences*, Basingstoke: Palgrave Macmillan.

Giddens, A. (1994) *Beyond Left and Right: The Future of Radical Politics*, Cambridge: Polity Press.

Gilbert, B.B. (1966) *The Evolution of National Insurance in Great Britain*, London: Michael Joseph.

Gladstone, D. (1999) *The Twentieth-Century Welfare State*, Basingstoke: Palgrave Macmillan.

Golding, P. and Middleton, S. (1982) *Images of Welfare*, London: Martin Robertson.

Goodman, A., Johnson, P. and Webb, S. (1997) *Inequality in the UK*, Oxford: Oxford University Press.

Gornick, J.C. and Jacobs, J.A. (1997) *Gender, Welfare State, and Public Employment: A Comparative Study of Seven Industrialized Countries*, Luxembourg: Luxembourg Income Study.

Gough, I. (1979) *Political Economy of the Welfare State*, London: Macmillan.

Gould, A. (1993) *Capitalist Welfare Systems: A Comparison of Japan, Britain and Sweden*, London: Longman.

Gupta, A. (1994) *The Changing Perspectives of the Welfare State: The Issue of Privatization*, New Delhi: Pragati Publications.

Guttmann, Amy. (ed.) (1988) *Democracy and the Welfare State*, Princeton: Princeton University Pres.

Handler, J. and Hasenfield, Y. (1991) *The Moral Construction of Poverty: Welfare Reform in America*, London: Sage.

Hansen, E.J., Ringen, S., Uusitalo, H. and Erikson, R. (eds) (1993) *Welfare Trends in the Scandinavian Countries*, Armonk, NY: M.E. Sharpe.

Hansen, H. (1999) *Elements of Social Security*, Copenhagen: The Damish National Institute of Social Research.

Hayek, Friedrich, A., von (1941) *The Pure Theory of Capital*, Chicago: University of Chicago Press.

Heikkilä, M. (ed.) (1999) *Linking Welfare and Work*, Luxembourg: Office for Official Publications of the European Communities.

Heikkilä, M. and Uusitalo, H. (eds) (1997) *The Cost of Cuts: Studies on Cutbacks in Social Security and Their Effects in the Finland of the 1990s*, Saarijärvi: Gummerus.

Held, D., *et al.* (1999) *Global Transformations*, Stanford: Stanford University Press.

Hernes, H. (1987) *Welfare State and Woman Power: Essays in State Feminism*, Oslo: Norwegian University Press.

Hills, J. (1993) *The Future of Welfare: A Guide to the Debate*, York: Joseph Rowntree Foundation.

Hjerppe, R., Ilmakunnas, S., Voipio, Iikk B. (eds) (2000) *The Finish Welfare State at the Turn of the Millennium*, Helsinki: Government Institute for Economic Research.

Howrath, C., Kenway, P., Palmer, G. and Street, C. (1998) *Monitoring Poverty and social Exclusion: Labour's Inheritance*, York: Joseph Rowntree Foundation.

Huber, E. and Stephens, J. (2001) *Development and Crisis of Welfare States*, Chicago: Chicago University Press.

Hurrel, A. and Woods, N. (1999) *Inequality, Globalization and World Politics*, Oxford: Oxford University Press.

Jamieson, A. (ed.) (1991) *Home Care for Older People in Europe: A Comparison of Policies and Practices*, Oxford: Oxford University Press.

Jones, C. (ed.) (1993) *New perspectives on the Welfare State in Europe*, London: Routledge.

Jorberg, L. (1982) *Swedish Economy in a Hundred years*, Stockholm: Swedish Economy.

Jordan, B. (1998) *New Politics of Welfare*, London: Sage.

Katz Olson, L. (ed.) (1994) *Graying of the World: Who Will Care for the Frail Elderly*, Binghamton, NY.: Haworth Press.

Kautto, M., Heikkilä, M., Hvinden, B., Marklund, S. and Ploug, N. (eds) (1999) *Nordic Social Policy: Changing Welfare States*, London: Routledge.

Kautto, M., Fritzell, J., Hvinden, B., Kvist, J. and Uusitalo, H. (eds) (2001) *Nordic Welfare States: In the European Context*, London: Routledge.

Kautto, M. (2001) *Diversity Among Welfare States: Comparative Studies on Welfare State Adjustment in Nordic Countries*, Helsinki: Stakes.

Kindleberger, C.P. (1967) *Europe's Postwar Growth*, Cambridge, Massachusetts: Howard University press.

Knudsen, T. (ed.) (1991) *Welfare Administration in Denmark*, Copenhagen: Ministry of Finance.

Kolberg, J.E. (ed.) (1991) *The Welfare State as Employer*, Armonk, NY.: M.E. Sharpe.

Korpi, W. (1983) *The Democratic Class Struggle*, London: Routledge.

Koslowski, P. and Føllesdal, A. (eds) (1997) *Restructuring the Welfare State: Theory and Reform of Social Policy*, Berlin: Springer.

Kosonen, P. (ed.) (1993) *The Nordic Welfare States as Myth and Reality*, Helsinki: University of Helsinki.

Kosonen, P. (1994) *European Integration: A Welfare State Perspective*, Helsinki: University of Helsinki.

Krauss, M.B. (1979) *The New Protectionism: The Welfare State and International Trade*, Oxford: Basil Blackwell.

Kremalis, K. (1991) *The Individual's Right to Social Assistance*, Athens: Sakkoulas.

Krieger, J. (1986) *Reagan, Thatcher and the Politics of Decline*, Cambridge: Polity Press.

Kuhnle, S. (ed.) (2000) *Survival of the European Welfare State*, London: Routledge.

Kumar, A. (1989) *State and Society in India: Making of the State's Agenda*, New Delhi: Radiant.

Kvist, J. and Sinfield, A. (1996) *Comparing Tax Routes in Denmark and the United Kingdom*, Copenhagen: The Danish National Institute of Social Research.

Lehto, J. (ed.) (1991) *Deprivation, Social Welfare and Expertise*, Helsinki: National Agency for Welfare and Health.

Leisering, L. and Leibfreid, S. (2001) *Time and Poverty in Western States: United Germany in Perspective*, Cambridge: Cambridge University Press.

Leonard, P. (1997) *Post-modern Welfare: Re-constructing and Emancipatory Project*, London: Sage.

Levitas, R. (1998) *The Inclusive Society? Social Exclusion and New Labour*, Basingstoke: Macmillan.

Lewis, J. (ed.) (1993) *Women and Social Policies in Europe: Work, Family and the State*, Aldershot: Edward Elgar.

Lewis, J. (ed.) (1997) *Lone Mothers in European Welfare Regimes*, London: Jessica Kingsley.

Lewis, J. (ed.) (1998) *Gender, Social Care and Welfare State Restructuring in Europe*, Aldershot: Ashgate.

Lødemel, I. and Trickey, H. (eds) (2000) *'An Offer You Can't Refuse': Workfare in International Perspective*, Bristol: Policy Press.

Mack, J. and Lansley, S. (1985) *Breadline Britain*, London: Allen & Unwin.

Marklund, S. (1988) *Paradise Lost? The Nordic Welfare States and the Recession, 1975–1985*, Lund: Arkiv.

Marmor, T.R., Mashaw, J.L. and Harvey, P.L. (1990) *America's Misunderstood Welfare State: Persistent Myths, Enduring Realities*, New York: Basic Books.

Marsh, A. and McKay, S. (1993) *Families, Work and Benefits*, London: Policy Studies Institute.

Marsh, Leonard, C. (1975) *Report On Social Security for Canada: With A New Introduction by the Author and a Preface by Michael Bliss*, Toronto: University of Toronto Press.

Marsland, D. (1996) *Welfare or Welfare State?* London: Macmillan.

McLaughlin, E., Millar, J. and Cooke, K. (1989) *Work and Welfare Benefits*, Aldershot: Avebury.

McMichael, P. (1996) *Development and Social Change*, Thousand Oaks: Pine Forge Press.

McQuaig, L. (1993) *The Wealthy Banker's Wife: The Assault on Equality in Canada*, Toronto: Penguin.

McQaig, L. (1995) *Shooting the Hippo: Death by Deficit and Other Canadian Myths*, Toronto: Viking.

Mead, L.M. (1985) *Beyond Entitlement: The Social Obligations of Citizenship*, New York: The Free Press.

Michie, J. and Grieve Smith, J. (eds) (1999) *Global Instability*, London: Routledge.

Misgeld, K., Molin, K., Aamark, K. (eds) (1992) *Creating Social Democracy: A Century of the Social Democratic Labor Party in Sweden*, Pennsylvania: Pennsylvania State University Press.

Mishra, R. (1977) *Society and Social Policy*, London: Macmillan.

Mishra, R. (1990) *The Welfare State in Capitalist Society*, London: Harvester.

Mishra, R. (1999) *Globalization and the Welfare State*, Cheltenham: Edward Elgar.

Mitchell, D. (1991) *Income Transfers in Ten Welfare States*, Aldershot: Avebury.

Mommsen, W.J. (ed.) (1981) *The Emergence of the Welfare State in Britam and Germany*, London: Croom Helm.

Moynihan, D.P. (1996) *Miles to Go: A Personal History of Social Policy*, Harvard: Harvard University Press.

Mullard, M. and Spicker, P. (1988) *Social Policy in a Changing Society*, London: Routledge.

Murray, C. (1984) *Losing Ground: American Social Policy, 1950–1980*, New York: Basic Books.

Murray, C. (1990) *The Emerging British Underclass*, London: IEA Health and Welfare Unit.

Nagel, S.S. and Mills, M.K. (1993) *Public Policy in China*, Westport: Greenwood Press.

Nussbaum, M. and Sen, A. (eds) (1993) *The Quality of Life*, Oxford: Clarendon Press.

Offe, Claus, *Contradictions of Welfare State*, Cambridge, Mass: MIT Press.

Olson, L.K. (ed.) (1994) *The Graying of the World: Who will care for the Frail Elderly?*, Binghampton, NY: Haworth press.

Palme, J. and Wennemo, I. (1998) *Swedish Social Security in the 1990s: Reform and Retrenchment*, Stockholm: Ministry of Health and Social Affairs.

Papadimitriou, D.B. (1994) *Aspects of Distribution of Wealth and Income*, New York: St Martin's Press.

Pasinetti, L.L. (1994) *Growth and Income Distribution: Essays in Economic Theory*, Cambridge: Cambridge University Press.

Pekkarinen, J. (1989) 'Keynesianism and the Scandinavian Models of Economic Policy', in Hall, Peter A. (ed.) *Political Power of Economic Ideas*, Princeton, N.J.: Princeton University Press.

Pekkarinen, J., Pohjola, M. and Rowthorn, B. (eds) (1992) *Social Corporatism*, Oxford: Clarenden Press.

Pen, J. (1971) *Income Distribution*, London: Allen Lane.

Pierson, C. and Castles, F.G. (eds) (2000) *The Welfare State Reader*, Oxford: Polity Press.

Pierson, P. (1994) *Dismantling the Welfare State: Reagan, Thatcher and the Politics of Retrenchment*, Cambridge: Cambridge University Press.

Ploug, N. and Kvist, J. (1996) *Social Security in Europe: Development or Dismantlement?*, The Hague: Kluwer Law International.

Powell, M. (1999) *New Labour, New Welfare State? The 'Third Way' in British Social Policy*, Bristol: Policy Press.

Rose, R. and Shiratori, R. (eds) (1986) *The Welfare State, East and West*, New York: Oxford University Press.

Rowntree, S. (1901) *Poverty: The Study of Town Life*, London: Macmillan.

Sainsbury, D. (ed.) (1994) *Gendering Welfare States*, London: Sage.

Salminen, K. (1993) *Pension Schemes in the Making: A Comparative Study of the Scandinavian Countries*, Helsinki: Central Pension Security Institute.

Salter, B. (1998) *Politics of Change in the Health Service*, Hong Kong: Macmillan.

Saltman, R. and Figueras, J. (1997) *European Health Care Reform: Analysis of Current Strategies*, Copenhagen: WHO.

Saltman, R., Figueras, J. and Sakellarides, C. (eds) (1998) *Critical Challenges for Health Care Reform in Europe*, Buckingham: Open University Press.

Schumpeter, J.A. (1968) *History of Economic Analysis*, New York: Oxford University Press.

Scott, A. (1990) *Ideology and the New Social Movements*, London: Unwin Hyman.

Segalman, R. (1986) *The Swiss Way of Welfare*, New York: Westport.

Shalev, M. (ed.) (1996) *The Privatization of Social Policy*, London: Macmillan.

Showstack Sassoon, A. (ed.) (1987) *Women and the State: The Shifting Boundaries of Public and Private*, London: Unwin Hyman.

Sipilä, J. (1997) *Social Care Services: The Key to the Scandinavian Model*, Aldershot: Avebury.

Spiro, Shimon E. and Yaar, Ephraim Yuchtman (1983) *Evaluating the Welfare State*, New York: Academic Press.

Stephan, Alfred (1988) *Democratising Brazil: Problems of Transition and Consolidation*, Oxford: Oxford University Press.

Sykes, R., *et al.* (eds) (2001) *Globalization and European Welfare States*, Basingstoke: Palgrave Macmillan.

Takahashi, Mutsuko (1997) *The Emergence of Welfare Society in Japan*, Aldershot: Avebury.

Tawney, R.H. (1952) *Equality*, London: George Allen & Unwin.

Teeple, G. (1995) *Globalization and the Decline of Social Reform*, Toronto: Garamond Press.

Theil, H. (1967) *Economics and Information Theory*, Amsterdam: North Holland.

Titmuss, R.H. (1958) *Essays on the Welfare State*, London: Allen & Unwin.

Titmuss, R.H. (1974) *Social Policy*, London: Allen & Unwin.

Townsend, P. and Davidson, N. (1982) *Inequalities in Health: The Black Report*, Harmondsworth: Penguin Books.

Tullock, G. (1983) *Economics of Income Distributions*, Boston: Kluwer Nijhoff.

UK, Department of Social Security (1998) *New Ambitions for Our Country: A New Contract for Welfare*, London: HMSO.

Venter, Albert J. (ed.) (1998) *Government and Politics in the New South Africa*, Pretoria: JL van Schaik Publishers.

Vivekanandan, B. (1991) *Pathfinders: Social Democrats of Scandinavia*, Bombay and New Delhi: Somaiya.

Vivekanandan, B. (1997) *International Concerns of European Social Democrats*, London and New York: Macmillan & St Martin's.

Vivekanandan, B. (ed.) (2000) *Building on Solidarity: Social Democracy and the New Millennium*, New Delhi: Lancer's Books.

Weir, M., Orloff, A. and Skocpol, T. (eds) (1988) *The Politics of Social Policy in the United States*, Princeton: Princeton University Press.

Wilensky, H. (1975) *The Welfare State and Equality*, Berkeley, CA: University of California Press.

Wilensky, H. and Lebeaux, C. (1958) *Industrial Society and Social Welfare*, New York: Russel Sage.

Wilkinson, R. (1996) *Unhealthy Societies: The Afflictions of Inequality*, London: Routledge.

Williams, F. (1989) *Social Policy: A Critical Introduction*, Cambridge: Polity Press.

Wistow, G., Knapp, M., Hardy, B., Forder, J. and Manning, R. (1996) *Social Care Markets: Progress and Prospects*, Buckingham: Open University Press.

Wong, L. and MacPherson, S. (eds) (1995) *Social Change and Social Policy in Contemporary China*, Aldershot: Avebury.

World Bank (1997) *World Development Report: The State in a Changing World*, New York: Oxford University Press.

Yeates, N. (2001) *Globalization and Social Policy*, London: Sage.

Index